FROM PROPHECY TO PREACHING

SUPPLEMENTS TO

VIGILIAE CHRISTIANAE

Formerly Philosophia Patrum

TEXTS AND STUDIES OF EARLY CHRISTIAN LIFE
AND LANGUAGE

EDITORS

J. DEN BOEFT — R. VAN DEN BROEK — W.L. PETERSEN
D.T. RUNIA — J.C.M. VAN WINDEN

VOLUME LIX

FROM PROPHECY TO PREACHING

A SEARCH FOR THE ORIGINS
OF THE CHRISTIAN HOMILY

BY

ALISTAIR STEWART-SYKES

BRILL
LEIDEN · BOSTON · KÖLN
2001

This book is printed on acid-free paper.

Library of Congress Cataloging-in-Publication Data

Stewart-Sykes, Alistair.
  From prophecy to preaching : a search for the origins of the Christian
homily / by Alistair Stewart-Sykes.
    p.   cm. — (Supplements to Vigiliae Christianae, ISSN 0920-623X ; v. 59)
  Includes bibliographical references and index.
  ISBN 9004116893
  1. Preaching—History. I. Title. II. Series.
  III. Series.

  BV4207 .S84 2001
  251'.009—dc21
                                                        2001035058
                                                        CIP

Die Deutsche Bibliothek – CIP-Einheitsaufnahme

Stewart-Sykes, Alistair :
From prophecy to preaching : a search for the origins of the Christian
homily / by Alistair Stewart-Sykes. – Leiden ; Boston ; Köln : Brill, 2001
    (Supplements to Vigiliae Christianae ; Vol. 59)
    ISBN 90–04–11689–3

ISSN 0920-623X
ISBN 90 04 11689 3

Cover illustration : Alje Olthof
Cover design : Cédilles / Studio Cursief, Amsterdam

PRINTED IN THE NETHERLANDS

For Teresa

CONTENTS

PREFACE

This work began when, as a doctoral student, I was invited, on the recommendation of Dr Iain Torrance, to co-operate in a book which would trace the history of the homily by writing the initial chapter, concerning homiletic origins. The book mutated and the final result was published by Brill as *Preacher and audience* in 1998, to which I submitted a chapter on Hermas and "Hippolytus". The following work is the chapter which I had intended to write, though I was at first I was unsure whether there was sufficient material to justify a chapter! This rather long chapter is a prehistory, rather than a history, of preaching. No other work deals with the subject, which is reason enough to attempt it, and so, even should I be shown to be entirely wrong in my account, I may claim at least to have raised the subject so that my account can be submitted to scholarly *diakrisis*.

The nine years which this work has taken have been marked by many vicissitudes. The *historia calamitatum* has not however been without blessings on the way. Special thanks are due to Jeff and Asha Golliher of New York for hospitality which enabled me to begin the work; much of the first chapter was written under their roof. Ellen Aitken also offered hospitality to a wanderer, and beyond that has been continuously supportive, assisting greatly in the supply of materials when I was far from any library. Towards the end of the pilgimage, Sven Erik Brod assisted me in reading the work of his colleague Ekenberg, and friends and colleagues in New York engaged in fruitful diatribe.

The work is dedicated to Teresa Stewart-Sykes, who not only unknowingly elicited from me the *hypothesis* of the work, allowing me to sort the mass of material, but has stood by me in the many trials which have accompanied our joint lives in the past nine years. I pray that the time of testing be at an end.

The Vicarage, Sturminster Marshall
Charles, King and Martyr, 2001

INTRODUCTION

There is hardly a document from the first two centuries of Christian discourse which has not been claimed at some point to be a homily. For all that there is little idea of what a homily would have sounded like in early Christianity, and no scholarly work has attempted to trace preaching before Origen, or to determine its origins.

On the basis of a examination of cognate activities in the ancient world which might have influenced Christian practice, which provide some formal guidelines, and on the basis of a narrative hypothesis on the nature of the development of Christianity, this book seeks to write a prehistory of Christian preaching. As the standard treatments of this subject begin with Origen, at which point the homily is formally and functionally established in Christianity, we conclude at that point, and seek to discover the process by which the homily known at that point had come to existence.

The first chapter sets out a *propositio* and as a *narratio* reviews the external evidence for Christian preaching before Origen, and the evidence of cognate activities in the Hellenistic world. The second chapter is the *probatio*; an attempt is made to determine what of the many documents from the early church which have claimed to be homilies were actually preached. A history is traced by which prophecy gives way to Scripture as the primary indication of the word of God under the influence of a process described as scholasticization. The homily is seen to emerge from the practice of submitting prophecy to judgement and application, which comes to employ Scripture and in time is employed on Scripture itself. The *conclusio* which forms the third chapter restates the *propositio* and provides an *exemplum* as narrative *probatio*, before concluding that the process of development in the first centuries of the church's life meant that the *oikos* became the *oikos theou* and that, as a result, converse (*homilia*) became discourse (homily).

CHAPTER ONE

PROLEGOMENA TO A PREHISTORY OF CHRISTIAN PREACHING

To deal with the problem of the preacher and the homily in the earliest church is to wrestle with the problem of evidence. As Brilioth puts it:

> The sources for a history of preaching in the post-apostolic era are very scanty. It is possible that a thorough consideration of the literary documents from the second century would be able to put together faint descriptions and similarities and thus make some contribution toward a clearer picture.[1]

This book is precisely such an attempt to contribute towards a clearer picture, and the main part of the work will be taken up with an examination of the literature which either reflects preaching, or which has been widely believed to have homiletic origins. This first chapter is intended to lay down some guidelines by which the examination of the literature may proceed. As a result of the paucity of evidence for early Christian preaching, histories of preaching typically devote a few pages to the origins of the homily and begin their real treatment with Origen;[2] it is at that point that this book concludes.

In the past it has been considered axiomatic that the earliest Christians preached, indeed for early form-criticism the sermon provided the rationale behind the shape of the New Testament documents. But for all that there is the working assumption that the earliest Christians preached there is nothing extant from the first two centuries which is self-confessedly a homily preached in the synaxis. The discussion, particularly with regard to preaching in the period of the New Testament, is confused by the number of activities which might be so described; in particular missionary preaching has been

---

[1] Brilioth, *Brief history*, 18.
[2] Thus, typically, Schütz, *Geschichte*; Edwards, "History of preaching"; Brilioth, *Brief history*; Old, *Reading and preaching*, is the exception, as he devotes a volume to this period. Sadly he makes no attempt to justify the classification of any of his examples as homiletic.

subsumed under the heading of preaching. But although both missionary preaching and preaching in the assembly are both forms of communicating the Christian message they should be distinguished carefully from one another since their audiences differ, as do their aims, and so the content of the messages is distinct to each. Thus Edwards makes the helpful functional distinction between liturgical, catechetical and missionary preaching.[3] The first takes place within the assembly, the third outside, whereas the second has the function of bridging the gap between those outside the Christian assembly and those within. Olivar makes a similar distinction, focusing on purpose rather than locus, in distinguishing between preaching intended to convert, preaching intended to catechize and preaching intended to confirm the faithful in their practice.[4] We shall observe in the course of this investigation that the aim of liturgical preaching is intended to confirm the faithful, and that Edwards' and Olivar's divisions are thus equivalent to each other.[5]

The focus of this study is liturgical preaching, that is to say we shall be solely concerned with preaching within the Christian assembly to those who are already Christians, and therefore exclude from consideration *ab initio* missionary preaching such as that found in *Acts* 2 and *Acts* 7. Whereas it is possible that these accounts may reflect something of the approach taken to preaching within the assembly, the fictive audiences are not believers and the aim of the addresses is therefore to convert rather than to edify a body of those who already believe.

The fact that there is no self-identifying homily extant is itself interesting, indeed it begs explanation. A similar situation exists with

---

[3] Edwards, "History of preaching", 184–185.

[4] Olivar, *Predicacion cristiana*, 35.

[5] These are more helpful than the distinctions made by Old, *Reading and preaching*, 8, who makes the generic distinctions between expository preaching, evangelistic preaching, catechetical preaching, festal preaching and prophetic preaching. What Old means by prophetic preaching (namely a challenge to the established order of things) is not what the early Christians would have understood by the term and so this is to be excluded from our consideration, whereas both expository and festal preaching might take place in the assembly, but need not be exhaustive as genres of preaching to be found there. The problem derives from the fact that, for Old, a scriptural basis defines preaching, whereas we shall note in the course of this investigation that this is neither a sufficient nor a necessary part of any definition. The result of this is that Old's generic distinctions are capable of including virtually any spoken communication within Christianity.

regard to the evidence for synagogue preaching, since no homily is undisputedly preserved intact from all the output of the Tannaitic preachers, even though there is ample external evidence of preaching.[6] This may derive from the suspicion with which writing was regarded by the Tannaim,[7] though there is no evidence that this suspicion was shared by Christians, but is more likely to derive simply from the fact that preaching was an oral event. Most particularly the extent of improvisation in public speaking in the ancient world should be noted, as well as the high regard in which the ability to improvise was held;[8] we may assume that this cultural norm was shared by Christians and that homilies as well as being oral in delivery were extempore in composition. This they hold in common with the eucharistic prayers of earliest Christianity. Thus were a sermon to be recorded it would have to be stenographically noted,[9] or revised from memory or notes for subsequent publication.

However much it was axiomatic for the earliest form-critics that the earliest Christians preached, no realistic attempt was made to discover the actual form of the sermons; so a homiletic *Sitz im Leben* for much of the New Testament was provided on the basis of assumption alone. The lack of any determination concerning the form of a sermon, combined with the readiness of the form-critics to classify units as such has led one critic to write of the "notorious ambiguity" of the term,[10] and another to suggest that the term "homily" is "so vague and ambiguous that it should be withdrawn until its literarily generic legitimacy has been demonstrated."[11] This work is intended to dispel the ambiguity. Since we will frequently confront

---

[6] Heinemann, "Proem", 106–107.

[7] On which see Strack and Stemberger, *Introduction*, 36–39, as well as our discussion below.

[8] Note e.g. Suetonius, *Augustus* 84. This is also noted by Siegert, *Drei hellenistisch-jüdische Predigten* II, 7–8 following Kennedy, *Art of persuasion*, 5. One may also note Quintilian *Institutio Oratoria* 4.1.54 where Quintilian suggests that a written speech may be given an extempore exordium in order to make the entire speech appear improvised.

[9] Olivar, "Preparacion e improvisacion", notes the evidence of extempore preaching in a later period.

[10] Black, "Rhetorical form", 2.

[11] Donfried, *Setting*, 26. It should be noted that we use the terms "homily" and "sermon" interchangeably here, despite attempts to distinguish them, originating with Norden, *Antike Kunstprosa*, 541. The Greek term ὁμιλία is discussed at 1.1.4 and 3.3 below.

the problem of definition we may start with a deliberately loose functional definition of a homily as "oral communication of the word of
God in the Christian assembly", and proceed from there to see
whether the evidence of this activity allows us any tighter definition
or makes it possible to supply generic criteria by which a homily
might be identified.

As has been noted, the main part of this work will consist of an
examination of the literary output of the earliest Christians in order
to discern the presence of homilies. Before this can be done, however, two things are necessary, namely the establishment of formal
criteria according to which a homily might be recognized and the
establishment of the fact that early Christians did indeed preach.
The tracing of a history of the sermon based on external reports of
preaching may moreover provide us with an underpinning narrative, what the ancients would have called a *hypothesis*, by which developments in preaching can be correlated with other developments in
the church's life. The two parts of this chapter therefore pursue the
two questions of external attestation for preaching and formal marks
of the homily. We begin by tracing references to preaching in early
Christian literature. This will at least enable us to determine whether
the earliest Christians preached and when they began to do so, and
may give some indication of the content of early preaching, which
might then be allied to formal observations in seeking out homiletic
strands and forms in the admittedly non-homiletic literature of the
first two centuries. In other words, even though it may not be possible to demonstrate the literarily generic features of the homily at
this stage, we may nonetheless attempt to discover the extent to
which preaching was a liturgical event in the life of the early church.

1.1. *The external evidence for Christian preaching before Origen*

According to Stowers the earliest certain evidence for a homily in
the Christian synaxis is that of Justin.[12] Salzmann similarly notes that
Justin is the first indisputable witness to a homily relating to a preceding scriptural reading.[13] Must we conclude that the earliest Christians
knew nothing of the sermon? Stowers suggests that attempts to see

---

[12] Stowers, "Social status", 70.
[13] Salzmann, *Lehren und Ermahnen*, 473.

preaching in worship before that time are anachronistic, "pathetic examples of special pleading", and that the descriptions of worship in *I Corinthians* preclude the possibility of a sermon in this setting. Stowers cites Delling as an example of that special pleading.[14] This is a grossly unfair assessment of Delling's argument; Delling argues that since the proclamation of the kerygma is an essential item in the life of early Christianity, that since both the pagan world and the synagogue both knew activities akin to preaching, and that since the later New Testament books appear to know something of the communication of the word of God in the assembly, this proclamation and communication might be part of the earliest Christian worship. But Delling is clear that there is no easy step from the pagan world or the synagogue to the Christian church, and is equally clear that there is nothing directly corresponding to the modern sermon in earliest Christian worship. Nonetheless, worship was a point at which the will of God for the congregation might be discovered. We may therefore begin our search for homiletic activity in the descriptions of worship to be found in the Corinthian correspondence.

1.1.1. *Preaching at Corinth?*

Delling had suggested that activity akin to preaching might form part of the worship at Corinth. Most significant for understanding the way in which this might have occurred is the activity of the prophets. It is clear that prophets functioned within the liturgical assembly at Corinth,[15] as indeed would seem to have been the case in the community known to the author of *Acts* or to his sources;[16] thus *I Corinthians* 14:29–31, in legislating for the involvement of prophets at the assembly, suggests that prophets should not interrupt each other but give way, so that the people might learn and be exhorted. This clearly implies that a prophetic message would be of some length and, especially since prophecy is contrasted with glossolalia, that it is comprehensible, and intended for the instruction

---

[14] Delling, *Worship in the New Testament*, 103. The point is that Justin witnesses to a homily based on Scripture, whereas Delling is in fact unsure whether Scripture was even used in the earliest Christian communities!

[15] A full treatment of prophetic activity in Corinth may be found in Gillespie, *First theologians*.

[16] See Ellis, "Role of the Christian prophet".

and edification of the people; it is thus akin to preaching.[17] On the
other hand it is clear that there is no set place for a homily in the
worship of the church, and certainly clear that there is no individual whose specific function it is to direct the church in this way. It
is possible that there is a group of prophets, but even this group
may be open-ended. Put thus we must agree with Delling that the
sermon in the earliest communities might not have the formality
which we would associate with preaching activity, but that this does
not mean that prophetic activity is not preaching, or at least preaching in nuce. When prophets instruct and encourage then they are
functionally preaching.[18] There is indeed wide agreement that prophecy
in the Pauline communities was functionally equivalent to preaching, the only dissenting voice being that of Forbes, who argues that
prophecy is necessarily the revelation of new material, whereas preaching is the repetition of previously revealed content.[19] However we
shall see below that the disjunction is artificial, and that prophecy
may well have reference to that which is already revealed. There is
also some terminological confusion in Forbes' argument, since when
he discusses preaching he is referring to missionary preaching, and
not to preaching in the assembly.

Here we should note the absence of any reference to the reading
of Scripture in the summary of Christian worship in the Corinthian
assembly. This is not an isolated instance, for one should also note
that there is no evidence that there was reading of Scripture in the
liturgy of the community addressed by the *Didache*. In the Corinthian
assembly the prophetic messages were "revelations" and so we should
note that apart from having a lesser degree of formality than the
homily this *diakonia* of the word of God was unmediated. On this
basis Delling doubts that Scripture formed any part of the Christian
assembly,[20] though Meeks finds this difficult to accept given the extent
of scriptural knowledge displayed or assumed in the Pauline correspondence.[21] However, Paul may simply have assumed scriptural
knowledge deriving from attendance at the synagogue. Ekenberg similarly asks how the Galatian problem might have arisen had the

---

[17] These points are noted by Müller, *Prophetie und Predigt*, 23–31.
[18] So Bauer, *Wortgottesdienst*, 55.
[19] Forbes, *Prophecy and inspired speech*, 225–228.
[20] *Worship in the New Testament*, 92–103.
[21] Meeks, *First urban Christians*, 146.

Pauline communities not known the Scriptures of the Old Testament;[22] the answer is that the opponents brought reflection on Scripture with them. It is thus to be noted that the main location for scriptural citations within the Pauline corpus is in the setting of arguments with opponents. It is even possible that Paul's conviction that God was doing a radically new thing meant that he did not communicate through means of the Old Testament Scriptures, believing that whereas they were of value to Jews they did not apply to gentile converts.[23] However, when his opponents employ scriptural weapons then he must respond in like manner.

Salzmann suggests that Scripture is not mentioned in the list of constituents of the Corinthian worship because the list is incomplete.[24] However, one would expect that if Scripture played anything like the role which it played in the synagogue then it would be mentioned. It is true that the argument for the absence of any scriptural reading in the worship of the Pauline communities is fundamentally an argument from silence, and that arguments from silence are always dangerous, especially when dealing with ancient liturgy where, as Bradshaw reminds us, the most common is usually the least mentioned.[25] Thus it would be illegitimate to conclude that the community of *Acta Johannis*, which likewise describes liturgies without mentioning scriptural readings, did not read Scripture in worship since the descriptions are brief, intending to set a scene for the narrative.[26] But when we deal with the Pauline corpus we are not dealing with a brief description of worship but, in *I Corinthians* in particular, with an extensive discussion of worship, in which context it would be exceedingly strange for the role of Scripture in the assembly not to be mentioned once, unless it had no role. We are able to build up a good picture of the Pauline assembly on the basis of what Paul

---

[22] Ekenberg, "Urkristen predikan", 19.

[23] This fundamentally theological argument is an updated version of that of Bauer, *Wortgottesdienst*, 19–20, who likewise doubts that the gentile communities addressed by Paul read Scripture in their assemblies.

[24] Salzmann, *Lehren und Ermahnen*, 68, 72–74.

[25] Bradshaw, *Search*, 76–77.

[26] For a discussion see Salzmann, *Lehren und Ermahnen*, 285–6, 288–89; Salzmann, in view of the absence of reference to Scripture in the preaching of *Acta Johannis*, thinks it possible that this community actually did not read Scripture in the assembly. Whereas it is possible, there is not the material on which to construct an argument, as the single *Gemeindepredigt* in these *Acta* is atypical, a farewell discourse rather than a sermon.

tells us, and may perceive that activity in the assembly might include
teaching and the communication of the word of God, but at no
point is there an indication that Scripture played a formal role in
that. The *Didache*, though not from a Pauline milieu, provides supporting evidence of this phenomenon. The argument from silence
can moreover be supported by the theological shape of the Pauline
gospel, and may further be supported by noting the question raised
by Bauer of whence and why the earliest gentile Christians might
acquire the expensive rolls containing the Jewish Scriptures.[27] Most
recently Stanley independently argues that it would be unlikely that
the Pauline communities would have ready access to the rolls containing Scripture,[28] and although he does not consider the implication of this for Pauline worship his conclusion that it is improbable
that the early Pauline households had any Scripture in their pos-
session would clearly impact upon worship in these households.

The need for public scriptural reading comes only when a generation grows up within the church which does not have this synagogal background, and when the church begins to remodel itself on
the synagogue under the pressure of maintaining its mission and
presence. This takes place within the Pauline communities at the
time of the production of the Pastoral Epistles. Prior to this, formal
reading from the Scriptures might well have been considered unnecessary. Similarly the *Didache* would seem to assume scriptural knowledge on the part of the original users. In time however it becomes
necessary for churches to model themselves on the synagogue, but
this synagogal influence is not found in the first generation of Pauline
Christians.[29]

Apart from the use of Scripture in the synagogue, it is possible
that the activity of the prophets which was, we have suggested, akin
to preaching, could relate itself to Scripture, in the significant role
of prophetic speech forms as reminders of the past.[30] Whereas this
might simply be a reminder of the past life of the Christian,[31] this

---

[27] Bauer, *Wortgottesdienst*, 40–45.
[28] Stanley, "Pearls before swine", 126–130.
[29] So Bauer, *Wortgottesdienst*, 19–20.
[30] This is noted by Müller, *Prophetie und Predigt*, 57–58 and by Furnish, "Prophets, apostles and preachers". See moreover 1.2.1.3 below.
[31] A form suggested by Dahl, "Form-critical observations." Note here the man-
ner in which preaching in the assembly might hark back to missionary preaching.

past could be scriptural, the prophet reminding his hearers of the past salvation of God, and so Scripture could easily begin to serve, if not as the basis for exegetical preaching, at least as a source of *exempla* in ethical παράκλησις. The unmediated word of God from the prophets might thus remain unmediated, whilst relating to Scripture. We may, however, conclude that although there was no scriptural reading in the worship of the Pauline churches, the assembly was a place at which the word of God was communicated, and that the means of this communication was prophecy.

1.1.2. *Preaching and prophecy in Acts*

When the activity of preaching is described in *Acts* it is not teaching in the liturgical assembly but missionary preaching.[32] A possible exception to this is the λόγος παρακλήσεως which Paul delivers in the synagogue at Pisidian Antioch, and with this we may note the (somewhat brief) sermon of Jesus at *Luke* 4. But although both are given a setting within the assembly they are both kerygmatic in content, and in both cases the "sermons" are against the expectations of the audience, because kerygmatic preaching would not normally belong in that setting.[33] Whereas their content is therefore no indication of the nature of preaching in the assemblies known to Luke, it is nonetheless noteworthy that both of these "homilies" find their setting in the synagogue, which opens the question of whether Luke is describing the practice of the synagogue as known to him or whether he is transferring the practice of the church as known to him to the synagogue. We shall see that it is quite likely that the homiletic practice of the synagogue had by the time of Luke been transferred to the church; fortunately we are not dependent entirely on Luke's account for either Christian or Jewish preaching.

---

[32] A difficulty which has been frequently noted, most recently by Wills, "Form of the sermon", 277. On the other hand one should note the missionary effect of prophetic preaching described at *I Cor.* 14:23–25.

[33] The blurring of the distinction between kerygmatic preaching and preaching in the assembly is useful up to a point, Paul for instance uses the verb κηρύσσειν at *Romans* 2:21 for what would appear to be moral exhortation in a synagogue setting, and Gillespie (*First theologians*) argues that prophetic discourses were kerygmatically based. One should note however that the only uses of κηρύσσειν in the second century are with reference to the preaching of the apostles or the ancient prophets (for references to which see Bartelink, *Lexicologisch-semantische studie*, 122–123). On Paul's "sermon" in *Acts* 13 see 2.2.1 below.

Although the synagogue homily of *Acts* 13:16b–41 is missionary preaching, the setting is the assembly, and so it is interesting that it should be introduced as a λόγος παρακλήσεως. The term παράκλη-σις had a long history in Greek; as McDonald[34] points out it orig-inally applied to the προτρεπτικοὶ λόγοι and as such is rejected by ps-Isocrates as a medium of moral teaching, the word παραίνεσις being preferred.[35] The word παραίνεσις however does not appear in a Christian author before Clement whereas παράκλησις on the other hand appears to have become in some circles a word with a par-ticular significance indicating prophecy or preaching. Apart from its use in *Acts* 13:15 we should note the self designation of *Hebrews* at 13:22 as a λόγος παρακλήσεως, together with the statement of Paul that the function of prophecy is παράκλησις (*I Corinthians* 14:4–5). Hill compiles further evidence for its use, which indicates that proph-ecy plays a role in *Acts* (or perhaps in Luke's sources) which is func-tionally similar to preaching.[36] So Barnabas is said to be a Son of παράκλησις. The name would be derived from *bar-nᵉbuʾah* or *bar-nᵉbiyya*; as such he is the son of prophecy and as a prophet he deliv-ers παράκλησις. The same term is used by Luke to describe the Baptist's proclamation and is employed again at *Acts* 9:31, where the church is filled with the παράκλησις of the Holy Spirit.

Hill goes on to state:

> At *Acts* 15.32 the phrase "they exhorted and strengthened the brethren" is specifically connected with the fact that Judas Barsabbas and Silas are themselves prophets. The same two terms are used at 14.22 with reference to the activity of Paul and Barnabas, both of whom must have been regarded, in certain aspects of their careers, as prophets (13.1); this verse (14.22) offers some insight into their παράκλησις: . . . strengthening the souls of the disciples, exhorting them to continue in the faith, and saying that through many tribulations we must enter the Kingdom of God. The prophetic ministry has the characteristics of pastoral preaching.[37]

It is on such a basis that Wills suggests that λόγος παρακλήσεως took on a fixed meaning, and is still employed in this fixed meaning as

---

[34] McDonald, *Kerygma and didache*, 69.
[35] ps-Isocrates *Ad Demonicum* 1.1.
[36] Hill, *New Testament prophecy*, 101–103.
[37] Hill, *New Testament prophecy*, 103.

late as the redaction of *Constitutiones Apostolorum* 8.5.[38] Thus it would seem that in parts of the early church at least, the communities founded by Paul and known to Luke being cases in point, that preaching was a function of the prophets. This does not mean that preaching was restricted to the prophets, in fact the evidence points to an overlap of functions in the church in the earliest period, nor does it mean that the functions of prophecy were necessarily restricted to those which may be designated preaching, but nonetheless it confirms the place that prophetic preaching held in the earliest communities, implies that preaching was considered an inspired activity, thus providing supporting evidence for our earlier suggestion that homilies in the earliest Christian communities were extempore, and indicates that the function of these prophetic sermons was the upbuilding of the believing Christian.

Apart from the reported sermons, teaching in the Christian liturgical assembly is referred to at *Acts* 20:7–12; there three words are used, conceivably of the same activity; διαλέγεσθαι, ὁμιλεῖν, and παρακαλεῖν. In this case however it is not clear whether διαλέγεσθαι and ὁμιλεῖν are being used in their conversational sense,[39] though given the extended length of the assembly it is quite likely that converse and teaching interrupt the formal preaching and prophecy. At 20:24, where Paul speaks of his missionary activity, it is clearly the case that conversation is intended, and here we may recall that cynic attempts at conversion were undertaken through conversation rather than through direct address.[40] The problem of distinguishing between preaching in the assembly and catechesis, either of groups or of individuals, is one which will confront us frequently. We shall see below that there is ordered catechesis in the community known to the Pastoral Epistles, but that the comparative disorder of the earlier references, such as those of *Acts* 20, indicates that earlier than the Pastoral Epistles there was no firm distinction, in that catechesis and preaching alike took place within the liturgical assembly. Similarly *Colossians* 3:16–17 seems to combine vocabulary associated with worship and catechesis, and easily passes from instructions concerning

---

[38] Wills, "Form of the sermon", 280.

[39] Donfried, *Setting*, 27 shares this uncertainty.

[40] Stowers, "Social status", makes much of this point. References may be pursued there.

worship into a *Haustafel* at 3:18. Thus there is early evidence of the *diakonia* of the word in the New Testament, but it points to a somewhat lesser formality than that which we would associate with the homily. The evidence of synagogue preaching, however, shows a greater degree of formality. In the diaspora Philo bears witness to the reading and exegesis of the books of the law in the synagogue[41] and elsewhere he refers to the scholastic activity undertaken there.[42] In Palestine likewise discourse on the law was given in the first century.[43] It is this formality which we seem to find in the Pastoral Epistles. The evidence of *Acts* thus supports our reading of the information found in the Corinthian correspondence in implying that prophecy functioned as preaching in the informal setting of early Christianity.

1.1.3. *Developments in preaching and the church in the first century*

At *I Timothy* 4:11ff "Paul" exhorts the hearer "Timothy" to the public reading of Scripture and to proclamation (παραγγέλειν) and gives his three main duties as ἀνάγνωσις, παράκλησις and διδασκαλία. We may reasonably take the reading referred to as a reading of the Scriptures,[44] παράκλησις as a reference to preaching in the assembly,[45] and διδασκαλία as a reference to the work of catechesis, perhaps still given within the worship of the church,[46] but distinguishable at least in principle from preaching more generally. At *II Timothy* 4:2 the addressee is thus similarly exhorted παρακαλῆσον. One thus sees the church at the end of the first century adopting the scholastic practices of the synagogue in the reading and explanation of the law, in contradistinction to the informality of earlier practice and the absence of the use of Scripture. Does this derive from the received practice of the church or is it an attempt to remodel the wor-

---

[41] *Apologia* 7.12.

[42] *De somniis* 2.127.

[43] Josephus *Contra Apionem* 175; note also TJ *Sotah* 1:4; Tosefta *Megillah* 2:18; Tosefta *Sotah* 7.9.

[44] ἀνάγνωσις is used of the public reading of Scripture in the synagogue at e.g. *Acts* 13:15, *II Cor.* 3:14, Josephus *Antiquitates Judaicae* 4.209.

[45] Our argument for seeing παράκλησις as a reference to preaching is strengthened by its association here with ἀνάγνωσις.

[46] On this passage see also Salzmann, *Lehren und Ermahnen*, 95–96, who sees it as a description of the responsibilities of one charged with the communication of the word of God in the worship of this community.

ship of the church on that of the synagogue? Is there indeed a "straight line from the worship of the synagogue to that of the early church", as Morris asserts,[47] or is the line more crooked and the route less direct?

The process leading to the establishment of the church at the time of the Pastoral Epistles is generally understood as "institutionalization";[48] according to this understanding the earlier informality of Christian worship becomes typified and habitualized. However, this description is an oversimplification, for not only had the earlier informality already led to social and theological problems, even leading Paul himself to encourage a process of institutionalization,[49] but the separation from the synagogue exposed a need for scriptural teaching that the church was not meeting, and which opened up the church to precisely the problems which Paul combats in his letters. Thus in time practice is borrowed from the synagogue, including practice related to the activity of preaching. Separation from the synagogue leads to a need for re-institutionalization, so although reading and preaching were not originally part of the practice of the church they very rapidly became so. In the earliest period of the Pauline mission the synagogue would provide the opportunity for the hearing of Scripture and its interpretation, and Christian assemblies were a supplement to the worship of the synagogue. When the ways began to part it became necessary for the Christian communities to absorb additional, synagogal, functions, and with these functions and liturgical forms come forms of organisation associated with the synagogue. For this reason we begin, in the Pastoral Epistles, to hear of πρεσβυτέροι and their duties.

It is this same movement, rather than the growing importance of ethical paraenesis,[50] ordering of worship resulting from institutionalization,[51] or decline in the expectation of the parousia[52] which accounts for the relative paucity of reports of prophetic activity in the descriptions of worship in the second and third centuries. Prophetic functions had become absorbed into preaching and teaching, which were

---

[47] Morris, "The Saints and the Synagogue", 51.
[48] So MacDonald, *Pauline churches*, passim.
[49] Macdonald, *Pauline churches*, 14, 65.
[50] Ekenberg, "Urkristen predikan", 9, 23, 31.
[51] Norden, *Antike Kunstprosa*, 539–540; also Aune, *Prophecy*, 204.
[52] Müller, *Prophetie und Predigt*, 238.

activities to which prophecy had always been related,[53] and just as
prophetic functions became absorbed into the activities of preaching
and teaching, so the prophets themselves, who functioned within the
household setting, were absorbed into the synagogal arrangement
with the corresponding growth in offices.[54] Thus prophets, who had
never held an office as such, became bishops, and bishops, who previously needed only be householders, became prophets and preachers
and teachers. Meeks is surprised how little imitation of the organization of the synagogue there is in the Pauline church, given the
close links between them,[55] but this derives from the foundation of
the church in private houses alongside the synagogue as supple-
mentary to rather than substitionary of those synagogues, and the
organisation which resulted from that household setting. Even when
the church within the Pauline tradition began to imitate the synagogue more closely, its foundation upon a household model was
already firm enough to allow certain elements deriving from this
foundation to survive.[56]

The household is thus the social construction which provides the
setting for the communication of the word of God in the Pauline
churches. The synagogue had itself derived from the household, but
by this time is sufficiently defined as to be recognisable as a separate social setting, one into which the Pauline communities grew,
but which might provide a basis for the social construction of other
Christian communities. The Graeco-Roman school likewise is a subspecies of the household, but had likewise by the first century developed into a distinct social reality, and may have provided a model
for Christians in the construction of their communities; in examining the literature we must have an eye on the social settings which
dictated the nature of the communication which occurred in these
groupings.

---

[53] For prophets as teachers see Hill, "Christian prophets as teachers or instructors".

[54] It should be stressed that there is no conflict in this absorption; prophets were
performing activities which were already parallel to those of the synagogue; it is
only their designation which changes. Thus in the second century Polycarp is
διδάσκαλος ἀποστολικὸς καὶ προφητικὸς . . . ἐπίσκοπος (*Martyrium Polycarpi* 16.2), Melito
of Sardis is likewise bishop (Polycrates at Eusebius *Historia ecclesiastica* 5.24) and held
to be a prophet (Jerome *De viris illustribus* 24).

[55] Meeks, *First urban Christians*, 81.

[56] Thus Verner, *Household*, 159–160 is able to see that the qualifications for leadership in the Pastoral Epistles are essentially those of a householder, but does not
note the absence of any analogy for the teaching functions put upon this leadership.

The process of synagogalization here has been observed solely in the Pauline and post-Pauline communities. In other communities there was a similar emphasis on prophecy in the early period: for instance, in the letters addressed by the seer of *Revelation* to the seven churches, Müller finds a prophetic form, the *Bußparaklese*.[57] Moreover, given that the function of prophets was παράκλησις, we may perhaps see the function of the παράκλητος in the fourth gospel as being the function of prophecy within the church. Like the prophet, the paraclete teaches, reminding the Johannine disciples of the sayings of Jesus[58] and bearing witness to Jesus through them.[59] The paraclete is a πνεῦμα, by whom the disciples are to function; this observation should alert us to the further possibility of finding prophetic homiletic traces in the Gospel, in particular in the mouth of Jesus, since the spirit of truth is another paraclete, like Jesus.[60] We shall explore in detail below the question of whether the Johannine communities underwent the same process of synagogalization undergone by the Pauline communities and find that although the process is harder to trace, because all the literature left by these communities comes from a time at which the church was already separated from the synagogue, there are some indications that analogous developments had taken place in these communities. Thus we may note the use of Scripture in the prophecy of the fourth Gospel along with the writer's characterization of himself in *III John* as a πρεσβύτερος.

Thus we find that at the end of the first century there has been some development in the church and that the church is on the way to becoming a scholastic organisation. Prophecy is still practised, but there is also reading of Scripture, which would inevitably impact on the communication of the word of God either in prophecy or through other means.

1.1.4. *Developments in preaching and the church in the second century*

Having suggested that the Christian homily is a product of the late first century, albeit building on earlier beginnings, we may extend

---

[57] Müller, *Prophetie und Predigt*, 57–76. A closer examination of Müller's arguments follows at 1.2.1.3 and 2.1.3 below.

[58] *John* 14:26. The prophetic function of recalling the past to mind is noted by Müller, *Prophetie und Predigt*, 57–58 and by Furnish, "Prophets, apostles and preachers".

[59] *John* 15:26; the prophetic role of the paraclete as the realization of Jesus in the church is noted by Panagopoulos, "Urchristliche Prophetie", 13–14.

[60] See on this 2.2.3.1 below.

our search for external evidence into the second century. Here one finds a few references to teaching activity, arguably including preaching. However, the fact that there is not much mention of preaching in the literature of the early centuries should not be taken to imply that preaching did not happen. Bradshaw reminds us that the fact that something is mentioned more often means that it is unusual than that it is commonplace, and that the common and familiar is often passed over in silence.[61] The nature of these references to preaching in the first centuries is as mentions in passing, implying that this was such a normal activity that it hardly needed to be mentioned. On the other hand the fact that this is the sum total of the external evidence means that our picture will of necessity be incomplete. Secondly we should note that the evidence is gathered from a variety of geographical settings, and thus that we should be aware of the danger of universalizing a local peculiarity.[62]

In turning to the evidence we may note first Justin's well-known description of Christian worship;[63] Justin describes for us an assembly at which, he tells us, the president (προέστως) gives a word of νουθεσία καὶ πρόκλησις after the readings, intending imitation of the good contained therein. The use of the term νουθεσία here reminds us of Paul's assertion at *Acts* 20:31 that he did not cease νουθετῶν ἕνα ἕκαστον, though this implies individual direction such as that practised both by cynics and in the schools of the Epicureans. Nonetheless it is possible that in Justin's school the techniques used on individuals have been turned on to the group.

Ignatius uses language reminiscent of homiletic activity in describing his letters. At *Ad Ephesios* 9 he describes himself through the writing as προσομιλῆσαι, and at *Ad Magnesianos* 14.1 he says παρεκάλεσα ὑμᾶς.[64] Because these letters were intended for reading in the assembly, we might well expect the writer to use language reminiscent of the language of a preacher.[65] That preaching, or at least a functionally equivalent activity, was established in the church of his period

---

[61] Bradshaw, *Search*, 76–77.

[62] A warning sounded by Salzmann, *Lehren und Ermahnen*, 28.

[63] *I Apologia* 1.67.

[64] Lightfoot reads παρεκέλευσα at this point, a reading with which Sieben, "Ignatianen als Briefe", 8 is unimpressed, since the word is otherwise unattested in the corpus of Ignatius, or in the New Testament. Cf. also *Ad Polycarpum* 7.3.

[65] This occurrence of the word is distinct from its usual epistolary use, (on which see Bjerkelund, *Parakalô*) which is otherwise the case in Ignatius' uses of the term.

may be assured through his reference to Onesimus speaking (λαλοῦντος) in the assembly,[66] though unfortunately this contains no indication of technical vocabulary. The possible conversational significance of all of these terms should also be noted, since preaching need not have been a formal event and prophecy has not yet ceased.

I Clement contains a number of references which may imply preaching activity. In the first chapter the writer describes the past good works of the Corinthians and states that:

> You enjoined (ἐπετρέπετε) the young to think in a moderate and seemly manner, you instructed (παρηγγέλετε) the women to do all things with a blameless, seemly and pure conscience ... and you taught (ἐδιδάσκετε) them to manage their households ...

Here there may be reference either to preaching or to catechetical teaching. Similarly at chapter 21 Clement refers to the work of παιδεία in Christ. These references however would all seem to refer more to systematic catechetical teaching than to preaching in the assembly. Support for viewing these references as references to catechesis may be gained from Hermas who, at *Vision* 2.4.3, is told to give a copy of the book containing his visions to Grapte, that she νουθετήσαι the widows and orphans, whereas Hermas is to read the book in the company of the elders of the patrons. In Rome at least it appears that there were separate catechetical groups for different categories of people; this may have been the case in Asia likewise, in view of the differing groups mentioned by Ignatius. Thus although Clement here gives us no information about preaching, we may observe that in either the Corinthian or the Roman community the scholastic activities of the synagogue have been adopted by the church, and that catechesis is now separate from the usual preaching within the assembly.

In the Latin tradition, we should note that Tertullian, at *Apologeticum* 39.3, speaks of *exhortatio* in the assembly, based on the Scriptures, intended to build up the faith, hope and Christian practice of the hearers. That preaching took place in his African assembly may also be gathered from his description of worship at *De Anima* 9.[67]

---

[66] *Ad Ephesios* 6.2.
[67] scripturae leguntur ... psalmi canuntur ... allocutiones proferuntur ... petitiones delegantur.

Unfortunately, although Tertullian's catechetical addresses on baptism and on the Lord's prayer survive, there is no surviving evidence
of African preaching from the period, though there is some evidence
of prophetic activity, albeit outside the main assembly.[68]

The final possible external reference to preaching in the second
century is left until the end. At Ignatius *Ad Polycarpum* 5.1 Polycarp
is told ὁμιλίαν ποιεῖν against the evil arts. Does this mean preaching or conversation (conversation being the usual and common meaning of ὁμιλία)? In contrast to the virtually unanimous opinion of
commentators[69] it will be suggested that this is not a reference to
preaching as such. Whereas a full discussion of the term ὁμιλία must
wait upon the substance of the work here presented a brief investigation is in order here, in which it is argued that ὁμιλία does not come
to mean "homily" until relatively late in the history of its usage.

Siegert's discussion of the term may be taken as typical of previous investigations. He suggests that the use of ὁμιλία to signify an
address is a product by and large of the second century.[70] However,
in this he is essentially following Norden who saw the ὁμιλία as an
instructional discourse, a usage which, he believed, derived from the
philosophical schools.[71] However, the classical philosophical uses to
which Norden has reference are all concerned with philosophical
companionship, and thus to philosophical conversation, and not to
public address. We may note with interest here Iamblichus' description of the philosophical life in the school where there take place
διαλέξεις καὶ τὰς πρὸς ἀλλήλους ὁμιλίας.[72] The nearer equivalent to
the Christian homily would be the διάλεξις, the address,[73] though

---

[68] On these addresses as sermons see Barnes, *Tertullian*, 117–118; Barnes refers
to these as "homiletic discourse" whilst wisely stopping short of suggesting that they
are homilies as such. This is entirely plausible. Salzmann, *Lehren und Ermahnen*, 473
similarly notes that these thematic addresses are not typical sermons. For the discussion of prophecy in Carthage and a hypothetical prehistory of preaching there
see 2.2.5 below.

[69] Lightfoot, *Apostolic fathers* II 2, 347; Donfried, *Setting*, 27; Bartelink, *Lexicologisch-
semantische studie*, 136–137; Schoedel, *Ignatius of Antioch*, 271; Brilioth, *Brief history*,
17–18; Siegert, *Drei hellenistisch-jüdische Predigten* II, 10; Camelot, *Ignace d'Antioche*, 175.
The only mildly dissenting voice is that of Salzmann, *Lehren und Ermahnen*, 193 n202
who, as a result of the context which mentions various other forms of educational
activity in the church, believes that this is a reference to catechetical teaching.

[70] Siegert, *Drei hellenistisch-jüdische Predigten* II, 10.

[71] Norden, *Antike Kunstprosa*, 541–544.

[72] *De vita Pythagorica* 104.

[73] Dillon and Hershbell, *Iamblichus*, 127 translate διαλέξεις here as "dialogues".

the close relationship between address and discussion is to be noted, as it is hardly likely that an address would be uninterrupted and undiscussed.

Norden's theory thus has a missing link, though the close relationship between philosophical converse and address here is to be noted, reminiscent of the use of both διαλέγεσθαι and ὁμιλεῖν at *Acts* 20:7–12. Conversation may well belong closely alongside address, as it would in a school, and so we should be alive to a greater informality in preaching in the earliest church than that with which we are familiar. But this does not make ὁμιλία mean "homily", even less does it enable us to understand ὁμιλία as a sermon of a particular type. Norden sums up his theory as follows:

> Da in dieser Art der Predigt das lehrhafte Moment im Mittelpunkt stand, so nannte man sie ὁμιλία, ein Wort in dem die Anschauung ausgesprochen liegt, dass der Prediger zu seiner Gemeinde in rein persönliche Beziehung trat, wenn er sie fast im Tone eines gewöhnlichen Gespräche belehrte.[74]

The evidence of classical usage will not however stand the weight which is being put upon it here.[75] Quacquarelli comes to similar conclusions on the basis of Cicero's distinction between *sermo*, which is a relaxed and discursive style of speech, and *contentio*, a more aggressive form.[76] Yet although the companionship of a school might lead to a relaxed style of speech, this is not ὁμιλία.[77]

There is moreover not the support to be found in the use of the term at Justin *Dialogus* 85.5 and 28.2 which Lightfoot and Bartelink would like to find.[78] Here the phrase is employed to mean an argument based on the prophetic Scriptures, but not a discourse. The setting is a dialogue, and the argument is worked out dialogically;

However not only would this be redundant in the paired phrase, but ὁμιλία alone is qualified with πρὸς ἀλλήλους. By the time Iamblichus is writing the term διάλεξις has come to mean an address.

[74] Norden, *Antike Kunstprosa*, 541.

[75] According to Donfried, *Setting*, 27 this classical usage is "tangential", and yet he feels that "Norden's impulse is sound".

[76] Quacquarelli, *Retorica*, 62–63, with reference to *De officiis* 2.14.48.

[77] At least it is not in the second century. Quacquarelli, *Retorica*, 63 is able to quote St Augustine's reference to "tractatus populares quos Graeci homilias vocant" (*Ep.* 224.3), but this is far too late to be useful.

[78] Lightfoot, *Apostolic fathers* II 2, 347; Bartelink, *Lexicologisch-semantische studie*, 136–137.

this is therefore not a reference to a homily in the assembly, but indicates that part of the ὁμιλία of the schools would involve argument, and that the term may thus be extended to mean an argument set forth in a dialogue. It is perhaps in this sense that Theophilus refers to his address to Autolycus as a ὁμιλία; it is part of the fiction of an address to an individual.[79] These uses remind us of the methods of the cynics in seeking converse with individuals. In seeing the term ὁμιλία as persuasive in intent rather than exhortatory, we may so understand the title of Hippolytus' ὁμιλία εἰς τὸν αἵρεσιν Νοήτου which so puzzles Quasten.[80]

By the time of *Acta Johannis*, which mentions a liturgy which includes a ὁμιλία, the word has clearly come to mean a homily, since it is addressed πρὸς τοὺς ἀδελφούς.[81] But there is no evidence that this usage would have been known to Polycarp. In time we will return to this passage to determine what "conversing against the evil arts" might mean in practice, but should conclude for the moment that ὁμιλία meaning "homily" is not a usage of the earlier part of the second century.

From the above summary of external references the breadth of terminology employed should be noted. However, within the breadth we should note the continuing usage of παρακαλέω and παράκλησις. Questions of terminology apart, we have nonetheless safely established that preaching activity occurs in the synaxis from the end of the first century, building on earlier beginnings, and in particular the activities of the prophets in proclamation. We have further suggested that preaching activity in some communities may have been undertaken in conformity with Jewish models as the church undergoes a process of re-institutionalization along Jewish lines as a result of the expulsion or departure of Christians from the synagogue.

1.1.5. *A conclusion concerning the beginning of preaching*

In the first part of this chapter we set out to establish whether the earliest Christians preached, and if so to discern when they began to do so. We have established that the earliest Christians were con-

---

[79] *Ad Autolycum* 2.1; Interestingly, the ὁμιλία is addressed to the ears. This is to be noted as further emphasizing the oral nature of the proceedings.

[80] Quasten, *Patrology*, 180 thinks there must be an error here.

[81] *Acta Johannis* 46.

cerned with the communication of the Word of God within their worshipping communities, and that this communication was fundamentally a work of the prophets. We have further suggested that the origins of formal Christian preaching might derive from the institutionalization of the church, with the ordering of worship on a synagogal basis, and in the adoption of the scholastic functions of the synagogue, which would extend to preaching as to catechesis. Thus although the practice of reading and preaching is a relatively late development within the Christian churches this later practice derived from the earlier activity of the proclamation of God's word in the assembly. Finally we have suggested that these were not exclusive forces, and that the two movements of institutionalization and synagogalization might meet, in that the institution which the church becomes might have some of the functions of the synagogue. In seeking to chart the origins of the sermon we should be aware that whereas the sermon might be expected to develop in different ways in different parts of the church, the extent to which preaching appears to have been a universal part of the experience of worshipping Christians by the end of the second century, at which point Justin and Tertullian have borne witness to preaching in their assemblies, is quite remarkable of itself.[82] The underpinning narrative of institutionalization, or more precisely scholasticization, as a means of understanding the development of preaching may thus provide a useful heuristic tool in seeking the origins of preaching, alongside the observation of formal criteria in the literature of early Christianity which is the task of the next part of this chapter.

1.2. *The search for formal criteria*

We have demonstrated that the earliest Christians preached, and may assume that preaching adapted existing forms and genres to itself. But if no homily survives it is hard to see how we are to picture the homily in the earliest church at all, and with no picture it is hard to see how we might recognize a homily if one exists embedded in another form. We may thus begin the search for the origins of preaching by seeking formal criteria by which a homily may be

---

[82] So Olivar, *Predicacion*, 47–48.

recognized. This is not the first attempt to discern forms by which
a homily may be recognized, and we shall observe that some progress
in this direction has been made. Of itself however the task of form-
criticism is beset by uncertainty. The narrative of the development
of Christian communication out of prophecy and converse into something more formal which was suggested in the first part of this chapter may however be used to undergird formal observations, by allowing
us to picture the forms which have been suggested within the Christian
assembly. We shall observe possible models for preaching which
might supply formal criteria, but because in the strictly formal task
of discerning the shape of early Christian preaching there have been
some attempts we may begin by reviewing the contributions made
to date.

1.2.1. *A brief Forschungsgeschichte*

1.2.1.1. *Reicke's form-criticism*
We begin with the attempt formally to classify early Christian sermons undertaken by Reicke.[83] He found four forms of preaching,
which he labelled 1) conversion 2) instruction and edification 3) testament and 4) revelation.

McDonald objects to each of these categories.[84] Firstly he notes
that conversion is not a category of preaching; whereas this is true,
Reicke surely intends missionary preaching by the use of this term,
and in subsuming this activity under preaching is doing the same as
earlier form-critics had done. However we have already noted that
missionary preaching is not to be confused with preaching within
the assembly since the two activities have different aims and different
audiences, and that for this reason, quite apart from problems of
authenticity, the speeches in *Acts* cannot generally be employed to
reconstruct the preaching of the assembly.

McDonald next points out that Reicke's second category, instruction and edification, is far too broad to be a useful form-critical category. This is likewise true. Edificatory discourse was known to the
Greek world as paraenesis or as παράκλησις,[85] and edification (οἰκοδομή)
was for Paul the object of the discourses of the prophets, but we do

---

[83] Reicke, "Synopsis".
[84] McDonald, *Kerygma and didache*, 9–10.
[85] See further the discussion of these terms at 1.1.4 above.

not know whether these discourses were intended to be paraenetic, nor do we know whether paraenesis necessarily was found as part of a homily in the assembly, and cannot assume that this was the case;[86] we have moreover observed that just as missionary preaching should be distinguished from preaching in the assembly so should catechetical preaching. It is possible that catechesis and homily stood beside each other in the earliest period of Christian communication,[87] but they remain separate activities even if found together, and are certainly distinguished by their occasion as well as by their content by the end of the first century.

McDonald goes on to suggest that whereas Reicke's second category is too broad his third is too narrow, the testamentary discourse simply being a subspecies of the epideictic genre. To an extent this is true, but one should note that a number of testamentary discourses give the initial impression at least of being homiletic. Thyen notes in this respect Mattathias' testamentary discourse in *I Maccabees* 2:50–68 and suggests that this has been coloured by the homiletic traditions of the synagogue.[88] He also suggests that *Testamenta xii patriarchum* are likewise homiletic in form and origin. This suggestion is followed by Collins, who suggests that there is a homiletic basis to the exhortations.

Collins finds three patterns within the *Testamenta*, namely the exposition of virtues with the aid of *exempla*, exhortation with the use of catalogues of virtues and vices, and treatments of ethical dualism.[89] He does not justify his assertion that these are homiletic in origin, though one should note that the use of catalogues and *exempla* is common in the diatribe, a form of discourse in the Hellenistic world which is often compared to the homily.[90] Paraenetic exhortation is not however necessarily homiletic. Critical moreover is the situation in which the farewell is delivered; unless the preacher were regularly to adopt as *prosopopoiia* the person of the dying man, which stretches credibility somewhat, these are not homilies, except of a

---

[86] Olivar, *Predicacion cristiana*, 35, assumes that this is the proper place of paraenesis, since paraenesis was intended to build up those who were already Christians (as opposed to converting or forming those who were not). Whereas this is a possible social location for the activity, the committed state of the audience is not part of any usual definition of paraenesis.

[87] See further on this the discussion at 1.1.2 above.

[88] Thyen, *Stil*, 18.

[89] Collins, *Between Athens and Jerusalem*, 158–161.

[90] The diatribe is discussed at 1.2.4.1 below.

very specific type.[91] In order to show that these discourses have a
homiletic origin it must be possible to show that the narrative context in which they are found is secondary. Thus, as McDonald points
out, the genre as it stands is too specific to be described as a category of preaching. There may be a relationship between the testamentary discourse and the homily but they are not identical. Thus
whilst recognising with McDonald that the testamentary discourse as
a form-critical category for preaching is indeed too narrow, it behoves
us nonetheless to ask whether the testamentary discourse might be
one of the roots of the homily.

The Greek farewell discourse, of which the testamentary discourse
is a variation, usually contained instructions, and often a retrospec-
tive of the life of the dying person. The instruction need not have
been ethical, and instructions were usually specific.[92] There is much
similar deathbed exhortation in rabbinic literature.[93] There appears
to have been something of a growth in the form, from παράκλησις
on specific points to more general paraenesis. The ethical pattern
which emerges from the farewell discourse would adapt itself readily to ethical preaching, the *exemplum* of the person making his farewell,
which would provide the springboard for paraenesis, being replaced
with other *exempla*, primarily scriptural. The literary form of the testamentary discourse might thus come to influence the homily. Thyen
however suggests the opposite, namely that the literary form of the
testamentary discourse, he uses that of Mattathias as his example,
has been influenced by preaching.[94] The question of whether it is
the literary farewell discourse which has influenced preaching or vice
versa is probably unanswerable, but whatever the direction of the
influence a testamentary discourse is not a homily. Thus the farewell
discourse of John in *Acta Johannis*, whilst it has the fictional setting
of a sermon in the assembly, is really purely a farewell.[95] For this

---

[91] One has in mind the farewell discourses of Jesus in *John*, of John at *Acta
Johannis* 106–107 and of Paul in Miletus at *Acts* 20.

[92] See on this Perdue, "Death of the sage".

[93] See especially Saldarini, "Last words and deathbed scenes". Saldarini suggests
that the developed form of the testamentary discourse is a product of the time after
the destruction of the Temple, and was essentially a social myth to maintain Jewish
identity. This may be true, but the form has a scriptural past and a present in the
wider Hellenistic world.

[94] Thyen, *Stil*, 18.

[95] *Acta Johannis* 106–107.

reason there is no reference to Scripture, since John's own life and experience is the exemplary springboard for the closing admonitions.

The fourth category which Reicke proposes is revelation, by which he means the activities of prophets. It is problematic whether this is to be counted as preaching, though we have already observed that similar vocabulary is used of prophetic activity and preaching, and that the functions of preaching are among the functions of the prophets.[96] However it is true that left as it is the category raises as many questions as it answers, in particular whether the form of the prophetic sermon was noticeably different from that of any other revelation of the Word of God. However, given the possible correspondence between prophetic and homiletic activity already observed, this insight is worthy of further investigation.

1.2.1.2. *McDonald's understanding of preaching as* paraklēsis

In direct response to Reicke McDonald proposes an operational model, dividing the articulation of the Christian message into semantic domains which he terms *propheteia, paraklēsis, paraenesis* and *paradosis*.[97] Preaching, according to McDonald, comes under the operational model of *paraklēsis*. This model is operational and as such does not intend to answer the form-critical question of how the homilies of the earliest Christians might be discovered.

It is possible to raise objections to McDonald's model, for the division between paraenesis and *paraklēsis* in the Hellenistic world was something of a fine one.[98] Even so, we have sought to make a corresponding distinction in the Christian context between catechesis and preaching, and may note the possibility that catechesis, by being persuasive in intent yet stereotyped in form, might be rather closer to paraenesis. Prophecy may be taken to indicate activity functionally equivalent to preaching and so it is as unwise to cordon it off from preaching as it is to lump the whole of prophetic activity in with that of the preacher. Finally, it is perfectly conceivable that the

---

[96] At 1.1.1 and 1.1.2 above.

[97] McDonald, *Kerygma and didache*, 10–11 and passim.

[98] Malherbe, "Exhortation", 239 traces the modern understanding of paraenesis in a narrow sense (narrower than the ancient understanding) to Dibelius. Malherbe uses paraenesis and exhortation interchangeably. Similarly in *Moral exhortation*, 121, Malherbe points out that the distinction between protrepsis and paraenesis was likewise fine. However Gammie, "Morphology", 52, is fairly clear that there was a distinction, albeit narrow.

transmission of tradition was part of the activity of a prophet. Nonetheless, although as a taxonomy of the whole semantic field of Christian communication McDonald's division may be problematic, his
observation that preaching belongs in the semantic domain of exhortation is useful, in that it fits in with the language employed in *Luke-
Acts* to describe prophecy and with the insistence of Paul that prophetic
activity in Corinth build up the church.

Although McDonald's intention is less to define preaching than to
sort out the possible domains of Christian discourse, he does attempt
the definition of a homily. This he sees emerging from the synagogue homily and the diatribe.[99] In essence his idea is that the homily
is a development of an initial thematic statement, which may be
scriptural (deriving from Jewish models) or ethical (deriving from
models in the wider Hellenistic world). In the event of the theme
being scriptural then the preacher uses the technique of "pearl-stringing", according to which a series of further scriptural texts are
employed, linked together to the first, in order to create a texture
of scriptural meaning. However we shall observe below that whereas
this technique may have been employed in preaching it is by no
means unique to that activity, and its presence may not therefore
be noted as a means of identifying a homily. McDonald suggests
that in ethical discourse the procedure runs along similar lines, in
that there is an opening statement of a theme which is developed
in various ways. Once again, however, there is nothing which leads
to the necessary conclusion that this is a homily. McDonald however, for all that his efforts may be judged unsuccessful, does show
the manner in which formal criteria may be sought from homilies
outside of the Christian tradition in order that we might seek them
in Christian writings, and we may follow him in seeking these criteria in synagogue preaching and in Hellenistic ethical discourse. We
shall find that McDonald's own examination of the Jewish and pagan
evidence, in which he is indebted to previous researchers in the fields,
does not convince, and so does not assist us distinguishing *paraklēsis*
from the other areas of Christian discourse, but we should note further that formal criteria alone are insufficient in the absence of a
hypothesis within which the development of Christian preaching may
be understood.

---

[99] McDonald, *Kerygma and didache*, 50–68.

1.2.1.3. Siegert's functional model of early Christian communication
Siegert similarly proposes a functional model for understanding Christian discourse which he attempts to sort into three semantic domains: kerygmatic, conversational and "Charismenlehre".[100] In time, Siegert suggests, the homily becomes the medium for all inspired speech; we may suggest that since "pastoral preaching"[101] is the fundamental content of the prophetic message the distinctions are already becoming blurred in the first century. Nonetheless Siegert's classification fits in with the suggestion made above that the import of the term *homilia* and its cognates is conversational, and that by the second century the domain of kerygmatic preaching is consigned to the past.[102] However, useful as Siegert's division is, it does not assist with the construction of formal canons by which it might be possible in turn to identify homiletic strands and excerpts in non-homiletic works.

Siegert does confront the problem of form, but concludes that such an approach is not useful. He begins by suggesting that since orality is definitory of homilies, and that since the documents of the New Testament are literary productions, there is therefore nothing in the New Testament that may accurately be labelled a homily. The stress on orality fits in with our earlier suggestion that prophetic activity and improvisation meant that we should not expect to find a homily as such in the New Testament but nonetheless that original oral homilies may have been redacted into the text. Siegert, like Black,[103] notes the strongly anachronistic tendencies of past critics who have sought to discern homilies in the ancient documents. His definition of a homily as a discourse delivered in the liturgical assembly (thus excluding for instance "missionary preaching") is reasonable enough,[104] but in going on to suggest that a "zahlreiche" congregation is necessarily part of the definition ("in einen Hauskreis kann man nicht predigen" he states) he is in danger of being as anachronistic as those he criticises. What else is Paul doing at *Acta Pauli* 3.5–7 in the house of Onesiphorus?[105] Again, we should not expect

---

[100] Siegert, *Drei hellenistisch-jüdische Predigten* II, 26–27.

[101] The term employed by Hill, *New Testament prophecy*, 103.

[102] As has already been noted, the only uses of κηρύσσειν in the second century are with reference to the preaching of the apostles or the ancient prophets. See Bartelink, *Lexicologisch-semantische studie*, 122–123.

[103] "Rhetorical form", 2.

[104] Siegert, *Drei hellenistisch-jüdische Predigten* II, 6.

[105] Similarly note *Acts* 20:20.

the degree of formality attaching to the twentieth century sermon
(or indeed the fourth century sermon) to be found in the manner
of delivery in the context of a first century church. Nonetheless the
presence of teaching activity in the household church, as in the
household synagogue, is established, as is prophetic activity an established practice in the Pauline communities. We have already indicated that this prophetic activity may be compared to preaching.

Siegert in stressing the oral nature of the early sermon, and thus
concluding that orality is essential to a definition, is unhappy about
giving a formal classification to the homily.[106] For him orality is the
key, and this can only be defined by internal indications and by ver-
bosity. However, indications of orality can be misleading. The letters of Paul were probably read aloud in the assembly and are thus
to an extent an oral event, but they are not sermons but letters. In
examining the work of Philo we may seek indications of orality in
the text but because it is a text published as a discourse there can
be no certainty that it derives from an oral original. This is likely
to apply to any other attempt to find traces of orality in the literary output of the ancient world, and comes about because of the
extent to which Graeco-Roman antiquity was an oral culture. When
Rhetorica ad Alexandrum 3.12.2 picks out poets which are suitable for
private reading rather than performance, these are the exceptions.[107]
Writing was undertaken in order to be read aloud, and so any literary work may be marked by "orality".[108]

Part of this oral culture was the practice of improvisation. We
have already suggested that preaching was a work of improvisation,
and although oratory becomes more "bookish" in the late Empire,
with notes being used and speeches even being read,[109] there is
equally extensive evidence of the continuing practice of improvisation
in speaking[110] which would surely be imitated as much by Christian
orators as much as pagan. This orality, with its accompanying evalua-

---

[106] "Festlegungen betreffs einer Struktur gehören nicht in unsere Definition."
Siegert, *Drei hellenistisch-jüdische Predigten* II, 6. Such observations may not belong in
a definition, but surely they are to be sought.

[107] Cited by Harris, *Ancient literacy*, 86.

[108] So des Places, "Style parlé et style oral". Des Places attempts to discover
traces of common spoken Greek in the literary works of the time, and comes across
this very problem.

[109] Harris, *Ancient literacy*, 223.

[110] Anderson, *Second sophistic*, 55–64.

tion of improvisation, thus emerges as the reason why homilies are not preserved for us intact, so confirming the suggestion made earlier. Orality is indeed a necessary condition of a homily, theologically as well as formally, but it is not in itself sufficient. Siegert thus points us in the direction of prophecy in seeking preaching activity in the early church, and gives us a salutary reminder that preaching is an oral event, but does not further the task of discovering the remains of preaching in the literary output of early Christianity.

1.2.1.4. *Wills, and other recent form-critics*

The last attempt formally to determine the shape of an early Christian homily with which we shall deal is the highly influential attempt of Wills.[111] Wills proposed a pattern that he termed the "Word of Exhortation"; he took this term from the description of the homily at *Acts* 13:15 as a λόγος παρακλήεως. This pattern is threefold, consisting of scriptural *exemplum* or *exempla*, a conclusion drawn from the *exemplum* and concluding paraenesis. These parts are joined together by inferential particles or phrases, and may stand alone as a single unit, or in a cycle of similar exhortatory forms. He finds this form exhibited not only at *Acts* 13:16b–41 but also in *Hebrews*, *I Clement* and a number of other early Christian documents. In support of Wills we may note that Mattathias' testamentary speech (*I Maccabees* 2:50–68) has similarities with this pattern, beginning with exhortation, going on to a long list of *exempla*, and returning to exhortation. We have noted Thyen's suggestion that the testamentary discourse had been influenced by preaching, but in view of the similarity between the testamentary discourse and the units of exhortation which make up, say, *Hebrews*, we must conclude that the presence of this form in a discourse does not mean that we are necessarily dealing with a homily.

We may however study the question of the testamentary discourse in more detail here since, as we have seen, Collins argued that *Testamenta xii patriarchum* contained a number of self-contained units which were, he suggested, homiletic in origin.[112] At that point we concluded that it should be possible to show that the literary setting was secondary before determining that the unit was self-contained.

---

[111] Wills, "Form of the sermon".
[112] Collins, *Between Athens and Jerusalem*, 158–161.

We return to the point here because Wills likewise suggests that there are self-contained units within the *Testamenta* which follow his proposed pattern, and which might therefore have reflected preaching in the Hellenistic synagogue.[113] This is thus a good opportunity to test the theories of both Collins and Wills, since there is some division between them as to what exactly the self-contained units actually are. For instance Wills suggests that *Testamentum Reuben* 5:1–5 is a unit[114] whereas for Collins 3:10–4:5 and 4:6–6:5 are each independent units.[115]

The pattern of this part of the *Testamentum* is as follows:

3:10 Injunction: Pay no heed to the sight of women . . .
3:11 Negative *exemplum*: Reuben tells of his encounter with Bilhah
4:1   Injunction repeated: "Pay no heed to the beauty of women . . . but walk in singleness of heart in the works of the Lord . . ."
4:2   *Exemplum* continued: Reuben speaks of his reproach in the sight of his father and brothers after his sin
4:5   Conclusion, with inference drawn using the phrase διὰ τοῦτο: "Therefore my children, observe whatever I command you, and you shall not sin."
4:6   Proposition: For fornication is the destruction of the soul
4:8   Positive *exemplum*: Joseph kept himself from women, and found favour with God, who delivered him
4:10 Conclusion: If fornication does not overcome your mind you shall not be overcome by Beliar
5:1   Injunction: Women are wicked and use trickery as they have no power
5:3   Authority (an angel): "This is what the angel of the Lord taught me when he taught me about women . . ."
5:5   Injunction: "Therefore, flee fornication . . ."
5:6   *Exemplum*: The watchers before the flood were led astray in this manner
6:1   Concluding exhortation and instructions with inferential particle: "Therefore beware of fornication."

Collins suggests that 4:6–5:5 is redactional. Certainly he is right that within the exhortation it appears to constitute a separate unit, since

---

[113] Wills, "Form of the sermon", 293.
[114] Wills, "Form of the sermon", 294.
[115] Collins, *Between Athens and Jerusalem*, 158–159.

3:10–4:5 continue the same *exemplum*, although it is possible that the two units together are both building up to the common conclusion. Wills' extraction of 5:1–5 as a unit would seem to be erroneous since the *exemplum* is weak (in fact it is the statement of an authority rather than an *exemplum*) and the injunction which for him is the conclusion is followed by a further *exemplum*.

This point has been followed at length because it illustrates the extent to which Wills' extraction of a pattern may mislead. Both here and in the testament of Mattathias there is exhortation preceding as well as following the *exempla*. Collins' extracted unit at least has the merit of being a discrete and understandable block of material, but this does not make it a homily.

A few further examples from *Testamenta Patriarchum* may be treated more briefly. Collins notes *Testamentum Josephi* 2:7–10:3 which follows a similar pattern.[116] It begins with a general statement that μακροθυμία is a great medicine and ὑπομονή gives many blessings. There follows an account of the trials and sufferings of Joseph from 3.1–9.5, which provides an extended *exemplum*, and then gives way to a general moralizing conclusion: "See now, children, how much is achieved by patience and by prayer with fasting . . ."

Wills notes that the *Testamentum Naphthali* uses two cycles together.[117] But although the testaments may be divided into units, there is still no evidence that these units are homiletic in origin, nor any evidence that the literary setting is secondary, and thus there is still no evidence which would enable us to recognise Wills' pattern or Collins' units as homiletic. The complexity of the units indicates that the *Testamenta* are literary productions, and that whereas they may reflect synagogue preaching this can only be a hypothesis. The complexity indicates that they are not themselves built out of sermons incorporated as self-contained units, but that any pre-existent material has been edited for inclusion to the extent that it is no longer possible to tell what is or is not pre-existent! Nonetheless the pattern observed by Wills is an observable phenomenon. Thus Black, in his response to Wills, conceded the fundamental form-critical point and sought

---

[116] Collins, *Between Athens and Jerusalem*, 156.

[117] Wills, "Form of the sermon", 295, with reference to 8.1 and 8.2, and 8.9 and 8.10. At each point, he states, "the author concludes what has gone before . . . and gives the exhortation."

to anchor the form in classical rhetoric.[118] Our examination of the pattern as found in *Testamenta Patriarchum* certainly enables us to see that it fits into the manner in which a θέσις may be proved, using *exempla* and (at *Test Reuben* 5:3) an authority. But this does not make the pattern homiletic.

According to Black, recognising a classical rhetorical shape in Will's pattern involves not being unduly restrictive in the definitions of dicanic, sumbouleutic or epideictic oratory. Sumbouleutic oratory for instance need not take place in an assembly, indeed according to Aristotle it may be private. Wills' threefold pattern may be expressed as *propositio* (the initial injunction), *narratio* (using *exempla*, which may, after the pattern of the treatment of *chreiai*, be extensive) and *conclusio*. The inferential particles joining the sections of the speeches accord with the advice of classical rhetoricians to engineer smooth transitions between parts of the speech. Thus Wills' analysis conforms to the canons of classical rhetoric. It is to be termed a λόγος παρακλήσεως because, one might suggest, it is a piece of sumbouleutic oratory.[119] This does not mean that a general method of exhortation might not be extended to being used in the homily, indeed the manner in which Maccabaeus' exhortation of his troops at *II Maccabees* 15:7–11 draws on Scripture as well as on a vision is particularly interesting for the manner in which a conventional occasion of oratory might become the opportunity for preaching. But although, as has already been observed, *paraklēsis* and preaching share common semantic ground, it remains to be proven that the literary form which Wills has isolated is actually employed in sermons. There is no doubt that the pattern observed by Wills recurs consistently, but no certainty that it is actually homiletic. Something of this kind is known in Palestinian Judaism also, in an incident of individual admonition[120] as well as in preaching.[121] Wills' pattern is certainly a method of exhortation attested in the first century, and is interesting in demonstrating the interplay of *exemplum* and citation, but exhortation was

---

[118] Black, "Rhetorical form".

[119] So, for instance, at Polybius *Historiae* 1.61.1 the term is used for the exhortation of troops.

[120] BT *Sotah* 7b directs that an adulteress is to be encouraged to confess through telling her of narratives and incidents as *exempla*. Thus Reuben and Judah are used as exempla of the value of confessing.

[121] Mishnah *Ta'anith* 2.1 supplies the example of the Ninevites as an encouragement to fast.

not limited to the address. Additionally it is clearly not the only form which a sermon might have taken. Siegert criticises Wills on the basis that his form does not correspond to the homilies that he (Siegert) has identified;[122] although Siegert's homilies do not actually derive from Christianity, one would anticipate that the form of the narrative encomium found in the homilies which Siegert discusses would be found in Christianity and might also anticipate that the exegetical tradition of Palestinian Judaism would have some effect on Christian preaching.

Nonetheless Wills' attempt does connect with other similar attempts to locate patterns of exhortation in homilies. We have noted the similarities between his proposed pattern and that of the testamentary discourse, which led to the suggestion of Reicke and Thyen that there is a relationship between the testamentary discourse and the homily, and we may note here that a similar suggestion is made by Balzer with regard to the covenant formulary. The covenant formulary is a form isolated by Balzer based on the covenant texts of the Hebrew Bible which has three parts. The first he terms "antecedent history" which is, he suggests, dogmatic in intent. This is followed by an ethical section setting out the obligations imposed by the covenant, and the third part consists of blessings and curses intended to encourage the maintenance of the covenant. Actually it is possible that there is a relationship between the testament and the covenant formulary, since Balzer suggests that the covenant formulary was closely associated with the testament in the Hebrew Bible, and it is this which association which leads to the appearance of the covenant formulary in *Testamenta Patriarchum*.[123] The stability of the form comes about through a *Sitz im Leben* of preaching, he suggests,[124] but the origin of the form is nonetheless literary. According to Balzer the "antecedent history" has, by the time of the *Testamenta*, changed its function to become exemplary;[125] this literary form then appears in a preaching environment in the Christian church. The parallels which Balzer adduces for the homiletic use of the covenant formulary are however far from convincing, for his examples, taken from *Barnabas*, *II Clement* and the *Didache*, are not proven to be homilies and the

---

[122] Siegert, *Drei hellenistisch-jüdische Predigten* II, 27.
[123] Balzer, *Covenant formulary*, 137, 141–145.
[124] Balzer, *Covenant formulary*, 167.
[125] Balzer, *Covenant formulary*, 179–180; isolated by Balzer.

parallels are partial only.[126] Nonetheless it is quite possible that the
testamentary covenant of the Old Testament conspires with the Greek
farewell address to produce the testamentary discourse as it is found
in Hellenistic Judaism. The earliest appearances, and the most complete appearances, of this form are literary, and so it is more probably the literary form which has influenced the homily rather than
the homily which left traces in the literary forms. We may be alive
to the possibility that the recorded farewell discourses contain homilies or fragments of homilies, but to demonstrate this it must be
possible to show that the farewell is secondary to the discourse. Unless
this can be demonstrated there can be no certainty that when the
pattern of the word of exhortation is met in literary works there is
an actual homily here. It is quite possible that the testamentary discourse does lie within the ancestry of the word of exhortation, and
that these are somehow bound up to the ancestry of the homily, but
this does not assist us with our fundamental task of tracing the development of the homily within the Christian church.

There are also similarities between Wills' word of exhortation and
the prophetic sermon form proposed by Müller.[127] Müller begins his
argument by locating preaching as an activity of the prophets in the
assembly. Like Hill he sees the function of the prophetic sermon as
παράκλησις and like Siegert he stresses the oral nature of the delivery. He suggests two possible forms for the prophetic sermon, the
direct word of salvation, and what he calls "Paraklese als Bußpredigt".
As an example of this form he takes *Revelation* 3:1–5,[128] where there
is a verdict over the congregation, followed by a reminder of past
history bound up to a call to reform, and finally specific directions.
It is interesting that he should take this letter in *Revelation* as an
example, since Balzer had taken this as an example of the use of
the covenant formulary.[129] However Müller's arguments here are
more convincing since not only does this congregational letter have
the same function as prophecy, namely *paraklēsis*, but the form is

---

[126] Balzer, *Covenant formulary*, 123–136. Donfried, *Setting*, 42 calls the parallel with
II Clement "strained and only partially correct." Nonetheless at *Setting*, 41–47, he
does discern a threefold pattern within *II Clement* which is comparable to that of
Balzer's covenant formulary. See further the discussion at 2.2.2.4 below.

[127] Müller, *Prophetie und Predigt*, 57–62.

[128] Müller, *Prophetie und Predigt*, 57.

[129] *Covenant formulary*, 163–166.

established as prophetic because the announcement of this *paraklēsis* is made by the spirit.[130] In this event we are dealing with something corresponding to the "word of exhortation" and doing so in a context which is both congregational and oral.[131] The word of exhortation may well then have been a form employed in Christian preaching, even when the prophets cease to be the main preachers in the church. Note should be taken here that even this prophetic form might have ethical content, which is sufficient to make it clear that the growth of ethical paraenesis is unrelated to the decline of congregational prophecy.[132]

Finally similarities may be noted between Wills' scheme and that applied to *Hebrews* by Attridge.[133] The outline according to Attridge is one of formal introduction, citation followed by expository comments on selected verses, exhortation and finally "festive prose". Citation, exposition, encomium and exhortation might all have a place in a homily, though the homily need not be the unique vehicle for these activities.

Attridge is writing partially in response to Gammie's tight classification of paraenesis according to the Aristotelian divisions of rhetoric[134] and suggests that the three-fold division of rhetoric has by the time of the first century outlived its usefulness and that the Hellenistic synagogue provides a new social setting for what is effectively a new rhetorical occasion. *Paraklēsis* therefore is a "mutant on the evolutionary trail of ancient rhetoric."[135] Although one may doubt the extent to which the Hellenistic synagogue is indeed a new social event since it is closely related to the school, and therefore the extent to which the homily is an entirely new rhetorical event, there is no question that the Aristotelian division is breaking down. We may nonetheless enquire how Christian preaching is to be fitted into this broad division. Siegert suggests that the teaching in the church was not necessarily of anything new, but might be the repetition of formulae intended not to impart new information or to alter behaviour, but

---

[130] We shall examine the examples of prophetic preaching provided by *Revelation* at greater length at 2.1.3 below.

[131] Müller, because he is dealing with prophetic speech forms, takes the criterion of orality with great seriousness.

[132] Cf. Ekenberg, "Urkristan predikan", 9, 23, 31.

[133] Attridge, "Paraenesis in a homily".

[134] Gammie, "Paraenetic literature".

[135] Attridge, "Paraenesis in a homily", 217.

to reinforce the convictions of the assembly.[136] If this is the case then preaching is to be understood as epideictic, which re-inforces the opinions of an audience, rather than seeking to change them. This fits in with Paul's comments concerning the edificatory function of prophets in the assembly. Prophetic addresses and homilies are new rhetorical events since Aristotle's classification and can combine elements from different genera, but in order for the categorization of preaching to have heuristic value it is necessary to determine the primary category into which it may fall, and in this case, in view of the primary aim of the preacher to reinforce values and beliefs in the congregation rather than to win converts, it must be stated that preaching is primarily epideictic.

Attridge's attempt to define the homily according to its social setting is not the first. For despite the formal uncertainty attempts have been made to classify the Christian homily with reference to the social setting of preaching. According to these theorists the adoption of a high preaching style, typical after Nicaea, derived from the adoption of more ornate and extensive buildings for the Christian assembly. The preacher would then adapt a more exalted tone. Popular preaching however would be more fitted to a less exalted setting. This may be traced back to Norden[137] but is adopted by Schneider and Siegert.[138] But we should remember that the second century was the age of popular rhetorical displays and that the division between high art and populist art is not a division which people of the second century would recognize. Melito of Sardis adopts a style of extreme Asianism, and yet there is no archaeological evidence that there was anything like a basilica for the use of Christians in Sardis in the second century, indeed such a thing would be most unlikely. We have moreover observed that the term ὁμιλία more probably refers to conversation than to preaching, and so the suggestion of Norden, adopted by Siegert, that an original informal style of address in Christian communities (the *homilia*) gives way to a more exalted style, and in turn that this is an indication of the changing

---

[136] Baeck, "Greek and Jewish preaching", 110, likewise suggests that Jewish preaching did not intend to proclaim new truth but to expound and spread "truth already proclaimed".

[137] Norden, *Antike Kunstprosa*, 541–544.

[138] Schneider, *Geistesgeschichte*, 3; Siegert, *Drei hellenistisch-jüdische Predigten* II, 11.

social status of the audience, may be seen to be without foundation altogether.

These recent form-critical efforts therefore fail on the basis of circularity. No self-confessed homily is extant, and so the critic is left to determine for her or himself the form or forms which one might expect to find in a homily, and then so to label any document in which they might be found.

1.2.2. *An impasse and a possible way out*

Although there has been no extended attempt to follow through the agenda proposed by Brilioth of investigating early Christian literature in search of evidence for preaching, there have been some efforts in the direction of seeking formal criteria in order to lend generic legitimacy to the term "homily". No attempt based on form-criticism however has succeeded in breaking out of the impasse caused by the absence of any homily which might provide a demonstrable incidence of such form; there is hardly a document in the output of the early Christians that has not at some point been claimed to be a homily, but without formal criteria we are in no position to judge these claims. The most useful effort is that of McDonald, who sought formal criteria through an examination of synagogue preaching and of the diatribe, a form of address in the Hellenistic world which has frequently been compared to preaching. The remainder of this chapter will follow McDonald in investigating the possible roots of Christian preaching in Judaism and in the wider Hellenistic world. This examination might in turn give us some formal criteria by which we might be in a position to seek evidence of preaching in the literary documents of Christianity.

1.2.3. *Synagogue preaching as a possible background to early Christian practice*

It is a reasonable assumption that the practice of preaching in the Christian assembly was in part an adoption of the practice of the synagogue: we need in turn to raise the question of whether the act of preaching alone was received into the church or whether the forms of preaching employed in the synagogue were likewise received. Observation of the forms of preaching known in Judaism in the period before the parting of the ways may make it possible to observe similar forms in the writings of Christians.

1.2.3.1. *The proem form*

The earliest efforts to discover the forms which Jewish preachers might employ were undertaken by scholars working on the homiletic midrashim;[139] two forms widespread in the rabbinic material were recognized as possibly homiletic, the proem form, by which a text was cited and then interpreted in small units through the medium of another text and the *yelammedēnu* form by which a halakhic question was put and then answered through scriptural citation. Here we deal with the proem form.[140] According to Maybaum the form has a stereotyped pattern which consists of:

a) text

b) connecting formula between text and proem

c) proem and exposition

d) connecting formula

e) text from pericopē repeated.[141]

The work thus begun was continued by Mann[142] who sought to locate the homilies of the midrashim in the lectionary cycle of Palestine. However, Heinemann has shown that there is no evidence for such a lectionary cycle in the earliest period.[143] Nonetheless, much as this criticism has validity for the treatment of Mann's particular theories, it does not affect the simpler thesis on which Mann built, namely that homilies might be constructed according to an exegetical method exercised upon a proemial text which is interpreted in sections. The form-critical work of Maybaum and Bacher was extended by Borgen,[144] who brought their studies to bear on Philo and the New Testament. In these he found something corresponding to the proem form; since Borgen the mantle of the proemic homily has

---

[139] Notably Maybaum, *Ältesten Phasen*, and Bacher, *Proömien*.

[140] We do not deal with the *yelammedēnu* form here as it is first found in the Tanhumatic midrashim, and does not significantly differ from the proem except that it takes off from a halakhic question. Although Maybaum *Ältesten Phasen*, 1–8 reckons the *yelammedēnu* older than the proemic homily, and Finkel, *Pharisees*, 169–170 claims that the *yelammedēnu* homily has its origin prior to the destruction of the Temple, the evidence which they cite points less towards preaching as to enquiry into the law in a non-homiletic setting. The methods may in time have entered the preacher's repertory, but do not appear to have done so at any time around the parting of the ways.

[141] Maybaum, *Ältesten Phasen*, 9.

[142] Mann, *Bible*.

[143] Heinemann, "Triennial lectionary cycle".

[144] Borgen, *Bread from Heaven*.

been taken up by a number of other New Testament scholars, notably Ellis.[145]

However, two particular problems are posed for anyone seeking to illuminate the practice of first century Judaism by the date of these Jewish homilies and through their preservation in what are certainly literary collections.[146] Firstly, the works preserved in the homiletic midrashim date from the fourth century at the earliest. Thus using the homiletic midrashim to guide us in discovering the form of Christian preaching in the first two centuries is a dangerous business; we most certainly cannot proceed directly from the reconstructions of Jewish homilies in the fourth and later centuries and then proceed to uphold these as ancestors of the Christian homily. The literary nature of the existing "homilies" is then a further problem. In particular one should note the brevity of the existing openings; so brief are they that it is hard to conceive that in themselves they might constitute a homily. They are moreover puzzling because they end, as well as begin, with the texts which they intend to treat. For this reason it was once widely held that these proems in themselves did not constitute homilies, but were simply introductions to homilies, which are themselves lost; to this the objection may be raised that the homilies themselves would hardly be lost were the prefaces retained. Additionally one should note that the proem constitutes a form complete in itself, and as such the proems would not simply constitute an introduction to a larger unit.[147] For these reasons Heinemann suggested that the proems were introductory not to homilies but to the reading of Scripture. They were not therefore homilies in that they preceded the reading of Scripture rather than following it, but that they were homiletic introductions to the readings. In support of his theory he is able to produce

---

[145] A distillation of his views may be found at Ellis, "Biblical interpretation in the New Testament church".

[146] Sarason, "Petihtaot", insists on the literary nature of the extant petihtaot. Siegert, *Drei hellenistisch-jüdische Predigten* II, 6, similarly insists that orality is essential to the definition of a homily and so discounts all efforts to discover homilies in these works on the grounds that they are literary. Siegert is correct, in that preaching is an oral form, but the midrashim may nonetheless contain distillations of preached sermons. Thus Strack and Stemberger, *Introduction*, 315, and Heinemann and Petuchowski, *Literature of the synagogue*, 110, suggest that they may be described as "desk homilies".

[147] Heinemann, "Proem", 104–107, following Bloch, "Studien zur Aggadah", 183–4.

evidence for such a practice.[148] Thus the first citation to be found
in the proem is, he suggests, not a citation of the Torah text at all
but a title, which later commentators have misread as part of the
homily proper. In conclusion he suggests that the complete proems
which are recorded are products of the third century. Heinemann's
theory also solves the question of the brevity of these proemic treatments, for although he is open to the possibilities that tastes may
vary and that brevity in itself is not a serious objection it is true
that the proems do not exhibit what Siegert calls the *copia verborum*;
it was hardly a homily like this that Eliezer delivered on a festival
day, which took an entire day and which caused the audience to
leave in stages due to the length of the homily.[149] If these are simply introductions to the readings then the problem of brevity is easily solved. However if they are introductions then their designation
as homilies is uncertain and, especially in view of their date, their
formal elements do not assist at all in setting criteria by which
Christian homilies might be recognized.

We will return to the rabbinic evidence, but have seen enough to
realize that this cannot be a starting point for the search for synagogal predecessors to the Christian homily. If these proems are a
product of the third or fourth century then they cannot have influenced
Christian preaching; this realization has in turn led to the scholarly
consensus that attempts to see a proemic homiletic form behind early
Christian literature are anachronistic.[150] Although we intend to reverse
this consensus, the strength of the arguments should not be ignored.
There is however a starting point for the search for Jewish predecessors to Christian preaching alternative to the rabbinic midrashim.

The proemic homilies as they are found in the later midrashim
show a great complexity through their concern to link Scripture to
Scripture and to open a text from the Pentateuch with a text from
the prophets but, as we intend to demonstrate from the work of
Philo, the form has grown from a simpler procedure, that of atomizing a text for treatment. This atomizing exegesis still stands at the
centre of the midrashic "homilies." We may thus agree with Goldberg
that the *petiha* and the *hariza* are distinct; the purpose of the *petiha*

---

[148] Heinemann, "Proem", passim.
[149] BT *Betzah* 15b.
[150] So, typically, Stegner, "Ancient Jewish synagogue homily", 66–67.

is to expound Scripture, and multiple proofs and demonstrations may be applied, which may include the method of *hariza*.[151] TJ *Hagiga* 2.1 tells of R Joshua and R Eliezer linking the parts of Scripture to one another, "from the Pentateuch to the prophets, and from the prophets to the writings", but this is in the context of private study, not that of the assembly, even less that of preaching. In the later homiletic midrashim *hariza* becomes all important for the construction of *petihtot*[152] but in this earlier period it is simply one technique which may be employed. The earlier method, on which the later "openings" are built, involved simply an atomizing of the text for sequential exegesis. It is this which we will seek to observe in Philo's works. Philo states that one of the elders in the synagogue would interpret the law καθ' ἕκαστον.[153] The object of our study of Philo is therefore to see whether traces of this procedure may be found in his works.

Borgen, one of the proponents of the antiquity of the proemic homily, claims to find the form exhibited in them,[154] and Ellis is in a position to say that the general outline of this pattern appears "quite frequently" in the New Testament.[155] Whether we can share this optimism is questionable, since to an extent scholars having sought the form are prone to find it, but the search is at least worthwhile. Even if the later proem-form is not revealed, we may nonetheless find some examples of the atomizing exegetical method on which the later proems were built. We may investigate the claim of Borgen that *Legum allegoriae* 3.162–168 contains such a homily.[156]

According to Borgen the first phrase of the quotation "Behold I rain upon you bread from heaven" is paraphrased and discussed in 162. The second phrase "and the people shall go out and they shall gather the day's portion for a day", follows in the paraphrase and discussion of 163–167b."[157] Secondly Borgen suggests that the final phrase of this section is again a paraphrase of the *Exodus* passage.

---

[151] "Petiha und Hariza", 211–218.
[152] On which see Stern, *Midrash and theory*, 58–62.
[153] *Apologia* 7.13.
[154] Borgen, *Bread from Heaven*, 29–33; compare this to the approach of Maybaum, *Ältesten Phasen*, 1, who suggests that Hellenistic Jewish preachers employed methods entirely different from those known in Palestine.
[155] Ellis, "How the New Testament uses the Old", 155.
[156] Borgen, *Bread from Heaven*, 29–31.
[157] Borgen, *Bread from Heaven*, 29–31.

Finally, he claims to find other relevant quotations of *Exodus* in this text, and claims these as the subordinate quotations of the later rabbinic homilies.

Thus Borgen observes a pattern in these passages from Philo which a text is cited and then broken down in paraphrase which is expository of the text, in a manner similar to that observable in the homiletic midrashim, the whole having a unity due to a certain similarity in opening and closing statements. Each finally has a subordinate quotation. We have already suggested that Borgen's formal analysis is too systematic; what we must do is enquire whether the exegetical method (a method which to an extent dictates a form) found in the midrashim is likewise to be found here, thus concentrating on exegetical method rather than seeking a strictly formal parallel. That such is the case is not inconceivable, given the witness of Philo that we have already noted to the seriatim treatment of Scripture.

Legum allegoriae 3.162 does indeed treat of heaven, and the rest of the passage may likewise be seen as a treatment of the second half of the phrase. The closing citation however is not really a citation at all, but a moralizing conclusion, which has several verbal references to the text. The treatment of the scriptural passage is moreover somewhat loose; one should note the disproportionate nature of the space allowed to the second part of the quotation. However, for all we know an Alexandrian synagogue homily may sit slightly more lightly on the scriptural text than those of the Tannaim. Conley objects that the homily cannot be the controlling form for this passage, since it is only part of a more extended treatment of the manna.[158] This is true, but a homily may nonetheless be inserted into the text at an appropriate time, and a homily, especially a homily several hours long, may even be thematic, built up of exegeses of discrete but consecutive texts.

Conley proposes an alternative method for understanding Philo's treatment of this text, which derives from the treatment of texts in the schools.[159] He suggests that this passage is an extended ἐπιφώνησις on the text, intended as a κατασκευή of the original text, namely *Genesis* 3.14, rather as Hermogenes suggests the *kataskeuē* of a *chreia*

---

[158] Conley, *Philo's rhetoric*, 56–62.
[159] Conley, *Philo's rhetoric*, 58–60.

should be undertaken. There is no theoretical reason why this should not be both at once, a treatment of Scripture according to the usages simultaneously of the synagogue and of the Hellenistic schools, since the interpretative communities share a scholastic setting. However the treatment of the text here is less verbally detailed than those we meet in the Tannaitic midrashim; on this occasion at least the rhetorical demands of the schools take priority.

Conley rejects all formal attempts to classify Philo's scriptural treatment, and suggests that they are formed as a direct response to the needs of the audience. This does not, however, allow sufficient significance to the formal aspect of ancient literature. The literary *diatribai*, for all their apparent reference to real life, are literary forms nonetheless, and the same must be true of Philo's work.

Ellis and Borgen each make further attempts to discern proemic homilies behind Philo's works. For instance Ellis cites *De sacrificiis Abeli et Caini* 76–87.[160] Borgen, in connection with his discussion of *Legum allegoriae*, cites also *De mutatione nominum* 253–263.[161] Here the basic exegetical method is in fact clearer, the text "Indeed yes, Sarah your wife shall bear you a Son" being divided into "Indeed yes" (253–255), and "Sarah your wife shall give birth to a son" (255–263).

Philo deals first with the Yes:

> How significant, and how full of meaning, is that "Yes." What is more fitting to God than to grant his good things, and to agree so to do so quickly! (253)

He goes on to contrast God's affirmative with the widespread rejection of virtue.

In treating "Sarah shall bear you a son", Philo then treats of Sarah as meaning virtue; virtue is begotten of itself. Whereas Hagar's child is a lower virtue which has to be taught and learnt, true virtue is absolutely a gift of God. He thus concludes:

> Virtue then shall bear you a son, legitimate, and male. (263)

However although the repetition of the text concludes this section, Philo goes on with his treatment of *Genesis*, dealing with the name Isaac, which he takes as signifying the true joy which is born of virtue, and the statement that Sarah should give birth "at this season",

---

[160] "Biblical interpretation", 706.
[161] *Bread from Heaven*, 31.

which is taken as a name of God, and "in the next year", which is taken as another aeon. The treatment of "Sarah your wife shall bear you a son" is thus simply part of a larger treatment of the text. Moreover this unit has a wider context, and that is Philo's argument that there is a virtue derived from instinct as well as one from learning. The citation from *Genesis* is a citation of an authority, which is in turn confirmed, as Theon suggests, with an extended simile.

Nonetheless this, as a subunit within a wider argument, has a degree of independence. As such it may have been imported from another source, conceivably a homily. It is also possible, given that there are a number of similar consecutive subunits, that a series of proems might have been built into an extended homily, representing an extended period of scriptural study. Insofar as this unit joins the method of exegesis subsequently used by the Tannaim with Hellenistic rhetorical practice it is of exceptional interest, since both have in common a scholastic basis for their treatment of texts.

There are moreover some hints of the diatribe in these parts of the discourses, which may be a pointer towards orality. The citation of a text at *Legum allegoriae* 3.165 (for Borgen a mark of the proemial homily) may be seen as a mark of the diatribe, the description of fleshly pleasures compared to heavenly is a favourite philosophical theme, and Philo's frequent addresses to the soul may likewise be perceived as diatribal. However, there are considerably more extended denunciations of fleshly pleasures elsewhere in Philo's work,[162] themselves more likely to have been homiletic in origin, and the relatively thin distribution of the typical diatribal elements in this passage is to be noted. At *De mutatione nominum* 253 a rhetorical question precedes the citation, and there is significant paronomasia at 254, where Philo says that those to whom God gives assent are nonetheless refused by every fool: ἅπας ἄφρων ἀνένευκε.

However, even if the strongest diatribal elements were present, this of itself would not provide definite evidence that this section actually is a homily. It must remain an unproven possibility that this section is modelled on the Alexandrian synagogue homily. The only way in which this could be argued is to observe marks of possible orality[163] and, accepting that this is enshrined in a literary setting,

---

[162] See on these Wendland, "Philo und die kynisch-stoische Diatribe".

[163] Conley indeed does this, noting Philo's use of pronouns, asyndeton and dramatizing prosopopoiia.

to suggest that the source of this method for attracting and holding the attention of the audience derives from the synagogue. This is all very circuitous, and is hardly a safe foundation on which to construct an argument. A further possible indication of a synagogal origin to Philo's work may lie in the fact that Philo treats only of the Pentateuch. This is attributed by Borgen to a "liturgical peculiarity" at Alexandria.[164] Though not a peculiarity of Alexandria (the Samaritans canonized only the Torah) this would accord with suggestions that only the Torah was accepted as canonical at Alexandria, on the grounds of the differing quality of the Septuagintal translation, an impression reinforced when it is observed that *Epistula Aristeae* is concerned only with the translation of the Books of Moses.[165] If this is the case then it alone would be employed in the synagogue, and thus there may be a connection between Philo's exegesis and synagogal practice.

Borgen's attempt at classifying this part of Philo's work is strictly formal; Thyen similarly had claimed that Philo's treatment of Scripture was homiletic, and similarly claims that his own method would be "streng Formgeschichtliche".[166] But rather than form, Thyen picks fundamentally on certain rhetorical aspects of the work, such as changes of address, catalogues, digressions and repetitions. As marks of a diatribal style they may reflect preaching but, once again, need not. Thyen admits in fact that the commentaries as they stand are literary products. However, apart from style, certain aspects of the commentaries do seem to reflect a liturgical background. These arguments are set forth by Freudenthal, whom Thyen follows in this regard.[167] So, for instance, at *Legum allegoriae* 3.40 and 3.104 Philo invites the reader/hearer to pray. For Thyen and Freudenthal this is best understood in the context of a liturgical homily stemming from the synagogue. Freudenthal[168] is most impressed by the invitation

---

[164] Borgen, *Bread from Heaven*, 55. See McDonald, *Kerygma and didache*, 165 for other suggestions. Borgen, *Bread from Heaven*, 38, also observes that Philo's subordinate quotations are from the Pentateuch. However, the presence of subordinate quotations as a necessary part of the form is not found at the time of the Tannaim, so this part of the reconstruction may be readily dispensed with. Mann subsequently insisted that the proems were built upon the haftaroth.

[165] So Anderson, "Canonical and non-canonical", 145–147.

[166] Thyen, *Stil*, 7.

[167] Freudenthal, *Herrschaft der Vernunft*, 137–141.

[168] *Herrschaft der Vernunft*, 139.

to prayer at *Legum allegoriae* 3.104, which seems to him to be a fitting conclusion to a homily.

However, none of these invitations actually issue into prayer, but rather the exposition continues uninterrupted. Paul breaks off into prayer in the course of his letters, but one would be unjustified on this basis alone to suppose that this is indicative of a liturgical or homiletic basis. Similarly Philo frequently seems to address his hearers, but Freudenthal is clearly aware of the downfall of his own argument when he characterizes this as *prosopopoiia*. At two points there appears to be an address to the reader of the synagogue to read the law;[169] however this too may be part of the characterization. Freudenthal and Thyen finally admit that the homilies have been redacted into a collection.[170]

On the grounds of hints of orality in Philo's discourse, and on the basis of the fact that his exposition is limited to the Pentateuch, it is likely that homilies, or parts of homilies, may have been worked into the commentary, and it is possible that as part of his *prosopopoiia* Philo has adopted the tone of a preacher in the Alexandrian synagogue: but none of this can be proved, and thus we cannot easily proceed from this hypothesis to a reconstruction of Alexandrian synagogue preaching. The exegetical method found also in the proemic homilies may lie behind Philo's work on occasion, but the exactitude of Philo's reflection of an Alexandrian synagogal preacher cannot be known with certainty.

Even were we to have certainty that Philo reflects the practice of preaching in Alexandria, it is a long way yet to claim that the same practice was taken up by the church. Nonetheless this may count as evidence of the existence of a "common homiletic pattern" which may have influenced Christian exegesis and may therefore have found its way into the preaching of the church.

This pattern was certainly taken up by the Tannaim, and in time became the basis for the later stereotyped proem. Two early examples are worth noting. The first is significant because it shows both

---

[169] Freudenthal, *Herrschaft der Vernunft*, 138. Thyen, *Stil*, 74 seems particularly impressed by this argument.

[170] As indeed does Borgen, *Bread from Heaven*, 43, who accepts a degree of literary shaping. Sterling, "School of sacred laws", 158, whilst recognizing that some redaction has been undergone in order to form the treatises as they stand nonetheless is convinced by Borgen that there is homiletic material here.

that the order of the text was maintained in exegesis and that preaching, albeit here in a school setting, might be the locus for such a treatment of Scripture. R Eliezer ben Hyrcanos is found by his father in the house of R Johanan ben Zakkai, and he is preaching on *Genesis* 14:15, taking *Psalm* 37:14 as the proem text. The text is taken into its constituent parts, The wicked, referring to Amraphel, had drawn their bow against the poor and needy, namely Lot and against the upright, which is taken as a reference to Abraham. But as the wicked shall be pierced by their own sword, so this is illustrated through a citation of *Genesis* 14:15 to complete the homily.

> ... His father came up to disinherit him, and found him sitting and lecturing (דרוש) with the greatest of the land sitting before him: Ben Zizzith Hakesth, Nikonemon ben Gurion, and Ben Kalgba Shabua. He was expounding (דרוש) this verse: 'The wicked have drawn out the sword and have bent the bow': this alludes to Amraphel and his companions; 'to cast down the poor and needy' to Lot; 'to slay such as are upright in the way' to Abraham. 'Their sword shall enter into their own heart' as it is written "and he fought against them by night, he and his servants, and smote them".[171]

A second example which we may cite is one of R Aqiba. *Genesis* 23:1 is explained through the citation of *Esther*. Sarah lived 127 years which is explained through the fact that Esther became queen of 127 provinces. Bacher[172] suggests that the citation derives from a homily on *Genesis* 27:1 using *Esther* as a proem.

> R Aqiba was once lecturing, and the congregation became drowsy. Wishing to arouse them he remarked: why did Esther deserve to reign over a hundred and twenty-seven provinces? The reason is this: Let Esther, the descendant of Sarah, who lived a hundred and twenty-seven years, come and reign over a hundred and twenty-seven provinces.[173]

This is particularly interesting because it raises the question of the audience to which these midrashic homilies were directed. For the tale appears both at *Genesis R* at 58.3, where Aqiba uses it to arouse his congregation, and at *Esther R* 1:1 (8), where a school setting is

---

[171] *Genesis Rabbah* 42.1; translation according to Freedman and Simon, *Midrash Rabbah* I, 340.

[172] Bacher, *Proömien*, 23.

[173] *Genesis Rabbah* 58.3; translation according to Freedman and Simon, *Midrash Rabbah* II, 510.

presupposed and Aqiba's pupils, rather than a synagogue congregation, are growing drowsy. Bacher suggests that the anecdotal settings are secondary, but the question is raised nonetheless. A school setting is presupposed by the story of R Eleazer, which takes place in Johanan's house among his pupils.

The question of the audience of the rabbinic midrashic homilies is well put by Hirschmann.[174] He suggests that there would be different homilies aimed at different audiences. However he freely notes the absence of any evidence to support this. Jerome complains at the popularity of preaching among the Jews of fourth-century Palestine[175] which would point to a popular audience for the homilies surviving in the midrashim, and the midrashim themselves speak of the popularity of certain preachers.[176] But Hirschmann also notes the importance of scriptural education in the transmission of the haggadoth. He suggests (and admits that this as an impression only) that the midrash is closer to primers for the academy than to the actual preaching of the synagogue,[177] and thus that the distillations that survive do not so much represent the actual preaching that was heard, but the material out of which the homilies were formed.

This impression may, however, be misleading since an exalted style is no necessary indicator of an exalted audience, for the evidence of the second sophistic is that cultivated Atticizing rhetoric attracted large and popular audiences.[178] Nonetheless it may be conceded that the homiletic elements in the midrashim are indeed distillations, and are therefore formed for the academy. This is only what we would expect, since the extant midrashim are, after all, literary works. As such we may not claim that a homily could be directly reconstructed from these distillations, but nonetheless that some reflection, however pale, might there be found. It may well be that set in the literary midrashim the *petihtaot* are not intended either to precede the readings, nor to follow them, but rather are cut off entirely from their original liturgical setting.

---

[174] Hirschmann, "Preacher".

[175] *Hom. in Ezekiel* 34.3 cited by Hirschmann, "Preacher", 112.

[176] BT *Sotah* 40a tells of the popularity of the haggadic discourse, with reference to a story of R Abbahu and R Hiyya b Abba. R Abbahu delivered haggadah, whereas R Hiyya delivered halakah. The people flocked to hear R Abbahu, which does not surprise Abbahu in the least.

[177] Hirschmann, "Preacher", 114.

[178] On which see Anderson, *Second sophistic*, 55–64.

However it is also possible that the distinction between the academy and the synagogue might be somewhat blurred, the synagogue itself being modelled on a school.[179] According to R Eleazar b A'zariah men study in the assembly, and women listen.[180] In this event the style of preaching need not differ overmuch in the different settings in which preaching might take place since there would be a degree of overlap between the houses and their functions.[181] The style adopted by a preacher is dictated by his audience, but part of this dictation is not simply the needs of this audience, but also their expectations; we may not make assumptions too readily about the expectations which the audience would have. The school setting of this exegetical method may provide the key to its use in the church, which itself may have been modelled on a school, as much as in the synagogue. Thus, although midrash as such was an activity of the school, midrashic methods are to be found in the targums, which are primarily a liturgical event in the synagogue, and targums likewise may be employed in a school setting.[182]

The fact that there are so few examples of the proem form extant from the earliest period might indicate that the form was unusual. On the other hand we should recall the fact that what is usually reported is the unusual, not the commonplace. In addition there is evidence of a strong degree of suspicion of written targums in the rabbinic period, which might easily have been extended to homilies, to which they are closely related. This, apart from their basic orality, is one of the reasons for the failure to preserve the homilies intact.[183] And yet, even if the proem form was unusual, we have at least made a case that the proemial homily, or rather a homily which

---

[179] Which is not to say that the houses of Knesset and of Midrash are absolutely identical. On this question see Urman, "The house of assembly and the house of study".

[180] Tosefta *Sotah* 7.9, a record of a *derashah*, given however in a school setting.

[181] Which goes some way to counter the criticism of Borgen, *Bread from Heaven*, by Donfried, *Setting*, 30, where it is suggested that Borgen has not properly distinguished a synagogal homiletic setting from a school, and that on this basis his "homiletic" pattern is not necessarily homiletic.

[182] So York, "Targum in the synagogue".

[183] The evidence is disputed. See Strack and Stemberger, *Introduction*, 36–39. This view of the writing ban is adopted by Zunz, *Gottesdienstlichen Vorträge*, 65, and Moore, *Judaism*, 299. The ban is disputed in the later sources, which may explain why it is that most of the evidence for synagogue preaching is Amoraic. The existence of the ban is a salutary reminder of the oral nature of synagogal activity.

like the *petihtot* is based on an atomizing exegesis of a text, might
have been transmitted to Christianity. This is one form only, and
its presence does not mean that we have an actual preached homily,
for such a form might equally be present in literary constructions;
however, this in itself points to the possibility that the use of a
proemic method as the basis for the construction of a homily was
known in the Christian church.

1.2.3.2. *Other homiletic forms in early Judaism*

The major concentration in the study of early Jewish synagogue
preaching has been on the *petihtot*. But this is only one possible
homiletic pattern. Moore notes that in the *Mishnah* there is no attempt
to regulate the *derashah*, which leads him to suggest that a degree of
variety must have been exhibited;[184] Heinemann similarly suggests
that a variety of sermon types might be found,[185] as does Zunz.[186]
But again we meet the question of how it is that we are to recognise them as such. Bloch for instance found survivals of a type of
homily he termed the exemplary homily, by which a figure is held
up as an example for imitation,[187] and what he termed the "strophic"
homily, which is in fact a proem homily which has undergone tight
internal organisation.[188] We have already noted the possible use of
exempla in preaching and the suggestions that *Testamenta Patriarchum*
may derive from precisely such Jewish exemplary preaching, so Bloch's
hypothesis of the exemplary homily is reasonable, but unfortunately
the exemplary homilies have effectively been lost due to their redaction into the rabbinic midrashim and there is no evidence that the
exemplary exhortations which survive, such as the *Testamenta*, derive
from preaching in the synagogue. We have noted that Maccabaeus'
exhortation of his troops at *II Maccabees* 15:7–11 has some of the
traits of a homily, in that it relies on citations from Scripture for its
rhetorical effect,[189] but it is also interesting that he should conclude

---

[184] Moore, *Judaism*, 505.

[185] Heinemann, "Preaching in the Talmudic Age", 995.

[186] Zunz, *Gottesdienstlichen Vorträge*, 353.

[187] See e.g. Bloch, "Studien zur Aggadah", 264–269 where Bloch suggests that
Pisqa 2.1 of *Pesiqta deRab Kahana* which opens with "O Lord, how many are my
foes! Many are rising against me; many are saying of me, there is no help for him
in God." (*Psalm* 3:2–3) retains traces of the use of David as an *exemplum*.

[188] Bloch, "Studien zur Aggadah", 173.

[189] 1.2.1.4 above.

his exhortation by recounting a vision which he had received. We might wonder what influence visionary prophecy might have had in the preaching of early Judaism. But although this narrative alerts us to the possibility of a variety in preaching there is insufficient evidence on which to ground any conclusion.

There is, however, sufficient evidence for the role of haggadah in preaching; R Meir[190] would devote a third of his address to haggadah. A homily of Eleazar haModai on *Psalm* 29 which is cast into narrative form has been reconstructed.[191] Here the setting is the giving of the Law on Sinai, which is causing the earth to quake, and the Kings of the earth to tremble in their palaces, and to sing hymns to the glory of God. They thus approach Balaam to enquire concerning the source of the noise, and Balaam tells them that God is revealing the law to Israel. The Kings then depart, blessing Balaam as they go. The text of the psalm is followed through, though apparently not in exact order, as each verse supplies an element of the narrative. For instance the statement that the Kings in their palaces (היכליהם) praise God is the opportunity to cite vs. 9b: "In his temple (בהיכלו) they all cry Glory" and the final verse, "The Lord will give strength to his people; The Lord will bless his people with peace" provides the concluding dialogue between Balaam and the Kings, with the first part of the verse interpreted as the giving of Torah, the second part being the parting blessing given by the Kings. There was moreover no distinction before the end of the Amoraic period between פתח and דרש,[192] all of which points to the role of narrative in preaching. However it needs to be shown that such a phenomenon might have been known in the first century so that it might have been adopted by Christians. Certainly haggadic discourse is early, for it was known to Philo,[193] but the question arises whether it was found in a homiletic setting.

We may start with the haggadic collection passed down among the works of Philo and known as *Liber antiquitatum biblicarum*. Although extant only in Latin, it reflects a Greek translation of a Hebrew (or Aramaic) original dating from the period before the destruction of

---

[190] BT *Sanhedrin* 38b.
[191] Petuchowski, "A Sermon attributed to R Eleʿazar haModaʿi".
[192] Heinemann, "Proem", 105.
[193] So Bamberger, "Philo and haggadah".

the temple.[194] *Liber antiquitatum biblicarum* is a retelling of biblical history from the time of Adam to the death of Saul, following the contours of the biblical text. At times the text is closely followed, though
citation is to be found alongside paraphrase alongside authorial expansion. However on occasions the author leaves the biblical text entirely
behind, adding legends and digressions which have only an oral basis.
Is this then a collection of homilies? Perrot suggests that it is a haggadic collection made for the benefit of "targumists and homilists",
reflecting the needs of the synagogue before the destruction of the
temple. It echoes these homilies, though falling short of being a collection. This hypothesis has the merit of explaining the rationale
behind what is otherwise a puzzling document; moreover, according to Perrot the pre-eminence of certain scriptural chapters, the
thematic construction, the stress on the order of feasts and the primary reference to the Torah might likewise be explained by seeing
ps-Philo as a collection reflecting homiletic practice before the destruction of the Temple.[195]

As an example of the manner in which the narrative both expands
and abbreviates the scriptural text in retelling we may note the beginning of the narrative of the giving of the law on Sinai. Ps-Philo
begins with the scriptural text of *Exodus* 19:1: "And in the third
month of the departure of the children of Israel from the land of
Egypt they came into the wilderness of Sinai". The remainder of the
chapter up until the beginning of the decalogue is then paraphrased.

> God remembered his words and said: I shall give light to the world,
> and I shall enlighten the inhabitable places, and I shall establish my
> covenant with the children of men and I shall glorify my people above
> all peoples; I shall put forth high and eternal things for them which
> shall be a light for them, but a punishment for the wicked. And the
> Lord said to Moses: "Behold, I shall call you tomorrow. Be ready and
> say to my people 'for three days a man shall not approach his wife.'
> and on the third day I shall speak to you and to them And after you
> have climbed up to me, and I shall give my words in your mouth,
> and you shall illuminate my people in that which I have given into
> your hands, which is an eternal law, by which I shall judge all the
> world. For this shall be a testimony, that if people say 'We have not

---

[194] With regard to date and original language we accept the arguments of
Harrington, Perrot and Bogaert, *Ps-Philon: Les antiquités bibliques* II, 66–77, where the
arguments and relevant bibliography can be found in more detail.
[195] Harrington Perrot and Bogaert, *Ps-Philon* II, 35–39.

known you, and therefore we have not served you' I shall take vengeance on them on the grounds that they have not known my law." (11.1)

Following the preparation and sanctification of the people, ps-Philo picks up with the narrative of the thunder and lightning of God upon the mountain. This is extended to describe the shaking and burning of the mountains, and the boiling of the depths, and the roaring of tempests . . .

> and the stars were gathered together, angels going before, as God gave the law of the eternal covenant to the children of Israel, and gave eternal precepts which will not pass away. (11.5)

In the narrative itself and in the implied admonition of the content of the narrative it is reasonable to hear the voice of the preacher. It is to be noted that whereas the approach to the text is so different from that of Eleazar haModai, in that there is considerably greater freedom, both are nonetheless dependant on the text, and both are concerned with the universal import of the law given to Israel.

Less certain of date are the homilies on Sampson and Jonah handed down in Armenian among the works of Philo which are presented by Siegert.[196] These are likewise free narrative retellings of the biblical story, which Siegert characterizes as "biographical encomia."[197] Among them are two on Jonah. In the longer, complete homily on Jonah the broad lines of the narrative are followed, but it is nonetheless difficult to discern the original text lying behind the homiletic retelling.

As an example we may cite the point at which Jonah boards the ship in order to run away from the Lord.

> As he was running back and forth beside the sea in his agitation, he saw there a trireme. He waved to the seamen, and called out "Where are you heading sailors? Where are you taking your ship? Do me a favour and bring me on board." They said where they were going, reached an agreement and pulled him on board the ship. As they did so the uproar of the sea became dangerous for the sailors. For as the prophet, the messenger to the town, boarded the ship, he found himself, because of his prophecy, in the waves of agitation. They took a stone onto the ship, in the shape of him who had taken on proclamation,

---

[196] *Drei hellenistisch-jüdische Predigten* I. According to Siegert *Drei hellenistisch-jüdische Predigten* II, 40–47, these may be dated from any time from 200 BC to 200 AD.
[197] *Drei hellenistisch-jüdische Predigten*, 2.

and were sailing against themselves. Instead of sailing over the waves, the waves were rolling over them.[198]

Predictably enough, the simple prophetic message of Jonah to repent is greatly expanded. Here we are as far from the unmediated voice of prophecy as it is possible to be!

In the fragmentary homily on Jonah the text may be discerned behind the retelling as it is followed with much greater fidelity; even the verse structure of the scriptural original may be found behind this fragmentary homily. And yet there is a jump in the story from *Jonah* 1:8 to *Jonah* 1:11.

> Like judges the seafarers asked: Where are you from and what is your people, and what is your business? (*Jonah* 1:8) When they had sought this out and discovered it they did not fail to act justly, quite the opposite, for they had read that whoever is judged should himself sit in judgement. They said "What shall we do with you?" (*Jonah* 1:11) You judge and decide![199]

This sheds light on the prescription of Mishnah *Megillah* 4:4 that a reader may not skip from place to place in the reading of the Torah, but may do so in reading from the prophets. Yet despite the uncertainty of date there is sufficient evidence here of the existence of a narrative homily pattern which is relatively early, and therefore might well have been imitated by the Christians. Indeed, although there are elements of narrative pattern in later rabbinic works which may reflect preaching, they are relatively rare. Jacobson suggests that this results from the canonization and guarding of the text within rabbinic Judaism which would lead to hostility to anything which might threaten the text by appearing too close to it.[200] Not only does this argument fit in with our earlier observations concerning the writing down of sermons and targums,[201] but may also lead to the subsequent prominence of the proem form with its stronger emphasis on the verbal detail of the text.

---

[198] Translation based on the German of Siegert, *Drei hellenistisch-jüdische Predigten* I, 12.
[199] Translation based on the German of Siegert, *Drei hellenistisch-jüdische Predigten* I, 49.
[200] Jacobson, *Commentary*, 213.
[201] At 1.2.3.1 above.

1.2.3.3. *Jewish Scriptures and Christian preaching*

We have thus discovered two exegetical patterns in Jewish preaching before the parting of the ways, which we may characterize as "proemic-exegetical" and "narrative". What both have in common however is a deep dependence on the scriptural text. We may ask in conclusion how it is that these forms of scriptural homily came about. A suggestion which comes immediately to mind is that these forms each derive from the targumizing process. The "proemic" form in the simple manner which is suggested here can readily be seen as deriving from the targum, as elements in the text can become the subject of independent exegesis in the course of translation, and the narrative homily can equally be seen as an expanded targum, extending beyond simple translation to retelling. In this respect we may note again Perrot's suggestion that this is the origin of ps-Philo. The freedom of this retelling should be contrasted to the relative conservatism of the later rabbinic targums. It is this freedom which one might expect the Christians to imitate.

The suggestion that synagogue preaching grew out of the targum is not new, it is made by Moore,[202] followed recently by Mack[203] and Salzmann.[204] Although the earliest use of targums in the synagogue is wrapped in the same obscurity as much else concerning synagogue worship, it would seem that it is an ancient practice from the manner in which Mishnah *Megillah* 4 assumes that the practice is ancient and legislates for their use.[205] Could not the practice of the targumist, following the contours of the text, explain the manner in which the text is taken apart for explanation and expansion in the exegetical homily, as much as its expansion in the narrative homily? The deep adherence of the Jewish homily to Scripture in both the exegetical and the narrative homily, including a fidelity to the order of the text, may be explained in this manner, as may the uncertainty about the propriety of writing down targums which we have noted in early Judaism. It is Scripture which takes precedence

---

[202] Moore, *Judaism*, 304.

[203] Mack, *Aggadic midrash literature*, 41.

[204] Salzmann, *Lehren und Ermahnen*, 457.

[205] Zunz, *Vorträge*, 64, accepts the antiquity of the targumic process, as, more recently, does Schäfer, "Synagogale Gottesdienst", 391–413. The Qumran targum however cannot be admitted into evidence as it is conceivably sectarian, and its liturgical use is not ascertained.

in the synagogue, and homiletic activity grows directly out of the encounter with Scripture.

Thus as the synagogue setting was adopted by Christians, so might Christian preachers adopt this theology of Scripture, with its attendant homiletic forms, in their intent to communicate the word of God to their audiences.

1.2.4. *Models of preaching in the wider Hellenistic world*

1.2.4.1. *The diatribe*

Late in the nineteenth century, research led to the delineation of a *Gattung* which came to be known as the diatribe. The diatribe has frequently been adduced as a possible source of the Christian homily and this idea is enshrined in a number of popular treatments of the history of Christian preaching.[206] Wilamowitz-Moellendorff had investigated the style of Teles, and concluded that this style was the result of the reflection of an oral *Gattung* in Teles' work, that of popular philosophical preaching.[207] Subsequently other texts were discovered to exhibit the same style, and the form itself became known as the diatribe, a term occurring in Diogenes Laertius and in the manuscript tradition of Epictetus.[208]

The particular characteristics of this style were defined variously, but outstanding features are stereotyped ethical themes and stylistic features, notably the use of *chreiai*, examples from the world of myth, everyday images, rhetorical questions, parataxis, asyndeton, catalogues, antithesis, word-play, citations (particularly of Homer) and most particularly dialogical engagement with an imaginary objector. The context for this style was the short address, dwelling on a philosophical, generally ethical, theme. The suggestion that the diatribe might have contributed to the Christian sermon actually originated with Wilamowitz-Moellendorff, but the suggestion was taken up by Wendland.[209] The term subsequently entered the common vocabulary of New Testament scholarship with the work of Bultmann, who sought to discover Paul's preaching style on the basis of diatribal

---

[206] E.g. Sedgwick, "Origins", Carroll, *Preaching the word.*
[207] Wilamowitz-Moellendorff, *Antigonos von Karystos*, appendix on Teles at 292–319. See further Stowers, *Diatribe*, 7–48 for a history of early scholarship on the form.
[208] The name was first given by Usener, *Epicurea*, LXIX. The term was not employed by Wilamowitz-Moellendorff.
[209] Wendland, *Hellenistisch-römische Kultur*, 75–96, especially 92–93.

elements in *Romans*.[210] It is also to be noted that Norden's understanding of ὁμιλία as meaning an informal address was formulated largely under the spell of the diatribe.[211] Clearly, if the diatribe was a literary (or rather oral) form employed in the Hellenistic world in a context similar to that of preaching then to seek the origins of Christian preaching in this form is not unreasonable. However there are particular difficulties in working with this *Gattung* which should be noted.

An obvious difficulty is that of tying down the diatribe on a formal basis. If the essence of the diatribe is fluidity, then this very fluidity makes form-criticism rather difficult. Although it is referred to as a *Gattung*, the defining characteristics of the diatribe are stylistic rather than formal, though the single extant ancient definition of the diatribe is an indication of length rather than of *Gattung*, which complicates matters further.[212] The stylistic phenomena mentioned are not, moreover, unique to the philosophical literature, but are common to much Asianist rhetoric. Citations and *exempla* in particular are part of the standard array of any Greek speaker.[213] Even the authors held to be representatives of the diatribe vary. On this basis, and in view of the fact that Maximus of Tyre referred to his own public philosophical lectures, (which are included in the diatribal canon, and being public philosophical lectures might seem to be diatribai pure and simple) as διαλέξεις, it might be questioned whether the diatribe ever even existed. Certainly they were not identified under that label, and apparently they were rarely identified at all.

However the phenomena noticed by the early critics do exist;[214] what is peculiar about the so-called diatribe is not the appearance of these particular stylistic elements but their concentration, and their discovery in a philosophical context. We may continue to talk of diatribe, but must be conscious that this is a modern term for an ancient phenomenon. Even then the difficulty of definition remains.

---

[210] Bultmann, *Stil*.

[211] Norden, *Antike Kunstprosa*, 541–544. See our comments on Norden's theory at 1.1.4 above and 3.3 below.

[212] Hermogenes *De methodo* 5, who states that it is a brief dilation on a particular sentiment.

[213] Mack, *Rhetoric*, 42–43.

[214] So both Schmeller, *Paulus*, 20, and Stowers, *Diatribe*, 49.

Rather than conventional form criticism a better approach might be
to find a social setting for the use of the diatribe, in order to assist
with the task of definition, and to assist in the identification of the
form outside the classical diatribal canon.[215]

According to Stowers the essential setting for the diatribe is the
schoolroom;[216] if he is correct that holds out hope that the diatribe
might influence discourse in the scholastic community of Christianity.[217]
He reaches his conclusion on the basis that the normal ancient usage
of διατρίβω and its cognates was scholastic. We should here note
that significant among uses of the term in a scholastic setting are
those of Xenophon, where the word διατρίβω is virtually synony-
mous with ὁμιλεῖν.[218]

He then goes on to suggest that this setting would fit comfortably
with each of the classical authors recognised as employing a diatribal style. The school setting of Epictetus is clear enough, but he
also suggests that Teles likewise was a teacher, that the diatribai of
Musonius derive from a time when he was employed in teaching,
and that Plutarch was employed for most of his life as student and
teacher. However, special pleading is required when Stowers comes
to deal with Maximus of Tyre, whose audience, although fundamentally made up of wealthy youth, was nonetheless public, and not
founded on a school as such. Even more special pleading is required
for Dio Chrysostom, whose diatribai are most certainly public. Thus
his conclusions are vigorously disputed by Schmeller, who suggests
that the scholastic basis for each of the authors mentioned by Stowers
is dubious.[219] The fact that διατρίβω in the ancient sources refers to
scholastic activity is for Schmeller neither here nor there, since the
term in its current usage is a construction of the nineteenth century
and thus provides no guidance. The term "diatribe" was taken from
Arrian, whose lectures are of a schoolroom nature, and to whose
works it may well have been applied in the ancient world, but this

---

[215] So Stowers, *Diatribe*, 48 following Schmidt, "Diatribe und Satire".
[216] Stowers, *Diatribe*, 48–78.
[217] Cf. Siegert, *Drei hellenistisch-jüdische Predigten* II, 7 for whom the schoolroom setting for the diatribe (he follows Stowers) excludes the possibility that the diatribe
might be related to the homily on the basis of the absence of a cultic setting.
However, not only might a school setting suit the context of a first century church
through scholastic activity, but the schools were no strangers to cultic activity.
[218] *Memorabilia* 1.2.3; 1.2.27; 1.2.39.
[219] Schmeller, *Paulus*, 47–52.

does not provide a basis for seeing other works in a nineteenth-century canon as likewise scholastic in origin. Schmeller thus re-asserts the public nature of the diatribal literature; although some of the writers who are perceived to employ a "diatribal" style had some involvement in teaching, this is by no means true of all of them.

A middle view between Stowers and Schmeller may be to see the diatribal style as having its origins in the schoolroom, in particular with Teles, where this style would have been particularly appropriate, and extending itself out from there into more public forms of discourse; the term, although modern, is derived from Epictetus who was a teacher, and the stylistic phenomena which are found in Epictetus' diatribai are singularly suitable for a schoolroom and are moreover those which are found most prominently in the authors who comprise the diatribal canon. So it is that the orations of Maximus of Tyre, even though they comprise a course in philosophy and may thus borrow the style of the schoolroom, are by virtue of their public nature known as *dialexeis* and not *diatribai*. Just as the first oration is of the nature of a protreptic, so the entire course may be seen as an extension of the sumbouleutic genre. The same may be said of Dio Chrysostom, whose use of diatribal techniques may be characterized as the borrowing of a schoolroom style for orations which are nonetheless public. In the ancient sense of the word therefore these are not diatribai, but they exhibit nonetheless common traits of style which we may recognise and on the basis of these common traits label them as diatribe. This common style they share with works which have a schoolroom setting by virtue of the origins of the style, and thus bring something of the flavour of the schoolroom into public address.

It is equally possible that the public sumbouleutic style might find its way into the schoolroom. Put simply, since Epictetus, whose *diatribai* are educational in setting and intent, displays the same stylistic elements as Maximus of Tyre, whose *dialexeis* are public events, to deny that one or other of these is a diatribe would be to engage in a fruitless *logomachia*. A variety of settings, public and scholastic, may be found for the diatribe; all of which adds to the problem of definition.

Finally one might suggest that the public philosophical lecture, although having its origins as part of the *genos sumbouleutikon*, might have been influenced by public epideictic, especially in the period of the second sophistic, the period at which the diatribe seems to flower after its early cynic origins. This would explain the heavy incidence of rhetorical device in what is intended to be a directly didactic work, as well as explaining how it is that the diatribe really comes into its own only in the Early Empire. This is the period in which the sophistic displays become an art form and in turn infect dicanic rhetoric, and spread their influence into philosophical discourse likewise.[220] In this climate the distinction between the philosopher and the rhetorician becomes a narrow one.[221] This stands by way of direct contradiction to Philostratus' definition of the second sophistic, which for him is characterized by the shift from philosophical to historical themes.[222] This social movement explains the manner in which the rabbinic homilies likewise come to betray hints of "diatribal" style.[223]

Since it is disputable even that the diatribe existed at all, and in any event is to be defined by its very fluidity, it is interesting that McDonald, following Bultmann,[224] suggests that in fact the diatribe did have a general outline. According to McDonald an ideal is set forth which is followed by a negative demonstration of the ideal; the philosopher finally restates his intention in a conclusion which very often reflects the opening. As examples of diatribai displaying this shape McDonald takes Epictetus *Dissertationes* 1.18, and 2.1, though there are many more.[225] This pattern may be found extended across the diatribal authors, yet there is nothing distinctly diatribal about it, unless it be the manner of the illustrations, since this is simply the normal process of proof of a *thesis* to be found in Greek rhetoric, *probatio* proceeding firstly by refutation and then by statement. These diatribai are simply discourses on a theme. It is unfortunate that having been misled by Bultmann into giving the diatribe a formal

---

[220] As pointed out by Reese, "Semiotic critique", 238–239; see also 1.2.4.3 below.

[221] Philostratus accepts certain philosophers as sophists and several of his sophists are also philosophers, e.g. Aristocles *Vitae sophistarum* 2.3.567, Alexander "Clay Plato" *Vitae sophistarum* 2.5.570.) Bowersock, *Greek sophists in the Roman Empire*, 11–12, cites evidence from inscriptions that sophistry and philosophy are not mutually exclusive disciplines.

[222] Philostratus *Vitae sophistarum* 1.481. It is Bowersock, *Greek sophists*, who shows that it is not themes which are distinct about the second sophistic but the social status of the sophists and the diffusion of their functions through society.

[223] On which see especially Marmorstein, "Background".

[224] McDonald, *Kerygma and didache*, 42–43.

[225] McDonald, *Kerygma and didache*, 41.

shape McDonald goes on to suggest that this very formal shape provided the model for the Christian homily;[226] this cannot provide a basis for recognising a homiletic pattern since it is based on a misapprehension.

Given the difficulties of definition we should be clear that we may continue to employ it in a loose sense, referring only to the concatenation of stylistic phenomena noted above, and without this implying any prior judgement about the setting of the discourse under examination. Although there is no doubt that diatribal elements find their way into New Testament writings this does not in itself make them actual diatribai. However the direct influence of the schoolroom is possible, and the style certainly conveys something of a "scholastic" preoccupation.

However, even were it possible to find a complete diatribe extant in early Christian literature that in itself would not mean that it was a sermon preached in the synaxis. The presence of a diatribal stylistic element in Christian literature is not sufficient on its own to make these documents sermons, or even reflections of sermons. There is no doubt that *Romans*, for instance, contains diatribal elements, and as such we may hear something of Paul's preaching style. But *Romans* is not therefore a homily, it is a letter.[227] We use *Romans* here firstly because it is a clear-cut case of a non-homiletic form employing diatribal techniques which have been frequently observed, and secondly because Bultmann believed that a study of the diatribal elements in *Romans* might provide a clue to Paul's preaching technique.[228] Simply because of the presence of diatribal elements we are not justified in assuming that the document in question is a diatribe in the narrow sense, even less that it was "preached". A similar case pertains in the classical evidence. Seneca's *Epistulae Morales* are indebted to the diatribe, but they are most certainly literary creations. Siegert is right in that orality is essential, and a written document in the

---

[226] *Kerygma and didache*, 50–68.

[227] Although Donfried, "False presuppositions", 112–118, goes so far as to argue that there is nothing even diatribal about *Romans* on the grounds that the diatribe is a literary fiction, we may maintain that there are stylistic elements which are held in common between *Romans* and the diatribal canon (which does not involve a judgement on the actual existence of diatribe as a *Gattung*) whilst agreeing with Donfried's fundamental point that these stylistic elements in no way affect the literary purpose of *Romans*.

[228] Bultmann, *Stil*.

style of a diatribe is not therefore a sermon,[229] even though its diatribal elements may give an impression of orality.

Because there is no formal shape that leads to the recognition of
the diatribe we are not able to use the form as a form-critical meas-
uring rod to assess the genre of the writings of the New Testament
or others of the second century,[230] and because the diatribal literature may be either public or scholastic in its orientation we cannot
use the presence of diatribal elements to reconstruct a setting which
may in turn point us towards the activity of a preacher, since the
reconstruction of occasion is partly the task that is at hand. When,
in cases like *Romans*, we know that we are not dealing with a homily
because the occasion or genre is recognizable, then its identity as a
diatribe can be easily denied; but that has already been done by
virtue of the recognition of the occasion and purpose. In the cases
such as *Hebrews* or *Barnabas*, where there is no certainty about the
setting, then because the setting is not known the identification of
diatribal elements does not give us any assurance that we are dealing with a sermon. Finally the fact that a document betrays diatribal
elements does not mean that it was ever preached, in that it may
be a literary construction entirely. On the other hand, if by other
means we are able to identify a document as a homily, then the observation of diatribal elements may assist us in an examination of
style, and in a reconstruction of the setting; the style is likely to have
been adopted from the schoolroom, the lecture hall, or from the
rhetorical displays of the sophists and each of these may with them
bring a social context. An examination of the extant literature may
then be alive to influences from the diatribe, but cannot use it as a
defining characteristic to assist in the recognition of a homily.

We may illustrate these observations with some comments on *IV
Maccabees*. Thyen baldly states that the book is a diatribe, and from
there proceeds to see orality in that very diatribal form.[231] Van
Henten agrees that the book has the literary form of the diatribe
but notes also that it has other influences, including the ἐπιτάφιος

---

[229] Siegert, *Drei hellenistisch-jüdische Predigten* II, 4–6.
[230] This was the fundamental mistake made by Thyen, *Stil*, for which he has
received near universal criticism. Proceeding on the assumption that diatribal style
was a mark of preaching, Thyen classifies works exhibiting such traits as homilies
on this basis alone. So, notably, Donfried, *Setting*, 28.
[231] Thyen, *Stil*, 12.

λόγος.[232] Lebram similarly takes this opening phrase as indicating that "IV Makk hat die Form einer philosophischen Diatribe",[233] but then goes on to see the strong influence of the ἐπιτάφιος λόγος, and that the whole is intended as epideictic. Those characterizing the work as a diatribe would have support from the opening verses where the author announces himself as φιλοσοφώτατον λόγον ἐπιδείκνυσθαι μέλλων. However, rather than use the disputed term "diatribe" we may less controversially call this an item of epideictic on a philosophical theme; thus although *IV Maccabees* starts out with the philosophical intention of persuading the audience of the Lordship of wisdom the overall effect of the work is that of epideictic. This is lent support by Freudenthal's analysis of the work as the proof of a θέσις, issuing out into an encomium, followed by his stylistic analysis of the work demonstrating a vast array of rhetorical techniques.[234] All commentators, ancient commentators included,[235] note the thoroughgoing rhetoric of the work. In particular it should be noted that this is not Atticizing rhetoric, but written in the *koinē*, with a tendency to neologisms, and thus Asianist in tone rather than Attic, which in turn brings the document close to the diatribal canon without making it a diatribe.

Freudenthal argues that we have an actual synagogue homily here. In support of his argument he notes the rhetorical opening, where the writer states λέγω of his activity, direct addresses to his audience both in the body and the conclusion, and the statement that it is being delivered at a καιρός.[236] With this latter argument Lebram is in agreement.[237] Finally Freudenthal suggests that this is not an isolated example from the pen of the anonymous author: he notes that the sermon is delivered ὅπερ εἴωθα ποιεῖν.[238]

Interestingly Freudenthal here raises the question of audience.[239] Could an ordinary synagogue congregation follow a homily apparently aimed at a literary and educated audience and delivered by a

---

[232] van Henten, "Datierung und Herkunft".
[233] Lebram, "Literarische Form", 81.
[234] *Herrschaft der Vernunft*, 18–19.
[235] So Freudenthal, *Herrschaft der Vernunft*, 3: most recently Klauck, "Hellenistische Rhetorik".
[236] *Herrschaft der Vernunft*, 12, with reference to *IV Maccabees* 1:10.
[237] Lebram, "Literarische Form", 88.
[238] *Herrschaft der Vernunft*, 16.
[239] *Herrschaft der Vernunft*, 15.

rhetorically trained preacher? He suggests that there is no reason why such might not be the case, since the homilies of Origen and the Cappadocians are similarly written in exalted style on exalted subjects. To this we may again add the caution that the evidence of the popularity of rhetorical displays is indication that "high" rhetoric does not exclude a popular audience. This is important because any study of homiletics should take into account the audience as well as the preacher. If our interest is in the audience as much as the preacher, then the style adopted by the preacher is one possible indication of the nature of their interaction. Thus Siegert infers an educated audience from the exalted Asianism of the ps-Philonic *De Jona*.[240] It is moreover true that the rhetoricians teach that a style fitting to the occasion should be chosen, and that one of the things which dictates the occasion is the audience. So Dionysius of Halicarnassus states that the style of Thucydides is inappropriate to addresses πρὸς τὰς ὀχλικάς, as indeed it is unsuited εἰς τὰς ὁμιλίας![241] But the evidence of actual practice militates against this idea of adaptation to an audience. Interesting sidelight is thrown onto this question by Quintilian, who suggests that ornament is not out of place in forensic oratory;[242] rhetoricians were thus free to employ ornament in their speeches, as long as this did not make their speeches less persuasive. So ornament, belonging naturally enough in religious discourse, would be employed in preaching regardless of the capacity of the audience. For Quintilian the style is dictated more by the *materia*, that of greater importance requiring a greater degree of ornamentation, than by the audience. However, this takes *IV Maccabees* away from the schoolroom, and thus away from an appropriate classification as diatribe.

Against the theory of a homiletic origin to *IV Maccabees*, Thyen notes the absence of any consistent treatment of Scripture.[243] However Freudenthal had already noted such a possible objection, suggesting that it is perfectly in order for *II Maccabees* to be the Scripture and noting that the New Testament itself quotes apocryphal works as Scripture.[244] However, he suggests that this is not an exegetical homily,

---

[240] Siegert, *Drei hellenistisch-jüdische Predigten* II, 51; however he is clear that this is an inference only as, at 40, he notes that indications of audience are notably absent.
[241] *Thucydides* 50.
[242] Quintilian *Institutio Oratoria* 5.14.33–35.
[243] *Stil*, 14.
[244] *Herrschaft der Vernunft*, 14–15.

but one of a different nature altogether.[245] This is not an inconceivable claim for, as we have seen, we should be open to a variety of forms of preaching, and in particular that a scriptural homily based on the narrative outline of the text was known in early Judaism. Within the canons of Hellenistic rhetoric, this would appear to be what the author of *IV Maccabees* is constructing.[246]

However, although Freudenthal appears to give a satisfactory analysis of the speech, one should note the manner in which the opening differs stylistically from the main body, the actual panegyric. The division point is again a reference to the καιρός, at 3:19.

> Already now the occasion calls us to give a proof of the narrative of the lordship of reason.

One should also note that here there is what amounts to a shift of genera, sumbouleutic giving way to epideictic, an epideictic *probatio* being based on the following narrative. The division point at 3:19 stands out strongly in Freudenthal's analysis, for whereas Freudenthal notes that there is a shift at this point from *quaestio* to *laudatio* the connection between them is not made clear.[247] According to Norden this meant that the work as it stands is composite.[248] However, in appending a previously existing speech to his philosophical considerations the author is effectively creating a new whole. This is not secondary redaction, but rather the deliberate amalgamation of two genera, somewhat in the manner of the diatribe. Just as this is a scriptural retelling along Jewish lines, it is put to philosophical use, as the story of the brothers, like that of David at 3:7–16, is employed as an extended *exemplum* of the philosophical principles outlined at the beginning. According to Thyen a further redactor has been at work, and that what stands is not the actual homily but an edited version;[249] however, apart from 3:19 there is no trace of redactional work. If *IV Maccabees* is a homily, it is a homily as it stands.

A significant question however is whether we are dealing with a desk homily here or with a homily that was actually preached. The

---

[245] *Herrschaft der Vernunft*, 17.
[246] The admixture of forms is however significant. Freudenthal, *Herrschaft der Vernunft*, 17, therefore distinguishes this work from the *De Jona* treated by Siegert, *Drei hellenistisch-jüdische Predigten*.
[247] Freudenthal, *Herrschaft der Vernunft*, 18–19.
[248] Norden, *Antike Kunstprosa*, 416.
[249] Thyen, *Stil*, 13.

question, as Freudenthal himself admits, is unanswerable, especially
if we discount Thyen's suggestion of a further redactor beyond the
division point at 3:19. The references to the καιρός which in part
led to Freudenthal's assertion that we have here a real homily could
well be a clever piece of *prosopopoiia* since a recommendation is given
in one rhetorical work that a speaker should set the occasion of his
speech as part of his *prosopopoiia*.[250] We might be particularly suspi-
cious of this, in view of the fact that the anonymous author has a
distinct agendum, namely to warn against the dangers of assimila-
tion.[251] However, the reference to a liturgical occasion, whether fictive
or real, is one indication that, whether *IV Maccabees* was produced
for reading or for delivery, or was produced for reading and subsequently delivered in reality, what is intended is a homily. Further
support to this is then given through the interesting combination of
epideictic and sumbouleutic. In this it differs from the suggestion
that in Philo we have remains of homilies, for here a Hellenistic
Jewish homily would appear to stand intact, whether or not it is a
"real" product.

This brief study of *IV Maccabees* has shown that, although a literary document, it nonetheless reflects a homily which might be preached
on a liturgical occasion. Its narrative thrust and philosophical intent
both point in that direction. However its possible classification as a
diatribe does nothing to support that conclusion. The search for an
origin to Christian preaching in the diatribal literature is thus in the
end an unproductive activity.

1.2.4.2. *Protreptic*

The past concentration on the diatribe is unfortunate, and in particular its inappropriate classification as a *Gattung*, rather than a form
of speech distinguished by style, content and social setting.[252] A num-

---

[250] So Emporius *De Ethopoiia*; he quotes Virgil here as an example: non haec
sollemnia nobis has ex more dapes . . . (*Aeneid* 8.185–186) The setting at a religious
festival as a possible ethopoiic setting is noteworthy in the light of *IV Maccabees*.

[251] So Klauck, "Hellenistische Rhetorik", 451.

[252] As noted above, what is peculiar about the diatribe is the concentration of
rhetorical techniques in a philosophical setting. Reese, "Semiotic critique", 238–239
notes this peculiarity, and seems to imply that as such it attains the status of a
genre; however, as such it is at best a sub-genre; if homily is likewise to be seen
as a sub-genre, as Gammie, "Paraenetic literature", 46–47 suggests, then it is certainly distinct from the diatribe.

ber of the works which have been taken as diatribai belong to a distinct *Gattung* moreover, namely the *protreptikos*. Essentially intended to win over the hearer to the pursuit of a certain mode of life, in time protreptic becomes a vehicle for paraenesis. In this connection then we should note again the specialist Christian use of the term παράκλησις which, we have seen, became a frequently employed, if not the normal, term for Christian preaching and the activity of the prophets. We have already noted that this term originally referred to the λόγος προτρεπτικός,[253] and may therefore suggest that the term came into Christian usage in this way. That is to say, it comes into Christian usage through its association with the philosophical schools and with the process of ethical persuasion.[254] One should also note that protreptic, in its philosophical guise, is fundamentally the literature of the schoolroom, and so suitable for use within a scholastic community. One should then contemplate the possibility that the earliest Christians understood the preaching in their churches as an extension of this genre. The *protreptikos* might be equally a diatribe. However, although in examining the Christian literature of the early centuries we may be alive to the possibility that this form may have had some influence, of itself it is no guarantee that we are dealing with a preached homily. Clement's *Protrepticus* is quite simply a literary work, and there are extended paraenetic sections in the New Testament letters, which are "real letters."

Because paraenesis might be one of the functions of a homily there has been a widespread tendency, some examples of which will be observed below, to assume that works whose primary function is paraenetic must therefore be homilies. It is however interesting to observe that the λόγος προτρεπτικός exercised some influence in

---

[253] McDonald, *Kerygma and didache*, 69.

[254] The other possibility is that the word is originally intended in the sense of "comfort". Zunz, *Gottesdienstlichen Vorträge*, 348, states that synagogue homilies might be known as נחמות ברכות, since according to *Pesiqta de Rab Kahana* 13.14.4 the prophets who began with rebuke were to end with words of comfort (דברי נחמות) and this practice was followed by preachers. Stein, "Homiletische Peroratio", states that this practice is known to the Tannaim, indeed *Sifre Deuteronomy* 342 credits Moses with the idea! That דברי נחמות might lie behind the early uses of λόγοι παρακλήσεως, and that the usage is derived from Judaism, is a tempting idea, but the evidence of Jewish usage comes from after the parting of the ways, and is therefore of such a date that the possibility that the term is Jewish in origin must remain a speculation only. It is also possible that both Jewish and Christian use of the term derive from the usage of the schools.

Hellenistic Judaism, such that we might seek influence within Christianity, though we should beware of assuming that the influence is necessarily homiletic.

Both of these points may be illustrated by reference to recent works on *Wisdom* which have concluded that it is protreptic, and thus that as such it has taken on some aspects of the diatribe.[255] Winston finds items of language and style typical of the diatribe, such as the imagined adversary, *exempla* and parataxis whilst adducing parallels from Aristotle's reconstructed *Protreptikos*, which is essentially a call to live the life of wisdom, while ps-Isocrates' *Ad Demonicum* supplies a parallel to the final promise of eternal life. Reese finds the omission of names significant, pointing rather to character types than individuals, as well as the employment of diatribal style and the use of warnings alongside *exempla*. However, generic and stylistic observations apart, it should be noted that there is nothing within the work which would enable us to actually go so far as to classify the work as a homily. There is certainly a "copia verborum", but no actual direct indication of orality, or of a synagogue setting. Formally it does not actually link to any kind of homily yet proven to have existed. This latter argument is of course difficult, since we must be alert to the fact that we know too little about preaching in this period to be able to make a comparison; and yet in the current state of our knowledge it is not even possible to classify *Wisdom* as a desk homily, and so, in the absence of evidence which allows us to assign an occasion to *Wisdom*, we must assume that it is a purely literary work.

Nor is it possible to find indications of homiletic origins within the alleged homily. Suggs finds one such at 2:10–5:23, based on the fourth servant song.[256] There is a citation of *Isaiah* it is true, and at times the language and thought is very close to that of *Isaiah*, but this is not sufficient for us to claim it as a homily without clear formal criteria and indisputable indications of orality and audience, especially since at times the author appears to have other texts in mind. Admittedly Thyen takes *Wisdom* as a homily in that he discerns the *pathos* of the preacher addressing us in the final chapters, thus concluding that the book is an example of Alexandrian synagogal preaching before Philo,[257] but this is a subjective judgement.

---

[255] So Reese, *Hellenistic influence*, 117–121, Winston, *Wisdom*, 18–20.
[256] Suggs, "Wisdom of Solomon 2:10–5".
[257] Thyen, *Stil*, 26; for Siegert, *Drei hellenistisch-jüdische Predigten* II, 6 it should be

It is possible that these chapters are an expansion of *Isaiah*, rather like a narrative homily, but a homily is not the only possible locus for such an expansion. Similarly the historical section of *Wisdom* may be indebted to the narrative homily, but the detail provided by ps-Philo is notably lacking here; one of the traits which makes the work comparable to the protreptic therefore makes it less comparable to the narrative homily.[258] Thus if *Wisdom* is indebted to homiletic practice, and of this there can be no certainty, it is so in its parts, and not in its protreptic whole.

Additional problems for charting the influence of protreptic are posed by the question of definition. Burgess points out the *protreptikos logos* is, like the diatribe, without formal definition in the ancient world,[259] though at least here we can be assured that it did exist! However the problem of definition again makes the genre a difficult one to employ in making form-critical comparisons. Burgess calls it a union of philosophy and rhetoric,[260] which is rather what we have seen the diatribe to have been. Like the diatribe it is rhetoric based around philosophical themes. From the clearest ancient treatment of the subject it is clear that it is considered part of sumbouleutic, concerned to show that a course of action is correct, good, honourable.[261] However, when Quintilian indicates that certain species are common to all three genera this is an indication that the Aristotelian trichotomy is breaking down;[262] when Menander classifies the protreptic as epideictic it would seem that the scheme has broken down altogether,[263] since the true protreptic, rather than a speech in protreptic shape being undertaken as a school exercise, is primarily defined by being delivered to an uncommitted audience and thus should be counted primarily sumbouleutic in tone.[264] To the suggestion that

---

noted that *ethos* is more significant for the early Christian homily, as indeed for the diatribe, than *pathos*.

[258] See Reese, *Hellenistic influence*, 91–98, for a discussion of attempts to classify *Wisdom* in whole or in part as a "midrash". The comments made there apply equally here, though one would wish to demur from the rigorous division of "Hellenistic" from "Jewish" which runs through Reese's work.

[259] Burgess, *Epideictic literature*, 229–230.

[260] *Epideictic literature*, 229.

[261] *Rhetorica ad Alexandrum* 1.1. Here sumbouleutic is summed up as being either παράκλησις or διακώλυσις.

[262] *Institutio Oratoria* 3.4.15.

[263] Noted by Gammie, "Paraenetic literature", 44–45.

[264] So Stowers, *Letter writing*, 92.

this is the intended audience for the protreptic Gammie raises the question of the mixed audience.[265] Again the social setting of the early Empire means that there is some fluidity in the generic categories, but nonetheless a speaker might have a primary audience in mind. In view of the primary function of protreptic as persuasory, its influence on preaching in the assembly should be discounted, although its influence may have been felt in missionary preaching. Like Maximus, Paul uses a hall for the delivery of his addresses,[266] and as such may have conformed his preaching to the sumbouleutic model. In this light one may view the Pythagorean *Bekehrungspredigt* adduced by Berger as a parallel to Christian models, noting with interest the scholastic setting which this piece would seem to indicate, as well as the manner in which ethical direction and theological proof are bound up.[267] Catechetical teaching likewise may have undergone such influence; if the paraenetic sections in the New Testament epistles illustrate catechesis then they would certainly indicate this probability.[268]

In conclusion we may therefore state that whatever influence the protreptic discourse might have exercised in early Judaism or Christianity, it does not affect preaching. However, our brief study of *Wisdom* indicated the possibility that the narrative homily might have exercised some influence, even if the book as a whole cannot be recognized as in any way homiletic.

1.2.4.3. *The influence of epideictic displays*

Our discussion of the generic classification of preaching above,[269] and the attempt to see the influence of protreptic, have pointed up the extent to which the strict divisions between the genera break down in the Early Empire, as any type of rhetoric might become the occasion for a display. Philostratus' *Vitae sophistarum* is an account of the

---

[265] Gammie, "Paraenetic literature", 43.

[266] *Acts* 19:9. Similarly note Polycarp at Eusebius *Historia ecclesiastica* 5.20.5.

[267] Berger, "Hellenistische Gattungen", 1368–1370. Berger claims on this basis that this sub-genre had a Pythagorean origin. Certainly the Pythagorean schools would influence forming Christianity, but need not be the only scholastic influence, nor the sole entrée of protreptic into the literature of conversion.

[268] Paraenesis is here defined by the presence of maxims, following Gammie, "Paraenetic literature", 51. This formal observation, together with the suggestion that *protrepsis* has a more sustained argument, indicates that the audiences are basically distinct, since the maxims would of themselves be unconvincing to the uncommitted.

[269] At 1.2.1.4.

success of a number of orators who through their art-form gained social standing, wealth and prominence. This movement, named following Philostratus as the second sophistic, has generally been presented as the result of the decline of political life in the Empire, which meant that the ability to speak and persuade, which was a necessary part of the education of a citizen in classical Greece (as in republican Rome), declined in the conditions of the Empire, when neither political oratory or forensic persuasion were useful, and became as a result a purely academic exercise. According to this narrative the sophists, whose previous function had been to train the orators who were necessary for the political and forensic life of the state, became instead a class of themselves whose sole purpose was the continuation and perfection of the pedagogic exercises (the *progymnasmata*) which were the stuff of the schoolroom, and which dealt solely with mythological themes rather than with the *realia* of the present. Thus Marrou notes the fine line between the performance of set exercises and the practice of sophistry at a professional level;[270] the one was the direct product of the other, and the whole system came about due to the decline of the state and the resulting withering of pedagogy on the vine from being the practical teaching of a life-skill to a skill of value only in itself.

There are many grounds to criticize this decline narrative, for although political oratory had a narrower purpose in the conditions of the Empire, civic life continued nonetheless; litigation likewise did not come to an end with the advent of the Caesars, and many of the sophists whose speciality may have been the schoolroom exercises were also successful forensic speakers. The subject and nature of the persuasion may have been different in the Asian *polis* of the second century from that required in the Hellenic cities of the fifth BCE, but it was a political activity nonetheless for which rhetoric was an essential tool.[271] Beyond this one may also note the intense popularity of sophistic contests which, although themselves not of utility, demonstrate that the audience of the set declamations was not restricted to a narrow and educated elite but that rhetoric had a life beyond the schoolroom. There have thus been a number of

---

[270] So Marrou, *Education*, 195.
[271] For the decline of political life under Roman rule see Jones, *Greek city*, 170–192; however Anderson, *Second sophistic*, 7–8, gives us some insight into the fact that this decline was not necessarily perceived as such by its contemporaries.

recent attempts to rehabilitate the second sophistic, notably that of
Bowersock who characterizes the second sophistic as "the union of
literary, political and economic influence."[272] In this characterization
Bowersock is close to Philostratus, who takes great delight in telling
of the triumphs and honours gained by the sophists. Philostratus
clearly has agenda of his own, but the characterization has some
merit nonetheless; the second sophistic was a social movement as
well as a literary event, and sophistry became a means by which
individuals of education could gain and maintain status.

It is this movement which, we suggested above, gave rise to the
diatribe and which, we suggest, might in turn have affected the
Christian sermon. It is only to be expected that a rhetorical practice widespread in the Empire would affect the manner in which
Christian preachers addressed their audiences. According to Norden,
the influence of panegyric on Christian preaching was a phenomenon of the third century,[273] but this opinion must be revised in the
light of the discovery of Melito's *Peri Pascha*, which is a highly wrought
rhetorical work; it is more than likely that the social influence of the
second sophistic influenced the style and manner of Christian preaching, and that it did so from the beginning. Apart from the significance
of the second sophistic as a social movement, there is the further
indication of cross-fertilization in the extent to which the ability to
improvise was held among sophists: we have already noted the probability that Christian preaching in the early centuries was largely
extempore.[274] Most significantly, however, it is clear that sophists took
on religious functions in the atmosphere engendered by the second
sophistic. Stewart-Sykes notes the story of Polemo's participation in
the dedication of the Temple of Olympian Zeus, in which Polemo
claims to be speaking under divine impulse and hymns the god, of
sophists who served in priesthoods, and more significantly as hierophants, of the sacred contest dedicated to the rhetorical praise of
Capitoline Iuppiter, as well as noting the production by Aelius Aristides of the ἱεροὶ λόγοι concerning the revelations he received from
Asclepius.[275] These sophists are as likely to supply pagan parallels to

---

[272] Bowersock, *Greek sophists*, 27.
[273] Norden, *Antike Kunstprosa*, 544.
[274] At 1 above.
[275] Stewart-Sykes, *Lamb's high feast*, 129–130, with reference to Philostratus *Vitae
sophistarum* 1.25.533, *Vitae sophistarum* 1.21.515, *Vitae sophistarum* 2.4.568, *Vitae sophistarum* 2.26.613, *Vitae sophistarum* 2.20.600–601; Quintilian *Institutio oratoria* 3.7.4.

Christian preaching as the authors of the diatribal canon, but unfortunately not only is hardly any of their work extant but there is no one form which one might expect to find enshrined in their output; the work of Aelius Aristides contains both prose-hymns and the autobiographical ἱεροὶ λόγοι. This could impact however on the style of preaching, for it is possible that the task of a preacher was viewed from the standpoint of the sophistic rhetorician, and that the significance of the religious function being performed dictated an exalted style, to the actual exclusion of the audience. It is also possible that preaching deriving from this milieu might exhibit extended *narratio* as the Christian homily develops in the atmosphere engendered by the triumph of epideictic. Although Freudenthal differentiates between *IV Maccabees* and *De Jona*, they are both works alive with the influence of Asianism, and each may equally be characterized with Siegert as "biographical encomia".[276] Might not the same influences have come into play within Christianity? Not only the narrative homily of the synagogue but the aretology of pagan religion might play their part in the formation of the Christian sermon. It is a live question whether gentile Christians of the third generation would even be able to distinguish between them.

Thus once again the attempt to find literary parallels which may assist in the assemblage of formal materials, which may then be used in a comparative exercise with a view to the discovery of material germane to Christian preaching, is frustrated. Nonetheless, the observation of the social significance of sophists in the second century lends further foundation to the *hypothesis* of scholasticization.

1.2.4.4. *Philosophical table-talk*

The diatribe, and to a lesser extent the protreptic discourse, would be the most obvious models in the wider Hellenistic world which Christians might imitate in preaching, particularly since both derive from the philosophical schools. But whereas McDonald states that "the church began in a cultural environment in which preaching was a basic mode of communication",[277] we may need to revision the context for philosophical discourse. Quite apart from formal settings, such as the instruction of the sophist, or public epideictic, the

---

[276] *Drei hellenistisch-jüdische Predigten* I, 2.
[277] McDonald, *Kerygma and didache*, 39.

philosophical discourse might find a home in more private, informal
settings, in the home of a teacher and at dinner. Given the domestic origin of Christianity and the centrality of the meal to early Christian worship it is this setting which would perhaps be more influential
than the diatribe conceived as a formal speech. We may have reference to Plutarch's *Quaestiones conviviales* as an example of the manner in which ὁμιλία within the household might progress. Plutarch's
work is a collection of dialogues on a variety of subjects such as why
older men hold a text at a distance to read it, the properties of ivy,
whether the chicken preceded the egg and whether sex should follow dinner, all of which discussions are set at the dinner table.
Whereas this is obviously comic and parodic, the comedy only works
because of its proximity to reality, and thus Plutarch provides with
a picture of Graeco-Roman philosophical dining conversation which
is useful background to that which might take place around the
Christian table.

The conversation is not made up however of short statements, but
of longer statements delivered without interruption. Although this
probably results from the written nature of the dialogues it may
nonetheless illustrate the Pauline insistence that prophets should not
be interrupted, and that those with a message should wait until the
previous speaker has finished. A similar pattern of longer statements
delivered without interruption in a Christian literary context will be
observed below.[278] Plutarch is clear that the philosopher has a place
at these gatherings,[279] and the discussion which takes place at these
gatherings is not moreover entirely divorced from the topics of the
schoolroom. Thus *Quaestiones conviviales* 3.6, the discussion on the right
time for coition, begins with the discussion of a text, Epicurus'
Symposium, and the issue of whether Epicurus was right to introduce
the discussion of sex into this context.[280] This is followed by a contribution from Zopyrus, another diner, who accuses those who had
raised the topic of misreading Epicurus, and suggested that Epicurus'
intention was that of moral persuasion against the practice of having
sex after dinner, a moral discussion which continued after dinner.[281]

---

[278] 2.1.4.
[279] *Quaestiones conviviales* 1.1.
[280] *Quaestiones conviviales* 653B–C.
[281] *Quaestiones conviviales* 653C–D.

Interestingly Zopyrus suggests that this is not suitable for daytime διατριβή, since one cannot be sure of the audience, but is suited to the closer gathering of the philosophical dinner party.[282] Further contributions from guests involve the citation of Homer, and in particular the absence of any *exemplum* recommending coition during the day is noted, apart from the negative *exempla* of Paris[283] and of Plato.[284] Thus we may see that the philosophical discussion of texts, an activity which may readily be compared to Christian preaching, is thoroughly at home in the setting of the table.

We may conclude this discussion of possible Greek precursors to the homily by discussing what impact it might have on our understanding of Ignatius' instructions to Polycarp that he should ὁμιλίαν ποιεῖν against κακοτεχνίαι.[285] In the discussion above it was suggested that Ignatius' instruction was that Polycarp should raise this issue in conversation rather than that he should formally preach on the subject. We may now note that if the function of preaching is principally epideictic then a formal sermon on this subject would be unusual. In a domestic setting however the instruction to make ὁμιλία may be understood easily, and may see that Polycarp's contribution to the discussion is to be compared to one of the contributions of Plutarch's diners. In conversation, albeit a conversation where individuals are allowed to discourse at some length without interruption, the lines between the genera may moreover be somewhat flexible. This conversation may not be preaching as such, but is the communication of the word of God in a liturgical setting, in a manner suitable to the households of the second-century church.

1.2.4.5. *"Preaching" in the Hellenistic world*

Although the diatribe, usually understood as a Hellenistic equivalent to the Christian homily, does not of itself provide formal criteria for observing preaching activity, as part of the armoury of discourse within the schools it might have had some influence.[286] In Palestine likewise there is evidence that in time the diatribe affected the activity

---

[282] *Quaestiones conviviales* 653D–E.
[283] *Quaestiones conviviales* 655A.
[284] *Quaestiones conviviales* 654E.
[285] Ignatius *Ad Polycarpum* 5.1.
[286] Cf. this account to that of Schneider, *Geistesgeschichte* II, 5, according to whom rhetoric enters the Christian homily through the medium of the synagogue homily.

of Jewish preaching;[287] since the synagogue and the church were likewise variations of the school, we may suggest that analogous processes
were undergone by each independently. The influence of philosophical discourse on Christian preaching was not however limited
to the diatribal address, as philosophical conversation, protreptic and
the rhetorical practice of sophists might each have been likewise
influential. Although this does not assist us with provision of formal
criteria by which we might recognize an early Christian sermon, we
should note that all of these phenomena derive from the growth of
education in the ancient world. That these are the obvious sources
on which Christians might draw in preaching is further support for
the underpinning narrative of scholasticization in Christianity proposed above.

1.2.5. *Formal models for preaching available to Christians*

We observed above that formal attempts to define a homily had
failed on the basis that forms found in homilies might also be found
in other genera besides, and that since there was nothing definitely
homiletic surviving from the earliest church there was no basis on
which to extract a shape which was distinctly homiletic. An examination of analogous activities in the wider Hellenistic world has indicated that a homily might take the shape of a scriptural narrative,
or might consist of seriatim exegesis of a scriptural text. It is also
possible that marks of setting in a Hellenistic schoolroom might indicate that a document is reflective of communication in the Christian
assembly and, in view of the role of prophets in communicating the
word of God in the earliest assemblies, that prophetic speech forms
might mark homiletic delivery. Of themselves however these forms
do not necessitate defining any document which bears these marks
as a homily. Alongside formal criteria functional criteria need to be
employed, and over and above this further evidence is required to
indicate that any document being discussed is derived from or reflective
of preaching in the assembly. This further evidence may be supplied

---

[287] Marmorstein, "Background"; Fischel, "Use of sortites", and Stein, "Homiletische
Peroratio", also deal with the appearance of certain diatribal elements in the midrashic
homilies; Stein, "Homiletische Peroratio", suggests that the lateness of the evidence
prevents certainty concerning the date at which the diatribe began to affect Jewish
preaching.

by the underpinning narrative or *hypothesis* proposed in the first part of this chapter, and which is now restated in greater detail.

1.3. *A conclusion and a restatement of a hypothesis*

In this first chapter we set out to establish whether early Christians preached, and on the basis that they did so to establish some formal guidelines, on the basis of which it might be possible to discover early homilies among the writings of the earliest Christians.

It was established that the activity of the prophets in early Christianity was analogous to preaching, and that more formal communication of the word of God in the assembly enters the post-Pauline communities at least at the end of the second century as a result of the split from the synagogue, which meant that Christian worship in turn became synagogalized. The earliest Christians studied and heard Scripture in the synagogue rather in their own assemblies, whose activities were not those of the synagogue. In time however Scripture is introduced from the synagogue with a measure of synagogal organization, which in turn impacts directly upon the media of communication in the Christian assembly.

On this basis models for Christian preaching in the Hellenistic world were sought. The scriptural basis of the synagogue homily and the pervasive influence of epideictic oratory in the first and second centuries were both observed, as a result of which certain formal criteria may be gathered from the precursors to the Christian homily in the ancient world which might assist us in recognizing homilies, or fragments of homilies, in early Christian writings. In particular the proemic form is a possible indicator of a homily, as is a scriptural narrative. The diatribe, however, which has often been claimed as a "Hellenistic sermon", does not provide formal criteria as it is a style, rather than a form, though the manner of discourse of the Greek schools might provide a social basis for understanding the church, even if it does not provide any formal anchorage. This observation of social structure is however significant, as it fits in with the *hypothesis* of scholasticization set down at the beginning of the chapter, and alerts us to the relationship of form and social setting. Finally, given the significance of prophetic activity in the earliest Christian communities, indications of prophetic speech forms may assist us in recognising homiletic activity. However, as was noted in criticism of earlier form-critical attempts to define a homily, form alone is insufficient to assure us that any document, or part of a document, is derived from a homily preached in the assembly, and so beside these formal criteria we need to observe the functional criterion derived from the work of McDonald,[288] namely that preaching is intended to confirm an audience in its opinions and to strengthen it, rather than to convert or to persuade.

Most important, however, for recognizing the shape of preaching in the earliest church is to see how formal and functional observations fit in with the overall developments in church life which would in turn impact upon the communication of the word in the assembly. At the beginning of this chapter a *hypothesis* was stated. Before going on to the search it is necessary to state that *hypothesis* in greater detail.

As the Pauline churches developed out of their original household foundations we observed a process which we termed "synagogalization", namely the adoption of the synagogal practice of reading and interpreting Scripture. The synagogue might provide one basis on which systematic exploration of Scripture within the church might continue, and it is not a setting inconsistent with the introduction of diatribal style.

However, apart from the evidence for synagogalization in the Pauline communities, there is evidence of a wider perception of the church as a scholastic community. The term "scholastic community" to describe the church is taken from Judge, who views the earliest Christians within the social framework of the first century.[289] Thus, according to Judge, Paul would be recognisable in the first century as a sophist with a network of patrons, and thus his activity would have a recognisable social setting. Judge's work is "impressionistic"[290] but it is possible to lend some more precision to the valuable points which he makes.

In the period of institutionalization the development of the Christian synagogue would scholasticize the Christian movement. We have noted the teaching functions which are pressed on "Timothy" in the

---

[288] Note the discussion of McDonald, *Kerygma and didache*, at 1.2.1.1, 1.2.1.2, and the discussion of the generic classification of preaching at 1.2.1.4.

[289] Judge, "The early Christians as a scholastic community".

[290] So Meeks, *First urban Christians*, 82. Meeks does not find the parallels particularly significant. Malherbe, *Social aspects*, 53, tends to agree with the broad outlines of Judge's view, though he holds that the issues confronted by Christianity were more than merely academic. The issues confronted by many of the schools however were likewise more than merely academic!

Pastoral Epistles, and noted that these are likely to include catechetical teaching outside the assembly as well as preaching within.
This suggestion finds support in the references to catechetical activity observed above in *I Clement* and *Pastor Hermae*. Yet even beyond
the *didaskalia* the preaching and worshipping activity of the church
might be perceived in scholastic terms. Not only is there a teacher
supported by patrons, but the whole is, like a school, located in a
household setting. So Judas teaches in a house,[291] as does Justin,[292]
and indeed Paul.[293] The scholastic activity of the synagogue might
the more easily be taken over by the church because of the household setting which they both share. Just as similar developments had
already taken place in the synagogue with the result that Philo is
able to refer to the synagogues as schools of the virtues[294] so the
church develops along similar social lines, adopting the teaching practice of the synagogue in catechetical teaching as part of the process
of institutionalization. Moreover just as the *derashah* belonged equally
in the school as in the synagogue[295] so the Christian practice of
preaching might equally be seen as a scholastic activity. For this reason we may see how diatribal style finds an easy entry, and may
note the emphasis on ethical exhortation,[296] recognizing this as scholastic influence. Thus when *Colossians* 3:16 speaks of mutual exhortation alongside worship this is more than reminiscent of the practice
of the Epicurean schools.[297] Thus scholasticization begins almost as
the church parts from the synagogue, in part as a need to establish
itself on a social model.[298]

---

[291] *Acta Thomae* 131.

[292] *Acta Justini* 3.3.

[293] *Acts* 20:7–12.

[294] *De vita Mosis* 2.216.

[295] Tosefta *Sotah* 7.9 retails a discussion concerning the exposition of the law
which had taken place that day in the house of midrash. Note also the discussion
at 1.2.1.1 above of the flexible boundaries between the activities of the *beit haknes-
set* and the *beit hamidrash* with reference to the repeated tale of Aqiba at *Genesis R*
58.3 and *Esther R* 1:1 (8), which is given a location both in a synagogue and in a
school. Thus York, "Targum in the synagogue", suggests that the targum had a
place in the school as in the synagogue. In both instances the *derashah* grows out
of the encounter with Scripture.

[296] Found significant by Malherbe, *Social aspects*, 51.

[297] So Philodemus *De libertate dicendi* 23, 25, 73. Even the vocabulary employed
is similar. See also De Witt, "Organisation and procedure". This development is
not restricted to the deutero-Pauline communities, as Ignatius *Eph.* 3.1 and *Epistula
apostolorum* (Coptic) 48 similarly indicate a degree of mutuality in νουθεσία.

[298] Cf. Wilken, "Philosophical schools", for whom the scholasticization of Christianity
begins only with Justin.

Evidence of this process of scholasticization is exhibited most clearly in the communities of Pauline tradition since within this tradition there is evidence of both household and synagogal organisation; here we have termed the process "synagogalization", and understood it as a movement away from the household origins of the church. This is not to deny that the synagogue is a subspecies of the household, but to affirm that it is a household with specific functions and with an organisation to match those functions as opposed to a purely domestic organisation in which leadership derives solely from the position of the householder. The same moreover is true of the Graeco-Roman schools, which were likewise household based, but which were likewise households with particular aims and with matching organisation. It is possible that in some Christian communities the impetus towards scholasticization might come from surrounding philosophical schools rather than the synagogues. In the study below we shall attempt to discern whether the predominant influence is Jewish or not, but we must recognize that in the world of the Hellenistic synagogue as inhabited by Philo, for instance, whose household was both a school and a synagogue,[299] it is extremely hard to tell the difference between Jewish and Greek philosophical influences on the forming Christian communities.

In the Johannine communities there is evidence of household organisation, particularly clearly in the Johannine letters,[300] but also evidence of a school setting, which whilst more prominent in the Gospel may also be perceived in the epistles.[301] The historical relationship between the epistles and the Gospel is a complex question,[302] but between them they provide the nexus in which we can see the

---

[299] So Sterling, "School of sacred laws".

[300] The Johannine epistles are interpreted against a household background especially by Malherbe, *Social aspects*, 103–110, Maier, *Social setting*, 148–150 and Lieu, *Second and third epistles*, 125–135.

[301] Brent, *Hippolytus*, 61–62.

[302] Lieu, *Second and third epistles*, 212–216, whilst chary of committing herself to a definitive answer and arguing for diversity within the Johannine communities, nonetheless tends to see the epistles as subsequent to the Gospel, a view which may be seen as a tempered version of the consensus; Hengel, *Johannine question*, 32–39, 72–73 and passim, however argues that the epistles represent an earlier stage in the Johannine tradition. He suggests that the Gospel, with its theological tensions, is a result of the resolution of the tensions within the wider Johannine community to which the epistles bear witness; Thomas, "Order", argues for a similar historical process. In either event we may perceive that the Johannine community is in the process of development and that both household and scholastic models are available.

Johannine community developing. Given the close relationship between households and schools one may well expect a degree of overlap, but the evidence of the later Johannine literature indicates that the process of development led towards scholasticization, that the process undergone within the Johannine community was one of forming itself into a more consciously scholastic community and building on its household origins. This tends to support the reconstruction of Hengel, who sees the letters predating the Gospel, for if the epistles are to be seen as pre-dating the Gospel then we may perceive the process of development occurring relatively early in the life of the Johannine community. Thus although the process is harder to determine because the relative dates of the literary evidence are less certain, we may nonetheless observe that the same process of scholasticization occurred in the Johannine community as in the Pauline communities. This is an understandable development given not only the extensive influence of Hellenistic schools which would be available in Ephesus, but also the mutual hostility between the Johannine community and the synagogue, which would lead to the formation of a Johannine counter-synagogue. There is no Johannine literature dating from the earliest period, and so we cannot tell whether when the reading of Scripture was introduced into these communities; the letters tell us nothing of Scripture, but by the time of the Gospel the practice is clearly well established. We shall observe below that the Hippolytean community, one ultimately derived from the Johannine mission, has formed itself most explicitly into a school,[303] but although this may derive in part from its Johannine foundations this may also have resulted from its place within Roman Christianity. The widespread scholasticization of Roman Christianity would certainly have reinforced this social construction.

That the church might be perceived as a scholastic society is not an insight of modern scholarship alone; such was the perception of Galen at least in the second century in Rome, as he refers to the church as the "school of Moses and Christ",[304] as of the proconsul who interrogated Pionius and his companions in the third century.[305]

---

[303] 2.2.4.3.

[304] For discussions of the passages in Galen see Osiek, *Rich and poor*, 101–102; Wilken, *Christians*, 72–93.

[305] *Passio Pionii* 19.6 See on this den Boeft, "Are you their teacher?" who refers to a "furor didacticus" in the second century church.

Within Christianity moreover there was a self-consciousness of being a scholastic community. Thus by the beginning of the third century Hippolytus is able to make the same observation on the church of Callistus, namely that it is a διδασκαλείον[306] and concerning his own church that it is a school of grace.[307]

Finally we may note that the place of the scriptural text in the church would increase the impression of a scholastic setting, since the place of Scripture in the teaching activity of the church might be compared to the place of Homer in the classical curriculum. We have observed the extensive use of *exempla* in the Hellenistic synagogue, and that the *exempla* employed are scriptural. In the "word of exhortation" we may observe phenomena of a similar nature in the Christian church of the first two centuries. This compares to the use of Homer in the moral discourses of the sophists, whose *exempla* and citations alike are principally Homeric.[308] In time exegetical methods refined on the Homeric text are applied to Scripture; this derives from a whole social setting, which might in turn affect the preaching activity taking place within the church, just as in the synagogue scriptural narratives, such as that of *IV Maccabees*, may be fitted into Greek rhetorical models.

We have noted the comparative disorder of the *diakonia* of the word in the earliest Christian communities, but have noted that the descriptions of *Acts* and the instructions contained in the Pastoral Epistles indicate that in a short time preaching became a more ordered activity. Moreover by virtue of the same movement of conformity to the synagogue or the school we may anticipate that some association of the homily with Scripture occurs. Certainly Scripture holds the key to the development of the homily in the synagogue, since it derived from the targum and, in the assembly, followed the reading of Scripture; thus both the narrative homily and the exegetical homily follow the contours of their controlling Scripture. If the development of the church into a synagogue is, as we have suggested, secondary, then the line from the scriptural synagogue homily

---

[306] *Refutatio* 9.7, 9.12.
[307] *Homilia in Psalmos* 12.
[308] See e.g. Dio Chrysostom *Oratio* 71 who in five pages of printed text employs five *exempla* of which three are Homeric (one other is mythological, the other historical). The Homeric *exempla* are treated at greater length, and include one direct citation.

to the Christian homily is not a direct one. In particular, the role of the prophet was most prominent in the earliest house-church, and whereas we shall observe below that prophetic communication of the word of God might have reference to Scripture, the communication is not tied to Scripture in the same way as the directly scriptural homily.[309] Thus Thyen notes that a distinct difference between Jewish and Hellenistic *diatribai* lies in that for the Jew it is sufficient proof to cite Scripture, whereas in Greek practice a citation requires further support.[310] Nonetheless insofar as Christians begin increasingly to employ Scripture as a control in their communication this activity may be viewed as scholastic.

The movement toward scholasticization would also impact on the personnel of the church and on the office and function of the preacher. Countryman notes the intellectual role of the bishops in the second century, and notes moreover that here there lies a distinction between the church and the synagogue in that the *archisynagogos* would not be expected to have a teaching function.[311] However the bishops originated as householders and patrons, and therefore functioned in much the same way that the *archisynagogoi* would function, only becoming intellectual leaders as a result of the subsequent scholasticization of the church, with the resultant necessity that they should be equipped to teach. The situation is also likely to be more complex; prophets, who did not hold office as such, and subsequently teachers, might seek office to accompany their charisma, which in turn might lead to conflict with structures of authority based purely on the household. Thus *Canones apostolorum* in (probably) the third century allows for the possibility that the bishop is illiterate and assumes the existence of the office of reader,[312] which would hold the potential for conflict between offices with very different qualifications. In third century Rome Hippolytus' *Traditio apostolica* similarly reveals some conflict between the teaching bishop and supporting patron-presbyters.[313]

---

[309] Groh, "Utterance and exegesis", 73–95, notes scriptural reminiscences in two Montanist oracles, and seems to imply that their use here is as proof texts. This is certainly possible, though it is also conceivable that they are employed as *exempla*. See further the discussion below at 2.2.3.6 and 2.2.5.

[310] Thyen, *Stil*, 71–72.

[311] Countryman, "Intellectual role", 262.

[312] *Canones apostolorum* 16.

[313] So Stewart-Sykes, "Integrity".

The existence of this very conflict is evidence that the *hypothesis* of movement from unqualified household to school may be sustained. The *hypothesis* has the further merit of explaining how it is that in the Pauline churches there is no office, whereas by the time of the Pastoral Epistles offices have come into existence which mirror in some way the positions of honour held in the synagogue; that is to say, the offices originate as positions of honour in a household setting as they had in the synagogue, and become more formalized offices as a result of the need for teaching functions to be carried out within the church and for persons to be qualified for those duties.[314]

We may conclude this chapter by summarizing the formal criteria which we may employ in identifying homilies in Christian literature as the presence of a seriatim treatment of Scripture, which may have a narrative form since the existence of narrative homilies which may have fed into the Christian tradition within the Hellenistic synagogue. Secondly we may observe the presence of prophetic speech-forms. Since preaching is an oral event indications of orality may be observed, though these are potentially misleading because of the extent to which all ancient discourse is a potentially oral event. Functional criteria should also be employed; since preaching is fundamentally epideictic we should look first for discourse intended to re-inforce the attitude of an audience, but as the lines between the genera were somewhat flexible by the first century, we may also seek evidence of moral exhortation, perhaps bound up to the form of the "word of exhortation." In all cases when dealing with functional criteria a degree of caution needs to be exercised, but especial caution is needed when dealing with ethical exhortation; we have already observed the confusion caused by the equation of moral discourse

---

[314] This thus resolves the debate between Campbell, *Elders*, and Burtchaell, *From synagogue to church*. Burtchaell reckons that the πρεσβύτεροι of early Christianity derived directly from the synagogue, but Campbell (at 203–204) points out that all the evidence for the development of early Christianity points to a domestic rather than to a synagogal setting. However, whilst correct in perceiving three stages in the development of the church, represented for him by the Pauline correspondence, *Acts* and the Pastoral Epistles (note the chart at *Elders*, 205), he is able to produce no real evidence for the existence of a named group of πρεσβύτεροι in the Pauline churches, and their sudden emergence is therefore problematic unless in some way based on the synagogue. The uncanny correspondence moreover between the existence of presbyteral positions in both institutions, which is the basis of Burtchaell's thesis, begs explanation. The thesis of synagogalization satisfactorily accounts for all these phenomena.

with preaching, especially when marks of the diatribe are also present. We need to seek indications that the discourse is indeed preaching, and that it is preaching in the assembly and not missionary preaching or catechesis carried on outside the main liturgical assembly. Beginning with the formal criteria identified in this chapter, but following the plan of observing increasing scholasticization, the following chapter seeks to trace the history of Christian communication from unstructured prophecy to scriptural preaching.

CHAPTER TWO

PREACHING IN THE PRIMITIVE CHURCH

In this second chapter we attempt to chart the history of the development of Christian preaching up to the time of Origen. This may prove possible since we are now equipped with criteria by which to determine which of the extant documents of these centuries are homilies, or reflective of homilies.

However, sorting the material for examination is not easy. For instance it is not possible to treat the prophetic homily separately from the scriptural homily, since we shall observe that one of the functions of prophets was the exegesis of Scripture. It is likewise not possible to treat ethical exhortation separately since this might likewise be a prophetic activity, and might in turn be bound up to the use of Scripture as a source of *exempla*. A chronological approach is equally difficult because as a result of the localized diversity of Christian origins it is difficult to chart developments and therefore impossible to reach any overarching or universally true conclusions. Some works may be related to one another but others stand on their own. The uncertainty in dating of so much of the material is a further reason for difficulty with a chronological approach. Finally the approach taken by Salzmann,[1] which is to sort material on the basis of later and artificial groupings, such as the New Testament and the "apostolic fathers", is potentially misleading as it can lead to associations which are simply not there. Paul occupies a different world from the author of *Hebrews*, and Hermas a different world from that of *II Clement*.

In the first part of the work we suggested formal characteristics by which preaching in the church might be recognised. However we also began to note the different models available to the church in its social organisation. In particular we noted that, as a result of the division between Christianity and Judaism, some parts of the church were obliged to adopt some of the scholastic functions of the synagogue, particularly in the public reading of Scripture and related

---

[1] Salzmann, *Lehren und Ermahnen.*

preaching activity. We might therefore expect Christian preaching in these communities to have a teaching function like that of the synagogue homily.[2] This observation led to the statement of a *hypothesis*, or overarching narrative, according to which households in different Christian communities transformed themselves into synagogues or schools. This narrative provides a context not only for understanding the development of Christian preaching but also for the organization of the material under examination.

Thus as we proceed to the exploration of homiletic forms in early Christian literature we may have in mind the formal basis on which the search might be undertaken. The formal search should be concentrated on scriptural treatments, and in particular narrative treatments and division of the text for exegesis καθ᾽ ἕκαστον. Prophetic speech forms may be observed, and in any event the activity of prophets may be an indication of congregational preaching. The presence of the "word of exhortation" may well be observed, even though of itself it does not guarantee the presence of a homily. Hints of orality, although potentially misleading, may also be employed as an additional criterion. Secondly, functional criteria are employed: the homily is most probably a subspecies of epideictic. This may have implications for form, for in the context of the essentially scholastic environment the function of preaching was that of reinforcing the beliefs and loyalty of its members, and thus we may look for an extended *narratio* as the means of the introduction of narrative homilies based on Scripture into Christianity which was not Jewish in its immediate genesis. But apart from these formal and functional observations the enterprise should include an attempt to see how the forms related to the social construction of the community in line with the *hypothesis* proposed; our examination of other purely formal attempts to classify primitive preaching have shown the many possible pits into which such efforts may fall if undertaken without reference to the context in which the forms developed.

The first basis on which the Christian church was organised was the household, and this is the social setting for the communication

---

[2] Müller, *Prophetie und Predigt*, 238, suggests that Christian homilies have this much in common with those of the synagogue, as opposed to prophetic proclamation, which is unmediated and the consists of the pronouncement of new things. However, one should note that it seems that, alongside preaching, prophets might take on the functions of a teacher also. So see Hill, "Christian prophets as teachers or instructors".

of the word of God which is examined first. Subsequently we examine preaching in the two sub-types of household which have taken
on scholastic functions, namely the Christian synagogues and schools.
The latter two developments are capable of further development by
transferring their functions out of the household to a separate building such as a hall. We have noted the sophistic use of halls for public lecturing, and we may notice that Christians acted similarly. So
Paul teaches in the school of Tyrannus,[3] and Polycarp likewise makes
use of a hall.[4] Jews similarly may have been influenced by this social
movement.[5] The social setting of the preaching thus gives an insight
into the expectations and aims of the preacher and audience; it may
also provide a clue to the development of the sermon, since, as we
suggested earlier, the scriptural homily was a development deriving
from the synagogalization and scholasticization of the church. We
shall argue that the prophetic message, the original form of communication, is replaced or supplemented with the scriptural message,
and in that event not only does the expectation of a targum in a
synagogal setting give rise to the expectation of a homily, but also
that the earlier practice of explaining, expanding and criticizing the
prophetic message leads to the insertion of a further word to the
congregation in this place. However development did not take place
evenly; in keeping with the diverse nature of Christian origins there
is a diverse development of preaching, though by the third century
a degree of uniformity is beginning to emerge. As a result of this
diversity the classification of Christian communities into households
and schools is not altogether tidy. We shall note a number of transitional situations below, though the existence of transitional situations should not be found surprising, given the essentially domestic
setting of the Christian, as of the Jewish, synagogue, as of the school.
A domestic synagogal setting is probably that in which Polycarp was
instructed ὁμιλίαν ποιεῖν against the evil arts,[6] in that whereas he is
leader of a church based on his household[7] he is also a teacher and

---

[3] *Acts* 19:9.
[4] So Eusebius *Historia ecclesiastica* 5.20.5.
[5] Atkinson, "Further defining", 496–497 notes the similarities between the synagogue at Gamla and the Graeco-Roman assembly hall.
[6] By Ignatius at *Ad Polycarpum* 5.1. See also the discussions at 1.1.4 above and
3.2 below.
[7] So Maier, *Social Setting*, 156.

a prophet.[8] The function of teaching points to scholastic activity, even though the social organization of the church was still that of the household; we may thus describe this church as synagogalizing. In time the church in Smyrna, to judge from its extensive literary output from the third century, became further scholasticized. This, in microcosm, is the development which, rather unevenly, came about throughout the church with resultant impact upon the communication of the word of God in the assembly. Given the expectation of conversation as part of Polycarp's communication of the word of God however, we should note that there is still some of the informality of the early house-churches to be found here.

Beyond the positive thesis argued here concerning the scholasticization of Christianity, we may finally hope that the form-critical undertaking will enable further research in this neglected field by providing a corpus of literature, the homiletic origin of which is assured.

2.1. *The homily in a household setting*

We begin our attempt to trace the earliest development of Christian preaching with an attempt to discern what kind of preaching took place within the setting of the household. We have already taken issue with Siegert's dictum that preaching is not possible in a household setting[9] by observing that the communication of the word of God took place within the household. It is time to give more detail to this picture.

2.1.1. *Pauline prophecy as domestic preaching*

The earliest documents in the New Testament are probably the letters of Paul; we have already suggested that they might provide us with evidence for preaching or equivalent activities within the setting of a household. Although, due to the diversity of early Christianities, there is no definite linear development in the social structures of Christianity so that we may say that churches without exception began with the household and became something else, nonetheless

---

[8] διδάσκαλος ἀποστολικὸς καὶ προφητικὸς γενόμενος ἐπίσκοπος (*Martyrium Polycarpi* 16.2).

[9] Siegert, *Drei hellenistisch-jüdische Predigten* II, 6.

the household may be stated to be one common early Christian
social structure, and the Pauline letters, with their household setting,
provide a convenient starting point for this part of our study; we
may moreover suggest that although there is no one linear development from household to synagogue the literature of the Pauline
communities provide evidence of movement towards synagogalization, a movement which is shared with other communities, and that
the Pauline correspondence thus provides the best evidence with
which to begin this examination. We will observe in greater detail
the practice of prophecy as the fundamental mode of divine communication, building on the brief discussion above.[10]

That the Pauline churches were based on the household is hardly
open to question. Paul in his greetings to various churches emphasizes the extent to which these Christian assemblies were based on
various households:

> Aquila and Priscilla and the church at their house send greetings (*I
> Corinthians* 16:19)

> My host, Gaius, in whose house the church meets, sends you his greet-
> ings (*Romans* 16:23)

> To our friend and fellow-worker Philemon and the church that meets
> in your house . . . (*Philemon* 1–2)

It is in the context of a large household that we should envisage the
gatherings of the Corinthians to eat the Lord's Supper,[11] and in this
context that we should view the activities of the prophets.

> When you meet for worship one person has a hymn, another a teach-
> ing, another a revelation from God . . . (*I Corinthians* 14:26)

> Two or three who are given God's message should speak, while the
> others are to judge what they say. But if someone sitting in the meet-
> ing receives a message from God, the one who is speaking should stop.
> (*I Corinthians* 14:29–30)

We have argued already that these prophetic messages represent
preaching in nuce in that they are meant to be ordered communications of the will of God given at some length.[12] If this is the case

---

[10] 1.1.1.
[11] So Theissen, *Social setting*, 145–174.
[12] 1.1.1.

then we should seek to discover whether any such prophetic messages are included in the Pauline corpus by employing formal criteria. This we shall undertake below. However another line of enquiry
has been followed in the search for Pauline homilies, and this should
be explored first.

Earlier in this work it was observed that Borgen in particular had
argued that a particular form of exegesis might be recognised as
homiletic; namely that the seriatim treatment of a short biblical text,
with the text standing at the beginning of the treatment, might be
a homiletic form.[13] It was concluded that although Borgen had placed
undue reliance on a number of secondary characteristics of later
homilies, and had as a result been misled into making his description of a homily more complicated than was necessary, nonetheless
exegesis of this nature might be a homiletic form.

Borgen discerned a number of these "proemic homilies" in the
Pauline letters and on the basis of Borgen's initial suggestion Wuellner,
Ellis and Branick have argued that *I Corinthians* 1–3 consist largely
of a homily which has been placed into its existing epistolary setting.[14] The homily, as Branick sees it, is built upon the citation in
I Corinthians 1:19 "I will destroy the wisdom of the wise and I shall
take away the understanding of those who understand." Branick notes
that in what follows there is a continual play on the catchwords
σόφος and σοφία as Paul treats the subject through the medium of
a text. Moreover the chapters are set between a pair of inclusions,
a repeated list of names at 1:12 and 3:22–24, and more importantly
a pair of texts at 3:19 and 3:20 which repeat the substance of the
opening citation. Branick has to excise parts of the letter in order
to reconstruct the homily, but is able to suggest that these result
from the secondary application of the pre-existent material in the
epistolary context of *I Corinthians*. The "homily" thus consists of
1:18–31, 2:6–16 and 3:18–23. It opens with the citation "I will
destroy the wisdom of the wise" and closes with the double citation

---

[13] 1.2 2.1 with reference to Borgen, *Bread from heaven*.
[14] Wuellner, "Haggadic homily genre"; Ellis, "Exegetical patterns"; Branick,
"Source and redaction analysis". There are slight differences between the treatments
of Ellis and Branick, but the overall approach is the same. A different treatment
of this passage is offered by McDonald, *Kerygma and didache*, 57–58, who argues that
the passage is illustrative of Paul's preaching style, but who suggests that formally
it is representative of thematic speech rather than a Scriptural homily. McDonald's
theory of preaching as thematic *paraklēsis* is criticized at 1.2.4.1 above.

"he traps the wise in their cunning" and "The Lord knows the arguments of the wise are futile."

In favour of Branick's reconstruction it may be observed that there is indeed a series of catchwords employed which build on the opening citation. There are a number of other texts built into the material which would indeed appear to chosen on the basis of a "pearl-stringing" technique, and the *inclusio* would appear to place limits on the original homily. Branick's excision of material which he believes to be Paul's own interjections into the original material is not undertaken in an irrational manner and the interpolations may indeed be explained, as Branick explains them, as a series of clarifications and interjections into the original "homily" in order to bring the message home. They tend to deal more directly with the issue at hand among the Corinthians concerning their preference for leaders who can exhibit sophistry; thus, according to Branick, Paul has employed a pre-existent scriptural homily which had a certain appropriateness already and has expanded it to meet the pastoral situation of the Corinthians. There are thus some grounds for accepting Branick's classification of the passage; it is true that an exegetical pattern has been employed here and that the passage as reconstructed stands as a complete treatment of the biblical doctrine concerning wisdom. What is less certain from Branick's treatment of the passage (and the same criticism may be levelled in particular at Wuellner, on whose suggestion Branick had built) is whether it is possible on these grounds to label the section as a homily.

Against such a classification one should note that there is no indication of orality within the section. Secondly there is nothing like a prophetic speech form within the whole which would indicate that this is the work of a prophet; this is significant since we have seen that the evidence of Paul's letters indicates that prophecy was the primary means of the communication of the word of God within the assembly. Thirdly, and perhaps most critically, we have already noted that there is no such thing as a homiletic treatment of Scripture in the worshipping life of the Pauline communities since this is excluded by the informality which would have been associated with communication in the assembly and even more by virtue of the fact that the public reading of Scripture did not play a part in the worship of the Pauline churches which means that a message built on Scripture is unlikely to represent a Pauline homily. Branick assumes that Scripture played a part in the Pauline gatherings, and suggests that its interpretation is the domain of the teacher;[15] however, as we have already argued, in the light of the absence of any mention of Scripture in the descriptions of the worship of the Pauline assembly and by virtue of the fact that the Pauline view of the Gospel for the gentiles would exclude the reading of the law, this is improbable.[16] Whatever the role of the teacher in Corinth, it is not the same as a Tannaitic rabbi. If catechesis took place in the context of the assembly then it is possible that the teacher had a role in this, and may even have used Scripture as a source, but Branick's reconstructed homily is not catechesis. Teachers are mentioned alongside prophets in Antioch at *Acts* 13:1, and their role might have corresponded to the rabbinate, but this does not reflect conditions in Corinth which, unlike Antioch, was essentially a gentile foundation, whereas the Antiochene Christians, deriving their foundation from the synagogue, would be subject to synagogal organization from the first. The Corinthians would not therefore have recognised this passage as a homily, and such a treatment of Scripture would not have been produced as a homily within the Pauline gentile mission. It is possible however that this is "recycled" material from the (originally Jewish) foundation at Antioch to which Paul had formerly belonged and that in this context it was a homily, but this can only remain speculative.

The scriptural treatment, of a kind that would in time be recognised as homiletic within the Christian community, is therefore probably best recognised as the product of a school setting. It is not therefore a homily, since part of the definition of a homily should be that it is delivered in the Christian assembly in the context of worship, and whereas other Christian communities might have organised themselves as schools and reflected this organisation in their assembly for worship, the Pauline community at Corinth did nothing of this kind. The classification of these texts as midrash, the word preferred by Ellis,[17] is probably as good as any and is in any case to be preferred to homily. Although the meaning of midrash as a literary form and its suitability as a term descriptive of New Testament texts is much debated, the term is preferred here because it locates this material within the house of midrash rather than in the assembly.

---

[15] Branick, *House church*, 102.
[16] See the discussion at 1.1.1 above.
[17] In "Exegetical patterns" and consistently through his work.

It is thus used not as a literary term but as an indication of the social setting of the exposition. It is interesting that Wuellner should see the "homily" as a response to the school setting of halakhic arguments at Corinth.[18] It is far more probable that the problem at issue is sophistry of a Graeco-Roman variety, and the response is that of the synagogue school which upholds the wisdom of God against that of the moral teachers.[19]

We have already argued that the scriptural homily, within the Pauline communities at least, is a product of the second or third generation when the church began to imitate the synagogue more closely as a result of the parting of the ways; there is nothing here to contradict this. It is possible that other churches were scholastic or synagogal from the beginning, but this is not the case with the Pauline churches. There was, we argued, within Judaism a degree of overlap between the two essentially distinct social settings of school and assembly, and in time this would become the case in the Pauline churches, but this does not take place at the time of Paul.

Similar considerations apply to those other "scriptural homilies" which have been recognised within the Pauline corpus. Borgen for instance identifies *Romans* 4:1–22 and *Galatians* 3:6–29 as following his homiletic pattern, both based on the text "Abraham believed and it was reckoned to him as righteousness."[20] He suggests that both open and conclude with this text, namely "Abraham believed God and it was reckoned to him as righteousness" (*Romans* 4:3; *Galatians* 3:3). The conclusions of these two extracted units however differ: *Romans* 4:22 is close to the opening with "That is why his faith was reckoned to him as righteousness" but the closing paraphrase at *Galatians* 3:29, "If you are Christ's you are the issue of Abraham and so heirs to the promise", is a loose one.

Borgen goes on to note summary statements and subordinate quotations in the course of the "homilies" and paraphrase of the proem text in the course of the statement. We have seen that a seriatim treatment of the original text rather than the citation of subordinate texts is the decisive factor in determining the existence of a scriptural homily. A seriatim treatment is to be found in the *Romans* pas-

---

[18] Wuellner, "Haggadic homily genre", 203.
[19] So Litfin, *Saint Paul's theology of proclamation*, especially 160–173.
[20] *Bread from heaven*, 47–51.

sage but Borgen is unable to find much evidence of a paraphrase of the text in the Galatian "homily". He concludes that this is because "the exposition is based on the specific problem."[21] In other words some of the key terms are employed in the exposition because this is simply part of an extended *probatio* within *Galatians*, addressing a particular issue within the Galatian community. We may thus conclude that we have only a pale reflection of the exegetical method employed, perhaps indicating a past in the schoolroom, but in no way a homily incorporated into the text.

The treatment in *Romans* is more faithful to the text, but we may conclude that this is because it is couched in the terms of a Jewish schoolroom. At this point in *Romans* Paul is engaged in an extensive diatribal debate with a Jewish teacher, a product of his *prosopopoiia*, and therefore, in the language and style of a Jewish teacher, he uses the methods of the Jewish schoolroom to refute the assertions of the Jewish teacher that Jews, by virtue of their descent from Abraham, have a particular advantage over gentiles.[22] It is the Jewish teacher who cites the text and Paul who expounds it. We thus have a good reflection of the schoolroom in this part of *Romans*. It is a Jewish schoolroom, moreover, which has digested the diatribal techniques of Graeco-Roman teachers, but the debate within this school is no reflection of preaching within the Christian assembly. Once again we are to prefer the term "midrash", used not to indicate a literary form but a social setting. As such we may agree with Forbes that, in the Pauline communities at least, inspired exegesis was not a function of the prophets,[23] much as it was practised in early Judaism.

Although these scriptural "homilies" have proved not to be homilies at all, there is an alternative approach which may prove fruitful. That is the analysis of prophetic speech forms within the Pauline corpus. We have observed already that prophecy is functionally close to preaching[24] and so should seek formal criteria for discovering

---

[21] Borgen, *Bread from heaven*, 50.

[22] So Stowers *A rereading of Romans* 36–38, 227–237.

[23] Forbes *Prophecy and inspired speech* 229–237. He has in mind particularly the arguments of Cothenet "Prophètes comme exégètes charismatiques" 85–90, who nowhere shows that the actualization of Scripture, which lies at the centre of midrash, is prophetic.

[24] So Cothenet, "Prophetisme et ministere", 43, on the Pauline evidence: "dans ce groupe de textes la prophetie est ainsi a rapprocher de la predication".

prophecy embedded in the epistles. In particular we may begin by
employing the criteria set out by Aune according to which a statement within an early Christian document might be recognised as
prophetic: namely a supernatural attribution of a particular speech,
for instance to God, Christ or the Spirit, the display of a supernatural knowledge within the content of the oracle or the use of an
introduction which would elsewhere indicate the beginning of a
prophetic speech.[25] In proposing these criteria Aune realises that they
are not "infallible", but he has nonetheless provided a valuable starting point for the discussion.

Employing these criteria he is able to uncover reports of prophetic
activity by Paul within the Pauline corpus such as *II Corinthians* 12:9,
Galatians 5:21b, *I Thessalonians* 3:4 and *I Thessalonians* 4:2–6.[26] Apart
from these reports of prophetic activity by Paul, we may also note
the evidence cited by Müller that prophecy was a vital part of Paul's
self-understanding.[27] Moreover, it is as a prophet that he receives his
initial call, which he describes in prophetic terms taken from the
Old Testament.[28] For these reasons we may seek to see the extent
to which Paul's writing reflects Paul's speaking. That there may be
a gap is implied by *II Corinthians* 10:10, and so it is better to err on
the side of caution, as Aune does in restricting his reconstructions
to those passages which are explicitly confirmed as prophetic.

The paraenetic content of the three reports of Pauline prophecy
Galatians 5:21b, *I Thessalonians* 3:4 and *I Thessalonians* 4:2–6 are noteworthy in that the reports imply that these paraenetic messages were
first given in the assembly. As such they are in keeping with Paul's
insistence that prophecy should be employed in the assembly for the
upbuilding of the people. However not all paraenesis is necessarily
prophetic, and so we should be cautious in assigning all material of
this nature to Pauline prophetic activity. This is the fundamental
criticism which Aune levels, correctly, at Müller's work. Müller, while
recognising the absence in much Pauline paraenesis of messenger
formulae or the like, nonetheless stands by his argument of functional equivalence between prophecy, paraenesis and preaching.[29] But

---

[25] Aune, *Prophecy*, 247–248.
[26] Aune, *Prophecy*, 247–262.
[27] Müller, *Prophetie und Predigt*, 109–117.
[28] Stendahl, *Paul among Jews and Gentiles*, 7–11.
[29] Müller, *Prophetie und Predigt*, 139.

although paraenesis may be prophetic it is not necessarily so, and whereas prophecy may be functionally equivalent to preaching, once again this is not necessarily the case. Thus even when Paul qualifies a statement as being through or from the Lord we cannot state with certainty that this is prophecy, for although Paul claims to speaking on behalf of Christ this does not mean that he is directly inspired.[30]

With these cautions in mind we may turn to the oracles identified by Aune. Aune attempts a reconstruction of the oracle embedded in the report at *I Thessalonians* 4:2–6 as an oracle of warning.[31] If he is correct then we have here a short oracle forming a relatively brief paraenesis:

> I command you in the name of the Lord Jesus:
> That this is the will of God,
> that you abstain from unchastity,
> that each of you know how to take a wife for himself in holiness and honour, not in the passion of lust like heathen who do not know God,
> that no man transgress, and wrong his brother in this matter,
> because the Lord is an avenger in all these things.

That this is an item of paraenesis with an internal unity[32] would lend support to Aune's view of this piece as an oracle. Indeed the continuation may likewise be seen as part of the prophetic activity:

> God did not call you to live in immorality but in holiness.
> Whoever rejects this teaching is not rejecting man but God, who gives you his Holy Spirit.

This latter appeal to the Holy Spirit is an authentication of the oracle as deriving from the Holy Spirit. Even if short, the oracle has a unity, and a context. What is strange, however, about this is the brevity of the oracle. As such it conforms to the brief oracles which were common in the Graeco-Roman world, but does not exhibit the *copia verborum* which we may associate with oral delivery, nor does it fulfil the expectation of relatively lengthy oracles which might be raised by the description of Corinthian worship. We are therefore led to enquire whether in delivery in the assembly the oracles were surrounded with other material.

---

[30] Cf. Müller, *Prophetie und Predigt*, 120–121.
[31] Aune, *Prophecy*, 260.
[32] As noted by Collins, "Unity".

In *II Thessalonians* 3 Aune identifies three short paraenetic oracles in a brief space.

> We command you in the name of the Lord Jesus Christ to keep away from any brother who is living in idleness and not in accord with the tradition that you received from us.

> . . . we gave you this command: if anyone will not work let him not eat.

> Such persons we command and exhort in the name of the Lord Jesus Christ to do their work in quietness and to earn their own living.[33]

Although these oracles are gathered together primarily because of their epistolary context in the closing exhortation of the letter, this gathering may reflect the manner in which paraenetic oracles might be delivered as a series, each concentrating on an aspect of the single issue. A single prophetic delivery might consist of a series of revelations, and might be accompanied by other, non-prophetic, teaching. Thus an *exemplum* of Paul himself among the Thessalonians intervenes between the first and second oracles noted above, and in *I Thessalonians* 4:1–8 Paul refers to his earlier teaching by way of introducing the oracle. This may be typical of the manner in which teaching which is not properly prophetic might break up the delivery of prophetic oracles, and would fit in with the description of household worship at *Acts* 20:7–12; there, it was observed, Luke talks of διαλέγεσθαι and ὁμιλεῖν alongside παρακαλεῖν, and given the length of the assembly described it was thought likely that conversation and non-prophetic teaching might take place alongside the delivery of oracles. Envisioning the Christian assembly in this way would answer the problem posed by the brevity of the oracles as against the anticipated length of the assembly as a whole: a brief oracle might give rise to significant conversation (ὁμιλία) and to further supporting revelations.

A final point to be observed with respect to the Thessalonian oracles is the prominent number of benedictions to be found in the letters. Jewett suggests that their provenance is liturgical, and in particular that they are indicative of a homiletic origin, since this reflects the worshipping context of their original delivery.[34] Although these benedictions are not closely tied to the identified oracles, the significant

---

[33] *II Thessalonians* 3:6,10,12, cited by Aune, *Prophecy*, 260.
[34] Jewett, "Form and function".

number which are to be found in this correspondence is an indication that a substantial amount of the content of these epistles is culled from teaching and proclamation in a liturgical setting, which in turn goes some way to confirming the suspicion that these letters reflect the manner in which Paul spoke. In this light we may agree with Salzmann that the parting exhortation of *I Thessalonians* might conceivably reflect prophetic speech given in the assembly:[35]

> We exhort you, brothers, admonish the idle, encourage the faint-hearted, help the weak, be patient with them all. See that none of you repays evil for evil, but always seek to do good to one another and to all. Rejoice always, pray constantly, give thanks in all circumstances; for this is the will of God in Christ Jesus for you. Do not quench the Spirit, do not despise prophesying, but test everything . . . (*I Thessalonians* 5:14–21a)

If this is not prophecy it is nonetheless an insight both into the function of prophecy and of Paul's attitude towards the activity.

Another possible approach to this problem may be explored with reference to an oracle uncovered by Aune at *I Corinthians* 15:51–52:

> Behold I tell you a mystery:
> We shall not all sleep
> but we shall be changed
> in a moment, in a twinkling of an eye, at the last trumpet,
> for the trumpet shall sound,
> and the dead shall be raised imperishable,
> and we shall be changed.[36]

Gillespie discusses the fifteenth chapter of *I Corinthians* as a whole and argues that as a whole it is a "prophetic discourse."[37] Sadly it is unclear what he means by this. He argues that the whole is intended as a discussion of the prophetic revelation with which the chapter concludes, and that the subject is raised because it arises from the discussion of prophecy, that the discussion is moreover motivated by what may likewise be a prophetic revelation that "there is no resurrection." The fact that the chapter is a discussion of a prophecy, which leads to another prophecy, explains the otherwise difficult transition from chapter 14, which concerns the practice of

---

[35] Salzmann, *Lehren und Ermahnen*, 77–78.
[36] Aune, *Prophecy*, 251; Müller, *Prophetie und Predigt*, 224–225, also suggests that this is a prophetic oracle on the grounds that it is the revelation of a mystery.
[37] Gillespie, *First theologians*, 220; see also Merklein, "Der Theologe als Prophet".

prophecy. In this sense the chapter may be described as prophetic, in that it is an example of the process of judgement which must be exercised on prophecies, and in that it concludes with a counter-revelation in prophetic form. It is also interesting to note that the revelation which is made is then supported by scriptural oracles, the new revelation being seen as a fulfilment and clarification of these oracles. As such the prophecy of Paul is put into a larger prophetic context; whereas the primary function of prophecy is new revelation and not exegesis, nonetheless the new revelation may be delivered in accordance with the old and demonstrated to be coherent with it.[38] All of this makes the chapter prophetic in a loose sense. The oracle with which the chapter ends is but the prophetic climax of the whole address.[39]

But Gillespie does not make it clear whether this discussion belongs purely in the epistolary context, and is therefore prophetic in the sense that it concerns prophecy, or whether we are to understand him as saying that this is an example of prophecy in action. He demurs from classifying the chapter as a sermon, whilst recognising the fine line which separated orality and textuality in the ancient world through the public reading of the letter, on the grounds that there is no corpus of homiletic literature with which the chapter may be compared.[40] However it may be possible to see the whole as homiletic in the sense that it is the work of a prophet submitting prophecy to judgement. In the description of Corinthian worship which precedes this chapter we are told that prophecies which are given are to be subjected to prophetic judgement and interpretation.[41] In what follows we may have such a prophetic judgement of a prophecy; the difficult transition may thus be explained in the manner Gillespie proposes, as a transition from a prophecy to a judgement of a prophecy in the way that was normal in worship.

---

[38] Cf. Forbes, *Prophecy and inspired speech*, 225–237, who denies any exegetical role to prophets whatsoever.

[39] Cf. Müller, *Prophetie und Predigt*, 224–225 for whom the absence of any introductory formula is reason to deny that this oracle was ever part of a congregational address. The absence of a clear introductory formula relating it to the needs of the congregation comes about because the whole discourse functions as an introduction to the oracle.

[40] Gillespie, *First theologians*, 220–221.

[41] διάκρισις need not mean only judgement but also interpretation and application. On this see Merklein, "Theologe als Prophet", 418–419.

As a judgement it may be idealised, in that it now found in an epistolary context, and it may be the epistolary context which provides the *narratio* in verses 1–11 of how the gospel came to the Corinthians, but nonetheless this chapter may give us an idea of what the prophetic judgement might have been like. A brief oracle is delivered, and then subjected to judgement and interpretation by another of the prophets.[42] As Merklein points out, the task of interpretation and judgement is not a separate undertaking from prophecy, and the interpretation is, moreover, to be undertaken by one of the prophets.[43] Interpretation of prophecy is likewise a charismatic form of speech. Forbes correctly argues that these "others" should not be restricted to a class of prophets, since any member of the congregation is potentially a prophet,[44] but given the strong link between διάκρισις and prophecy which Forbes himself notes we may see that interpretation was a prophetic function, and since in practice not all were actually prophets, so it fell to those who were in practice prophets to deliver the verdict.

The chapter as it stands has a complete rhetorical form, proceeding from the *narratio* of the kerygma to the final exhortation to be steadfast;[45] this is probably the result of its inclusion in the letter, but for the Corinthians to recognise the judgement of an oracle it must have some link with normal practice. A possible form that the judgement might take would be the *topos*, which is what this chapter would form were it shorn of its *narratio*.[46]

The chapter is also characterized by a number of diatribal techniques such as the objector ("Someone will say 'How are the dead raised? With what kind of body will they come?' You fool ...",[47] the common image of the seed growing,[48] the catalogues ("Another

---

[42] *I Cor.* 14:29: οἱ ἄλλοι.

[43] Merklein, "Theologe als Prophet", 419.

[44] *Prophecy and inspired speech*, 265–269 contra Aune, *Prophecy*, 221.

[45] Mack, *Rhetoric*, 56–59. Cf. Gillespie, *First theologians*, 219, who finds Mack's analysis "unconvincing" because of the admixture of judicial and hortatory genera. We have already seen that the generic distinction was breaking down.

[46] For Gillespie, *First theologians*, the expression of the kerygma is one of the characteristics which makes the chapter prophetic. Without disputing Gillespie's assertion that a prophet should be guided by the kerygma, we would not expect the kerygma to be restated with every prophetic judgement. The kerygma is restated here as part of Paul's epistolary strategy.

[47] *I Corinthians* 15:35.

[48] *I Corinthians* 15:37–38; cf. Epictetus *Diss.* 4.8.36; 1.15.7; Seneca *Epistulae Morales* 38.2.

for men, another for the flesh of animals, another for the flesh of birds, another for fish . . .")[49] and antitheses ("It is sown in dishonour, it is raised in glory . . .").[50] Although this impression of orality is to an extent artificial, since it is now located in a written letter, it may give us an idea of the procedure by which prophecy was delivered and judged. That is to say the original prophecy consisted of a short oracle, or a series of oracles, perhaps interspersed with other material such as teaching or praise, which might then be taken up and expanded for the building up of the congregation. The manner of the judgement might well draw upon the resources of the Graeco-Roman schoolroom as on Scripture, as well as on other prophetic messages that had been received.

It is interesting that part of the alleged "homily" at *I Corinthians* 1–3 discussed earlier, *I Corinthians* 2:6–16, is a reflection on the prophetic task of interpreting oracles, where Paul states that the wisdom he speaks is God's hidden purpose, the same μυστήριον which is revealed as a word of prophecy in *I Corinthians* 15:51. According to Merklein 2:10–15 contain the interpretation of the scriptural citation in 2:9b.[51] Since there is no attempt to give a seriatim exegesis and the connection with the scriptural citation is loose we cannot accept this, but the whole is nonetheless an interesting reflection on the role of the prophet in διάκρισις. It is moreover interesting to observe that the discussion of the interpretation of oracles nonetheless draws upon Scripture, both at 2:9b and at 2:16.

A picture of the delivery of the word of God in the Pauline assembly thus begins to emerge. Prophecy, together with interpretation and the judgement of prophecy, functioned as the homily in time would function, as the communication of the word and will of God for the edification of the congregation through new revelation and through the critical and paraenetic exposition of revelation previously given. That is not to say that these prophecies and the treatments of prophecies are actually homilies, but that they provide the origin of the homily. In particular the taking up of a prophetic oracle and the resultant discourse in judgement or expansion of the oracle provides a bridge to the scriptural homily of the later Pauline

---

[49] *I Corinthians* 15:39.
[50] *I Corinthians* 15:41–43.
[51] Merklein, "Der Theologe als Prophet", 425.

church, in that a pattern of oracle followed by exegetical discourse
was thus established in the Pauline churches independently from the
synagogue. Once that was established then it was easier for the corresponding synagogal device of reading followed by exegetical treatment to make an entrée into the Pauline churches, the Scripture
taking the place of the word of prophecy. Moreover the familiarity
of the Pauline churches with further citation of Scripture as part of
the διάκρισις might lead to a more ready acceptance of Scripture
as normative for the assembly and indeed prepare the church to
adopt the synagogal practice of *hariza*, since this practice might be
seen and accepted in the light of the addition of scriptural citation
as a means of interpreting oracles.

One may thus conclude that although the earliest Pauline house
churches did not know preaching as such, and in particular did not
know scriptural preaching, there was communication of the will and
the word of God of a sort which functioned as preaching, that this
was the work of prophets, but that the prophecy in turn had to be
submitted to judgement, including judgement by Scripture. As the
household becomes a synagogue, the process of judgement might be
turned upon Scripture, as the word spoken by the prophets of old
and spoken again in the assembly replaces the word spoken in the
moment by the prophet.

However, there were churches based on the household model quite
apart from the Pauline churches. The next part of our task is to see
whether the same procedure of communication, and the same process
of synagogalization, might be observed in other households.

2.1.2. *Hermas' revelation-reports as domestic preaching*

The Pauline churches were clearly at an early stage of development,
and may be described as households without qualification. As a result
of the internal challenge caused by the parting of the ways they
underwent a process which we have termed synagogalization. To
find a further example of a household setting in which we may learn
something of the way in which the word of God was communicated
within the assembly it is necessary to turn our attention away from
the canonical New Testament to the work of Hermas. Here we seek
to show that a pattern of prophetic communication which is functionally equivalent to preaching is known in Hermas' household community, but at the same time there is already a degree of tension

between this prophetic household and Christian communities showing signs of scholasticization.

Hermas' work may be dated to a time around the turn of the
second century,[52] and located on the basis of internal clues to Rome.
Although *Pastor* is thus of a later date than most of the canonical
writings of the New Testament, it nonetheless derives from a household setting. Hermas is the father of a household church, one among
a number of similar churches within Rome, perhaps based on different
ethnic or socio-economic groups among the Roman Christians.[53]
There are frequent appeals for unity among the leaders of the Roman
churches in Hermas, along with a variety of terms employed to
describe those leaders,[54] both of which would imply a decentralized
Christianity in the city. The early pluralism of Roman Christianity
to which Jeffers attests[55] would thus seem to have held into the time
of Hermas at least, and a variety of churches might thus be found
in domestic settings throughout the city. Although not all of these
need be house churches in the narrow sense, as some may have
been organised on a scholastic model, it would nonetheless be probable that homes predominate. Even if this is not the case, they certainly predominate in Hermas' thinking. Thus the virtue of hospitality,
which is an indication of a domestic Christianity, is exalted, and the
location of this hospitality is said to be the homes of the leaders.[56]
From this Maier deduces reasonably that the references to leaders
and churches in Hermas are references to "various house churches
and their patrons".[57] In this light we may follow Young in reading
the frequent allusions to Hermas' οἶκος and his family as references
to his leadership of his household church.[58] This church was one
among others in the city of Rome. Each elder is a patron and householder, and Hermas, a man of property, is numbered among them.

The preaching of Hermas, insofar as it can be recovered, is to be
understood within this setting, once again giving the lie to the dic-

---

[52] There has been extensive discussion of the dating of Hermas' work. However
the discussion has been transformed by the work of Hahnemann, *Muratorian fragment*, and in particular his discussion of the date of Hermas at 34–72. There is little point in repeating his extensive arguments here.
[53] The conclusion of Stewart-Sykes, "Hermas the prophet", 62.
[54] Campbell, *Elders*, 224.
[55] Jeffers, "Pluralism".
[56] *Sim.* 9.27.2.
[57] Maier, *Social status*, 63.
[58] Young, "Being a Man", 240–245.

tum of Siegert that one cannot preach in a household setting. Hermas
is leader of his Christian community by nature of his social position
as householder and *paterfamilias*, but he is not necessarily the preacher
in his household by virtue of his household leadership, as in the case
of Hermas we may note that the role of leadership in the family is
allied to a charism as a prophet, and it is both as prophet and as
paterfamilias that he addresses the word of God to his erring children.
These addresses may be understood as homilies in that they are the
work of a prophet with a paraenetic aim. It is interesting that this
household setting should be the basis for prophetic communication
of the word of God in the same way as the Corinthian households
were, as this is an indication that this mode of address is particularly suited to a gathering of this size and nature.

The reason for seeing Hermas as a prophet is thus partly functional, as his intention in addressing his congregation is to strengthen
them, to exhort them to ethical behaviour, and to declare to them
what God desires of them. However, as we have already seen, not
all paraenesis is necessarily homiletic, not even if it is paraenetic
prophecy. In particular one should note that the first visions which
Hermas receives are made public not through the means of preaching in the assembly but through catechetical instruction, with the
instruction that Grapte communicate them to the women and children.[59] However Henne has shown that whereas the purpose of the
Visions is catechetical, that they are intended to encourage conversion and baptism,[60] the *Mandates* and *Similitudes* explore the themes
of the *Pastor* in greater detail, and are suited for delivery to a more
advanced audience. Hermas thus has prophetic aims and functions;
significantly his means of inspiration is equally prophetic, since all
he has to say to the church is given him in visions.[61]

Apart from the prophetic and homiletic aims of the *Mandates* and
the *Similitudes*, they may be seen as homiletic on formal grounds.
Once again we have reference to the work of Aune, who has exhibited a number of prophetic speech forms in the *Mandates* and *Similitudes*

---

[59] *Vis.* 2.4.3.

[60] Henne, *Unité*; cf. Salzmann, *Lehren und Ermahnen*, 216, who deduces from references to the unbaptized hearing the *Visions* that those unbaptized were admitted
to hear the homily.

[61] So Salzmann, *Lehren und Ermahnen*, 213.

of Hermas.[62] In doing so Aune admits that these oracles "exhibit many features of the style of the Hellenistic-Jewish homily" and admits further that had not Hermas prefaced these oracles with a commissioning formula it would be "virtually impossible to distinguish them from homiletic . . . paraenesis", and suggests that the Christian sermon was a source for Hermas' prophetic rhetoric and diction. In this he is picking up the observations made by Thyen, who had likewise noted a similarity in style between the paraenesis of Hermas and the stylistic tendencies of a number of early Christian and Jewish paraeneses, which led him to classify them as homiletic.[63] Thyen's arguments however were purely functional, whereas Aune, through insistence on the presence of formal criteria such as a commissioning formula or self-introduction of an agent of revelation (such as the angel of repentance) and the turn from address in the second person singular to the second person plural, is able to anchor his insights more firmly.[64] Once the presence of oracles is form-critically anchored then functional arguments, such as the presence of paraenesis, may be employed. Stewart-Sykes, on the basis of Aune's work, was thus able to suggest that the *Mandates* and the *Similitudes* not only reflected the preaching of Hermas, but were actually redacted in part from the preaching of Hermas in his household assembly.[65] Apart from noting the formal and functional characteristics which make the *Mandates* and *Similitudes* in part homiletic, he notes the extent to which the oracles which Aune identifies are nearly contiguous. Five of the six prophetic oracles identified by Aune in the *Similitudes* are in *Similitude* 9, and the two oracles discovered by Aune in the *Mandates* are both in *Mandate* 12, enabling us to read the entire *Mandate* as one single homily. These oracles are not oracles in isolation like those to be found in Old Testament prophets, but are worked into a more extended piece of prose.

Stewart-Sykes then adds two further arguments for his suggestion that *Pastor* is constructed out of only slightly redacted homilies. Firstly

---

[62] Aune, *Prophecy*, 299–310, following Reiling, *Hermas and Christian prophecy*, 166–170.

[63] Thyen, *Stil*, 23–24.

[64] Cf. Brox, *Hirt*, 259–260, who charges that Aune has neglected any formal criterion, and that the contents of Hermas' work are therefore no guide to the true speech of the prophet described in the 11th *Mandate*. This not only ignores what Aune has done, but fails to explain the contents and integrity of the prophetic work of Hermas.

[65] Stewart-Sykes, "Hermas the prophet", 39–40.

that the *Visions* themselves would appear to have been addressed at some point to a congregation as Hermas, in describing his visions, three times addresses himself to ἀδελφοί (*Visions* 2.4, 3.1.1, 4.1.1), and at *Vision* 3.3.1 he tells the ancient lady that he intends to announce these visions to the brethren, in order that they might rejoice the more and know the Lord; these aims, he suggests, are homiletic aims. Secondly he notes Hippolytus' report from the Book of Elchasai that in the reign of Trajan a second repentance was preached, which implies to him that these messages were received in an oral and ecclesial setting.[66]

Most of these oracles are unmediated pieces of moral exhortation. However it is also noteworthy that Hermas includes a proemic homily in his collection. This is *Mandate* 7 which, Stewart-Sykes demonstrates, is a general treatment of the fear of the Lord, beginning with a citation of *Ecclesiastes* 12:13 (fear the Lord, and keep his commandments) then proceeding with a treatment of the term φοβήθετι (fear) and concluding with a reworking of the text and a general application.[67]

> "Fear the Lord and keep his commandments"
>
> If you keep the commandments of God you will be strong in everything that you do. If you fear the Lord you will do all things well. This is the fear with which you should fear, and be saved. Do not fear the devil. If you fear the Lord you will have power over the devil because there is no power in him. Where there's no power, there's no fear . . . So fear the Lord and you shall live for him. And whoever fears him and keeps his commandments shall live to God. (*Mandate* 7.1–2, 4)

By beginning with a citation, breaking it up into sense units for the purpose of interpretation and application, and then concluding with the reworked text, this mandate follows the norms for a proemic homily suggested in the first part of this work.[68] As it derives from Hermas we may be clear that this is not a school exercise but a genuine homily delivered by the prophet Hermas and that it therefore reflects a transition of the school's methodology into the house-church. Although Hermas is leader of a household church, and

---

[66] Hippolytus *Ref.* 9.13.4; the word employed is εὐαγγελίσθαι.
[67] Stewart-Sykes, "Hermas the prophet", 41.
[68] In particular at 1.2.3.1 above.

indeed registers something of a protest against the scholasticization of some Roman churches, his own community is not immune to synagogalization. Although the *Mandate* is addressed to Hermas the proemic shape indicates that this is a homily which has been separately shaped and included in the narrative frame of the *Pastor*. That Hermas the prophet should use Scripture in his addresses in this way is interesting. For although one of the possible functions of a prophet was the treatment of Scripture[69] this is not a primary function, nor is this manner of seriatim exegesis typically prophetic. In the process of submitting prophecy to judgement we have already seen that Scripture may be employed, but this is a different use, since here it takes the place of the oracle rather than following it by way of support. This was a tendency which could only grow as the second century proceeded and Scripture moved to a more central place in the life of the church. However at the point of development at which we find Hermas there is not a great deal of scriptural influence. That Hermas should be aware of and employ this Jewish form of preaching is not surprising, since Hermas displays an extensive debt to Jewish traditions, but it is an unusual proceeding nonetheless.

The essential message of Hermas to the church is a warning against the dangers of riches and luxury, and a call to charity on the part of the rich, combined with a promise of forgiveness in return for repentance. Osiek suggests that the contrast here with the conventional paraenetic topic concerning the compatibility of wealth and salvation is a clear indication that the paraenesis is not conventional, but one which is closely bound up to the social situation of Hermas and his audience.[70] One may further deduce that this is because of the homiletic setting of Hermas' paraenesis. In similar light one may note what Hermas has to say about τρυφή; although this is a common theme of the diatribe, it is particularly appropriately aimed at freedmen, and so with Osiek we may read Hermas' audience as being fundamentally made up of freedmen. The absence of artifice in Hermas' rhetoric befits Hermas' own social background, but also that of his audience, and is seen by Stewart-Sykes as an indication of social homogeneity between Hermas and his audience. The parae-

---

[69] Groh, "Utterance and exegesis", Cothenet, "Prophètes Chrétiens comme exégètes charismatiques" and our discussion below.
[70] Osiek, *Rich and poor*, 91.

netic warning addressed to the freedmen on the dangers of wealth
and business, with the accompanying exhortation to charity and
promise of forgiveness, which might in turn encourage the freedmen
to continue their social support of the church,[71] is the essence of
Hermas' preaching.

Hermas' preaching employs Scripture, but not significantly. Rather,
in keeping with his prophetic means of inspiration, his addresses are
direct reports of the word of God as he has received it. We do not
know whether the worship of Hermas' community included the reading of Scripture. It is possible, given the strong links between Hermas
and Judaism,[72] that Scripture was employed, but it is equally possible that as this Christian community emerged from Jewish communities it preserved the traditional presupposition that scriptural education
might be received in the synagogue separately from the Christian
gathering and is therefore not continued in the household; obviously
this is not a situation which could continue indefinitely but just as
it is reflected at Corinth so this transitional phenomenon might be
reflected in the early part of the second century at Rome. A picture of worship in a rival Roman community is perhaps provided
by the eleventh *Mandate*, which concerns a false prophet. Here it is
noteworthy that the false prophet is seated on a teacher's chair, and
the listeners on a learner's συμψελλίον.

> He showed me men sitting on a bench and another man sitting on a
> chair, and says to me "Do you see the men sitting on a bench?" "Yes
> sir," I said, "I can see them." "These," he said, "are faithful and the
> one sitting on the chair is a false prophet, who destroys the under-
> standing of the servants of God" (*Mandate* 11.1).

This picture led Jay to ask: "Could the man seated on the καθέδρα
be the monepiscopus of the Church at Rome?"[73] Jay cannot think
of any Roman bishop in the second century who would fit this
description, and so Stewart-Sykes follows Maier in suggesting that at
the time of Hermas there was no bishop.[74] Given the nature of the
furniture it is possible that Hermas' description is that of a church
organised on a scholastic basis, as compared to his own household;

---

[71] The insight of Lampe, *Stadtrömischen Christen*, 71–78.
[72] On which see Brox, *Hirt*, 49–51.
[73] Jay, "From presbyter bishops to bishops and presbyters", 145–146.
[74] Stewart-Sykes, "Papyrus Oxyrhynchus" following Maier, *Social setting*, 53, 59–65.

that it should be the διάνοια of the faithful that is destroyed is a
further indication that a school setting is intended, since the faithful are presumably seeking understanding. By contrast to the practice of the false prophet the work of a true prophet is described,
whereby the Spirit chooses the one who is to prophesy.

> When the man who has the divine Spirit comes into the assembly of
> just men who have faith in the divine Spirit, and intercession is made
> to God by the assembly of those men, then the angel of the prophetic
> Spirit which rests on him fills the man and the man who is full of the
> Holy Spirit speaks to the congregation ... (*Mandate* 11.9)

There is no indication here that the inspiration derives as a response
to Scripture, but the picture is entirely consistent with the household setting which we have suggested was the setting for the prophecy
of Hermas, and indicates a degree of informality with regard to the
communication of the word of God. As Young points out, there is
a deliberate contrast between Hermas' own behaviour as a prophet
and that of the false prophet. So Hermas' prophecy is public, whereas
that of the false prophet is private, that of Hermas is inspired, whereas
the false prophet is empty, Hermas is humble, whereas the false
prophet is haughty.[75]

We may hesitate to draw general lessons for the development of
the homily from this one example, but it is possible nonetheless that
Hermas represents for us the most primitive stage in the communication of the word of God in the household of God, a situation in
which the word is unmediated, is the word of the Spirit, and is delivered in a situation of great informality by the one to whom the
Spirit had directly addressed himself. Hermas however is also aware
of Christian communities organising themselves on a scholastic basis,
and the possibility that this is likewise an early development in Rome
may be suggested in the light of the prominence of Jewish teachers
in Rome at the time of Paul.

Stewart-Sykes' study concentrates on the *Mandates*, appropriately
since, as Dibelius notes, these are "extended paraenesis".[76] They
begin with a general statement by the revealer, but go on to work
out in detail the implications for the audience. Once more we may
suggest that it in doing so they illustrate the manner in which prophecy

---

[75] Young, "Being a man", 243.
[76] Dibelius, *James*, 3.

might be worked into a homily by process of expansion and elucidation. Henne likewise perceives that the *Mandates* reflect the homiletic
practice of Hermas' church.[77] Because of their paraenetic function
and prophetic origin there is a prima facie probability that the
Mandates might be homiletic; however given that the *Similitudes*, according to Henne at least, have the same function within the church as
the *Mandates* it is possible that these too had a homiletic origin. Given
Hermas' close links to Judaism and given that parables might themselves have a homiletic setting in the Jewish world,[78] this may count
as further evidence for seeing the *Similitudes* as homiletic.

Further to this the content of a number of the *Similitudes* might
indicate a homiletic origin within Judaism. Stewart-Sykes has observed
that a significant number of elements in the fifth *Similitude* may be
found in the rabbinic parabolic tradition.[79] The parables in the earlier part of the *Similitudes* which concern trees might also be indebted
to a homiletic tradition employing images of trees. The *Apocalypse of
Moses*, a narrative expansion of the story of the fall, tells us that the
trees shed leaves at the eating of the forbidden fruit, but put forth
again at the appearance of God in the garden.[80] Likewise they did
not fruit when Abel died, but put forth leaves at the birth of Seth.
A similar tradition would seem to be indicated when the cedars of
the Temple were said to grow fruit when the incense was offered
in the Temple, but that they withered when Manasses introduced
an idol into the Temple.[81]

Apart from the context of their delivery and the content, the form
of the *Similitudes* might likewise betray some trace of homiletic origin. The *Similitudes* vary in complexity but in essence consist of:

(1) a parable followed by
(2) an explanation, or a series of explanations, and concluding
with
(3) application.

The sections may be broken up with dialogue.

---

[77] Henne, *Unité*, 111.
[78] According to BT *Sanhedrin* 38b R Meir would devote a third of his addresses
to משלים.
[79] Stewart-Sykes, "Christology of Hermas", 280.
[80] *Apoc. Mosis* 14 cited by Ginzberg, *Legends* I, 96, 97, 112.
[81] Ginzberg, *Legends* III, 163.

The double parable of the trees (*Similitudes* 3–4) for instance follows this pattern:

  1a) The shepherd shows Hermas some trees; he says that these are the people who live in the world. Hermas asks why they are withered.
  2a) The shepherd explains that in the world the righteous and the sinner cannot be told apart.
  1b) The shepherd shows Hermas other trees.
  2b) The shepherd explains that in summer the fruit of the righteous is revealed, but the trees which do not bear fruit are burnt.
  3a) Hermas is warned to bear fruit.
  3b) A warning about business is added.
  3c) A generalized application that all those who follow the shepherd's instructions will bear fruit.

A more complex example of this is the fifth *Similitude*. As it stands the *Similitude* is the result of a complex redactional process, but its basic parable nonetheless may be said to have close links with Jewish *meshalim*.

  1) The parable is told by the shepherd, and is introduced when Hermas is fasting. The parable is then introduced, and said to concern fasting. (5.2.1) A man has a vineyard and goes away. He chooses a servant, and tells the servant to fence the vineyard. If he does this he shall receive his freedom. The servant fences the vineyard, and then went on to exceed his instructions, by digging over and weeding the vineyard. When the master returns he is pleased, calls his son and his counsellors, and makes the servant joint heir with the son. Following this he gives a feast, and sends food to the servant. The servant shares this food with his fellow servants. On learning of this the master is still further pleased with the servant, once again assembles his counsellors, and all rejoice the more that the servant has been made joint heir with the son. (5.2.2–5.2.11)

  2a) The shepherd points out that the slave went beyond the master's commandments by seeking to please him further.

  3a) Hermas likewise is to do more than simply keep the commandments. (5.3.1–5.3.9)

  2b) After an extended dialogue (5.4.2–5.5.1) the shepherd finally consents to give a further ἐπίλυσις of the parable, from 5.5.2–5.5.3). The field is the world, the master is the Creator, the son of the parable is the Holy Spirit, the servant is the Son of God, the fences are the angels, the weeds are the sins of the people of God, the food sent from the supper is the commandments of God, and the friends and counsellors are the angels. Hermas asks why the Son of God in the parable is given the form of a servant (5.5.5). The Shepherd goes on to explain that the Son does not have the form of a servant but has great power, because, having had the vineyard handed over to him the Son appointed the angels to watch over his people and cleansed them of their sins. Having cleansed them of their sins he showed them the ways of his Father (5.6.1–5.6.3). Then the shepherd goes on to state why the Lord took his Son and the angels as counsellors (5.6.4). That is because of the Holy Spirit God made to dwell in the flesh which he willed. The flesh in which the Holy Spirit dwelt served the Spirit well and thus received its reward (5.6.4–5.6.8).

3b) From this the shepherd concludes that all flesh which co-operates with the spirit will be rewarded.

3c) Hermas is further exhorted to keep both flesh and spirit pure.

In both cases we may observe that each *mashal* is given an extensive treatment, the details being explained and gone over in a variety of ways. Whereas this is the result of the literary redaction of Hermas' work we may nonetheless suggest that the basic pattern of *mashal*, explanation and application reflects the manner in which a *mashal* might be used in preaching in a household setting, as in response to the questioning of the audience, a questioning reflected in the questioning to which Hermas subjects the revealer figures. The parable is explained in phases of meaning, concluding with ethical exhortation, and the questioning may function not only as a means of establishing meaning but also as a means of examination to ensure that the oracle is truly of God.[82] As such it may be described as prophetic conformity with the will of God. This questioning may further be taken as an example of prophetic ὁμιλία. In particular these final exhortations of these parables go beyond the conversation of the shepherd and Hermas and give the strong impression of generalized ethical exhortation of a manner entirely fitting a homiletic context.

---

[82] A suggestion of Salzmann, *Lehren und Ermahnen*, 215 based on *Vis* 2.4.2–3.

Therefore, if you do these things, you will be able to bear fruit for
the age to come; indeed, whoever does these things will bear fruit.
(*Sim.* 4.8)

This is how you must observe these things with your children and
your whole household, and in observing them you will be blessed;
indeed, all those who hear and observe them will be blessed, and whatever they ask from the Lord they will receive. (*Sim.* 5.3.9)

In this latter instance it is noteworthy that Hermas is specifically
commanded to proclaim the message within the context of his household church; it is this teaching which forms the basis of his homiletic
message, just as the same concerns for the salvation of the wealthy
and those engaged in business, which form the central concern of
the *Mandates*, continue to be addressed in the *Similitudes.*

We may thus conclude that Hermas' work provides a further example of the prophetic communication of the word of God in the household assembly. Although we have observed a slight degree of
synagogalization here it may be noted that there is a tension between
the household of Hermas and Christian communities based on a
scholastic model, which may indicate that something akin to synagogalization is happening in some Roman churches rather more
quickly than it is occurring in Hermas' household. It should also be
noted that the use of a *mashal* as the raw material for preaching may
be seen as a synagogal device, as may the occasional use of Scripture.
It is thus entirely possible that at a later date in its development the
community of Hermas underwent this process of development, even
though such a thing cannot be considered assured. Prophecy was
still practised in Roman Christianity late in the second century,[83]
and the corps of prophets then looked back to Hermas as a model
of true prophecy. Yet even as the Roman prophets claim to have a
διαδοχή akin to the succession of teachers to be found in other
Roman churches, they are themselves accepting into themselves a
scholastic expression of Christianity.

As far as the preaching of Hermas is concerned, apart from noting the loose relationship to Scripture, the prophetic inspiration and
the informality with which it might be delivered in a household setting, we may conclude by observing the essentially paraenetic con-

---

[83] Stewart-Sykes, "Papyrus Oxyrhynchus 5"; See also Robeck, "Irenaeus and
prophetic gifts" on the continuing practice of prophecy in the late second century.

tent of preaching in this community, in conformity with the prophetic messages of Paul. The wide distribution of the book shows moreover that this was a voice and a manner of address which was congenial, and presumably readily recognizable, to a wide circle of Christians, casting light not only on the preaching of Hermas in Rome but arguably on the nature of preaching more widely.[84]

2.1.3. *The prophecy of John of Patmos as domestic and synagogal preaching*

We have now observed prophecy in a household setting in two groups of communities, namely in the Roman household addressed by Hermas and in the households which were under the influence of the Pauline mission. In both instances it was observed that the words of the prophets functioned homiletically, but that movement towards synagogalization might be betrayed. However, before this chapter may be concluded we may observe a further extant example of prophecy which is probably delivered in a household setting and which is thus a reflection of the homiletic activity of these communities,[85] but in which there is no indication of scholasticization, even though they are organized, in a sense, as counter-synagogues.

The book of *Revelation* explicitly describes its contents as prophecy.[86] Since van Unnik's identification of the instruction given to John at 1:19 to write down both what is now and what is to come as a description of the work of a prophet on the basis of his observation that the work of pagan prophets is described in contemporary sources using similar language,[87] recent studies of *Revelation* have proceeded on the basis that the book is in essence a work of prophecy. Since it is a work of prophecy we may also explore whether it is also a work of preaching. Aune suggests that the whole of the apocalypse, since it was intended for delivery in worship, functioned in the place of a prophetic sermon which would otherwise have been delivered

---

[84] A suggestion of Salzmann, *Lehren und Ermahnen*, 218.

[85] Fiorenza, "Apokalypsis and propheteia", 136–137, denies that *Revelation* is in any way homiletic because of the manner in which Scripture is employed. However she is working with a definition of homily as scripturally based which is too inflexible to deal with Christian communication in the earliest communities.

[86] 1:3; 22:7.

[87] van Unnik, "Formula"; Aune, *Prophecy*, 280, notes that the designation of Christ as ὁ ὤν καὶ ὁ ἦν καὶ ὁ ἐρχόμενος is thus an indication of himself as the source of prophetic revelation.

by a local prophet;[88] as such it is what we would call preaching. Bauckham differs from Aune in emphasis only, suggesting that the book is a substitute not for the activity of a local prophet but for the voice of John as a wandering prophet, since *Revelation* is a circular letter sent to seven Asian churches, of each of which churches detailed local knowledge is demonstrated.[89] Since John mentions the role of other prophets and numbers himself among them we may deduce that whereas John was a wandering prophet who functioned in all of the churches,[90] there were nonetheless local prophets as well, and yet that John represents a charismatic leader among them, whose voice might rise above theirs, as it did on this occasion. This is a different claim from that of Hill, who ascribes a complete uniqueness to John;[91] although not unique qua prophet the fact that his message may replace theirs on this occasion is an indication that there is some hierarchy of prophets and that although the whole church may be considered prophetic in this circle[92] we may suggest that just as the voice of John rises over that of any local prophet so the voice of those who were congregational prophets would rise above those of others.

However, we are not permitted on this basis to assume prophetic governance of the church, or even that there was an office of prophet within the church's governance and organisation.[93] As Aune makes clear, John tells us nothing about the organisation or polity of the churches he addresses;[94] all we may gather is that prophecy was prominent within them. The probability is that the churches addressed are households, essentially on the grounds that the churches in the

---

[88] Aune, *Prophecy*, 275.

[89] Bauckham, *Theology*, 3.

[90] So Aune, "Social matrix", 26–28; similarly, though with slightly different argumentation, Fiorenza, "Apokalypsis and propheteia", 145–146.

[91] Hill, *New Testament prophecy*, 87–89.

[92] Bauckham, *Climax*, 161–162, observes that witness to Jesus is equated with prophecy (19:10, 11:3) and the whole church is a witnessing church (12:17). However he accepts that this is a potential situation and does not imply that all were prophets all of the time. Cf. Satake, *Gemeindeordnung*, 47–63, who finds reasons at every point that prophets are mentioned to distinguish them from other groups in the congregation on the assumption that the prophets hold office.

[93] As does Satake, *Gemeindeordnung*; thus (at 60, on 19:10) "Von anderen Ämtern in der Gemeinde ist hier wieder nicht die Rede. Die einzigen Amtsträger sind die Propheten." This is fundamentally an argument from silence based on dubious assumptions.

[94] Aune, "Social matrix", 23–26.

same area addressed in a later era by Ignatius were likewise households. We may moreover note that prophecy continued to be prominent in these households at the time of Ignatius, and yet that there
is no office of prophet as such manifested within them. There may
have been some attempt within these households to claim charismatic authority on the basis of prophetic gifts,[95] and so Ignatius himself prophesies in order to gain support for the message of obedience
to the bishop which he is delivering,[96] but we cannot be assured that
it was normal procedure for structures of authority to be charis-
matically legitimated. The balance of probabilities is that they were
not, and that household leadership came with ownership of the house
and headship of the household. The absence of reference to household leaders need not invalidate this hypothesis; the silence is plausibly interpreted by Aune as an implication that John is concerned
not to alienate this leadership because these leaders would provide
patronage and hospitality to the prophets, and in particular to the
wandering prophets,[97] and slightly less plausibly by Fiorenza as an
indication that the communities to which John writes effectively dis-
regard the bishops.[98] Fiorenza slightly overstates the case here, as it
is difficult to see how a householder could be ignored in a domestic ecclesial setting, but it is true to say that John opposes rival
prophetic groups rather than the officials of the church, and that
structures of authority are not his concern.[99]

It is also possible that the churches addressed were organized as
synagogues, in view of the proximity to Judaism of the Christianity
preached by John who, for instance, forbids the eating of meat offered
to idols, and who describes the established synagogues of Smyrna

---

[95] So Trevett, "Prophecy and anti-episcopal activity". One cannot however deduce
from this that prophecy was opposed to episcopacy as does Trevett; it is equally
possible that rather than the principle of episcopacy being opposed, members of
the household other than the bishop were seeking episcopate for themselves on the
basis of their charismatic qualifications.

[96] Ignatius *Ad Philadelphios* 7.

[97] Aune, "Social matrix", 26.

[98] Fiorenza, "Apokalypsis and propheteia", 143–144.

[99] Fiorenza, "Apokalypsis and propheteia", 145. On occasion at this point she
appears to be operating on the assumption, derived from Satake, *Gemeindeordnung*,
and ultimately from nineteenth-century German liberalism, that (bureaucratic) episcopacy came to replace (charismatic) prophecy as a means of ecclesial organisation.
There is however no reason to suggest that the two could not, in principle at least,
co-exist and that they had co-existed from the beginning.

and Philadelphia as "synagogues of Satan."[100] However even if John's communities are counter-synagogues the probability is that they are small, household synagogues, concerned to maintain separation from the prevailing culture in contrast to the accommodation which the synagogue had reached with the Roman authorities in Asia.[101] We may moreover note that in our examination below of the use to which John puts scripture in his communication of the word of God there is nothing typically scholastic or synagogal about his procedure.

We have noted that *Revelation* describes its contents as prophecy; to this observation of its prophetic content may be added the formal insights of Müller. Earlier in this work we gave brief notice to his identification of two forms of prophetic sermon within the Johannine apocalypse, which he termed the *Heilspredigt* and the *Bußpredigt*.[102] Müller argues that the seven letters found in the second and third chapters of this work are written oracles which nonetheless function orally, since the author was prevented from delivering them in person.[103] The oral character is to be observed in the injunction delivered at the end of each oracle to *hear* what the Spirit is saying to the churches. According to Müller and Aune, each oracle has three broad stages. First is the section termed by Aune as the commissioning formula, which serves to identify the speaker in the oracle.[104] This speaker is the risen Christ, who, in the concluding part of the discourse is identified with the Spirit. Thus the letter to the church at Sardis begins: "These are the words of the One who holds the seven spirits of God, the seven stars . . ." and concludes "Hear, you who have ears to hear, what the Spirit says to the churches." This conclusion is a standard closing, which may be classified as a *Weckformel*. Between the opening and conclusion is the substance of the oracle.

Between the opening and conclusion Müller identifies two possible forms of homiletic oracle, the *Heilsorakel* (oracle of salvation) and the *Bußparaklese* (call to repentance). The *Heilsorakel* he finds in pure form in the letter to the church at Smyrna:

---

[100] *Revelation* 2:9; 3:9.
[101] On the opposition of the communities to their surrounding culture see Michaels, *Interpreting the Book of Revelation*, 38–39. On Jewish rapprochement with surrounding Asian society see Trebilco, *Jewish Communities*, 173–183.
[102] 1.1.3 above.
[103] Müller, *Prophetie und Predigt*, 48–50.
[104] Aune, *Prophecy*, 275.

I know how hard pressed you are, and poor, and yet you are rich. I
know how you are slandered by those who claim to be Jews but are
not; they are the synagogue of Satan. Do not be afraid of the suffering
to come. The Devil will throw some of you into prison, to put you
to the test. And for ten days you will suffer cruelly. Only be faithful
until death, and I will give you the crown of life. (2:8–11)

Here there is an assurance of salvation given to the recipients, and
encouragement in the midst of their suffering.

The oracle of repentance (*Bußparaklese*) Müller finds represented in
the letter to the church at Ephesus:

I know your ways, your toil and your fortitude. I know you cannot
endure evil men; you have put to the proof those who claim to be
apostles but are not, and have found them false. Fortitude you have;
you have borne up in my cause and never flagged. But I have this
against you; you have lost your early love. Think from what a height
you have fallen. Repent, and do as you once did. Otherwise, if you
do not repent, I shall come to you and remove your lamp from its
place . . . (2:2–7)

Here the promise of salvation is conditional upon repentance, and
the form consists of a) accusation b) admonition and c) Threat of
judgement.

However the basic forms identified by Müller more often occur
in mixed forms in these oracles, which limits the usefulness of this
form-critical classification.[105] The offer of salvation and the threat of
judgment are both conditional either on the maintenance of good
conduct or on repentance. For our purposes however, this criticism,
whilst entirely justified, is relatively insignificant. Given the explicit
identification of the speaker as a supernatural being and the concluding *Weckformel* which, as Aune notes, functions in the same way
as the proclamation formula of Old Testament,[106] it is hardly deni-
able that these are examples of prophecy. Although prophecy is not
to be directly identified with preaching Aune notes that "the function of these salvation-judgement oracles . . . is not distinctive to
Christian prophecy but permeates the kind of religious and moral
discourse exhibited in the surviving letters and homilies from early
Christianity."[107] In other words the prophetic form and hortatory

---

[105] So Aune, *Prophecy*, 277.
[106] Aune, *Prophecy*, 278.
[107] Aune, *Prophecy*, 277.

function of these oracles enable us to recognise them as representing a sermonic form in the communities within the sphere of influence
of the seer of the apocalypse, and to recognise that the preaching
and communication of the will of God undertaken in these communities was essentially an unmediated word of prophecy. This conclusion stands at odds with that of Aune who seems to think that
the emergence of a prophetic form in this context points to a crisis
of leadership in the communities of the apocalypse, which has led
to the emergence of prophetic leadership.[108] In view of the prominence of prophetic forms of preaching in other primitive Christian
communities this is an unnecessary conclusion. Rather, for these
Asian communities, prophetic communication of the word of God
is normal.

Müller attempts to trace the prophetic tradition found in *Revelation*
back through a Deuteronomic tradition with roots in the Old
Testament, seeing in the paraenetic sections of *I Enoch* in particular
a tradition of hortatory prophecy in apocalyptic form from which
the prophecies of the apocalypse have derived. Aune criticizes this
attempt on the grounds that there is nothing particularly prophetic
about *I Enoch* 91:3–10 (the passage which Müller selects as his example) and on the grounds that Christian prophets might equally have
been indebted to Graeco-Roman oracular forms.[109] It is possible to
answer Aune's criticisms here by suggesting that there is no reason
why the seer might not be open to Graeco-Roman forms whilst
standing in a fundamentally Hebrew and scriptural tradition, and
that the visionary context and ethical intent of the paraenetic sections of *I Enoch*, rather than its eschatological framework, is in itself
sufficient to enable us to recognise this particular section as prophetic.
However a more significant difference between *I Enoch* and the apocalypse than those noted by Aune is the obvious one, that *I Enoch* is
an anonymous and pseudepigraphical production whereas John names
himself as the seer.[110] Because John names himself and tells about
the circumstances of his visions and of the delivery of his vision
reports we have an assurance that the setting of the delivery of the

---

[108] Aune, *Prophecy*, 277–278.
[109] Aune *Prophecy*, 276–277.
[110] On this difference between *Revelation* and other apocalypses see Bauckham,
Theology, 11.

oracles to the churches was originally cultic, and that they therefore functioned as a sermon; the fictional setting of the oracles in *I Enoch* means that we cannot have a similar certainty. Müller sees a similar form set into a speech of Joshua in pseudo-Philo's *Liber antiquitatum biblicarum*;[111] although we have suggested that *Liber antiquitatum biblicarum* reflects some kind of preaching, this reflection lies in the fact that ps-Philo's work is narrative rather than in any prophecy, or other discourse, which might be secondarily included. Nonetheless it should be observed that Joshua describes a night vision and exhorts the people of Israel on the basis of his vision report and that there are thus grounds on this basis for seeing this speech, as Müller argues,[112] as prophetic exhortation (though its setting as a farewell discourse is not relevant). However, although there are some similarities with the vision reports of *Revelation*, and although the pattern of exhortation might reflect preaching in a synagogue, the narrative frame means that we are at one remove from the synagogue itself. The same might be said of Maccabaeus' exhortation of his troops in part on the basis of Scripture and in part on the basis of a vision of Jeremiah he had received in a dream.[113] It is possible that both of these reports reflect visionary prophecy functioning in early Jewish worship in the way that it functioned in the churches of the seer, but because the narratives are not set in synagogues we cannot be confident. Thus although it is possible that this section of *I Enoch* reflects a sermon which was originally orally delivered[114] we cannot be sure that this was the case. Since it is a work of prophecy which explicitly locates itself in worship we may share the certainty of Müller and Aune that *Revelation* typifies a type of prophetic preaching in a particular Christian community, though we cannot be so sure, even though it is a strong possibility, that it derives from a tradition of Jewish prophecy.[115]

---

[111] Müller, *Prophetie und Predigt*, 86–88, with reference to *Liber antiquitatum biblicarum* 32:4–13.

[112] Müller, *Prophetie und Predigt*, 87.

[113] *II Maccabees* 15:7–11.

[114] So Müller, *Prophetie und Predigt*, 80.

[115] Müller's claim that the prophetic practice of *Revelation* grew out of that of sectarian Jewish groups is more tenable than that of Hill, *New Testament prophecy*, 87–89, who, on theological rather than historical grounds, tries to envisage John's prophecy as deriving directly from the Old Testament rather than being mediated through any tradition.

In the light of his conclusion that *Revelation* is essentially a prophetic work Aune discovers other oracles in this text beyond the messages addressed to the individual churches. The single criterion which he sees as a reliable indication of prophetic content is the explicit attribution of an oracle to a divine or quasi-divine agent of revelation.[116] Because John is a prophet of a visionary type, Aune's restriction of oracular material to that which is explicitly stated as deriving from supernatural sources is a reasonable criterion to employ for the identification of individual oracles within the overall visionary prophetic message, but insofar as the whole of the book is essentially a substitute for oral prophecy in the worship of the community our understanding of his preaching is not to be limited to the individual oracles which he reports but the extended reportage of the visions in which the oracles are embedded. Hill notes that the function of the seven letters is to warn and to encourage the hearers, and that these are prophetic, as well as paraenetic, aims.[117] We may also suggest that they are homiletic aims, and that this aim extends beyond the letters to the individual churches and provides a framework of understanding for the entire book; the purpose of *Revelation* is to assure the hearers that God's judgement is being pronounced and that victory has been won by the lamb, and in this light to encourage them to continued faithfulness.

Among the oracles identified by Aune two are of particular interest. The first is actually a pair of oracles which have been linked.

> Behold he is coming with the clouds, and every eye will see him, every one who pierced him; and all tribes of the earth will wail on account of him. Even so. Amen

> "I am the Alpha and the Omega" says the Lord God, who is and who was and who is to come, the almighty. (1:7–8)

Standing near to the beginning here are two formulae of prophetic identification; one is the messenger formula which is familiar from many Old Testament prophetic collections. But there is also a formula of self-identification in the "I am" form. This is a form of self-identification and commendation which is found frequently in prophetic works from an Asian provenance. So we may note:

---

[116] Aune, *Prophecy*, 279–280; cf. Hill, *New Testament prophecy*, 76–79, who sees a number of stock phrases of John as being prophetic.
[117] Hill, *New Testament prophecy*, 85–86.

I am the Lord God, the ruler of all . . . (Montanus fr. 1)

I am not a wolf, I am word and spirit and power (Maximilla, fr. 5)[118]

I am the way, the truth and the life . . . (*John* 14:6)

I am the word . . . (*Epistula Apostolorum* 10)

I am your forgiveness, I am the Passover of salvation (Melito *Peri Pascha* 103)

This formula is repeated before the delivery of the seven oracles to the churches, serving as a reminder to the assembly of the identity of the speaker. Coming in the context of a vision report it is quite unusual,[119] but is a clear indication nonetheless of the prophetic nature of the communication. But although prophetic we may note that there is an allusion to Scripture in the statement that those who pierced him will look upon him and mourn him,[120] the significance of which scriptural allusion we shall note below.

The "Amen" with which the first oracle concludes is in part a device of oracular speech, but also reflects the worshipping context of the delivery of the oracle. It is noteworthy that this is the beginning of the prophetic content of the book after the epistolary opening, an indication that the prophecy is being begun and that as prophecy begins the assembly gathered to hear the words of the prophecy is gathering as for a liturgy. A similarly liturgical context is to be found in the oracle which concludes the book, which according to Aune is a combination of a series of literary forms:

Oath Formula
I warn everyone who hears the words of the prophecy of this book:

Threat of Judgment
If anyone adds to them, God will add to him the plagues described in this book,
And if anyone takes away from the words of the book of this prophecy, God will take away his share in the tree of life and in the holy city, which are described in this book

---

[118] Following the numbering of Heine, *Montanist oracles*.
[119] Cf. Hill, *New Testament prophecy*, 149, who makes the appearance of the formula in *Revelation* normative for its usage.
[120] The allusion is to *Zechariah* 12:10.

Oath Formula
He who testifies to these things says,

Promise of Salvation
Surely I am coming soon.[121] (*Revelation* 22:18–21)

An "amen" stands at the conclusion of this oracle, but outside the oracle itself, as it is attached to a prayer; "Amen, come Lord Jesus". This is a prayer summing up the community's response to the visions of eschatological hope which have been received in the assembly, and concluding the prophetic content of the book, before the very brief epistolary conclusion, indicating again the liturgical setting of the delivery of this prophecy.

We have described John as a visionary prophet. That means that his means of inspiration are visions received outside of the context of worship, the contents of which are subsequently reported to the community.[122] We have observed that Hermas is a prophet of this type, and may note at least one other Christian prophet of this type at work in Asia, as well as one in Africa.[123] We may thus suggest that John stands at the head of a tradition within Asian Christianity of a type of inspiration, and alongside Christians in other areas.[124] Having been inspired through a "vision trance" the prophetic delivery of the visionary prophet reports what he has seen and heard in his vision. Thus the content of his prophetic preaching consists of reportage of his visions, as well as the oracles which revealer figures articulate in the course of his visions.

But having determined the prophetic content and cultic context of *Revelation* we need to be cautious in suggesting that as a work it typifies the communication of the word of God in the assemblies

---

[121] Cited following Aune, *Prophecy*, 288. Aune notes that the repeated oath is a verification of the authenticity of the content of the oracle, and that this is of interest because it is taken in the name of the prophetic speaker. We may see this as an indication of the nature of the authority which is claimed by John, which as we shall note below is of a peculiar kind.

[122] On prophecy of a visionary type see further Stewart-Sykes, "Condemnation", 4–5.

[123] Quintilla (cited at Epiphanius *Panarion* 49.1); the anonymous sister described by Tertullian at *De Anima* 9.

[124] Cf. Hill, *New Testament prophecy*, 76–77, who, in trying to fit the seer into a tradition of Old Testament prophecy where he does not belong, tries to claim that the inspiration is auditory only and that the visionary material is secondary, and the result of the apocalyptic framework of the book.

known to John in Asia. This is because, although a work of prophecy, it is also a letter, and although designed for oral delivery in worshipping congregations it has been written down, and we may assume has undergone some revision in this process. However, in order for it to be recognized in the congregations in which it was read as an act of prophecy it cannot be too distinct from the prophecy with which they would be familiar, nor can John be too different from the prophets with whom they would be familiar. Whilst proceeding with some caution in reading *Revelation* as prophetic preaching we must also be careful not to exaggerate the differences. Nonetheless the written nature of the prophecy does put distance between it and the oral practice of John's communities, and so some degree of caution needs to be employed in seeking to use the book as a mirror to the communication of the word of God in these assemblies. However, insofar as certain details of the prophecy coincide with what we know of Christian prophecy from elsewhere in early Christianity, we may note, with Hill, certain common features in the prophecy. We have already observed that prophecy has an overall function of exhortation, and that the oracles of chapters two and three fulfil this prophetic function; beyond this Hill suggests that the interpretation of Scripture was a function of the prophets and that this prophetic activity may be discerned in this book.

We have already taken issue with Cothenet, and suggested that exegesis is no part of the activity of a prophet in the Pauline communities.[125] However the same need not apply to the community addressed by the seer. None of the examples cited by Cothenet is actually prophetic, since realisation of Scripture is at the heart of midrash, but the exegetical method of *Revelation* is not midrashic. Whereas there are frequent allusions to the Hebrew Scriptures, and in particular to the prophetic books of the Hebrew canon, there is no formal exegesis of the kind we would recognise from the synagogue by which individual texts are subjected to detailed examination. The seer's allusions to Scripture mean that the earlier message is now appropriated to the present community which he addresses.[126] Typical of this is the reference to *Zechariah* which we noted in the oracle with which the book opens, in which the fulfilment of the

---

[125] 2.1.1, with reference to Cothenet, "Prophètes Chrétiens comme exégètes charismatiques".

[126] As Hill, *New Testament prophecy*, 91 notes.

words of prophecy is announced in words which are themselves
prophetic. Similarly typical is the reference to *Isaiah* 22:22 at 3:7.
The risen Christ describes himself as having the key of David, but
this is only an opening to a wider reference to the whole of the
story in *Isaiah* to which he alludes here. The message to Philadelphia,
in which the allusion is found, is an assurance that the Philadelphian
believers will triumph, and remain in that place that they have taken
over from the Jews. The whole is a realization of the story from
Isaiah, which concerns the taking over of the office by Shebna from
Eliakim. The theme of supersession is introduced by allusion, and
whereas a typology may be seen lying behind the oracle it is not
made explicit. Because of the nature of his use of Scripture John is
fruitfully compared by Hill to the Teacher of Righteousness "to
whom God made known all the mysteries of the words of his servants the prophets" (1QpHab VII 5).[127] Fiorenza however disputes
this characterization, suggesting that the teacher of righteousness
interprets Scripture primarily whereas John interprets the current situation.[128] But this is precisely the reason why the comparison is so
apt, since the Teacher's insights, like John's, go beyond the written
Scriptures and behind them to consist of new revelation rooted in
the old.

Thus, insofar as this method may be called exegesis it must be
described as *charismatic* exegesis. The scriptures are of secondary
importance in the light of the visions which are communicated, providing only a background against which the prophet may deliver the
new message of God for the community; this new message is described
in an unqualified manner as the Word of God and the testimony
of Jesus, a testimony which is equated with the prophetic spirit. This
observation lends support to the general thesis which we have suggested that Scripture is not significant as the basis of preaching and
proclamation in the earliest Christian households but has secondary
significance nonetheless. However, although John's hermeneutic is
like that of the teacher of righteousness and is a spiritual insight into
the meaning of the prophets and the events that are to come given
in an unmediated way by God,[129] and although the manner in which

---

[127] Hill, *New Testament prophecy*, 91.
[128] Fiorenza, "Apokalypsis and propheteia", 136.
[129] So, on the teacher of righteousness, 1QpHab 2.8–10; CD 1.12–13.

the prophecies of old are applied to the present situation of the community is also comparable, the actual exegetical books from Qumran show a much more synagogal procedure through atomization of the text (albeit employing the unique "pesher" technique) or, as Vermes notes, through *hariza*.[130] The insistence of the Community Rule on Scriptural study[131] is likewise reminiscent of later rabbinic academies. The formal procedure of the Habbakuk commentary thus differs from that of John even if there are certain hermeneutical presuppositions held in common, and so we cannot say that there is anything distinctly *prophetic* about the exegetical procedure of the Qumran sectaries. However, John's procedure is, as we shall observe below, paralleled among Christians by the Montanists.

Secondly we may note the absence not only of any indication that the oracles are to undergo any critical examination within worship of the kind observed within the Pauline households; rather, as Hill observes, the statement from God that the words are faithful and true, and the warning that nothing is to be added to or removed from the prophecy, are indications that the prophecies are unquestionable.[132] This bears witness to the very primitive nature of the communities of the apocalypse, and their communication of the word of God. One of the differences which may be noted between *Revelation* and other apocalyptic literature is the virtual absence of dialogue between John and the revealer figures whom he meets.[133] This may be contrasted with the extensive dialogue not only in Jewish apocalypses but also in Christian prophetic reports such as Hermas' reports of his visions, and the dialogue between the apostles and the risen Christ in *Epistula apostolorum*. Whereas the genre of "revelation dialogue" has been proposed as a description of this procedure it is suggested by Stewart-Sykes that a dialogue might be the usual manner in which a revelation might be reported in early Christianity;[134] indeed we may observe here that this is ὁμιλία. A reason for this dialogue may be that it reflects the way in which a prophetic oracle might be explored in early Christianity. The conversations which take place within visions may be read as anticipations of the questions

---

[130] Vermes, *Dead Sea scrolls*, 291.
[131] 1QS 8.15.
[132] Hill, *New Testament prophecy*, 87.
[133] Aune, "Social matrix", 18; Bauckham, *Theology*, 9–10.
[134] Stewart-Sykes, "Asian context", 427 and references.

and objections of the audience, and the dialogue which takes place
in the delivery of an enthusiastic prophecy, such as that met in the
Epistula apostolorum and in the fourth Gospel, might likewise be an
indication of the process of questioning which might be undergone
by a prophet as part of the determination that his message is genuine. The nature of John's prophetic authority is such that there is
no questioning of his authority nor doubt cast on the genuineness
of his visions; such few expansions and explanations of the visions
that exist are volunteered by the revealer figure, an indication that
the revealer is entirely in control of the proceedings, just as the
reporter in the assembly is unquestioned. Although this may be
unique to John himself, a reflection of his own charismatic authority in the churches, so denying us the assurance that the activity of
local prophets would be received in the same way, given the high
regard accorded to the prophetic spirit we may be assured that having been recognised as authentic prophecy their words would be
given the same high accord that in time would be afforded to Scripture
in the developing Christian synagogues.

As we have seen, it is possible to exaggerate the difference between
John and the local prophets, as Hill does by casting him more as a
prophet in the Old Testament mould, rather than the Christian
prophetic mould. The fact that he is a member of a prophetic circle[135]
is an indication that even if a leader among them he is still a prophet
among prophets, and the event of his prophecy being written is more
probably a product of circumstance than any conviction that written prophecy is in any way distinct from or superior to oral prophecy.
One of Hill's reasons for seeing John as a "free prophet" of the Old
Testament type is his observation that, unlike the congregational
prophets described in *I Corinthians*, his prophecy is not subjected to
judgement and examination. Whereas this may be an indication that
the practice of examining oracles is alien to this community it is
equally likely, as we have already suggested, to be a reflection of his
charismatic authority. Aune picks up hints of opposition to John
among the churches at 2:14 and 2:20–23, where other (presumably
local) prophets are tarred with the brush of false prophecy under
biblical pseudonyms;[136] the fact that John needs to oppose prophecy

---

[135] So Aune, "Prophetic circle", 103–116, "Social matrix", 18–19, with reference
to 22:9 and 22:16.
[136] Aune, "Social matrix", 22.

with prophecy is an indication that only a prophetic message carried authority in these communities, and that having been received the prophetic messages of "Balaam" and "Jezebel" were acted on. John needs to bolster his own charismatic authority, and this can only be done in prophecy. Similarly there is some indication that Ignatius' prophecy in Philadelphia was doubted, but the manner in which its divine origin is stressed is an indication of the expectation of these communities that there should be prophecy among them and that this prophecy should be authoritative. Paul states that the διάκρισις of prophecy is as much a work of the Spirit as the original prophecy, and in observing one Pauline διάκρισις we have found it to be prophetic at heart. There is no necessary contradiction between charismatic and authoritative prophecy and authoritative and charismatic interpretation.

Quite regardless of its date,[137] the Johannine apocalypse thus enables us to see the church functioning at its most primitive level in terms of the manner in which the word of God was communicated to the community. The *kairos* is near at hand, and the words of the prophet carry urgency and unique authority in the assembly. Perhaps one hundred years later, this is still the case in one part of Asia at least, namely the community from which *Acta Pauli* derived.

2.1.4. *The survival of domestic prophetic ὁμιλία*

We observed above that Paul, in *Acta Pauli*, preached in a house.[138] We may further observe that this community, which is household based, is also well acquainted with the practice of prophecy within the assembly. According to Tertullian, *Acta Pauli* originated in Asia, apparently late in the second century.[139] Certain correspondences with Montanism, beside the practice of prophecy, such as the encratite emphasis, the significant role played by women in the church and the emphasis on fasting would tend to support Tertullian's testimony.[140]

---

[137] Michaels, *Interpreting the book of Revelation*, 43–46, notes attempts at dating varying between Nero and Domitian; because of the diversity of early Christianity the "primitive" nature of John's communication does not impinge upon the question, and does not necessarily imply an earlier date.

[138] 1.2.1.3 in response to Siegert's asseveration that one cannot do so!

[139] *De baptismo* 17; Schneelmelcher, *New Testament apocrypha*, 214–215, finds no reason to question this.

[140] These correspondences are pointed out by Rordorf, "Was wissen wir", 76–78. The correspondences do not however necessitate Montanist influence, as these are simply common Asian Christian practices and beliefs.

We may thus see that the practice of prophecy, despite the problems caused by the new prophecy, did not die out altogether in second-century Asia. This is a vital witness not only for the practice of
prophecy as the means of conveying the message of God in the
assembly, but also for the manner in which prophecy was received
and adjudicated.[141] It is to be noted that the adjudications, as one
might expect from the Pauline evidence, are considered as much
inspired as the original message. The following exchange takes place
during worship at the house of Epiphanius in Corinth.[142]

> ... Paul, full of the Holy Spirit, said: "Brethren, be zealous about
> <fasting> and love. For behold, I go aware to a furnace of fire <...>
> and I am not strong except the Lord <grant> me power. For indeed
> David accompanied Saul <...>, for Christ Jesus was with him <...>.
> <The Grace of> the Lord will go with me, that I may <fulfil> the
> <...> dispensation with steadfastness." But they were distressed and
> fasted.

It is to be noted that Paul's prophetic message cites the *exemplum* of
David's presence with Saul as the way in which Christ is to be with
him. The use of a scriptural *exemplum* is not alien in the prophetic
word. The response of the congregation however is to refuse the
message, and so the Spirit is obliged to come upon another of those
present in order to confirm the message.

> Then Cleobius was filled with the Spirit and said 'Brethren, now must
> Paul fulfil all his assignment, and go up to the <...> of death <...>
> in great instruction and knowledge and sowing of the word, and (must)
> suffer envy, and depart out of this world.' But when the brethren and
> Paul heard <this> they lifted up their voice and said: 'O God, <...>
> Father of Christ, help thou Paul thy servant, that he may yet abide
> with us because of our weakness.' But since Paul was cut (to the heart)
> and no longer fasted with them, when an offering was celebrated by
> Paul ... <lacuna>

A further prophetic proof is subsequently required. Before observing
this however we may also note that there is no particular order

---

[141] Vouaux, *Actes de Paul*, 276–277, suggests that the whole scene is based on the
prophecy of Agabus in *Acts*. Whereas there may well be some influence from *Acts*,
in particular with regard to content, the procedure of confirmation of the oracle
which is described in such detail is indicative that the scene is drawn on the basis
of experience.

[142] Papyrus Hamburg page 7, cited in the translation of Schneelmelcher, *New
Testament apocrypha* II, 257–258.

apparent in which the prayer of the congregation, the sacramental action of the congregation and the word of the Lord addressed to the congregation is to be found.

> But the Spirit came upon Myrta, so that she said: 'Brethren, why <are you alarmed at the sight of this sign?> Paul the servant of the Lord will save many in Rome, and will nourish many with the word, so that there is no number (to count them) and he (?) will become manifest above all the faithful and greatly will the glory <. . . come> upon him so that there will be great grace in Rome' and immediately, when the spirit that was in Myrta was at peace, each one took of the bread and feasted according to custom <. . .> . . .

In distinction to the procedure assumed by *Revelation*, the question of the validity of the prophecy may be raised, even if it is subsequently confirmed. This process of prophecy followed by confirmation by various parties could well be described as prophetic ὁμιλία, and coheres with the picture derived from the Pauline households of inspired speech being confirmed by further inspired speech. The manner in which each speech goes uninterrupted and is held at some length conforms with the directions given by Paul for the manner in which prophecy is to be delivered and is reminiscent of the dialogues described by Plutarch in *Quaestiones conviviales*. This indicates the manner in which this scene of *Acta Pauli* betrays the nature of prophecy in the household and is thus an indicator of the manner in which the homily grows from these prophetic origins.

2.1.5. *Preaching and the synagogalizing community of* I Peter

We have observed that the Roman churches underwent a process of scholasticization which, although similar to the process of synagogalization we have observed in the Pauline churches, is not quite identical. We have moreover observed that the communities addressed by John in *Revelation* show no evidence of a move in that direction. However it is possible that John, who displays conservative tendencies in other respects, is an exception in a general drift within the churches to some form of scholasticization, either Jewish (described therefore as synagogalization) or one reflecting more closely the wider Graeco-Roman context. There were other exceptions; we have already noted that *Acta Pauli* still knows the practice of prophecy at the end of the second century, and that here the movement from house to house-synagogue was not complete. We shall moreover note below that Montanism is in its prophetic practice a conservative movement within the church of second century Asia.[143] But in spite of exceptions, and in spite of the fact that the process of scholasticization took place more quickly in some communities than in others, the movement is as near to universal as anything in ancient Christianity. As evidence of this we may note that a process of synagogalization apart from that undergone by the Pauline households, and distinct from that undergone by the Roman households of which Hermas betrays some knowledge, may be observed in the Bithynian communities addressed by the first letter of Peter.[144] There have been attempts to see this document as homiletic and, although we will show that there are insufficient grounds for this classification, the study of the document is still worthwhile because it illustrates the process by which households reformed themselves.

We may begin our examination of these communities with reference to the work of Elliott, who sums up the purpose of *I Peter* as the formation of an οἶκος. In particular he notes that the addressees of *I Peter* are those who are without a home, those marginalized within the setting of the Empire; however those *paroikoi* who converted in the hope of finding security and a "place of belonging" find that they are still *paroikoi* since their conversion, for their conversion had led to further hostility, with consequent disillusionment.[145] "Peter" intends to encourage the Christian community to understand that it is itself an οἶκος, and that its self-definition derives from the conflict with outsiders in which it finds itself.[146] The use of the term *oikos* does not however mean that Peter is envisaging an ecclesiology narrowly based on the household, since the household which the *paroikoi* are to form is a household specifically of faith, and by virtue of the *paroikia* of the recipients it is a household outside of the normal Graeco-Roman setting. So although they are described and addressed as an *oikos*, the household communities to which this letter is addressed are in a process of change, a change which the

---

[143] 2.2.3.6.

[144] It is possible that the letter is written from Rome (such being the usual understanding of the coded reference to "Babylon" at 5:13) but even if this is the case the writer appears to be addressing a situation in the communities to which he is writing rather than in the Roman churches, and therefore reflects the situation in these Asian churches rather than the Roman churches.

[145] Elliott, *Home*, 101–106.

[146] Elliott, *Home*, 148–150.

letter intends to encourage. Because the *oikos* is a substitute for a more conventional *oikos*, it is not a household based on the normal network of family but one based on belief. As such it has more in common with the synagogue than with the household.

Support for this characterization of the households of which *I Peter* speaks may be gained by observing the extensive debt which the epistle owes to Scripture. From this Schutter deduces that the author is Jewish, and that it is through the synagogue that he has gained his expertise in Scripture.[147] We may therefore safely characterize the community which he is seeking to form in the same way. That this process of synagogalization should take place explains the hermeneutical methods employed by Peter, such as the use of hariza in 2:3–9, a process including the identification of similar words (χρηστός and Χριστός at 2:3) and actualization of ancient texts, such as the application of the epithets of biblical Israel to those addressed as chosen race, royal priesthood and holy nation (2:9).[148] However, the actualization of ancient texts extends even to the word of God itself; in quoting *Isaiah* at 1:24–25 the author suggests that the abiding and enduring word of God is the Gospel which was preached. The author is not so much devoted to scripture as to the Gospel, which is being scripturalized.[149]

But although we may agree with Schutter that this indicates synagogalization, and a hermeneutic which broadly speaking may be called midrashic, it is not possible to follow him in seeing *I Peter* partially representing the shape of a synagogue homily. Schutter seeks to perceive the same proemic shape described by Borgen in *I Peter* 1:14–2:9. In this light he suggests that 1:16, a citation of *Leviticus* 19:2, is the proemial text. Beyond the obvious subordinate quotations, he perceives allusions to this chapter of *Leviticus* behind a number of other points in the epistle.[150]

- An allusion to *Leviticus* 19:18 at 1:22
- The command to fear father (19:3) and fear God (19:14) behind 1:17
- The prohibition of idolatry in 19:4 lying behind 1:18

---

[147] Schutter, *Hermeneutic and composition*; conclusions at 82–84.
[148] Schutter, *Hermeneutic and composition*, 93–94.
[149] Cf. Old, *Reading and preaching*, 227, for whom this passage is simply a witness to "Peter's" devotion to "Scripture".
[150] Schutter, *Hermeneutic and composition*, 95–98.

- The use of the Temple community tradition in 2:5–9 deriving
  from the Levitical directions concerning sacrifice
- The denunciation of sin (19:11f) summarized in the catalogue
  of vices at 2:1
- Several significant verbal tallies such as σκάνδαλον (19:14) at
  2:8 and κατασπερεῖς (19:19) at 1:23

In isolation these allusions might well be seen as fortuitous or forced,
but their cumulative effect in the light of the opening citation is
impressive. *Leviticus* 19 plays a significant role in the body opening
of *I Peter*, and midrash may provide a key to open up the wealth
of allusions. This much admitted, the question arises as to whether
the midrash is necessarily homiletic. The problem lies in the very
depth and subtlety of the allusions. "Peter" does not proceed in the
manner of the extant Tannaitic preachers by a verbal analysis of an
opening citation, but rather produces his own piece of exhortation
with an eye on a particular passage of *Leviticus*. This procedure, whilst
perhaps based on the same hermeneutical assumptions as the synagogue homily, would be more appropriate in a literary work or a
school exercise than in a homily addressed to an audience on a single occasion, and betrays a mind working with a fair degree of
reflection rather than a preacher extemporizing on a text.

I Peter as it stands is self-consciously a literary work, for the author
concludes by stating that he is writing.[151] It is a letter sent on a circular route around various congregations in Asia,[152] and if Elliott is
in any way right it is intended to meet a particular set of pastoral
issues in the Asian churches to which it is addressed. Were Schutter
correct in classifying the letter as a homily, then disregarding the
letter opening, *I Peter* would have to have been a homily which was
originally independent of the current epistolary context, which had
been turned into a literary work through a secondary epistolary situation. But not only do the subtlety of the scriptural allusions remind
us more of a literary work than a homily, the very suitability of the
"homily" to the pastoral situation which it addresses, namely the
paroikia of the recipients caused through the hostility of a surrounding population, militates against this possibility. If we have any kind

---

[151] ἔγραψα, *I Peter* 5:12.
[152] Hemer, "Address", proposes a plausible route for the letter carrier beginning
at Amisus. The puzzle is why the route should begin there.

of homily here then it is a "desk" homily, written against the background of a process of synagogalization. Support for this characterization may be found in the author's description of his literary purpose as παρακαλῶν, which indicates that the letter may serve as a written substitute for a homily (*I Peter* 5:12) and his self-designation at a συμπρεσβύτερος at *I Peter* 5:1, which constructs a picture of *presbyteroi* co-functioning in the assembly. The letter may reflect something on the nature of preaching in the community from which it is sent, be it Asian or Roman, in that it informs us to an extent of the use to which Scripture may be put and in that it manages to combine an epideictic strategy and the accompanying festive prose with elements of paraenesis, but we cannot say that it is typical of a homily addressed to the faithful in the assembly and cannot therefore draw conclusions from the nature of the preaching in that community. *I Peter* may represent an ideal type of sermon, and may even stand in a tradition of instruction given in the assembly through its use of traditional material,[153] but that is the best that can be said: it does not enrich our understanding of the form of the sermon in the first century. Rather its greatest value lies in the insights which it gives us into the nature of the synagogalization process, which would in turn impact on preaching.

An alternative way in which *I Peter* has been viewed as a homily has been to understand it as a baptismal homily. Most consistent of these attempts is that of Bornemann.[154] He views the body of *I Peter* as a baptismal homily based on *Psalm* 34. However there is no introductory citation of the psalm, and only six possible citations in the course of the letter, a number of which are inexact and a number of which may be co-incidental (such as the epistolary blessing formula εὐλογητός ὁ θεός (1:3) which, according to Bornemann, is a citation of *Psalm* 34:2 εὐλογήσω τὸν Κύριον.[155] Even less credible is his attempt to find traces of the creed in the letter.[156] There are undoubtedly allusions to the Pascha in the letter,[157] and language which harks back to baptism;[158] however the absence of evidence of

---

[153] So Salzmann, *Lehren und Ermahnen*, 105–106.
[154] Bornemann, "Erste Petrusbrief".
[155] Bornemann, "Erste Petrusbrief", 149.
[156] Bornemann, "Erste Petrusbrief", 151–153.
[157] See e.g. Leaney "I Peter and the Passover".
[158] Note the comments of Lohse, "Paraenesis and kerygma", 48 n50.

an association of Pascha and baptism in the earliest centuries rather
weakens any classification of *I Peter* as a paschal baptismal homily
on this basis.[159] The paschal references are part of the epideictic
strategy of the author who uses the suffering of Christ remembered
at Pascha as a means of encouraging the Christians he is addressing in their trials, whereas the baptismal references may best be
explained with reference to the traditional nature of the paraenesis
which the writer has taken over,[160] which was probably used as part
of baptismal catechesis. This in turn is employed as part of the
writer's purpose in helping the recipients understand themselves as
a sanctified household of faith, and need not be taken as an indication that baptism has just taken place. Bornemann's work has been
taken as an example of a number of attempts to discern a paschal
or baptismal homily in the letter[161] because it has at least the merit
of attempting to find a scriptural basis by which it might be considered homiletic. Best's verdict may be passed on all these attempts:

> The real reason for arguing for a sermon in 1:3–4:11 is to provide
> an explanation for the presence of baptismal references; this section
> has never been considered to be any kind of sermon but a *baptismal*
> sermon. If however the baptismal allusions can be equally accounted
> for by the use of traditional material, hymns, creeds, catechisms then
> there seems to be no reason to maintain the argument that the ear-
> lier part is a sermon.[162]

In the light of Schutter's work this verdict has to be revised, since
the underlying synagogal hermeneutic of *I Peter* provides a possible
reason to consider it is as homiletic, but even then we have concluded that this is probably not the case. As far as the theory of
I Peter as a baptismal homily is concerned Best's verdict still holds.[163]

---

[159] On which absence note Hall, "Paschal baptism".

[160] On the traditional nature of the catechesis see Lohse, "Paraenesis and kerygma",
49–51.

[161] Such as that of Beare, *First epistle*, 25–28. According to Lohse, "Paraenesis
and kerygma", 38, these attempts originate with Perdelwitz's attempt in 1911 to
link *I Peter* with the mystery cults.

[162] Best, *I Peter* 27; Brox, *Erste Petrusbrief*, 23–24, reaches similar conclusions.

[163] A related effort is that of Old, *Reading and preaching*, 236–238, who, in the light
of the extensive traditional catechesis in *I Peter*, holds that it is a summary of catechetical preaching. But although catechesis may occasion a homily, this is not representative of the usual preaching of the church. There is by no means sufficient
here to enable us to see *I Peter* as in any way representative of preaching in the
assembly.

However, even if *I Peter* has not been shown to be a homily it remains a useful pointer to the ways in which households might transform themselves into synagogues. Peter's use of Scripture may be seen as part of his overall rhetorical strategy, since the transformation of these communities into synagogues would in turn transform their media of communication from those received by prophets in the present to those received by prophets in the past, which are to be actualized in the present, and the process of inquiry would be transferred from an inquiry into the meaning and appropriateness of the prophetic message given within the meeting of the community into an enquiry into the meaning of the writings of prophets of old. Exegesis as a prophetic activity has been observed, and the process of realization of old prophecies into new prophecy was particularly marked in the circle of the seer of *Revelation*. There, however, the very exegetical procedure was prophetic and the exegesis charismatic; here the procedure may better be described as rabbinic.

We are thus equipped to explore the communication of the word of God within churches whose organisation is scholastic. Here we may primarily seek the forms of homiletic communication which are betrayed within the later Jewish synagogues, on the basis that as Scripture comes to replace prophecy, so the process of enquiry which took place into the words of the prophets might become a process of enquiry into the Scriptures, and διάκρισις become midrash. This however is only part of a generally scholasticizing movement within early Christianity; the inspired *diakrisis* which was the work of prophets is transferred to those equipped as teachers to interpret the sacred texts.

2.1.6. *Preaching in the household*

In the households of the Pauline churches, of Hermas and of the seer of the apocalypse we have found evidence of the communication of the word of God principally through prophecy. Whereas this is not preaching as such it functions in much the same way, and can be seen as a root out of which later practice might grow. In particular prophecy was subject to subsequent examination, which might take the form of conversation, or ὁμιλία, and here likewise we may discern a base from which the later practice of preaching might grow. At the same time it was proving difficult to sustain the church as a simple household, and just as the Pauline churches and those addressed by the author of *I Peter* were in the process of becoming synagogues, there is evidence in Hermas' writings that other forms of scholastic community were forming within the church. This would not mean an instant end to prophecy and ὁμιλία, since we have already observed that table-talk might be found in an scholastic environment,[164] but increased concentration on a sacred text would inevitably alter the mode, as well as the subject-matter, of Christian communication.

2.2. *Preaching in scholasticized communities*

Our study of the communication of the word of God in a household setting has indicated that this communication was primarily prophetic and therefore surrounded with a lesser formality than we would expect of a homily, even though prophecy might be functionally equivalent to preaching. It has also lent support to our *hypothesis* that the process undergone by some Christian households might be termed synagogalization or scholasticization, and that this process led to emphasis on Scripture in the development of preaching as the scriptural text moved to the centre of Christian worship. Alongside this a process of appraisal and elucidation, which had been applied to oracles given within the assembly, became applied to Scripture.

The homily preached by Paul in the synagogue at Pisidian Antioch is frequently claimed as a Christian synagogue homily. Although we shall observe below that it is no such thing, nonetheless this provides as good a starting point as any for the investigation of synagogalization, though it is better seen in the context of the whole of *Luke-Acts*.

2.2.1. *Christian synagogal preaching in* Luke-Acts

If the Emmaeus pericopē is a reflection of worship in Luke's church,[165] it may well be that the pattern of scriptural reflection, including, we should note, ὁμιλία, and a meal, is an indication of a household undergoing synagogalization, as the rituals themselves lead to community foundation. The motif of hospitality may indicate a house-

---

[164] 1.2.4.4 above.
[165] So Betz, "Ursprung und Wesen", discussing *Luke* 24:17–32.

hold setting, and the conversation which would seem to be envisaged in the discussion on the road may indicate that some of the informality of the house-church remains, but the preliminary reading of Scripture which provides the basis for the discussion is something that comes in with the second generation. One might thus anticipate that Luke's church is one which knows the practice of preaching within the church. Luke moreover has the beginnings of a pneumatology of preaching, by which the Holy Spirit enables the preacher in particular ways, such as giving insights and the power of boldness.[166]

For all this, however, the only commonly recognised homily in the *Luke-Acts* corpus is that which is put into the mouth of Paul and is located in the synagogue at Pisidian Antioch, where Paul is invited to give a λόγος παρακλήσεως after the reading of Torah and *haftarah*. The description of the speech as a λόγος παρακλήσεως may indicate that a homily is to follow, but although these words may indicate that Paul is being invited to give a homily in the assembly, this is not what is forthcoming. What we hear in *Acts* 13:17–41 is missionary preaching. Ellul makes it clear that the narrative context and expectation of a normal homily is precisely what gives bite to the ensuing missionary discourse.[167] Whether or not Luke has employed a source, and whether or not Paul preached in Pisidian Antioch, the combination of the speech and setting are Lukan literary devices; when McDonald comments that "it probably passed, in the synagogue setting, as a sectarian address" he is missing the point that the emphasis is entirely on the new thing that God has done.[168] Moreover we should be clear that although both *paraklēsis* and exegesis are possible prophetic functions, there is nothing prophetic about what follows;[169] for this reason likewise it is difficult to see that this is a homily.

Nonetheless Bowker, largely indebted to Mann, has perceived a proem form here.[170] This form would not necessarily be expected, since missionary preaching need not follow the rules of scriptural

---

[166] See Turner, "Spirit of preaching", 69–70.
[167] Ellul, "Antioche de Pisidie".
[168] McDonald, *Kerygma and didache*, 51–52.
[169] Cf. Cothenet, "Prophètes Chrétiens comme exégètes charismatiques", 91, who classifies this as "une lecture prophétique de l'écriture".
[170] Bowker, "Speeches in Acts".

preaching in the assembly. Further difficulty in identifying the proem form is caused in that the lections for the *haftarah* and Torah are disputed. Whereas this may reflect a situation where a lectionary had not yet been established, given that the proem is not obvious, it may equally well indicate that this is not a proemic homily at all! Bowker answers this problem with reference to the art of *hariza*, which he sees underlying the "homily"; the whole, he reckons, is an oblique reference to *II Samuel* 7:6–16, a suggestion originally made by Doeve[171] and, apparently independently, by Cothenet.[172] Certainly there is some indication that *hariza* is employed in this passage, but this does not mean that we are dealing with a homily since *hariza* is not the point of preaching, but simply an exegetical strategy based on hermeneutic assumptions. *Hariza* may underlie the construction of a homily, but not a homily only. It may be possible to construct what is occurring here as midrashic, in the broadest sense of the word,[173] but midrash it is not.

The first citation of a text is found at 13:22: "I have found David son of Jesse to be a man after my own heart who will carry out all my purposes." Whereas this is probably a conflated and targumized version of *Psalm* 89:20 and *I Samuel* 13:14,[174] this very conflation makes it improbable that this is the proemic text. This leads Bowker to suggest that it is quoted in a targumic form.[175] This begins to sound like special pleading; a more probable explanation of the form of the citation is that this is the result of collecting testimonia,[176] which is not an exercise related to preaching. The most problematic item about this text, however, is that is found relatively late in the "homily" and not at the head at all. According to Bowker the homily "starts with a proem text"; but this is not the start of the homily, as Bowker is himself clear. He later refers to the earlier verses as an introduction[177] which makes it unlike a proem homily.

---

[171] Doeve, *Jewish hermeneutics*, 172–175; it is important to note that Doeve was simply pointing out the debt to Jewish exegetical strategies, and not trying at all to see this address as a homily.

[172] Cothenet, "Prophètes Chrétiens comme exégètes charismatiques", 91–92.

[173] In common with Cothenet, "Prophètes Chrétiens comme exégètes charismatiques", 91–94.

[174] So Bruce, *Acts*, 305.

[175] Bowker, "Speeches in Acts", 104.

[176] So Albl, *And Scripture cannot be broken*, 195–198.

[177] Bowker, "Speeches in Acts", 103.

He is eventually led to conclude that it is not a "pure" proem homily, but that it has characteristics of a proemic homily. To add to the confusion he purports to see *Deuteronomy* 4:37–8 as an underlying *seder*, which underlies the homily. Whereas the author of *Acts* 13 may have been a master of *hariza*, one may still reasonably ask what text he is actually interpreting. However, apart from the fact that the text is prefaced by an introduction, and indeed that it is unclear what exactly the proemic text is, there is a more telling objection to such a classification of this passage. Namely this passage lacks the most distinctive and primitive mark of a synagogue homily in proemic form, which is an ordered and verbatim exegesis of the text. To say, as Bowker does, that the sermon is "on the relationship . . . between David and Jesus"[178] is inadequate; the proemic method involved attention to the verbal detail of the text which is under consideration, not a generalized treatment of the theme.

Similar objections to Bowker are noted by McDonald who, as we have seen, argued on the basis of Bultmann's formal theory of the diatribe that the Christian homily was in its origins precisely such a thematic speech, and finds that the address in *Acts* 13 fulfils this shape.[179] He can account for the scriptural elements by suggesting that this is something of a stock device for the purpose of missionary preaching, and that the speech thus demonstrates "the prime example of the formal transition from the proem type synagogue homily to Christian *paraklēsis*, consisting of a thematic address or sermon."[180] We have already seen that his formal classification of the diatribe is erroneous[181] and we may now see that the conclusions he draws from this classification are likewise erroneous, since this address is not representative of preaching in the assembly. We shall observe that Scripture continues to provide a basis for Christian preaching, and thus that the transition from *petiha* to *paraklēsis* of which he talks is purely imaginary. If the role of Scripture within preaching does change in the early centuries it changes by becoming more central to the purpose of the homily.

Given that the purpose of *Acts* 13:17–41 is missionary preaching, and granting, in the light of the targumic citation, that the whole

---

[178] Bowker, "Speeches in Acts", 102.
[179] McDonald, *Kerygma and didache*, 51–52.
[180] McDonald, *Kerygma and didache*, 52.
[181] 1.2.4.1 above.

has some life previous to Luke's inclusion of the "homily" in *Acts*, the most probable solution is that this is a remainder of exegetical activity which took place in a missionary context, but not a homily at all, rather a piece which employs some of the techniques of homilists. Bruce suggests that it would certainly be fitting as an example of "preaching to a synagogue congregation",[182] and his observation that the citation at 13:22 may result from a collection of *testimonia*, in the light of the similarity with *I Clement* 18.1 is a helpful one.[183] But for these very reasons it cannot be said to typify a synagogue sermon either Christian or Jewish.

An alternative analysis of this speech is offered by Wills in accordance with his perceived pattern of (scriptural) example, conclusion and exhortation.[184] So, according to his analysis, 16b–37 is a collection of *exempla*, 38–39 comprises the conclusion, "Let it be known to you therefore that through this man forgiveness of sins is proclaimed to you", and this is followed by a final exhortation. This is Wills' first example, and he himself admits that this is a missionary sermon, and that only the setting is what leads one to expect a "typical synagogue homily".[185] Once again we must note that there is nothing here which is necessarily homiletic. The fact that this writing, together with others of a similar shape, are "often considered to be 'homiletical'"[186] points only to the complete uncertainty of critics as to what constitutes a sermon in this period, which is the very uncertainty which Wills was attempting to correct.

We have earlier noted Black's criticism of Wills by suggesting that this thematic approach does not do sufficient justice to the use of the rhetorical models which would be readily at hand; the speech may be classed as epideictic, or, Bailey and Vander Broek point out, as deliberative.[187] Either would fit with the pattern of *narratio, probatio* and *exhortatio*. This may be Luke's own work, or, in the light of the possibility to which Bowker adverts that Luke is using a source, it may have come to him from the tradition of Christian controversy within Judaism. The concentration on the Davidic descent of

---

[182] Bruce, *Acts*, 303.
[183] Bruce, *Acts*, 305–306.
[184] Wills, "Form of the sermon", 278–279.
[185] Wills, "Form of the sermon", 278.
[186] So Wills, "Form of the sermon", 279.
[187] *Literary forms*, 168.

Jesus is not a fundamental theme of Paul's teaching in the letters, and so the source is probably not Pauline; Davidic descent is a basic item in the kerygma, but for this reason Lukan composition must remain the most probable option since, as Ellul points out, the result of the treatment of David in the "homily" is actually a rejection of Davidic claims in the light of the newer and greater revelation of Christ.[188] In either event the interplay of Scripture as authority and Greek rhetorical forms within early Christianity is interesting as indicating a possible line which preaching in the assembly might follow. But this is not an example of preaching in the assembly.

Nonetheless we may seek to see whether this marriage of Scripture and rhetoric, a marriage which we have seen to have taken place within the Hellenistic synagogue, might have taken place in the preaching of Christian communities which modelled themselves on the synagogue.

A better indication that *Acts* 13 of the nature of preaching in Luke's church is perhaps that of the Baptist in the third Gospel.[189] Turner characterizes this as "prophetic preaching" in that the Baptist is a prophet, but his teaching is not a string of prophecies as such, but a "more general proclamation and ad hoc application of the truths revealed to them."[190] What is particularly noticeable about this "preaching" is the manner in which it is directed to different groups. It is general ethical guidance with a religious basis, which is in turn applied to various groups; that is to say, it is paraenesis. But paraenesis is not necessarily homiletic. One of the besetting problems with the study of early Christian preaching is the assumption made that paraenetic documents are homiletic on the basis of their contents. The Lukan corpus shows us that paraenesis may be found in a homily, but a homily is not its exclusive domain, nor is paraenesis the only possible content of a homily.[191] We shall see that this confusion has led to the probably inaccurate representation of *James* and *II Clement* in particular as homilies.

We may however examine the Baptist's paraenesis further, not least since it is described as παρακαλῶν (3:18). The Baptist is addressed

---

[188] Ellul, "Antioche de Pisidie", 8–9.
[189] *Luke* 3:7–18.
[190] Turner, "Spirit of preaching", 71.
[191] Such is the conclusion of Salzmann, *Lehren und Ermahnen*, 43, on the basis of the reports of preaching in *Acts*.

as διδάσκαλε (*Luke* 3:12), which is a reflection of the synagogal origin of this picture, but the context is therefore as likely to be catechetical as homiletic since the manner in which the Baptist answers
specific questions is reflective of the schoolroom. Nonetheless we
noted above that catechesis might stand alongside more directly
homiletic address within the assembly at one stage in the development of Pauline and deutero-Pauline communities, and this could
be the stage of development of the Lukan synagogue reflected in
this pericopē. Thus the Baptist's preaching may reflect in some way
the communication of the word of God within the Lukan assembly,
but is not part of the line of development which led to the homily.
That line of development is bound up to the use of Scripture.

It is however important to note that significant as Scripture is in
communication within the Christian synagogue as described by Luke
it is not the beginning point. As such it may be seen to have some
linkage with the use of Scripture in the households as part of the
means of adjudicating the content of prophecies. Rather than taking Scripture as a starting point the nature of the scriptural reflection
which is betrayed by the Emmaeus pericopē is one which begins
with the situation of the community, namely the events surrounding
the death of Jesus, and goes on through reflection on the Old
Testament to see that this present situation has come about in
fulfilment of the prophetic Scriptures. A similar hermeneutic is demonstrated in the speech at Pisidian Antioch, even though it is not
homiletic, since for all the reference to Scripture what is significant
is the kerygma, which is then shown to be the fulfillment of Scripture.
Similarly we may note the manner in which James, at *Acts* 15:13–21,
adjudicates the report of Paul and Barnabas (both of whom, inci-
dentally, are prophets) by noting the extent to which what they say
agrees with the scriptural prophets, and concludes his judgement
with a citation. Once again this is not a homiletic setting, but this
procedure may nonetheless reflect the hermeneutic which would
underlie preaching in these developing Christian synagogues and the
description of the meeting may well be modelled on the manner in
which the word of God was addressed and adjudicated in these
assemblies.

Thus rather than the speeches of *Acts*, whose purpose is evangelistic, a better reflection of the manner in which the word of God
is communicated in the community of *Luke-Acts* may be provided by

the paraenetic communications of the prophets. In this light an exploration of the relationship between paraenesis and homily is needed.

2.2.2. *Paraenesis and preaching*

A number of paraenetic documents from early Christianity have been claimed to be homilies, principally because of their paraenetic content. Because these claims have been so persistent the arguments need to be examined, even though we shall conclude that they are either pale imitations of preaching, or are not homiletic at all. Nonetheless they may cast some further light upon the process of synagogalization, since all would seem to derive from Christian communities which have either derived directly from the synagogue or which have organized themselves as alternative synagogal communities.

2.2.2.1. *The epistle of James as synagogue homily?*

Our further exploration of the relationship between paraenesis and homily may be begun with an outstanding example of paraenesis in a Christian synagogal setting which has frequently claimed to be a homily, or made up of redacted portions of homilies. That is the *Epistle of James*. That *James* is formed out of homilies is at least possible since as it stands it is paraenesis. This does not gainsay the observation of diatribal elements in *James*, for even though Ropes rejects the hypothesis that *James* is paraenetic because he felt that a paraenetic collection should be calmer in tone than a diatribe, a diatribe is quite capable of being a vehicle of paraenesis.

In claiming that *James* is paraenesis it should be clarified that the term is used simply to describe moral exhortation, marked by the presence of maxims. We have already seen that the modern definition of paraenesis, which may be traced to Dibelius' commentary on *James*, is somewhat narrower than the ancient definition;[192] this has led to the discussion of whether or not various documents are paraenesis in the modern sense, when it is clear that they qualify under the broader ancient criteria. So, for instance, Wessel argues that *James* is not paraenesis as Dibelius understands it because there is more than simply stereotyped material and that it meets a real situation.[193]

---

[192] 1.2.1.2 n98 above.
[193] Wessel, *Enquiry*, 77–78.

Similarly McDonald argues that *James* is not a homily as it stands because the whole does not exhibit the nature of organisation which one would expect of a homily; in his assessment of the organisation of *James* McDonald is indebted to Dibelius, part of whose definition of paraenesis is the absence of order.[194] Whereas Dibelius may be in error at this point, and it should be noted that the question of whether there is organisation in *James* is a currently live one as recent studies have sought rhetorical organisation behind the letter,[195] we should be aware that even were it possible to find a rhetorical shape to the letter that does not therefore mean that it reflects the rhetorical shape of a homily.

However, before examining the question of what *James* can tell us about Christian preaching it is necessary to determine its social setting. At 2:3 James refers to a συναγωγή. Whereas this may be a neutral term for the assembly of people there are indications that this term is employed because the assembly envisaged is synagogal in the technical sense of the term. Although Davids suggests that the use of this term by Hermas and Polycarp indicates that an assembly in the neutral sense of the term may be envisaged,[196] both Hermas and Polycarp are closely connected to Judaism. The usage of Hermas in particular, who refers to the συναγωγὴ ἀνδρῶν δικαίων at *Mandate* 11.9 and 11.14 is felt by Salzmann to be a specific reminder of Jewish usage.[197] Thus the very use of the term in *James* is a prima facie implication that the user derives from a Jewish context.

The συναγωγή described here is a public assembly, and hence anyone might enter, either a rich man or a poor man. Whereas we may assume that a cultic gathering is being described, for such is the "common and traditional interpretation",[198] a number of recent commentators suggest that the function of the synagogue here is judicial rather than cultic.[199] Ward presents extensive evidence for the custom of judicial matters being considered in Palestinian synagogues, and a depth of rabbinic material which seems to be making the

---

[194] McDonald, *Kerygma and didache*, 62.
[195] E.g. Cargal, *Restoring*; Thuren, "Risky rhetoric".
[196] Davids, *James*, 108.
[197] Salzmann, *Lehren und Ermahnen*, 207.
[198] Ward, "Partiality", 87.
[199] So, following Ward, Davids, *James*, 107–108; Maynard-Reid, *Poverty and wealth*, 54–58; Martin, *James*, 61.

same point that James makes, particularly alluding to the questions of sitting and standing.[200]

Although the disparity in dates between *James* and the rabbinic evidence means that the parallels are not absolutely convincing, it is possible that the same fund of conventional wisdom is being employed by James as by the rabbis, as there is clearly a wealth of rabbinic reflection on the question of equal justice. The synagogue described is the synagogue of the addressees, but it is difficult to imagine legal matters being considered in a Christian gathering; although Davids points to the "church court" of *I Corinthians* 6:1–11,[201] and Martin to *Matthew* 18:15–20,[202] as examples of church courts these are courts which are dealing with matters purely within the church, and do not consider the structures of the society outside, as the example given by James would seem to indicate. If the gathering is legal rather than cultic then we may deduce that, rather than discussing the situation of his own church directly, James is adopting the same previously cast piece of paraenesis which is referred to in the rabbinic parallels which are quoted by those arguing for a judicial setting here. If it is the case that James has taken a piece of pre-existing paraenetic wisdom and is simply repeating it, then, although the original situation envisaged was legal, James, in re-addressing it to his own assembly, might be imagining a cultic gathering. One of the reasons which led to the suggestion of a legal setting is the difficulty of imagining strangers entering a Christian gathering seeking economic justice. This led Dibelius to suggest that the situation was entirely unreal,[203] which led Ward in turn to counter that if the setting is unreal then the paraenesis contained would not therefore be convincing. But Ward is at a loss to explain how it is that a wealthy Christian of James' community might be engaged in

---

[200] *Aboth de R Nathan* 10.1.2 concerns the questions which arise when a rich and a poor litigant appear together. R Meir interprets *Deuteronomy* 12:17 to mean that one should not stand whilst the other sits. R Judah would allow both to sit, but reckons it forbidden that one should sit whilst the other stood. (The source is R Judah b El'ai at *Sifre Leviticus* on 19:5). Note also BT *Shebuoth* 30b cited by Maynard-Reid, *Poverty and Wealth*, 57: "Rab son of R Sherabya had a case before R Papa. He told him to sit, and told his opponent also to sit; but the attendant of the court came and nudged the illiterate man and made him stand up."

[201] Davids, *James*, 107.

[202] Martin, *James*, 61.

[203] Dibelius, *James*, 129.

legal actions within the ecclesial setting and finding preferential treatment. That this might be a traditional *topos* transferred would be a
solution to this problem. The example is unreal, but is convincing
because it has a traditional basis. The repetition of what would
become rabbinic tradition is thus itself an indication of the synagogal setting of *James*, and that fact that James can envisage a cultic
gathering termed a συναγωγή, which would be implied by the manner in which he does not recast the paraenesis, indicates his understanding of Christian gatherings. Thus, although James elsewhere
refers to his own assembly as an *ekklesia* (5:14) the reference to the
synagogue, and the possibility that a piece of conventional Palestinian
wisdom is being repeated, point to a synagogal and Palestinian life-
setting for the materials employed in the construction of the letter.

Apart from this reference to a synagogue there is other evidence
of a primitive and Palestinian origin to the epistle. This is suggested
by Davids on the grounds that the wealthy are those of agrarian
wealth.[204] Whereas, as he admits, there are many other places in the
Empire where there is agrarian wealth, the setting fits Palestine very
well. One may note in support of this characterization that the
wealthy are not absent from the audience envisaged by the writer,
and so the landlords are not absentees as in so much of Asia.
Moreover there is no paraenesis addressed to slaves or slave-own-
ers.[205] Those who work the land are therefore rural poor.[206] This
does not fit the situation in Italy where the *latifundia* were worked
by slaves. As the reference to the synagogue would imply, the situation envisaged is one within Judaism, where the religious situation
prevented extensive slave ownership, and Palestine would be the
obvious setting of this Judaism, for here there is agrarian wealth concentrated in a few hands but no slavery. This may be given yet further support by the climatic conditions which are presupposed by
the letter, which would point particularly to a Palestinian agricul-
tural setting.[207]

There is thus ample evidence for a primitive Palestinian origin to
James, which would indicate that this community is synagogal in
organisation. Beyond this we may note that whereas James' *ekklesia*

---

[204] Davids, *James*, 30–33; also Martin, *James*, 174–175.
[205] Wessel, *Enquiry*, 209.
[206] Wessel, *Enquiry*, 212.
[207] So Robinson, *Redating*, 120.

may have a cultic function its fundamental orientation is scholastic. The officers of the assembly are known as teachers, and so we may envisage that the gathering of his community places the highest value on teaching and instruction. The assembly envisaged by James is thus synagogal not only through its derivation from Judaism but in that it is scholastic in orientation. It is possible, on the basis of the Palestinian background that has been proposed, that James' *ekklesia* is a synagogue not because it has developed into one in the way we suggested that the Pauline churches reformed themselves on a synagogal model, but either because it has not yet fully distinguished itself from its Jewish origin, or because it has grown out of an original Jewish foundation from which it is now religiously distinct but to which it is socially and, through its emphasis on teaching, functionally identical.

Although it is possible that James' communities did not undergo the process of synagogalization observed in the Pauline communities, a process akin to synagogalization is offered by Martin as a suggestion which explains the process by which the canonical epistle was constructed. According to Martin *James* is the product of a two-stage process of editing: the original material of James (the just) was carried out of Palestine and put into a form by which an apparently apostolic letter might be the means of legitimating the authority of certain teachers among those who looked back to a more "charismatic" form of church organisation.[208] This explains the emphasis which the letter places on the role of the teacher in the community. In this way Martin suggests that it is possible to account both for the depth of traditional Palestinian material as well as the proper objections which have been raised to Jacobean authorship such as the exalted Hellenistic style of the letter, the difficulty of squaring the view of the law contained in the letter with what is known of the attitudes of the historical James, and the problems caused by what would appear to be a polemic against a later Paulinism.[209] Martin suggests that a similar setting is known from the *Didache* and the first Gospel, and on the basis of a possible link between these documents and Antioch suggests that Antioch is likewise the place of *James'* synagogalization. This is perhaps being over-precise

---

[208] Martin, *James*, lxxvi.
[209] Martin, *James*, lxix–lxxiii.

as the links between *Matthew*, the *Didache*, and Antioch are not certain, and may be equally attributed to a common use of traditional material. However, Martin's suggestion has the merit not only of explaining the synagogal organization of *James*, but also much of its content.

The amount of traditional material is overwhelming, and insofar as the role of the teacher is addressed the attention paid to this role is relatively insignificant compared to the amount of material concerning social tensions within the community caused by wealth and poverty. But the traditional material may well be brought to bear on a situation as envisaged by Martin because it is also of relevance to the dispute concerning organisation within the community. Those in the community who are wandering from the truth are a primary focus of the epistle in the light of the final injunction and in the light of the characterization of its recipients as a diaspora.[210] Those who are wandering are also apparently well-off members of a merchant class. The use of traditional material legitimates the teachers as those with access to the tradition, whilst its content is particularly suitable as a weapon against the wealthy. If Corinth is in any way typical of the ancient church then the wealthy might well be concerned to uphold a "charismatic" element of organisation in the church.[211] In the absence of a hierarchy the social structures of the surrounding society will serve, and a primary qualification of leadership would thus be personal wealth and the status of a householder rather than any objective criterion of learning claimed by a teacher.

Thus the social organisation of James' church may properly be described as synagogal, whether because it is an organisation that has grown out of the synagogue, and is in contact with Jewish synagogal organisation, as would be indicated by the traditional material indicating a Palestinian life-setting, or because it is a community that is undergoing synagogalization, either at Antioch or elsewhere. Beyond the scholastic functions of the synagogue we can only speculate whether there was cross-fertilization between the two aspects of midrash and knesset, but we may assume that the assembly gathers primarily for instruction.

The synagogue is the social setting in which we may envisage the instruction given in *James* originating, but this does not necessarily

---

[210] This aspect of *James* is brought out by Cargal, *Restoring the Diaspora*, 45–51.

[211] See Chow, *Patronage*, 184–185, for the possible connection between high social status and the use of charismatic legitimation.

mean that the canonical epistle is in either form or content homiletic. Were we to see *James* as a synagogue homily one might look first to see whether there is any typically synagogal treatment of Scripture.

Gertner perceives a homiletic exposition of *Psalm* 12 lying behind *James*, whilst admitting that it has been "de-midrashized" in its current epistolary context.[212] There is no doubt that themes touched on in the psalm are also the principal themes of *James*, namely double-mindedness, the boastful tongue, faith and its outcome, and the necessity of care for the poor and needy. Gertner is however less successful in demonstrating a consistent application to the words of the psalm. The letter touches on all these themes, but not in the order which Gertner seeks to discern; insofar as the psalm represents common religious and moral concerns of early Judaism we may suggest that *James* does the same, and that although it is conceivable that James had the psalm in mind in much the same way that, following Schutter, we suggested that the author of *I Peter* had an eye on *Leviticus* 19, and although similar hermeneutic patterns may be observed (אמונה, which is taken in the psalm to refer to relationships between people, is taken in *James* to refer to faith in God)[213] the problem is one of the subtlety of the allusions, which suit a literary work rather than a real homily. Gertner suggested that a homily provided the *Vorlage* of *James*, and that the process of editing is what gives *James* its current shape. If this is so the editing process has been so radical that it is the letter, rather than any homiletic *Vorlage*, which lends shape to the current treatment of Scripture. In this event it is better to see *James* as a literary work from the beginning, and observe that Scripture functions within the epistle but not in the way that it would function in a homily. However, although Gertner's attempt is ultimately unsuccessful, this does not mean that there is no basis to the suggestion that *James* represents redacted fragments of homilies; it may be that the need of ethical exhortation within James' community outweighed the need for a "rabbinic" fidelity to the Scriptures. It is this same need for exhortation which leads to the employment of Scripture as a source of *exempla*, such as those of Abraham and Rahab,[214] in the same way that the warning to the people given at M *Ta'anith* 2.1 employs the example of Jonah.

---

[212] Gertner, "Midrashim", 284–291.
[213] So Gertner, "Midrashim", 285.
[214] *James* 2:21–25.

Despite this significant difference between *James* and the synagogue homily as described originally by Bacher, there have been numerous attempts to see *James* in the light of synagogue preaching.[215] We may begin with the work of Wessel, perhaps the first to attempt to link *James* specifically to the synagogue homily. Wessel has been followed more recently by Davids.[216]

In arguing for this position Wessel first takes issue with the characterization of *James* as a diatribe. As long ago as 1916 Ropes claimed that "the epistle is a diatribe",[217] and there are indeed a significant number of diatribal elements. One may note with Ropes the dialogical elements (2:18), the direct address (1:16) rhetorical questions (2:20) and the use of *exempla* (2:21f). Thyen likewise believed that *James* was a diatribe, and it is on that basis that he counted it among his "homilies" and noted stylistic points in common with the other "sermons" which he uncovered.[218] However the equation of diatribe and homily cannot be sustained, as we have already seen, and although these diatribal elements may hint at orality, this does not mean that it is homiletic.[219] Thyen's case is further weakened in that he is indebted to the theory of Meyer that *James* is a lightly Christianized version of a testamentary discourse, the James of the superscription being the patriarch James, and the discourse being addressed to tribes in turn concerning particular appropriate virtues and vices.[220] Although we have already observed the possibility of some relationship between testamentary discourses and the ethical exhortation of the synagogue, the nature of the relationship remains uncertain, and is in any event not pertinent in this case as Meyer's hypothesis has not won much acceptance; the identification of various virtues and vices with Jacob's sons on which his hypothesis depends is often tenuous.

Wessel suggested that *James* is not a diatribe because he intended to argue that it was a synagogue homily, and he felt that the dia-

---

[215] Church, *Forschungsgeschichte*, 157–202, cites many examples, few of which add particularly to our understanding. We may take Agourides, "Origin" and Forbes, "Structure" as two typically unenlightening examples.

[216] Wessel, *Enquiry*, 71–112 followed by Davids, *James*, 23.

[217] Ropes, *James*, 17.

[218] Thyen, *Stil*, 14–16.

[219] Interestingly, Davids, "Epistle of James in modern discussion", 3630–3631, on the basis of the diatribal elements to be found in *James*, describes the origin of the contents of the epistle as "oral discourse".

[220] Meyer, *Rätsel*.

tribe, being a typically Hellenistic form, necessarily excluded the synagogue homily. *James* is essentially a Jewish work and therefore, Wessel felt, would not employ a Hellenistic form.[221] This exclusive view of the relationship between Greek and Jewish literary forms and styles cannot now be sustained. Diatribe and synagogue homily are not opposites; indeed, given the scholastic origin of the diatribe a diatribal style fits in well with the synagogal setting. The style had crossed over from the Graeco-Roman school to its Jewish equivalent since, despite the differences which inevitably derived from their differing religious bases, the synagogue and school had equivalent social functions. James, in using scriptural *exempla* and diatribal style, shows how the marriage of rhetoric and scripture found in the Jewish synagogue crosses over into the synagogal gatherings of the Christians.[222] There is diatribal style in *James*, but this is entirely appropriate in the light of James' exaltation of the teaching office, and his own implicit acceptance of this role.[223]

Having suggested that attempts to classify *James* as a diatribe are unfounded, Wessel argues that *James* is a homily on the grounds that it has in common a number of stylistic traits with synagogue homilies.[224] His main evidence for this is derived from the work of Marmorstein discussed above.[225] There is no doubt that *James* and the synagogue homily hold in common a number of stylistic traits, but these are likewise stylistic traits of the diatribe, namely the imaginary objector, harsh speech and the use of such stylistic techniques as alliteration. The appearance of these traits in Jewish homilies of the Tannaitic period is simply an indication that diatribal style had crossed the linguistic divide, and therefore cannot be used to suggest that *James* is not a diatribe but a synagogue homily. Other indications of Jewish homiletic style adduced by Wessel, such as the address to the audience as ἀδελφοί and the eschatological conclusion, are not necessary indications that the context is homiletic. They may be found in homilies, but preaching is not their exclusive domain. Wills' form of the *logos parakleseôs* is likewise to be found in *James*, but once again we note that this does not mean that we can say

---

[221] Wessel, *Enquiry*, 72–75.
[222] So Wifstrand, "Stylistic Problems".
[223] So Church, *Forschungsgeschichte*, 66.
[224] Wessel, *Enquiry*, 78–91.
[225] Marmorstein, "Background".

with certainty that *James* is a homily, or even formed out of homilies.

Despite the problems with Wessel's hypothesis, it largely adopted by Davids, who, on the basis of Wessel's work, argues that *James* is a complete literary work but that it has been formed out of homilies.[226] But arguing that *James* is a literary work formed out of homilies is different from arguing that it is a homily; in seeing the work as formed out of homilies Davids adds nothing to the arguments of Wessel. If a two-stage editing of *James* is to be envisaged, as it is by Davids, Martin and Church,[227] then the current rhetorical shape of the document is not pertinent to an exploration of James' preaching, since the literary shape would betray the hand of the editor rather than the voice of the original preacher.

It is possible that as paraenesis it may reflect the style of the preaching that was known in James' Christian synagogue; we may assume that preaching occurred in James' synagogue since the synagogue is a possible social and liturgical setting for preaching. It is also possible that catechesis was likewise given in the context of synagogal gatherings, that this too adopted a paraenetic style, and that this was a function of the teacher. As such however the raw material of *James* would not be homiletic in the usual sense. In the light of James' diatribal style, a style shared by the Jewish preachers of Palestine at a later date, it is more than probable that his preaching would be diatribal in effect, and in view of the scholastic bias of this synagogal setting the adoption of diatribal style would be only reasonable, but it is not possible to go beyond these possibilities. The best that Wessel can do is to quote Stevenson: "Look at it as a collection of little sermonettes, or sermon notes, and you feel at once that you are sitting in the synagogue, and hearing the very tones in which the dear old saint addressed his readers . . ."[228] Whereas it is possible that James is indeed repeating points made previously, in particular doing so with his picture of the rich and poor in the synagogue, this does not mean that he is recycling homilies.

A final attempt to locate *James* in the homiletic tradition of the synagogue which we should examine is that of Wifstrand based on his study of the nature of James' language.[229] He describes it well

---

[226] Davids, *James* 12–13, 23.
[227] Church, *Forschungsgeschichte*, 202.
[228] Stevenson, "St. James' Sermon Notes" quoted by Wessel, *Enquiry*, 78.
[229] Wifstrand, "Stylistic Problems".

as the "edifying language of the Hellenized synagogue". He argues that it differs from the diatribe as represented by Epictetus in that there is more use of abstract nouns, more frequent use of imperatives and more extensive short metaphors; this he suggests comes directly from the synagogue. Although he has no direct evidence for this there is a prima facie probability that this is the source of the diction of the paraenetic writers of the New Testament. Certainly a comparable style is to be found in the moral writings of the Septuagint such as *Wisdom*, and in *Testamenta xii patriarchum*, but our examination of these documents has failed to show with certainty that they are actually homiletic.

Thus whereas it may be attractive to see *James* as a document formed out of homilies and reflecting the preaching of his synagogue it is purely speculative. Paraenesis may have a variety of settings, cultic and educative, quite apart from the homily. Organised catechesis of those preparing for baptism is a possible setting,[230] as is more advanced teaching of groups and individual exhortation. Although all of these are possible settings, we cannot say which of these activities took place in James' synagogue. The author considers himself a teacher, which may mean that he is also a preacher, but preaching probably does not exhaust his activities since one might expect a teacher to be engaged in catechesis. Perdue's study of the social settings of paraenesis may however help, for whereas liminality, which is one of the social settings he describes, may describe the situation of catechumens,[231] he also suggests that paraenesis may contribute to community formation through socialization or through the legitimation of authority structures. Perdue does not make any concrete suggestion concerning the original setting of *James* in the light of his study, though he suggests that the context might be that of the separation of James (by death or distance) from his disciples.[232] Whereas these are both possible, they are not entailed by *James'* paraenetic character; however if Martin's suggestion concerning the

---

[230] So Popkes, *Adressaten, Situation und Form*, 126–146; Popkes reaches his conclusion on the basis of the manner in which *James* appears to be an address and on the basis of its paraenetic content and sumbouleutic character.

[231] Camp, "Paraenesis: a feminist response", 244, suggests that Perdue's concentration on liminality may lead one into the expectation that all paraenesis took place in the context of rites of passage, which is improbable. However, a passage (quite apart from its rite) may be an extended process.

[232] Perdue, "Paraenesis and James", 250–251.

social formation of James' community is accepted then *James* may
be seen as a primarily paraenetic document concerned to legitimate
the new leadership. We have seen that preaching is primarily epideictic, whilst containing paraenetic elements. *James* however is primarily paraenetic, and therefore is probably not a sermon. Elements
may have been lifted from pre-existent sermons but seeing the provenance of the traditional material as sermons is speculative only; the
document as it stands is not a sermon but a paraenetic discourse.
The elements out of which it is formed may indicate orality, and as
oral material may be catechetical, or may be homiletic.

Thus although it is possible that Stevenson's instincts are sound,
and that *James* indeed does reflect homilies given in the synagogue,
there can be no certainty in this respect because the preaching is at
one remove. All we can say is that the function of *James* is paraenetic, and whereas paraenesis may be homiletic or prophetic these
are not the only contexts in which paraenesis may be found. We
have already noted that ethical guidance might be found in a variety of contexts in the Graeco-Roman world, and the same is true
of the church. The paraenetic preaching put into the mouth of the
Baptist may more probably be homiletic since it is described as *paraklēsis*, and in that the Baptist is a prophet. But although closer to
demonstration than any supposition about the origin of *James*, even
this is far from certain. For although the Baptist's proclamation is
prophetic, and although it is described as *paraklēsis*, it lacks any reference to Scripture. As such it may reflect the practice of an earlier generation than that of Luke, since as paraenetic guidance given
in a series of pronouncements it is similar in form to that noted
in the Thessalonian correspondence. But is unlikely to be reflective
of the preaching of the Christian synagogue at the time of Luke
since the Emmaeus pericopē's concentration on Scripture might lead
us to anticipate some scriptural content.

2.2.2.2. Hebrews *as a λόγος παρακλήσεως*

We have thus gained an impression of the way in which preaching
might occur in the early Christian synagogue, namely that it is a
reflection on the life of the community in the light of Scripture, and
a reflection on Scripture in the light of the community's experience,
but have failed to discover any example of homiletic communication within these communities. There is another New Testament document deriving from a social setting which may be broadly described

as synagogal and which is frequently understood to be a homily on similar grounds to those adduced for *James*, namely *Hebrews*. We intend to suggest that here there are good grounds for reading this document in the light of preaching within the Christian synagogue, and that this reading confirms the suspicions which have already been reached concerning the nature of preaching in these communities.

In 1964 Grässer can speak of a consensus that *Hebrews* is a homily.[233] In doing so he has particular reference to the work of Thyen, who takes *Hebrews* as another example of a Hellenistic synagogue homily. Although he was not the first to do so, his work is nonetheless the starting point for most recent treatments of *Hebrews*. Thyen's reason for seeing *Hebrews* as a homily is essentially that 13:22ff, the epistolary conclusion, is a post-script to the original homily; for him this is an indication that what has gone before is not a letter. He then finds evidence for a homiletic origin in the personal manner of the address of the writer, in particular in the shifts from "I" to "we" to "you".[234] Throughout his work he subsequently has reference to the similarities between *Hebrews* and his other "homilies", such as the use of Scripture for *exempla*, the use of inferential particles, and stylistic phenomena held in common with the diatribe. Finally he notes that the concluding doxology at 13:21 reflects the synagogue liturgy.[235] Swetman likewise largely follows Thyen, differing from him only in warning against "too facile a separation of *Hebrews* from the 'Palestinian' tradition of Jewish homily in favour of the 'Hellenistic' tradition."[236]

Despite the obvious circularity of Thyen's procedure and the severe doubt which must be placed on the assumption that there is any equation between the diatribe and the homily, this consensus remains in place. Most recently both Attridge and Lane fundamentally follow Thyen. Whereas Attridge is largely content to follow Thyen[237] Lane adds some interesting additional points.[238] In particular he points to indications of oral delivery within the text, such as

---

[233] Grässer, "Der Hebräerbrief, 1938–1963", 160.
[234] Thyen, *Stil*, 17–18.
[235] Thyen, *Stil*, 68. In this he is mistaken, since a benediction may likewise close an epistle.
[236] Swetman, "Literary genre", 267.
[237] Attridge, *Hebrews*, 14.
[238] Lane, *Hebrews*, lxxi–lxxv; also at "Sermon in search of a setting", 14.

... the world to come, about which we are speaking (2:5)

and

Even though we speak like this dear friends (6:9)

Whilst also allying himself to the formal and stylistic investigations of Thyen and Wills, Lane thus sees the indications of orality as the primary indications of homiletic form. In the context of noting orality he is able to note the range of rhetorical devices displayed in the document. McDonald similarly, in concluding that *Hebrews* is a homily, points out that the writer thinks of himself as a speaker, and his hearers as listeners.[239] It is interesting that orality, rather than strictly form-critical observations, should become the fundamental argument by which Lane accords to *Hebrews* the status of a homily. But we have already seen that this is a difficult concept, because the distinction between orality and textuality in the ancient world is a difficult one in that all literature, quite apart from genres which today would have a primary tendency to be orally delivered, was essentially oral in its conception because of its intention to be delivered by the spoken voice. So for instance the alliteration which for Lane is a clear mark of oral delivery may be paralleled from non-oral sources in the ancient world. Because the distinction between oral and literary delivery is not clear in the ancient world, indications of orality in a text cannot be held to be sufficient for a classification of that text as a homily, or any other public oral event.

Lane also takes note of Wills' uncovering of a common homiletic pattern and sees the presence of this pattern in *Hebrews* as supportive of his argument,[240] suggesting that this is an example of an interrelationship between exposition and exhortation which is particularly suited to oral delivery. Certainly it is true that the interrelationship between exposition and exhortation is suited to oral delivery and is the kind of thing which might be expected in a homily, but once again we should firstly recall that no evidence has been found according to which documents demonstrating Wills' pattern may be classified as homiletic and secondly may suggest that a pattern of argumentation suitable for oral delivery should not surprise us in a culture

---

[239] McDonald, *Kerygma and didache*, 172 n153.
[240] Lane, *Hebrews*, lxxiii–lxxv, with reference to Wills, "Form of the sermon".

which was primarily oral. *Hebrews* figures large in Wills' attempt to perceive a common homiletic pattern in early Christian literature, but there is an initial assumption in his discernment of the pattern that *Hebrews* is a homily which makes any attempt to use his arguments in support of seeing *Hebrews* as homiletic as necessarily circular. McDonald similarly attempts on formal grounds to test his hypothesis that *Hebrews* is a homily, and sees this in terms of his suggestion that a homily took the form of the exposition of a theme statement, or a series of theme statements.[241] But once again we may recall our argument above that there is nothing necessarily or specifically homiletic about this procedure.

There have been other attempts at perceiving a homily behind *Hebrews*. Buchanan sees *Hebrews* as a "homiletical midrash" on *Psalm* 110.[242] Apart from missing the fact that there is much in *Hebrews* apart from the exegesis of the psalm, there is nothing like a complete running commentary in *Hebrews*, nor is there anything resembling the exegetical methods which we meet in the later homiletic midrashim. Nor for that matter does Buchanan seek to locate any. The comment of Hughes may be aptly quoted here: "The thesis is assumed rather than argued. Nowhere is any explanation offered of the fact that no elements of Psalm 110 other than verses 1 and 4 . . . are ever alluded to by the writer."[243] More convincing is the effort of Hill who, whilst noting the stylistic arguments, employs arguments which are largely functional. *Hebrews*, he notes, is concerned with the upbuilding of a Christian community, which is likewise a function of prophetic preaching, and does so moreover on the basis of scriptural exegesis.[244] We shall examine these arguments below, and find that whereas they are not finally convincing there is something in Hill's assertions.

These attempts all fundamentally stem from the self-designation of *Hebrews* as a λόγος παρακλήσεως. The normal understanding which stems from this is well summed up by März who recognising the paraenetic content of *Hebrews* and noting its self-designation describes the work as a "gesandte Predigt."[245] An almost identical term is

---

[241] *Kerygma and didache*, 59–60.
[242] Buchanan, *Hebrews*, xix.
[243] Hughes, *Hebrews and hermeneutics*, 144 n11.
[244] Hill, *New Testament prophecy*, 142–144.
[245] März, *Hebräerbrief*, 11–14.

independently employed by Grässer who calls *Hebrews* a "zugesandte Predigt".[246]

There is no doubt that in its self-description as a λόγος παρακλήσεως *Hebrews* intends to reflect the language of a preacher and thus refers to itself as a homily. It has already been argued that λόγος παρακλήσεως is a term referring to preaching,[247] and it may be that in this light the author was even more conscious of the result of oral delivery than any other ancient writer. But this does not necessarily mean that it is a homily which has been stenographically recorded and subsequently sent on. It is equally likely that it is a written communication intentionally reflecting a homily; we may note that the purpose of an ancient letter was as a substitute for the personal presence of the writer and so, rather as has been suggested for *James*, it is possible that a homiletic-type text has been produced in order to answer a series of issues in a community from which the writer was removed. Even were *Hebrews* to conform to an agreed form-critical set of definitions of a homily, internal literary criteria alone would not be able to answer the question. For instance Lane notes the degree of uncertainty about whether *Hebrews* may be classified as deliberative or epideictic.[248] On the one hand *Hebrews* is attempting to inculcate a set of attitudes, the basis on which Attridge sees *Hebrews* as "clearly" epideictic, and yet there is also an eye to the future action of the hearers (4:14–16, e.g., contains two hortatory subjunctives), which leads Attridge to suggest that *Hebrews* may have something in common with protreptic.[249] As we have seen, the two categories may coalesce, and so this in itself cannot determine the answer to this question. However Lindars, on the basis that deliberative rhetoric is intended to advise and dissuade, sees *Hebrews* as deliberative because he can perceive a definite situation to which the letter was addressed, and suggests that because *Hebrews* is addressing itself to a real situation it must therefore be a letter.[250] Attridge,

---

[246] Grässer, *An die Hebräer*, 15.

[247] Cf. Cothenet, "Les prophètes chrétiens comme exégètes charismatiques", 80: "L'épitre aux Hébreux . . . est qualifiée par son auteur de λόγος τῆς παρακλήσεως. Traduire sermon . . . c'est affaiblir la portée du texte. 'Parole d'exhortation' est déjà mieux. Il faudrait paraphraser: 'Faites bon accueil à ces paroles d'exhortation basées sur les écritures', en se souvenant du Rom. 15:4" It is hard to see what a word of exhortation based on the scriptures might be if it is not a sermon.

[248] Lane, *Hebrews*, lxxix.

[249] Attridge, "Paraenesis in a homily", 212.

[250] Lindars, "Rhetorical structure".

whilst admitting that it was "probably sent from a distance", nonetheless argues from its structure and techniques, and in particular from the manner in which exhortation is linked to scriptural exegesis, that it is a homily,[251] and that its primary characterization is epideictic, whilst admitting sumbouleutic elements.[252]

The obvious argument against Lindars' characterization of *Hebrews* as a letter, and the basis for the whole "literary riddle", is the absence of an epistolary opening.[253] However, Lindars argues that the opening functions rhetorically to prepare the listener for the weighty and lengthy discourse that is to come.[254] Cosby similarly suggests that the paronomasia of the opening sets the scene for the discourse that is to follow.[255] As such an epistolary opening might therefore be redundant. We should moreover note that the letter was read in the assembly, and that the context of the first reading might therefore also make an epistolary opening redundant. It is even possible that there was an original covering letter which was not transmitted with the larger letter.[256] As it stands the opening is a strange one. According to Attridge the opening verses form "an exordium which encapsulates *Hebrews'* major themes". As such it is as much a *propositio* as an exordium but as Attridge notes, the wealth of rhetorical embellishment in these verses provide a fitting opening to the document.[257] Insofar as the key themes of the completeness of the work of Christ and the faithfulness of his people are gathered together here the verses function as an introduction which in the setting of the assembly and in the historical situation to which *Hebrews* was sent, might speak for itself. The epistolary conclusion, despite the absence of a letter opening, is thus sufficient to anchor the document as properly a letter.

The epistolary conclusion tells us that the letter is sent to those who are in danger of falling away from their initial profession of faith (13:8); in this light they are to remember those who first preached the faith to them and the effect of faith on their lives. This fits in with the exhortations within the letter not to drift away from what

---

[251] "Paraenesis in a homily", 216–7.
[252] Attridge, "Paraenesis in a homily", 214.
[253] Noted particularly by Attridge, "New covenant christology", 89.
[254] Lindars, "Rhetorical structure", 390.
[255] Cosby, *Rhetorical composition*, 4.
[256] Suggested by Ellingworth, *Hebrews*, 62.
[257] Attridge, "New Covenant Christology", 92.

they have heard nor to neglect the message of salvation (2:1–3) not
to lose hold on faith (4:14), not to be unproductive but to continue
in good works (6:7–12). Beyond this anything which is to be said
must be deduced from the content of the letter. The answer is in
essence that the work of Christ is all-sufficient and that faithfulness
such as that shown by the ancestors is the proper response to this,
but this answer could be posed to a number of questions. The question proposed by Lindars, that the problem of post-baptismal sin is
disquieting some who are seeking recourse in the Jewish sacrificial
system, is perhaps better than that of Grässer, who sees the situation as an existential crisis caused by the failure of the parousia with
the resultant falling off of expectation,[258] because it at least bears
some connection with the text,[259] but it does assume that the sacrificial
system of the Temple is still in place when the letter was written.[260]
Whereas this is not impossible, there is no external evidence to support the assertion.

But it is not necessary to follow Lindars in his reconstruction of
the situation of the readers to agree that the situation to which the
letter is addressed is a real one, and that as such *Hebrews* is primarily to be understood as a letter. However, the conclusion that as it
stands *Hebrews* is not a homily does not follow as necessarily as might
at first appear to be the case. We have already noted that the situation of the community might be the starting point for homiletic
communication based on an exploration of the Scriptures; this is
what *Hebrews* does. It meets needs in the life of the community and
explores the situation of the addressees with reference to Scripture.
Thus insofar as it performs some homiletic functions, albeit at a
remove, and describes itself using homiletic language, it may be
described in terms similar to those of Grässer, though slightly more
nuanced, as an "epistolary homily", a letter which performs a homiletic function and which reflects preaching practice in part at least
of the church.

Specifically this part of the church may be said to be the Christian
communities which had grown out of the Hellenized synagogues of
the diaspora; this is argued by Lindars on the basis of his recon-

[258] Grässer, *Glaube im Hebräerbrief*, 200–203.
[259] Hughes, *Hebrews and hermeneutics*, 137–142, suggests that Grässer's arguments
are loose, and largely circular.
[260] Lindars, "Rhetorical structure", 403.

struction of the situation of the readers but need not depend on this. As Ellingworth puts it: "In *Hebrews* the evidence is overwhelming that the author expected his readers to be thoroughly acquainted with Old Testament persons, institutions and texts . . . Moreover the argument of *Hebrews* is marked at many places by typical if not uniquely rabbinic procedures".[261] Whereas this need not mean that the community was exclusively Jewish in origin it does indicate a synagogal basis to the intellectual life of the community. Thus although the writer of *Hebrews* is clearly rhetorically trained in the Greek language, employs diatribal elements in his discourse and is perhaps theologically influenced by the *koinē* of Hellenistic culture,[262] it is the extent of the scriptural grounding of this author which allows us to see him growing out of a synagogal setting. In this light we may understand the reference to Christian meetings by the author of *Hebrews* as ἐπισυναγογαί as specifically synagogal in the sense of a gathering for the study of Jewish Scripture based on a Jewish model which had been inherited.[263] We may also see the plural terms used for the leaders of the community as indicating something like a synagogue council.[264] Insofar as it has reference both to Scripture and to the life of the community it may be described as homiletic, and be seen as relating to synagogal scriptural study; indeed Vanhoye may be correct in speculating that it was read after the liturgy of the word in the Christian assembly.[265] There is however no specific Scripture to which it can be said to relate, which may tend to diminish its value as typifying a sermon in this context.

Though not a typical sermon because of its epistolary character, because (perhaps as a result of its epistolary character) it relates to a series of scriptural texts chosen for a theological purpose rather than to any one particular scriptural text, and because of its sumbouleutic function (which again comes about because it is a letter

---

[261] Ellingworth, *Hebrews*, 23.

[262] So Windisch, *Hebräerbrief*, 119–122, who sets the redactor in a context of educated Hellenistic Judaism.

[263] Ellingworth, *Hebrews*, 26, suggests that not too much should be read into this reference and sees the gathering which *Hebrews* addresses as something more like a Corinthian house-church. Lane, "Sermon in search of a setting", 16, similarly assumes a household setting for *Hebrews*. Whereas the setting of the synagogue is probably domestic, it is not however an unqualified household.

[264] Cf. *I Clement* 1.3, 21.6.

[265] Vanhoye, *Structure and message*, 45. Vanhoye describes it as a "priestly sermon".

addressed to a particular situation), *Hebrews* may nonetheless provide some evidence for preaching in Jewish-Christian communities modelled on the synagogue.[266] In particular this reflection is to be sought in the interplay of exposition and exhortation, since we have seen that exposition of Scripture is central to the synagogue homily and that exhortation was one of the functions of preaching in the church, though here we should be clear that the two are not of necessity always joined in a homily.[267] Whereas the exhortatory aspect of *Hebrews* was sufficient to allow Thyen to classify it as a homily[268] we may respond that exhortation was not uniquely a homiletic exercise any more than was scriptural exposition, but it is the interplay of these addresses with the expository aspects of the work which are more probably homiletic.

We may take as an example the expository section concerning the Son of God contrasted with the angels (*Hebrews* 1:5–2:18)[269] with its accompanying exhortations. The passage is based on a *hariza* starting with the citation of *Psalm* 2 at 1:5 and bounded with an *inclusio* with a citation of *Psalm* 110 at 1:13.[270] However this essentially academic procedure is then interrupted at 2:1 with a warning to the listeners not to reject the word of God, on the basis, as Guthrie notes, of an a fortiori argument that if rejection of the word declared by angels deserved punishment then rejection of that spoken by the Son of God merits even greater punishment.[271] But although the exhortation differs from the exposition it depends on it not simply for its content but also for its rhetorical effect, due to the extent of semantic borrowing between the two sub-units.[272] As soon as this brief exhortation is complete the author goes on to a further exposition with a new text, *Psalm* 8:4–6 (cited at 2:6–8) which links with the psalm citation on the other side of the exhortation through the

---

[266] Which is not the claim of Attridge, "New covenant christology", that it is "the best example we possess of an early Christian homily." Similarly Thyen, *Stil*, 106 reckons it unique as a completely preserved first-century homily.

[267] Which would be to be misled as are Wills, "Form of the sermon", and those who follow him.

[268] Thyen, *Stil*, 85–110, concentrates on the manner in which the speakers in his "homilies" address their audiences directly.

[269] Here the division of *Hebrews* into expository and hortatory units is that suggested by Guthrie, *Structure*, 117.

[270] Guthrie, *Structure*, 77, following Vanhoye, *Structure and message*, 74.

[271] Guthrie, *Structure*, 128.

[272] So Hughes, *Hebrews and hermeneutics*, 7–9.

common concluding words τῶν ποδῶν; this text is then interpreted to explain the incarnation of the Son, with the citation of further texts but building on the basic note of *Psalm* 8 that he became "lower than the angels". This, at verses 17–18 leads to a conclusion that he was like his brethren in temptation, which in turn opens the way to a new unit of exhortation beginning at 3:1, linked by a parae-netic οὖν, which encourages the hearers to remain faithful. But despite the paraenetic οὖν, the connection with the foregoing is relatively loose, as here a new *exemplum*, that of Moses, is introduced. Exhortation relates to exposition to rhetorical effect, but it actually slightly more complex in its relationship than the isolation of Wills' "common homiletic pattern" would lead us to expect; the expositions are com-plex, being built of *hariza* rather than seriatim exposition and the relating exhortations are more than simply the selection of some aspect of the text as exemplary. But because of the complexity of the semantic borrowing the effect is more telling. This then goes to support the conclusions reached earlier, that although the pattern that Wills uncovers is not of itself the form of a homily, and is inad-equate as the defining form of a homily, it may be nonetheless be a pattern of persuasion or of attitudinal reinforcement, which was available to preachers, and which could be used in the construction of a sermon.

Thus although we are forced to conclude that *Hebrews* is not a homily as such because it is sent from a distance, on the basis of its self-designation as a λόγος παρακλήσεως and on the basis of the manner in which there is an internal interrelationship of exposition and exhortation we may suggest that it nonetheless provides a reflection of homiletic practice in the particular synagogal Christian commu-nity from which it is sent, and conceivably that it reflects a similar practice in the receiving community, whose specific situation is being addressed through an extended reflection on Scripture, and who are being exhorted on the basis of that scriptural judgement. That we do not know where these communities lay geographically is there-fore somewhat frustrating. Apart from its internal contents, *Hebrews* also betrays significant information about preaching in the assembly through its references to worship. Thus the exhortation not to stay away from the assemblies at 10:25 is linked to the mutual encour-agement of the members, an indication that this is a primary func-tion of the assembly and of the fact that the role of encouragement need not be restricted to any one individual. The festive prose of

12:22–24 is likewise not only a reflection of the festive prose which might be part of a homily in this community but moreover refers to a πανήγυρις as part of the festive gathering.

As part of its reflection of preaching it is possible that previously existing homiletic material has been incorporated into the epistle as it stands, as McDonald suggests.[273] Although he sees that the letter has a definite structure, he reckons that this does not preclude the incorporation of other homiletic material. An example of this may be provided by *Hebrews* 11, which stands out as a unit in itself.[274] This is partly undermined by Cosby's study of the unit which shows that the rhetorical function of similar example lists in antiquity is in the literature of persuasion;[275] thus according to Cosby the chapter is "designed to instill bravery".[276] So he observes the asyndetic list from 32–40, a rhetorical technique which, he argues, follows the advice of Quintilian on the effect desired when special vigour in speaking is required, which then turns in verse 40 to the language of exhortation. His own recognition of the persuasive nature of this chapter rather goes to undermine his continual reference to *Hebrews* as a sermon[277] intended to "inspire a tenacious faith in these faltering believers".[278] More importantly he is able to see that this chapter contributes to the overall purpose of *Hebrews* through the use of historical exemplars who showed the faithfulness which is now required of the recipients of the letter. This very conformity to the overall purpose of *Hebrews* makes it in turn less likely that pre-existent homiletic material has been taken over here.

A further question raised by the conclusion that *Hebrews* may reflect the practice of preaching is whether it is intended to reflect a single homily, or whether the reflection extends only to technique and manner, rather than to length and complexity of content. Wills notes that his pattern recurs in a series of cycles; the question is one of the nature of that recurrence. Wills stops short of stating that *Hebrews* is an actual homily; rather he suggests that it is a redactional com-

---

[273] McDonald, *Kerygma and didache*, 172.
[274] As such it is treated by Schille, "Katechese und Taufliturgie", who fantasises concerning its use in catechesis, and suggests that it is a Jewish creed for use by proselyte baptisms taken over for Christian use.
[275] Cosby, *Rhetorical composition*, 49.
[276] Cosby, *Rhetorical composition*, 65.
[277] Notably at *Rhetorical composition*, 85–86.
[278] Cosby, *Rhetorical composition*, 4.

position, a "complex sermonic text".[279] However, since the whole
was designed for public reading, even in its complexity and length
it may reflect the homily. Lindars estimates that it would take an
hour to deliver,[280] but this *copia verborum* may well be appropriate in
a culture well used to listening to complex rhetorical productions.[281]
The fact that individual thematic units, such as the eleventh chapter, may be seen in the light of the overall purpose of the epistle
once again makes it probable that insofar as *Hebrews* is reflective of
preaching it reflects a single homily rather than a "homiletic hariza",
that sermons in this community at least were considerably longer
than the bald summaries which we otherwise possess might lead us
to expect, and that Wills' homiletic pattern, insofar as it occurred
in preaching, would be used in the complex manner in which *Hebrews*
uses it. Jewett notes that the letter closes with a "homiletic benediction", and sees this as an indication that *Hebrews* is a homily.[282]
We need not follow him in concluding that *Hebrews* is a homily without qualification if we note that this benediction comes only at the
conclusion of an extensive discourse, and that therefore, insofar as
Hebrews is representative of a homily, it is the entirety of the discourse, marked by its homiletic conclusion, which is supposed to represent the homiletic teaching of its anonymous author.

In conclusion we may state that whereas *Hebrews* is not a sermon
it is something more like a "real" homily than simply a desk homily.
Attridge attempts to deal with it in the context of paraenetic literature and finds that it does not fit these categories;[283] this is because,
despite its fundamentally sumbouleutic aims, it engages in a great
deal of festive prose more suited to an epideictic occasion and, despite
the occasional occurrence of ethical maxims, is not primarily a piece
of paraenetic literature. Because it is not primarily paraenetic it is
therefore closer to a homily than *James*, and thus provides a picture,
albeit an idealised one, of preaching in a particular Jewish Christian
community. It is difficult to describe its social aims without a com-
mitment to a solution of the particular issue which it is confronting,

---

[279] Wills "Form of the sermon", 283.
[280] Lindars, "Rhetorical structure", 385.
[281] Hill, *New Testament prophecy*, 143, considers that an hour is not particularly
long for a homily!
[282] Jewett, "Form and function", 30.
[283] Attridge, "Paraenesis in a homily", passim.

but it is noteworthy that none of the social aims of paraenesis as
described by Perdue, namely protreptic, socialization, legitimation
and conflict, readily fit.[284] Once again this is an indication that *Hebrews*
reflects a homily more closely than other paraenetic literature; whereas
paraenesis may have a place within a homily it is a secondary element
in the primarily epideictic whole. What is more significant is the
manner in which *Hebrews* reads the situation of the community alongside Scripture, and Scripture alongside the situation of the community.

2.2.2.3. *Paraenetic preaching in the Pastoral Epistles?*
Our study of *Hebrews* has served to confirm our earlier conclusions
that, whereas paraenesis might find a place within a homily, it is
not definitory of a homily and that, although homily and paraenesis might cover some common ground, the two forms of communication are by no means coterminous. However, in discussing the
occasion of paraenesis and the possibility that it might find a location in a homily, we may observe with interest the suggestion of
Quinn that the Pastoral Epistles contain paraenesis deriving from
the liturgical events of baptism, ordination and marriage.[285] In these
settings the setting of the paraenesis may be akin to a homily, even
if not a homily of the usual synaxis, yet nonetheless a message delivered in the assembly on a liturgical occasion. Although directed
towards a particular occasion, rather than deriving either from the
inspiration of the Spirit or the reading of Scripture, these paraeneses may be described as homiletic in that they are expressions of the
will of God given in the assembly.

We have already observed that the Pastoral Epistles demonstrate
the process of synagogalization within the Pauline tradition through
the development of the reading of Scripture within worship, and in
that context have also noted the instructions given to "Timothy"
that he is to instruct the congregation and that he is to engage in
the work of *paraklēsis*.[286] Here we may further note that the epistles
demonstrate some traits of synagogalization through the development
of a πρεσβυτέριον instead of the relative lack of organisation which
marked the governance of the Pauline churches. Within this synago-

---

[284] So Attridge, "Paraenesis in a homily", 218–221, with reference to Perdue,
"Social character".
[285] Quinn, "Paraenesis".
[286] 1.1.3.

gal setting Quinn claims a number of texts as deriving from traditional sources, seeing the citation of traditional material as a means by which the pseudonymous writer may claim authority. We may examine three of Quinn's specific claims, namely that *Titus* 3:4–7 is from a didactic baptismal oration,[287] that *I Timothy* 6:11–16 is a citation from a liturgical charge at ordination[288] and that *I Timothy* 2:11–3:1a is a citation from the liturgy of marriage.[289] These are selected because they are the largest blocks of material which he treats.

Titus 3:4–7 is described as a λόγος which is πιστός, given force, according to Quinn, by being enclosed in a before/after schema. The description of this saying as a λόγος indicates the possibility that a preached homily is being cited, and the trinitarian nature of the passage (all three persons are mentioned) indicates that the homilist is paraphrasing some content of the liturgical act of baptism. We have already observed moreover that the church of the Pastoral Epistles was one which was accustomed to the act of paraenesis as well as *paraklēsis* in the assembly; this passage may give some insight into the nature of that preaching.

I Timothy 2:11–15 is likewise described as a πιστὸς λόγος, an indication that a sermon is being quoted. Quinn argues that this is a charge to a wife since here the term γυνή is used in the singular, whereas the more general paraenesis to women in which this unit is set uses the plural term; he suggests that it derives from a marriage liturgy because it describes duties and a situation (namely childbearing) which specifically belong in the marital context. The charge that the wife is to be a submissive learner within the marriage is then legitimated by an *exemplum*, that of Adam and Eve. The unit does not have a concluding exhortation, in the way in which Wills' homiletic pattern might lead us to expect, but this is may be an indication that the paraenesis as it stands within the epistle has been excerpted from a larger unit; it is at present to be found embedded in a general paraenesis, but has been taken out of its liturgical context in order to supply reinforcement for the wider context of the writer's purpose in enforcing order.

These two paraenetic excerpts are, as we have seen, each described as a πιστὸς λόγος, a term which appears five times in the Pastoral

---

[287] Quinn, "Paraenesis", 196.
[288] Quinn, "Paraenesis", 198.
[289] Quinn, "Paraenesis", 199–201.

Epistles. Quinn suggests that it is an idiom which is particularly indebted to the language of prophecy and apocalyptic. He notes that 1Q27 1.5–8, from the "Book of Mysteries", gives an apocalyptic description of the triumph of righteousness which concludes with the statement that "the word will assuredly come to pass and the prediction is certain".[290] He also notes that *Revelation* describes Christ as the faithful witness, and that more specifically he is described as faithful and true (πιστὸς καὶ ἀληθινός) (3:14; 19:11). The words of prophecy which he speaks are described using the same terms (21:5; 22:6),[291] enabling us to see that, in common with the usage at Qumran, this is an authenticating formula which may be used of the words of prophecy. Similarly in *II Corinthians* 2:1–18 the faithfulness of God is seen to authenticate the words of Paul. This πιστὸς λογός is thus being claimed as having a prophetic as well as a paraenetic character, which is in keeping with the character of Paul's prophecy as found in the Thessalonian correspondence. We may add to Quinn's observations on this point that Maccabeus describes the dream of Jeremiah which he had received, and which he employs in the *paraklēsis* of his troops, as ἀξιόπιστος;[292] that is to say, this is a prophetic phenomenon which qualifies for acceptance.

Quinn speculates that, in the context of the Pastoral Epistles, the term designates a collection of liturgical and catechetical texts, but given that the term is used here to describe a παράκλησις which is to be accepted, given that this *paraklēsis* was a prophetic function in the wider church, and given the prophetic context of other uses of the word in early Judaism and early Christianity, it may be that the term here is a direct indication that the words are words given in this context, designating a prophetic utterance. The practice of prophecy had not died out in the church of the Pastoral Epistles, as *I Timothy* 1:18, 4:1 and 4:14 bear out. The words to be believed are prophetic messages which have been tested, which in turn confirms their homiletic provenance.

I Timothy 6:11–16 was first recognised as part of a liturgical ordination charge by Käsemann.[293] It begins with a series of imperatives to pursue ethical qualities, and then the apostle, in the first person,

---

[290] Quinn, *Titus*, 230.
[291] Quinn, *Titus*, 231.
[292] *II Maccabees* 15:11.
[293] Käsemann, "Formular".

urges the man of God to keep unblemished the charge which has been given. The passage concludes with a doxology, which Quinn suggests has derived from Hellenistic synagogal liturgy.[294] This fits with the evidence that we have already noted of the possible role of blessings in preaching. Given the personal tone (note the first person singular in παραγγέλλω) with which "Paul" reminds Timothy of the witness he gave at ordination we can hardly doubt that this passage, with its summary, its personal appeal and its closing benediction is taken from the conclusion of an ordination address. More specifically it may be suggested that this address was prophetic. 4:14 speaks of the gift of God given to Timothy διὰ προφητείας alongside his commissioning by the laying on of hands. Although this appointment by prophecy is to be seen as primarily the choice of Timothy through the voice of a prophet, linked to the laying on of hands as a sign of appointment, one may suggest that as part of the same liturgy there was a prophetic homily which concerned the duties which Timothy was to undertake and exhorted him to be faithful in his duty, and that a fragment of precisely such a charge is now to be found in the sixth chapter. The liturgical elements thus point to the role of prophets not only in exhorting and in decision-making but also in prayer.[295]

Further evidence of prophetic activity is to be found at *I Timothy* 4:1 where a prophecy is cited that:

> In these latter times some people, who dote on seductive spirits and demonic doctrines, will apostasize from the faith.

That this is a prophetic oracle may be seen not only from its content but from the attribution which is made to "the Spirit" without mediation. This oracle is then interpreted in terms of the enemies of the church at the time who deny marriage and teach abstinence from various foods; finally, in the light of "Scripture", the interpretation of the oracle is proved when it is stated that in Scripture God's word may hallow these things. We may thus see that, although

---

[294] Quinn, "Paraenesis" 198.

[295] Dekkers, "ΠΡΟΦΗΤΕΙΑ-PRAEFATIO", suggests from the later Latin usage of the term "praefatio" that the principal reference is to the prayer of consecration said by the prophet. Brox, "προφητεία", however is correct in pointing out that the evidence for this usage is too late to be useful. Nonetheless there is sufficient evidence in the liturgical content of this paraenesis to see prayer joined to prophecy as equal forms of inspired speech.

the Pauline household has developed into a synagogue, the Pauline practice of prophecy continues to be the basis of preaching, and that the preaching may still embrace paraenesis; Scripture however now stands alongside prophecy as a source of authority within the church. The paraeneses are moreover recognized as πιστοὶ λόγοι; although the origin of these λόγοι is prophetic, the possibility of their becoming stereotyped would inevitably arise as a result of being enshrined in the tradition of the community through their recognition as faithful and true. As this happens so the possibility of catechesis separate from the liturgical homily could begin to develop in this community, as clearly it did in others, since the living voice of the prophet in worship was no longer needed to instruct the community, as the recorded words of prophecy could become part of the tradition. The Pastoral Epistles thus show that although prophecy might still be valued in a synagogalizing setting, that very setting would make the continued practice of prophecy unnecessary, and thus lead to its decline.

2.2.2.4. II Clement *a homily?*

Such a process of the routinization of recorded prophecy may perhaps be observed in *II Clement*. This is a further fundamentally paraenetic document, frequently claimed as a homily, whose setting may reasonably be claimed to be synagogal. We intend to argue here that it not a typical homily, but is wedded much more closely to catechesis. It may however be seen as illustrative of the development of communication of the word of God in synagogalized Christian communities.

In supporting the characterization of the church as synagogal, we may note that the church is institutionalized to the extent that it has πρεσβύτεροι;[296] this is an indication that its household was developing in a synagogal direction. We may also note a number of references to Scripture, which indicate that some use of sacred texts had come about within the community, though it will be noted below that their primary function is that of testing a pronouncement according to its conformity with Scripture, rather than being themselves the starting point of preaching. *I Clement* gives a picture of a church governed by a presbyterate, and whereas *II Clement* is less explicit

---

[296] *II Clement* 17.3.

concerning governance it is to be noted that exhortation is particularly the role of the *presbuteros*; if the Pastoral Epistles are in any way representative of institutionalizing Christianity then exhortation was not the preserve of the *presbuteros*, but was a presbyteral function, whereas governance was certainly bound up to office. There is no particular philosophical vocabulary in *II Clement* nor any startling rhetoric, although the author employs the typically diatribal image of the athletic contest at chapter 7. Nonetheless the author's use of Scripture is sufficient for us to observe a degree of scholasticization in this community.

The discussion of the genre of *II Clement* may begin with Lightfoot who argued that "the work is plainly not a letter but a homily, a sermon."[297] Certainly it is not a letter, since it lacks epistolary characteristics altogether,[298] but although Lightfoot's suggestion in time became the consensus,[299] it was this consensus which caused Donfried to ask the searching questions which we observed above concerning the possibility of recognizing a sermon from the earliest centuries.[300] Lightfoot argued that *II Clement* is a homily on the basis of the address at various points to "brothers and sisters", on the basis of the reference at 17 to νουθεσία by the elders, and on the basis that 19 refers to the address as an ἔντευξις which is being read so that the audience might pay attention to the things which have been written (τὰ γεγραμμένα). This last reference he takes as a reference to the Scriptures, the reading of which would have preceded the homily. To illustrate the enduring force of Lightfoot's arguments we may note that Graham follows a similar line of argument.[301] However, for all that Lightfoot argued for his position we must suspect that it is the paraenetic content which led to the supposition that *II Clement* is a homily, through the virtual equation of paraenesis and homily.[302]

---

[297] Lightfoot, *Apostolic fathers* I.2, 194.

[298] Donfried, *Setting*, 21–25.

[299] To such an extent that Norden, *Antike Kunstprosa*, 541–547, used it as the prime example of a homily; among others who accepted its homiletic origin we may note Windisch, "Christentum" and "Bemerkungen", and Knopf, *Lehre*, 151, for whom it is "die älteste christliche Homilie die wir besitzen". Most recently Salzmann, *Lehren und Ermahnen*, 219–232, has accepted this classification.

[300] 1 above; see also Stegemann's critique at *Herkunft*, 106–117, of the many unreflective attempts at labelling *II Clement* as well as other early Christian documents as homilies.

[301] In Grant and Graham, *Apostolic fathers*, 109.

[302] This at least is the basis on which Olivar, *Predicacion cristiana*, 51, accepts the

This is not sufficient reason to recognize *II Clement* as homiletic. Here it will be argued that *II Clement* is not a homily from the assembly but a catechetical and exhortatory address to those preparing for baptism. That such a life setting was known to the church from which *II Clement* derived is probable given the range of educational activities ascribed to the Corinthians in *I Clement* 1. As a catechetical address it owes something to the homily in its shape, and like a homily is an oral address to an assembled group in the church, but it is not a normal homiletic address to the assembly. This understanding of *II Clement* explains its structure, its contents and the reason for its preservation.

Lightfoot's arguments for a homiletic origin are far from secure. An address to "brothers and sisters" does not determine a homily since a similar address may be found in *Romans*, for instance, which is a letter. The reference to γεγραμμένα by no means necessarily refers to scripture, since *I Clement* refers to itself as τὰ γεγραμμένα, and Donfried plausibly suggests that this usage is being imitated by *II Clement* to refer to *I Clement*.[303] The term ἔντευξις, as we have seen, does not figure among the terms generally employed in the early church to refer to preaching.[304] νουθεσία likewise, although part of the field of vocabulary which potentially refers to preaching (we may recall at this point that Justin refers to a word of νουθεσία καὶ πρόκλησις after the scriptural readings),[305] is not restricted to preaching in the assembly.

By contrast to Lightfoot's arguments, Donfried suggests that our understanding of the genre of *II Clement* should be guided by the manner in which it describes itself.

There are three relevant points:

- At 15.1 Clement states that he has given συμβουλία concerning self-control

---

classification; similarly Ekenberg, "Urkristen Predikan", 30, for whom *II Clement* is "without doubt a paraenetic sermon".

[303] Donfried, *Setting*, 14; this point will be discussed further below. For the moment we may simply note that the term γεγραμμένα here does not *necessarily* refer to Scripture and therefore cannot be used as an argument in presenting *II Clement* as a homily.

[304] 1.1.4.

[305] *I Apologia* 1.67.

– At 17.3 Clement states that νουθεσία is being given by presbyters through *II Clement*

– At 19.1 Clement states that he is reading an ἔντευξις

The first statement is clearly asserting that *II Clement* is to be considered as a member of the *genos sumbouleutikon*. In this light Donfried
notes Aristotle's use of the term νουθετοῦντες to mean those who
give advice through speeches at *Rhetorica* 2.18.1, and his use of the
term ἔντευξις in a rhetorical context as meaning an address. Here
he also notes Dionysius of Halicarnassus' comment on Thucydides'
style that it is not suitable for speeches to the crowds (ὀχλικὰς ἔντευ-
ξεις), indeed that it is not suitable for sumbouleutic purposes at all.[306]

Donfried may be said to have established the sumbouleutic character of *II Clement*. He thus describes it as "oral exhortation to an
assembled Christian congregation."[307] Put thus it is hard to see how
this differs from a homily, except that Donfried's description does
not refer to any occasion. However, we may suggest that whereas
persuasion to a particular course of action may be the occasion of
a homily, it would not be a usual homiletic procedure. *II Clement* is
also unusual because it is written, whereas a homily would normally
be delivered extempore.[308] Nonetheless Wengst, in giving assent to
Donfried's characterization of *II Clement* as a *Mahnrede*, comes to see
that this functionally is identical to a homily[309] and Lindemann likewise, whilst recognizing its sumbouleutic character, nonetheless refers
to *II Clement* as a "Predigt".[310] Further refinement is needed if Donfried
is not to be trapped in contradiction, and the refinement may come
through better understanding the nature of the assembled Christian
congregation.

In pursuing the question of the *Gattung* of *II Clement*, Donfried suggests that it has a tripartite structure rather like that of the covenant

---

[306] *Thucydides* 50; we might also recall, from the observation of this passage at
1.2.4.1 above, that Dionysius also states that it is also unsuitable for private conversations (ὁμιλίας . . . ἰδιωτικάς).

[307] Donfried, *Setting*, 48.

[308] Though Donfried, *Setting*, 36, does note that written compositions were not
unknown, we may nonetheless suggest that written compositions, which explicitly
state themselves to be written, are exceptional given that even those orators who
wrote would be at pains to disguise the fact that they are reading. Siegert, *Drei hel-
lenistische-jüdische Predigten* II, 18, doubts whether *II Clement* is a homily precisely
because it is written.

[309] Wengst, *Schriften*, 214–217.

[310] Lindemann, *Clemensbriefe*, 190.

formulary which, Balzer had argued, was a major influence on the
formation of Christian discourse.[311] Thus, according to Donfried, it
has a theological section, followed by an ethical section which sets
forth the consequences of the theological truths expressed, and an
eschatological conclusion. Whilst there is a certain similarity with the
covenant formulary in that *II Clement* indeed does begin with a theological section, to which the ethical sections surely relate, Wengst
notes that the eschatological section (15.1–18.2 according to Donfried)
is hardly pure of exhortation,[312] and that the ethical section is not
free of eschatological import. *II Clement* moreover extends beyond
the "eschatological section" to engage in further exhortation.[313] We
noted above that it is hard to see how the formulary might enter
Christian moral discourse and that Balzer's analysis of *II Clement* was
inadequate; Donfried misleads himself through his indebtedness to
Balzer. We may now moreover see that a better analysis is readily
at hand.

In beginning this analysis we may agree with Donfried that the
first two chapters form a "theological section" distinct from the rest
of the document. Donfried argues that the following sections are "an
interpretation and correction" of the theological section, and of the
hymnic opening in particular. If Donfried is correct it is possible to
argue that the ethical section relates to the confession with which
II Clement opens as a διάκρισις on a prophetic oracle relates to the
oracle which it is expanding. *II Clement* is thus shaped as a homily
in that it expands and interprets a statement which is not itself part
of the homily, though the *diakrisis* here is not on a prophecy but on
a confession. Prophecy has apparently ceased to be a live event in
this community, but the procedure of testing has remained, as has
the high respect given to the prophetic speaker, though this respect
is now transferred to the presbyter.[314]

---

[311] Balzer's theory is discussed at 1.2.1.4 above.

[312] Wengst, *Schriften*, 215.

[313] A similar criticism may be levelled at Baasland's observation ("Zweite Klemensbrief", 102) that the conclusion might owe something to the homiletic conclusion intended to give comfort; the possibility of salvation set alongside exhortation
runs through the entire homily.

[314] So Salzmann, *Lehren und Ermahnen*, 230, suggests that the manner in which *II
Clement* 17.5 addresses the hearers is an implication that Christ is speaking through
the presbyters, and that this derives from a tradition of prophetic preaching.

The opening confession reads as follows:

> Brothers, we must think of Jesus Christ, as of God, as the judge of
> the living and the dead.
> And we must not think little of our salvation.
> For if we think little of him we shall hope to receive little.
> And those who listen as though these were minor matters are sinning,
> as we sin if we know not from whence
> and by whom
> and to what place we were called,
> and how great the sufferings which Jesus Christ bore for our sake.
> What return then shall we make him,
> or what fruit worthy of that he has given us?
> How great a debt of holiness do we owe him!
> For he gave us the light,
> he called us sons as does a father,
> he saved us while we were perishing (ἀπολλυμένους).
> What praise, what gift should we render him for what we have received?
> We were maimed in our understanding, worshipping stones and wood
> and gold and silver and bronze, the works of human hands.
> Our whole life was nothing but death.
> We were covered with darkness
> and our eyes were full of mist;
> but we received our sight,
> and by his will cast off the cloud which covered us.
> He pitied us and in his mercy saved us,
> seeing the great error and destruction which was in us
> lacking hope of salvation except through him.
> He called us from non-being,
> and willed that out of nothing we should come to be. (*II Clement* 1)

Donfried notes that this section is distinct in style and theology.
Stylistically he notes the manner in which participles are heaped up
in the opening section, and that there is significant vocabulary
employed in this section which is not found elsewhere in *II Clement*.[315]
Formally we may recognize this section as a kind of credal statement,
having similarities to the Pauline confession of *I Thessalonians* 1:9–10.[316]
We may also observe that it is hymnic in character, and may thus
recognize it as a hymnic confession of the congregation.[317] Thus far

---

[315] Donfried, "Theology", 488–489.

[316] On the identification of this *credo* as pre-Pauline note the arguments of Best,
Thessalonians, 85–87; the similarities are probably to be attributed to a common use
of (Old Testament) prophetic language concerning idolatry interpreted in a Platonizing
framework.

[317] On the hymnic character of this opening see Donfried, *Setting*, 103–109.

on to suggest that although the opening *credo* states that Christ has
already worked salvation, and that the hearers are thus already saved,
the remainder of *II Clement* goes on to offer a corrective in that it
argues that repentance and good works are necessary in order that
the salvation won by Christ might be attained.[318]

To see this as a correction might be an overstatement, but certainly
there is a case for seeing *II Clement*'s exhortation as related to this
opening. In particular we must observe that the "theological section"
is not exhausted by the opening statement, but that it is followed
by a scriptural citation which is then given a seriatim treatment.

> Rejoice, barren one who has not given birth, break forth and cry out,
> you who have not laboured, for the children of the deserted are many
> more than those of her who has a husband.
>
> In saying "Rejoice, barren one who has not given birth" he is speaking
> of us, for the church was barren before children were given to her.
>
> In saying "Cry out, you who have not laboured" he means this: that
> we should offer our prayers before God in simplicity, not growing
> weary as women who are in labour.
>
> In saying "For the children of the deserted are many more than those
> of her who has a husband", he means that our people seemed deserted
> by God, but now those who believe are become more than those who
> only seem to have God. And another Scripture says: "I have not come
> to call the righteous but sinners". He means that those who are perish-
> ing must be saved. For it is great and wonderful to give strength not
> to those things which are standing but those which are falling. Thus
> Christ willed to save those who were perishing, and he saved many,
> coming and calling us who were already perishing. (*II Clement* 2)

This procedure of interpreting Scripture in sections may be indicative of a homily, but the fact that the credal statement is followed
by scriptural citation is itself more directly indicative of a homiletic
procedure, in that Scripture is presented as the basis by which a
preliminary judgement on the *credo* might be made. That this is the
relationship between the opening statement and the scriptural section may be shown through the connections between the scriptural
passage and the opening theological statement shown by Donfried,
where he observes "a curious parallelism here as well as an inter-

---

[318] Donfried, "Theology", passim.

esting repetition of the verb ἀπόλλυμι which suggests that our author is interpreting the hymnic confession of chapter 1 in chapter 2."[319]

1.7 ἔσωσεν ... μηδεμίαν ἐλπίδα ἔχοντες σωτηρίας	2.5 δεῖ τοὺς ἀπολλουμένους σώζειν
1.8 ἠθέλησεν ἐκ μὴ ὄντας εἶναι ἡμᾶς	2.7 ἠθέλησεν σῶσαι τὰ ἀπολλύμενα
1.8 ἐκάλεσεν ἡμᾶς οὐκ ὄντας	2.7 καλέσας ἡμᾶς ἤδη ἀπολλυμένους

The reliance on Scripture to undergird a statement exhibited here is not a typically synagogal procedure, though it points in the direction of synagogalization. Here Scripture has a definite place of honour, but is not yet the subject of preaching but the means by which διάκρισις might be made. Following the demonstration of the agreement of Scripture, the *diakrisis* may extend further by bringing out the ethical content which is implicit in the statement and applying it to the hearers. However, this observation does not enable us to suggest that the same is true of normal preaching in the assembly, since, as we intend to argue, this is not a normal homily.

II Clement thus owes something to homiletic procedure in its form and shape, in that it is a wider consideration of a text, albeit a confession rather than a prophecy or a biblical text, and in that it supports the confession principally with reference to Scripture. Donfried further notes that the same procedure is followed in microcosm within a number of chapters in *II Clement*, where a citation is followed by a drawing out of an ethical lesson.[320] Donfried notes that it is far from co-incidental that the citations come from authoritative texts from the Jewish Scriptures or authoritative traditions from Christianity. He sees that they stand somewhere between being illustrations and proof texts, but is unclear how they function within the work.[321] We may now see that they are brought forward as further proofs of the overall thesis, and serve then as the basis for further illustration of the paraenetic aim of the writer. This is the way in which a preacher would expound a text.

II Clement is thus a work of homiletic character and technique, yet it is not a typical homily since, as we have seen, it is sumbouleutic

---

[319] Donfried, *Setting*, 39.

[320] Donfried, *Setting*, 96–97; as an example we may note *II Clement* 6, where the saying that nobody can serve two masters is the springboard for a wider reflection on the differences between Christian life and the life of the world.

[321] Donfried, *Setting*, 97.

in intent; indeed, as Baasland suggests, it may be placed in, or at least influenced by, a particular subspecies of sumbouleutic, the protreptic.[322] On the basis of rhetorical function, whilst yet recognizing *II Clement* as an address to a congregation, we suggest that *II Clement* functioned as a *Mahnrede* specifically intended for those preparing for baptism. Here then we part company further with Donfried in his view of *II Clement* as a correction of the theological statement with which it opens by suggesting that its purpose in the Corinthian church was not, as he thinks, related to the crisis of which *I Clement* informs us, but had a broader occasion and liturgical purpose.

Donfried theorizes that *II Clement* is an address to the congregation by the same presbyters whose overthrow was the occasion of *I Clement*. He finds a number of phrases in *II Clement* to support this supposition.[323] At *II Clement* 19.1 he reads the passage μισθὸν γὰρ αἰτῶ ὑμᾶς as a request by the presbyter for (financial) compensation for having been overthrown from his previous office.[324] However this totally ignores the context, in which the reader is exhorting the hearers to be saved, and through their salvation to be the salvation of the reader. The μισθός is the reward which is the salvation of the reader through having successfully brought others to salvation. A speaker who describes himself as a πανθαμαρτωλός would hardly be so arrogant in demanding compensation from the congregation. At 13.1, when the presbyter is talking about the blasphemy heaped upon the name of God, he cites *Isaiah* 52:5 "Every way is my name blasphemed among all the heathen", and then begins to unpack this statement in homiletic style. "In what way is it blasphemed? In that you do not do what I desire . . ." Donfried reads this as a statement of the presbyter making demands upon the congregation. However, the subject of the passage is prophetic oracles from Scripture, which the reader goes on to discuss. The "I" of this statement is surely not that of the reader but that of God, given the prophetic context of the preaching. The question and the answer are simple cases of *prosopopoiia*. Although prophecy in the congregation is clearly already subservient to Scripture, scriptural prophecy continues to be understood and used as congregational prophecy had been understood and used, as the direct voice of God, which nonetheless needed appli-

---

[322] Baasland, "Zweite Klemensbrief", 105, 108.
[323] Donfried, *Setting*, 10.
[324] Graham, *Apostolic fathers* II, 131, seems to read the phrase in the same way.

cation. Scripture is seen as prophetic and functions as prophecy had done; for this reason the prophetic books predominate in the speaker's use of Scripture.[325]

The essence of Donfried's theological argument is that the credal confession is phrased in the aorist, telling what God has already done, whereas the following exhortation makes salvation rely upon the obedience of the congregation. These are the grounds on which he suggests that the opponents had an over-realized eschatology, of which *II Clement* is a gentle correction. This is to read too much into the situation. If the intention was to correct a seriously imbalanced theology one would expect more direct confrontation of the theology being opposed. The same consideration applies to Salzmann's understanding of the purpose of *II Clement*, which is opposition to Valentinianism;[326] certainly there may be some anti-Valentinian language but that does not of itself explain the contents of the address as a whole. A recognition of the form and technique of *II Clement* as *diakrisis* like that exercised on the prophetic oracles enables us to see that the writer's expands and applies, rather than corrects, the credal confession which he is treating. Donfried's concern to see *II Clement* as a correction of the confession is what prevents him from seeing that the *Sitz im Leben* of the *Mahnrede*, as of the original confession, might be baptismal. He attributes the somewhat basic nature of the material which the author is treating to a fundamental misunderstanding, particularly tending to an over-realized eschatology, and assumes that the hearers are already baptized,[327] whereas it is far simpler to see the moralizing tone and the fundamental nature of the contents as fitting an unbaptized audience receiving the same kind of ethical catechesis as that which appears in the *Didache*.

It is as a pre-baptismal *Mahnrede* that *II Clement* warns the hearers to keep the seal of baptism intact;[328] if this is its purpose we may moreover understand how *II Clement* manages to combine elements of sumbouleutic with elements which Baasland recognizes might actually alienate a pagan hearer, such as the appeal to Scripture as an authority.[329] Donfried recognizes that baptism might be the *Sitz im*

---

[325] As Knopf, "Anagnose", 270, observes.
[326] Salzmann, *Lehren und Ermahnen*, 226.
[327] *Setting*, 126–128.
[328] *II Clement* 6.9; 7.6; 8.6 which all exhort the hearers to keep the seal intact.
[329] Baasland, "Zweite Klemensbrief", 107.

Leben of the original hymn with its emphasis on conversion and salvation,[330] but does not seem to recognize the possibility that the following exhortation might have the same function. Seeing the whole
of *II Clement* as an address preceding baptism also rescues it from
the contradiction perceived by Windisch and Knopf. They find the
sudden call to repentance at the beginning of the eighth chapter
odd, and suggest that missionary preaching has been uncomfortably
combined with congregational paraenesis.[331] If the audience were
indeed baptized then it would be odd indeed, but the oddity comes
from the assumptions that the earlier part is addressed to the baptized, and that a call to repentance is necessarily directed to those
who are not only unbaptized but unconverted. A warning to keep
the baptismal seal intact followed by a call to repentance is not con-
tradictory when addressed to those converted but not yet baptized.
Donfried is correct in seeing that the "brothers" addressed in chapter eight must be the same brothers who were addressed earlier, and
his recognition that the outside pagan world would not be addressed
in this fashion is certainly in order,[332] but in seeing the sole alter-
natives as unconverted pagans and baptized Christians he is failing
to see all the possibilities, and failing to see the significance of his
own recognition of the sumbouleutic nature of *II Clement*. If an audience of those preparing for baptism is assumed, then the contradiction
perceived by Windisch[333] between the rigorist assertions of *II Clement*
combined with the possibility of repentance fall away. There is a
possibility of repentance for those unbaptized, but those who are to
be baptized are warned nonetheless that they must keep the seal
intact. The contradiction between the assertions of the first chapter
that the audience is already saved and the promise of future salvation which is found later in the speech is solved through recognizing with Donfried that the first chapter is a citation of a *credo* of the
congregation rather than strictly part of the address.

To see *II Clement* as a generalized *sumboulia* concerning repentance
accords with the shape of the document as a *diakrisis* of the fundamental creed of the Corinthian church and in turn enables us to
escape from speculation concerning the causes of *I Clement*. Donfried's

---

[330] Donfried, *Setting*, 109.
[331] Windisch, *Taufe und Sünde*, 329–339; Knopf, *Lehre*, 164–165.
[332] *Setting*, 130–131.
[333] *Taufe und Sünde*, 339.

connection of the occasion of *II Clement* with *I Clement* has the advantage of explaining the association between the two which is found not only in the manuscript tradition but in citation extending back to Eusebius, who refers to two letters of Clement.[334] However, if a Corinthian origin to *II Clement* is sustained[335] the connection may continue to be explained in that both are key documents in the life of the Corinthian congregation, and that both moreover major on repentance. Donfried agrees with Beyschlag[336] that *I Clement* is a tract on second repentance, and rightly sees *II Clement* as similarly a call to repentance.[337] If it is a sumbouleutic exhortation to those approaching baptism, it may however simply be a call to repentance in baptism, rather than to a second repentance. Finally this view of *II Clement* explains the connection to *I Clement* without obliging us to tie the occasions together as Donfried does. The two documents may be found together in Corinth as being central and foundational documents and both in their ways dealing with the necessity of repentance. *I Clement* was used in a period beyond the crisis which it immediately addressed,[338] otherwise it would not have been preserved, and may indeed have been used in a similar way to *II Clement*, as an address within the congregation urging repentance, even after

---

[334] Eusebius, *Historia ecclesiastica* 3.38; admittedly there is no certainty that the second letter referred to is *II Clement*; on the manuscript tradition see Donfried, *Setting*, 20–21, and on the history of citation as well as the manuscript tradition Stegemann, *Herkunft*, 62 (in summary).

[335] Corinth is the most probable place of origin. Lightfoot, *Apostolic fathers* I.2, 197, is followed by Donfried, *Setting*, 1–7, (and refs) in noting the universal connection with *I Clement*, and argues that since this latter was written from the Roman church to the Corinthian church a certain priority has to be given to one of these two places. Determinative of Corinth, rather than Rome, is the reference at 7.3 to those who sail in for the games. Whereas athletic imagery is common enough in early Christian literature the reference to sailing without indication of any particular direction would point most obviously to Corinth, and to the Isthmian games. Although this argument is not totally secure since, as Stanton, "2 Clement VII", argues, καταπλέω is susceptible of a range of meanings and the reference may simply be to the effort expanded by some people in attending games, any explanation of the provenance of *II Clement* must account for the connection with *I Clement*. Thus the argument of Stegemann, *Herkunft*, 29–30, that virtually any coastal city which celebrated games might be intended fails because it takes no account of the relationship with *I Clement*. Stegemann's own suggestion, that *II Clement* was conceived as some kind of appendix to *I Clement*, is speculative in the extreme.

[336] Beyschlag, *Clemens Romanus*, 145.

[337] Donfried, *Setting*, 13; Windisch, *Taufe und Sünde*, 329, similarly characterizes *II Clement* as a *Bußpredigt*.

[338] Eusebius, *Historia ecclesiastica* 3.16.1–2 records that it is still read in the Corinthian church assemblies.

II Clement ceased to be used in the context of preparation for baptism.[339] In this way it is possible to account for *II Clement* having
been written down and preserved.[340]

If this is the case then some agreement may be found with
Stegemann's suggestion that *II Clement* properly ends with chapter
18, and that the final two chapters are a post-script intended to close
not only *II Clement* but *I Clement* as well.[341] If this is the case then it
is to be noted that the reference to the reading of the ἔντευξις is
found in these closing chapters, which is an indication that *II Clement*
need not have originated as a written homily but may have been
an originally entirely oral event.[342]

To conclude this consideration of *II Clement* we should observe
that Scripture plays a key role in the community of *II Clement*, in
that it provides the basis on which statements may be judged,
expanded or corrected, and in that scriptural prophecy has come to
function in the community in the same way that congregational
prophecy had done. On this basis it is possible that τὰ γεγραμμένα
to which the reader refers, is indeed a reference to Scripture, albeit
not to any preceding scriptural reading, though it is still possible that
it is a self-reference to the *enteuxis* which is being read.[343] But beyond
this we should note that there is not the evidence which would enable
us to confirm that scriptural reading followed by homiletic comment
was a regular feature of the worship of this community, even though

---

[339] Chapter 19 states that the repentance of the hearers might be an example to
the νέοι; this is an indication that when this chapter was added the whole was not
read to those about to be baptized, for they who are about to become νέοι themselves are hardly likely to be setting an example in this way.

[340] An issue which Salzmann, *Lehren und Ermahnen*, 220, sees as vital in the literary problem of *II Clement*.

[341] Stegemann, *Herkunft*, 99–105. There are certainly stylistic and linguistic distinctions between these chapters and those foregoing. This is not to adopt the whole
of Stegemann's theory concerning the origin of *II Clement*, the independent origin
of which should be maintained, but is perhaps a useful speculation on the *Nachleben*
of the document.

[342] Whereas this is not the place to discuss in detail the problems posed by the
final chapters, we must register disagreement with Baasland's characterization of
them as *peroratio* ("Zweite Klemensbrief", 116) on the principal grounds that, through
mentioning Scripture, they bring *II Clement* into accordance with Justin's report of
preaching in Rome. There is no particular reason why *II Clement* should accord
with Justin, and so this cannot supply a reason for the retention of the final chapters. Salzmann, *Lehren und Ermahnen*, 222–224, agrees that the final chapters are a
post-script.

[343] So Stegemann, *Herkunft*, 101; Praetorius, "Bedeutung", 523, considers this possibility, though rejects it.

the small pieces of interpretation to be found in *II Clement* point in this direction. The "homily" is based on a *credo* of the congregation, rather than on Scripture, and so there is little point seeking the reading which preceded it; unlike a scriptural homily, which depends on the preceding reading, *II Clement* is self-contained.[344] Knopf reckons that preaching based on a preceding Scripture would be usual on the basis of Justin's report, according to which a reading is followed by a word which draws out the ethical lesson for the hearers;[345] these perhaps are the grounds on which he favours a Roman origin. But it is to be noted that even though the latter part of *Isaiah* figures large in *II Clement* the relationship between exhortation and the scriptural text is not that of exhortation deriving from the scriptural text but Scripture providing the proof of a *credo*, which in turn can become the subject of exhortation. *II Clement* is in no way an expository homily.[346]

II Clement, whilst a homily of sorts, is therefore not a typical homily of its community. In its structure, particularly in the manner in which the speaker employs Scripture to judge the *credo* and to draw ethical lessons from the original citation, in the manner in which it breaks down Scripture for consideration and in its attitude towards scriptural prophecy it may convey some indirect information about congregational preaching, though even this is far from secure, and can only be understood as such in the light of what has already been discovered, whilst adding no new information or understanding of its own.

2.2.2.5. *Paraenesis, preaching and prophecy*

In *Hebrews* and *II Clement* we have some indication of the manner in which preaching might take place in a Christian synagogue, though the extent of the paraenetic content might not be typical[347] since

---

[344] So Stegemann, *Herkunft*, 113; Salzmann, *Lehren und Ermahnen*, 229.

[345] Knopf, "Anagnose", 266–267.

[346] So Praetorius, "Bedeutung", 524, who whilst thinking that *II Clement* followed a scriptural reading recognizes that there is no direct reference to it. Cf. Old, *Reading and Preaching*, 278–284, who sees *II Clement* as an expository proem homily, with *Isaiah* 54:1 as the proemic text and with a bridging text provided by the use of the citation of *Matthew* 9:13 at *II Clement* 2. Not only does this ignore the structure of *II Clement*, which does not introduce itself with the text, but ignores any research on the form of synagogue homilies undertaken since Moore and Mann!

[347] Praetorius, "Bedeutung", 522, likewise warns of the dangers of extrapolating generalizations from the unusual and unique *II Clement*.

both are addressed to particular situations in the Christian community, *Hebrews* probably to give encouragement to those who are harking back to former Jewish practices, *II Clement* to encourage a congregation to repentance, probably in baptism. The very fact that they are preserved in writing should be warning enough that they are atypical, since their written nature means that they are not simply homilies preached in the assembly, which were oral and extemporaneous. Similar considerations apply to the paraenetic oracles uncovered in the Pastoral Epistles, since these are addressed to particular contexts in the worshipping life of the Christian community.

Thus none of the paraenetic documents studied in this sub-section are typical synagogue homilies. For this reason they fail to demonstrate what one would anticipate as the typically synagogal procedure of preaching on the basis of Scripture. Rather the starting point is the situation of the church which is judged in the light of Scripture, just as prophetic messages were adjudicated according to their conformity with Scripture, in the manner in which we observed James, at *Acts* 15:13–21, judging the report of Paul and Barnabas.[348] This comes about because each is addressed to a particular situation. *II Clement* is perhaps slightly exceptional in that the community's creed, rather than an oracle or a situation, provides the basis for homiletic reflection. But we may see that the *credo* is treated as a prophetic oracle may have been treated in an earlier period, first being submitted to a test of scriptural conformity and then used to draw out ethical and religious applications for the audience.

However in one respect these paraenetic addresses give some indication of the manner in which preaching would develop. For in the case of the prophetic διακρίσεις of the household, as in the case of James giving judgement through Scripture on the report of Paul, the judgement and expansion is made by someone other than the prophet. In *James* and in *Hebrews* however the paraenetic injunctions are supported through Scripture by the same person who had delivered the original injunction. In *II Clement* we are to assume that the whole was delivered by a single presbyter, the *credo* as well as the following expansion. We may thus see the manner in which there is development away from ὁμιλία as prophetic dialogue to homily as scriptural monologue; even if *II Clement* is not a sermon, it betrays the same

---

[348] 2.2.1 above.

process of concentration of communication in the assembly in the hands, or rather the mouth, of one person.

Finally, our recognition that the paraeneses of *James* and *II Clement* are not by their very nature homiletic leads to a further reflection on the ongoing search for early Christian preaching. For according to Ekenberg, whose fundamental evidence is Justin's report that a word of νουθεσία was given, and that these words were given from Scripture for the imitation of the audience, ethical interests became predominant in preaching in the second century; he sees this is something of a departure from the earlier period.[349] One must be aware that there may be some apologetic interest in Justin's words, since Philo writes similarly of the function of the synagogue at *De specialibus legibus* 2.61–62 when stating that its function is schooling in virtue. Moreover in observing Mishnah *Ta'anith* 2.1 and BT *Sotah* 7B we must be aware that a similar pattern of exhortation might be found within Judaism, since the words spoken here are words of admonition. Further to this we have also found that prophecy in the assembly is quite capable of conveying paraenesis. Ekenberg is singled out for criticism here because he lays bare his assumptions and argues for them. However there is an underlying assumption which equates paraenesis and preaching and which is not laid bare in the work of Thyen, whose "homilies" are predominantly paraenetic, even to the extent of including the first six chapters of the *Didache* in his collection of homiletic material.[350] The same assumption that the fundamental concern of early Christian preaching was ethical, and thus that there is a virtual equation of paraenesis and preaching, would appear to be operating in the work of Wills, whose pattern of exhortation (through which he defines a homily) is fundamentally ethical, and among all those who have assumed that *James* and *II Clement* are homilies on the basis of their paraenetic content. Our examination of these paraenetic documents has shown that although catechesis might take place within the assembly in the earliest period as a result of the informality of communication which would take place in a household gathered around a table, and although prophecy might include paraenesis, paraenesis and preaching cannot be equated.

---

[349] Ekenberg, "Urkristen predikan", 9, 23, 31; a similar view is expressed by Brilioth, *Brief History*, 20: "prophecy has been silenced and replaced by teaching and a sober paraenesis."

[350] Thyen, *Stil*, 21–22.

It is possible that the equation has derived from the equation of diatribe and homily, in that the concerns of the diatribe are principally ethical, though it is equally possible that the diatribe was only identified as the Hellenistic equivalent to the sermon on the basis of its ethical content. But whatever the direction of influence, just as diatribe and sermon cannot be equated, nor can paraenesis and preaching. Both formally and functionally they are different.

2.2.3. *Preaching in the Christian schools of Asia*

In the first chapter of this work we argued that prophecy was a primitive form of Christian communication akin to preaching. Subsequently we have argued that although in some settings there was potential tension between the prophetic and the scriptural forms of homiletic communication, a process of development was more common in which the two, being treated as on a par, form a relationship according to which prophecy becomes a means of interpreting Scripture and Scripture a means of testing prophecy. We have also seen that prophecy as a form of communication was known in both household and synagogal ecclesial organisations. In this part we intend to demonstrate that it was also possible for prophecy to find a place in a school setting apart from the synagogue, and that in this setting the role of the prophet as exegete came to prominence, until prophets were eclipsed by teachers performing an analogous exegetical function.

Firstly we will examine the schools of Asia Minor, represented by the fourth Gospel, by the anonymous author/redactor of *Epistula apostolorum* and by Melito, each of whom stand in the Johannine tradition, by the anonymous author of a homily on the Pascha and by Papias. In each instance we will discover some evidence of prophetic activity within a school setting. Asia was a place where the second sophistic was a powerful phenomenon, and the influence of the Asian rhetorical schools might be expected to influence the organisation of the church. It is for this reason that the Johannine school has been classified here as a school rather than a synagogue, despite the strong synagogal links of that community, and despite the rather fine line which has already been noted between the synagogue and the school. Beyond the earliest generations of Johannine Christians we will find evidence of a fairly thoroughgoing imbuing of Asian Christians with the rhetoric of their day, which we may anticipate would influence their preaching.

2.2.3.1. *Prophecy, exegesis and preaching in the Johannine school*

We may begin with noting the role of prophecy in the Johannine school. There we will find that the prophetic generation of scriptural exegesis is the essence of the communication of the word of God in this community.

Debate about the role of Christian prophets in the formation of the sayings of Jesus in the Gospel tradition has largely centred on the synoptic Gospels. That concerning the fourth Gospel is an entirely separate issue, and so we may proceed without regard to the arguments which centre on the synoptic Gospels. In particular we may note that the fourth Gospel, in contrast to the synoptics, enunciates a theology of prophetic communication such that it is reasonable to blur any distinction between the historical Jesus and the voice of the risen Christ speaking through his prophet. John's narrative of Jesus is termed by Smith a "metahistorical narrative", by which he means that the Jesus depicted is at one and the same time the historical Christ, speaking in the past through the narrative frame of the Gospel, and the exalted Christ, speaking through his Spirit to the church of John's day.[351] When the exalted Christ communicates through his prophets moreover it is possible to identify this prophetic speech as that of Jesus because the communication of the exalted Christ takes place through the medium of the paraclete, the *alter ego* of the risen and exalted Jesus.[352] The communication of the paraclete through the Johannine prophet is functionally equivalent to the communication of Jesus because of the functions which are ascribed to the paraclete, which closely mirror the functions of Jesus among his disciples.[353] Thus the paraclete teaches the disciples, reminding them of what Jesus taught (14:25), bears witness to Jesus (15:24), convicts the world of sin (16:8), speaks the words of Jesus, guides the disciples into all truth, and glorifies Jesus (16:13–14). The paraclete is the means by which the exalted Christ addresses the people of God, and

---

[351] Smith, "Presentation of Jesus", 184–186.

[352] So Smalley, *John*, 232, summarizing much previous discussion.

[353] So Brown, "Paraclete"; Bornkamm, "Paraklet", 69; Ashton, *Understanding*, 420–425.

the statements of the paraclete, made through the prophets, are thus
functionally equivalent to the voice of Jesus. For this reason John
may be at perfect liberty to project these prophecies back into the
historical realm of the earthly Christ. Thus we may observe that
Jesus in the fourth Gospel is depicted as a prophet. He employs
prophetic speech forms, hears heavenly voices, has visions, is described
as omniscient[354] and undergoes disturbance at the time of delivery.[355]
We intend to argue that this takes place because John is himself a
prophet, and because the speeches of the Johannine Jesus are themselves John's prophetic speeches, spoken in the persona of Christ
through the inspiration of the paraclete.

The word "paraclete" was chosen, as we argued above, to indicate the one who gives *paraklēsis* in the church;[356] because *paraklēsis*
was a prophetic function we may state that it is the function of the
paraclete to convey the speech of Jesus through the prophets. Johnston
similarly argues that the word is chosen as meaning *paraklēsis* in the
sense of preaching and proclamation.[357] These functions may be
classified separately as preaching, teaching and prophecy, as Johnston
does, but since the teaching envisaged is teaching within the assembly they may all be considered as functionally equivalent communications of the word of God and described as *paraklēsis*, or prophetic
preaching. This leads Boring, who is a proponent of the view that
much of the synoptic tradition is formed out of the work of Christian
prophets, to sum up the situation with regard to John thus: "The
fourth Gospel is composed in such a way as to frustrate any effort
to distinguish between the sayings of Jesus and the voice of the
prophetic/apostolic community."[358] This is because, as we have already
observed, the distinction between the voice of Jesus and that of the
prophet in the community is a false one.

Two significant objections have been raised to this understanding
of Johannine prophecy. Firstly, Hill denies the prophetic basis of the
Johannine discourses on the grounds that the speaker in the Gospel

---

[354] On omniscience as a prophetic mark see van Unnik, "Greek characteristic".
Significantly this is also attributed to the paraclete.
[355] Thus at the Last Supper, in the course of the delivery of the farewell discourses, Jesus is disturbed (ἐταράχθη) in the spirit. (*John* 13:21)
[356] At 1.1.3.
[357] Johnston, *Spirit Paraclete*, 128–130; similarly Cothenet, "Prophètes Chrétiens
comme exégètes charismatiques", 80–81.
[358] Boring, *Continuing voice*, 268.

form is the earthly Jesus and not the risen Christ who speaks in
Revelation, and that in the apocalypse there is a clear distinction
between the voice of Jesus and the voice of the seer.[359] To this we
may respond that the distinction between the earthly Jesus and the
heavenly Christ is a false one in the context of the Johannine presentation of Jesus and its resultant christology. It is possible for John
to depict the communications of the exalted Christ as the communications of the earthly Jesus because of the essential continuity
between them. Secondly we may respond that the John of *Revelation*
is a visionary prophet, and that this is a separate kind of inspiration
from the "enthusiastic" evangelist. For this reason the speeches are
reported in the context of a vision report rather than being direct
speech in the mouth of the prophet. Secondly, with primary reference to the synoptic Gospels, Dunn suggests that prophetic speeches
should be introduced by a statement clearly indicating that what follows is the voice of the Lord and that in the absence of such an
indication speeches in the "I-form" cannot be attributed to prophets.[360]
He has reference to the canonical prophets of the Old Testament,
whose speeches in the "I-form" are clearly introduced with an indication that what follows is an oracle of God. However this is the
literary context only; in practice, if the one who spoke was known
as a prophet and was speaking in the manner appropriate to a
prophet then there would not be a problem in determining that the
content was prophecy. Certainly Dunn is right in stating that there
was no anonymous circulation of prophecies, but in the case of the
Johannine school these prophecies were not anonymous because of
the towering significance of the founding elder in this context.

Thus when the discourses of Jesus in the fourth Gospel are accompanied by formal indications of prophetic delivery we are on safe
ground in arguing that the voice heard in the text is the voice of
the paraclete as he spoke through the prophets of the Johannine
community, and may properly describe these discourses as Johannine
prophetic sermons. In doing so we may have in mind that this manner of prophetic proclamation within the Johannine churches was
not restricted to the earlier generations; we shall note below that the
Epistula apostolorum, Melito and the Montanists use the same means
of prophetic communication.

---

[359] Hill, *New Testament prophecy*, 149; a similar point is made by Dunn, "Prophetic
'I' sayings", 180.
[360] Dunn, "Prophetic 'I' sayings", 180.

These general observations may be illustrated by an examination of *John* 6:25–58. There are two grounds for viewing this as a Johannine prophetic sermon. In the first instance it is given in the "I form", which as we have seen is a formula of self-identification which is an indication of prophetic delivery. More tellingly this passage has been identified as a homily by Borgen, who observes a proemic pattern.[361] According to Borgen the discourse follows the classical shape of the proem form. The proemial text is cited at the beginning in the form:

> He gave them bread from heaven to eat.

The text is then broken up into two constituent parts for exegesis, first "he gave them bread from heaven" and then "to eat". The whole is summed up in the conclusion at 58:

> This is the bread which came down from Heaven. Unlike the bread which the ancestors ate and died, whoever eats this bread will live for ever.

In its narrative setting the text is cited by the Jews. Jesus then begins the interpretation, repeating the key words in the text:

> Truly, truly I tell you, Moses did not give you the bread from heaven, but my father gives you the true bread from heaven. For the bread of God is that which comes down from heaven and gives life to the world.

Through use of the prophetic saying "I am the bread of life", Jesus then explains that his coming down from heaven is the true meaning of the text. He then begins to interpret the term "to eat":

> Your ancestors ate the manna in the desert and they died. This is the bread coming down from heaven, so that whoever eats of it might not die.

The occurrence of homiletic exegesis, bound up to the prophetic "Amen" saying and the "I form" found at verses 35 and 48, is a clear indication that this is a homily delivered by one acting in the capacity of prophet. Whereas Borgen's arguments have not convinced all critics, nobody who accepts that a proem homily was a real phenomenon doubts that this chapter is a clear example of the form. In addition to observing the proem form here we should also note

---

[361] Borgen, *Bread from heaven*, 59–98.

that the extensive debt to material deriving from traditional haggadic exegesis[362] makes it probable that this is a discourse deriving
from a homiletic tradition. Finally we should note that the discourse
is explicitly described as a synagogue homily at the conclusion of
the chapter when John records that it is given in the synagogue at
Capaernaum (6:59).[363]

But although there is widespread agreement among those who
accept the form-critical basis of Borgen's work that this chapter constitutes a homily there is some dispute about where exactly the homily
ends. We have already observed that Borgen sees the summary passage at verse 58 as the conclusion to the homily; but there is also
a summary passage at 51a–b which provides an equally suitable conclusion to the formal homily by recapitulating the original Scripture.

> I am the living bread which came down from heaven. Whoever eats
> this bread shall live for ever.

This argument has been brought into play by Richter as part of the
wider argument concerning whether 51c–58 is an interpolation.[364]
Richter suggests that, since the homiletic pattern may be shown satisfactorily to conclude at 51b with a citation, the latter section of
the discourse may be seen as a post-script to the original homily,
added by the hand of a later redactor.[365] Without following Richter's
redactional arguments entirely, Schnelle also notes that 51b likewise
forms a satisfactory conclusion to the discourse.[366] Into this argument
Richter brings the tensions that had previously been noticed between
the two parts of the homily as reconstructed by Borgen, such as
slight variations of style, the addition of αἷμα to the σάρξ and the
substitution of τρώγειν for φαγεῖν. He also points out the discrep-
ancy that whereas the giver is said in 31–51a to be God himself, in
51b–58 Jesus is himself the one who gives.[367] Thus, according to
Richter, the homily has a sapiential interest in the earlier part,

---

[362] On which see especially Gärtner, *John 6 and the Jewish Passover.*

[363] McDonald, *Kerygma and didache*, 48–49, notes the significance of this clue.

[364] Richter, "Formgeschichte". The literature on the subject of whether these
verses are interpolated, and the theological consequences of such an interpolation,
is immense. Works cited here should provide sufficient further reference.

[365] Richter, "Formgeschichte", 23–31; Richter actually argues that the form is
better represented were the homily to end at this point, but here he overstates his
case.

[366] Schnelle, *Anti-docetic Christology*, 201.

[367] Richter, "Formgeschichte", 25.

whereas the latter part is explicitly eucharistic and therefore secondary. Dunn however points out that eucharistic interest, whilst present in 53–58, is secondary even in these verses compared to the significance of following Jesus and being one with him;[368] the essence of this post-script is, he suggests, anti-docetic,[369] rather than, as Richter would like to see, the result of a dispute over the eucharist itself.[370]

This is not the place to become involved in the greater argument concerning Johannine eucharistic theology, but it is important that the extent of the original homily be determined. Thus although we may agree with Dunn and Schenke that in the final product of the Gospel the discourse is to be interpreted as a whole,[371] our concern is not with the correct interpretation of the fourth Gospel but with the prehistory of the units out of which it is constructed, in order that the extent of the original Johannine homily may be determined. The chief argument against seeing 51c–58 as an interpolation is that this part of the discourse is so thoroughly Johannine in its style;[372] although Bornkamm discounts such arguments, given the significant differences in theology which he perceives between the eucharistic section and the rest of the fourth Gospel,[373] it remains an argument which cannot be satisfactorily answered by those who perceive the hand of an ecclesiastical redactor here. Jeremias answers this objection by suggesting that the "appendix" is part of a separate Johannine homily which has been added by a redactor employing Johannine material.[374] Although may agree with Jeremias that verses 51c–58 are the work of a reviser within the Johannine school, we intend to suggest that the situation differs from that which he envisages, namely that it is verses 31–51b that are the original and distinct homily and that the postscript has been composed in homiletic style in order to bring the earlier homily into the narrative frame of the Gospel.

Although there are inconsistencies between 31–51b and 51c–58, the latter section does have some consistency with the earlier part

---

[368] Dunn, "John 6".
[369] So Schnelle, *Anti-Docetic Christology*, 202, 207.
[370] Richter, "Formgeschichte", 43.
[371] Dunn, "John 6", 330; Schenke, "Formale und gedenkliche Struktur".
[372] This has been frequently observed. McDonald, *Kerygma and didache*, 49, expresses the situation well: ". . . on strictly literary criteria the contrast between this passage and its context is very slight; the entire sequence is thoroughly Johannine . . ."
[373] Bornkamm, "Eucharistische Rede", 163–164.
[374] Jeremias, "Joh 6:51c–58: Redaktionell?".

of the chapter, the feeding of the 5000. Although the eucharistic language of this story has been exaggerated[375] we may reasonably assert that it this interest in eating which is picked up by the post-script to the homily. Moreover it is to be noted that in the feeding miracle it is Jesus himself who gives the bread directly to the people, by contrast to the synoptic Gospels, who have the bread mediated through the disciples. In concentrating on the action of Jesus the feeding narrative reflects the theology of 51b–58, where Jesus himself is the giver, rather than of 31–51b. It would thus seem that 51c–58, if a postscript, has been composed in order to expand on the matter of the sign which preceded. This post-script must, moreover, have been composed by someone with some understanding of the form of the proem homily because of the appropriateness of the conclusion and because it is possible (as Borgen does) to read this as a continuation of the exegesis of φαγεῖν. Whatever other tensions may be discerned in the passage, not only is the language Johannine, the form likewise is complete and undisrupted. The redactor not only has an understanding of Johannine language but also of the means of communication of the Johannine school.

The tensions between 51c–58 and the rest of the discourse are undeniable. But the connection between 30–51b and the preceding material of the chapter is also somewhat obscure. Schnelle suggests that the preceding miracle is "forgotten" here,[376] and Borgen notes that the references to eating in this part of the passage are minimal.[377] The implication of this is that since 31–51b is not altogether consistent with the foregoing sign, the feeding of 5000, it has not been composed for the purpose of inclusion in the Gospel. For this reason we may state that this passage, but not 51c–58, is pre-existent and independent material, and that this passage was a Johannine prophetic homily which has been redacted into the narrative, whilst the post-script to the homily is intended to supply anchorage of the original homily to the narrative setting.

If 51b is seen as the conclusion to the original homily, then the role of 51c needs to be examined. Whereas it is widely assumed that this formed part of the post-script, Schürmann suggests that it belongs

---

[375] Dunn, "Eucharistic discourse", 332–333.
[376] Schnelle, *Anti-docetic Christology*, 201.
[377] Borgen, "Unity", 278.

to the earlier passage.[378] If he is right then it is added on to the concluding citation of the homily, which would be unusual to say the least. Theologically Schürmann is correct; the emphasis of the verset, whilst having passing overtones of eucharistic imagery, is the death of Jesus, and as such it looks back to the role of the father of sending Jesus, which is the essential subject of the earlier homily. But if a compositional process is envisaged it is entirely reasonable to see with Schürmann that it is the vital link between the two parts of the discourse because of the way in which it connects the substance of the earlier part of the discourse with the eucharistic language of the latter part, but unnecessary to conclude with him that the whole discourse is an original unity,[379] but rather to suggest that this is the point at which the redactional material begins. The addition to the homily is not an afterthought but is an addition nonetheless, the result of careful redactional activity, a careful redactional activity which includes the provision of verses 26–29, an opening statement which, in discussing the difference between ephemeral bread and the food of eternal life, prepares the way for the eucharistic section which follows.[380]

All of this indicates that the redactional work has been undertaken by the original evangelist, and results from the first incorporation of the material into the narrative framework of the Gospel.[381] A unity has been constructed, but some of the material employed originated separately from the Gospel form with a homily preached in the Johannine community. The redactional history for this chapter which is envisaged here fits in with the three-stage redactional history for the Gospel as a whole which is proposed by Schnackenburg.[382]

Schnackenburg envisaged pre-Gospel material as a first stage, which at a second stage is put into a Gospel setting, followed by a further redactional effort which lends final shape to the Gospel. The steps envisaged in the production of the sixth chapter are the first two, as an original Johannine homily is incorporated into the narrative frame which is constructed at the second stage; verses 26–29 and

---

[378] Schürmann, "Schlüssel" followed by Anderson, *Christology*, 127–134.
[379] The conclusion of Schürmann, "Schlüssel", 262.
[380] Schürmann, "Schlüssel", notes the significance of these verses; Schnelle, *Anti-docetic Christology*, 195, argues for their redactional character.
[381] So Schnelle, *Anti-docetic Christology*, 195.
[382] Schnackenburg, *John*, 59–74.

51c–58 are provided at this stage as a fence around the homily which allow its inclusion. The eucharistic postscript may therefore be seen as an addition made to a pre-existent homily in order to lend the discourse conformity with the narrative setting and enable the whole chapter to be interpreted as a whole.[383] It is the very presence of redactional material which alerts the reader to the presence of the original homily embedded in the text. Since the major part of the discourse had independent existence of the Gospel this implies that it was a real homily preached in the Johannine community and not a desk homily, since were a desk homily to be supplied for the literary occasion we would would expect it to fit more neatly into the surrounding narrative. It is possible that in the process of recording some abbreviation may have taken place, but certainly in its elements and outline this may be taken as an example of Johannine preaching.

The narrative context into which it has been placed provides interruptions and objections, ending with an internal dispute in which the Jews ask "How can this man give us his flesh to eat?" Richter attributed this question to internal divisions within the Johannine community,[384] but although we can only speculate here, it is quite possible that this, and the other objections found in the course of the homily, are narratized versions of diatribal objections with which the discourse was broken up, and so their existence does not provide an objection to seeing the passage as a homily,[385] but rather provides evidence that such an origin is quite conceivable. The scholastic setting of Johannine Christianity would lead one to look for diatribal elements in its preaching, and so these objections may well have been formed out of the characters of imaginary opponents, including Jewish opponents, both within and without the Johannine school. Diatribal style is united with prophetic speech forms and a proto-rabbinic hermeneutic to form the Johannine sermon, as the interplay between discourse and dialogue, though now stylized through being written, may give us a picture of the interplay of διάλεξις and ὁμιλία in the Johannine school. Recognizing the questions and interruptions as signs of diatribe also lends grounds to assert that 51c is

---

[383] In agreement with Schnelle, *Anti-docetic Christology*, 202–206.
[384] Richter, "Formegeschichte", 43; also Schnelle, *Anti-docetic Christology*, 208.
[385] Lindars, *John*, 51, sees this as a potential objection.

the beginning of the following section, the eucharistic discourse, rather than the conclusion of what preceded. For Barrett argues that although the discourse is constructed around the objections "the division at this point is not entirely satisfactory, for it means that after one short sentence Jesus breaks off, the Jews ask their complaining question and the discourse then resumes with a reiteration of the reference to σάρξ."[386] Schenke similarly sees the *Vorgeschichte* of *John* 6 as dialogue, breaking up the discourse into various elements divided through the objections and interruptions.[387] This may anticipate a greater tidiness than is necessary. Recognizing the interruptions as indicative of diatribal technique means that they are to play no role in the construction of the passage except as signs to the hearer that a new theme has begun already. The precise point of the interruption at verse 52 is not therefore that Jesus breaks off after one sentence but that he is interrupted (or rather an interruption is made by the speaker in the *persona* of a hostile audience) which means that the reiteration of the theme can be read as an answer to the objection and taken in a new direction.

But apart from the homiletic elements provided by diatribal technique and prophetic speech forms (neither of which guarantee the presence of a homily) the essential ingredient for this homily is provided by Scripture, which is interpreted in the manner of the synagogue. The homily takes off from a text from *Exodus* 16. According to Abrahams this was the Torah for the second year in the first weeks of Iyyar,[388] the time of the barley harvest, and so fits in with the (springtime) references to the plentitude of grass and to the fact that the loaves mentioned are barley loaves (the first weeks of Iyyar are the time of the barley harvest.) However not too much should be made of the barley loaves, since these are more probably a detail taken from *II Kings* 4:42–44, where Elisha similarly feeds a crowd. Moreover it is unsafe to ground any firm conclusion on the basis of a lectionary theory due to the uncertainty whether there was any fixed lectionary in use at the time.[389]

---

[386] Barrett, "Flesh", 40.

[387] Schenke, "Literarische Vorgeschichte", building on his claims in "Formale und gedenkliche Struktur". Schenke hardly gives a satisfactory account, however, of what kind of material was employed in John's construction of his dialogue.

[388] Quoted by McDonald, *Kerygma and didache*, 166.

[389] Heinemann, "Triennial lectionary cycle".

The text informs us that the Pascha was near. This, together with the wealth of paschal reference in the discourse and in the sign, would seem to imply a setting in the month of Nisan rather than Iyyar. Further evidence of this may be presented by the depth of eschatological feeling which is betrayed in the narrative. In John's version of the walking on the water the disciples are in the boat; John stresses the darkness, and then goes on to say that "Jesus had not yet come to them",[390] an implication that the disciples are actually expecting the coming of Jesus. This expectation is satisfied not only in the divine epiphany on the water, but in the subsequent discourse. This may well represent a *Sitz im Leben* of Johannine paschal worship, a nocturnal waiting for the revelation of Jesus of the sort that was practised by the Quartodeciman communities of Asia in the second century, who were themselves heirs to the Johannine heritage. The discourse is in part the satisfaction of the expectation of revelation of the presence of Jesus among them, through the paraclete speaking in the mouthpiece of the Johannine prophet.

However the Johannine community, as well as practising prophecy, was well aware of the dangers of false prophets. We have observed that prophecy in the Pauline community was tested, and that the criterion employed was its coherence with past revelation, and in particular its coherence with scriptural revelation. Dunn notes that a similar procedure was carried on within the Johannine community with the essential criterion being a matter of whether the prophecy given was coherent with the central Johannine conviction that Christ had come in the flesh.[391] There is however no evidence that these prophetic discourses were tested beyond the ὁμιλία which interrupts the delivery.

In part this derives from the fact that they are already based on Scripture, but also we suggest that it is a result of the school-setting in which the preaching takes place, which was itself the guarantor of the prophecy. Culpepper defines the characteristics of ancient schools as the pursuit of the ideal of fellowship or friendship embodied in communal celebration, a sense of tradition as the means of passing down the wisdom of a founder, a concern for discipleship as the outworking of philosophical wisdom, a pre-occupation with

---

[390] *John* 6:17.
[391] Dunn, "Prophetic 'I'-sayings".

reading, teaching and study, and an ambivalent attitude to those outside the school, who whilst potential converts or learners are nonetheless defined as those who are not members. Whereas not all of these characteristics are exclusive to ancient schools since, as Culpepper notes, a number of these characteristics are shared by sects,[392] the simultaneous appearance of these characteristics in any ancient social group provides us with a good case for viewing that group as a school.

Culpepper argues that the Johannine community shares sufficient numbers of these characteristics to properly be classified as a school. In common with Epicurean communities the members are known as brothers and friends, there is emphasis on the ideal of fellowship which is re-inforced by the practice of common ritual and esoteric use of language, there is evidence of literary activity within the school since the Gospel itself shows evidence of revision, there is emphasis on the role of the founder, the beloved disciple, and there is evidence in the Gospel text which shows that there has been sustained reflection on the Scriptures.[393] Culpepper concentrates on the role of the beloved disciple, who is, he suggests, an idealization of a historical personage. He notes that the beloved disciple performs the same functions within the community that are attributed to the paraclete.[394] He also notes that these roles of teaching, guiding and reminding the disciples of Scripture are the central functions of the Johannine community, which are in essence scholastic; this explains the interest in the Gospel in the teaching role of Jesus.

If the Johannine prophetic discourses are from the mouth of the beloved disciple then, because of his unquestioned authority within the school, there would be no need to test the contents of the message; the beloved disciple is the embodiment of the paraclete, and is perfect in his relationship to Jesus as Jesus was perfect in his relationship to the father (each reclines on the breast of the other). The need to test the spirits comes when others take up the practice of the beloved disciple in the extended Johannine communities.

In keeping with this scholastic organisation we have already seen that John's preaching, like that of which we know within the syna-

---

[392] Culpepper, *Johannine school*, 259.
[393] Culpepper, *Johannine school*, 262, in summary and 264–279 in detail.
[394] Culpepper, *Johannine school*, 267–268.

gogue, is tied closely to Scripture. That this should be the case does not however contradict the prophetic element of Johannine preaching. Teaching was a function of a prophet in the primitive church and is described as one of the functions of the paraclete. So when Johnston is unclear about whether the words of Paul at *I Thessalonians* 4:15 are those of a prophet or of a teacher,[395] we may reply that in a first-century context the distinction is artificial. More particularly we should note that one of the prophetic roles of the paraclete is to remind the disciples of the teaching of Jesus. The paraclete reminds the disciples of the teaching of Jesus, and the teaching of Jesus in turn is recorded as reminding the disciples of the teaching of Scripture. Prophecy therefore does not cut across scriptural preaching, but the prophecy nonetheless is not unmediated as it had been in the Pauline communities. Rather the prophetic element in Johannine preaching provides John with a hermeneutic. Preaching in this school is therefore at one and the same time a scholastic reflection upon Scripture and an inspired discourse.

Borgen's treatment of chapter six as a homily is accepted by Lindars.[396] But according to Lindars this method of exegesis and exegetical preaching is not restricted to Scripture; the discourses of the fourth Gospel may be explained as being built up out of homilies, including homilies preached on items of the Jesus tradition.[397] As an example of this he takes *John* 8:31–58, and concludes that the form and methods employed by John are those of a preacher, that "the discourse is . . . not a report of an actual debate . . . it is a sermon addressed to the Christians in order to deepen and strengthen their faith".[398]

Lindars suggests that the homily begins with the dialogue in 31–33, in which the themes of the discourse are laid out. But then he goes on to suggest that verse 34, the statement that anyone who sins is a slave, is the foundation of the argument, together with an accompanying parable in verse 35 concerning the slave and the son; a slave has no permanent place in a household whereas that of a son is permanent.[399] The "homily" is thus based on this text, and we

---

[395] Johnston, *Spirit-Paraclete*, 129.
[396] Lindars, *John*, 47–50.
[397] Lindars, *Behind the fourth Gospel*, 43–60.
[398] Lindars, *Behind the fourth Gospel*, 47.
[399] Lindars, *Behind the fourth Gospel*, 44.

may recognise the earlier dialogue as a narrative device employed
to fix the homily in place.

The first part of the homily concerns the descent of the Jews and
of Jesus, and picks up on the (unmentioned, but surely present) father
in the household of the parable. Jesus and the Jews argue concerning the true father of Jesus, as of the Jews, be he Abraham (the first
claim of the Jews), God (Jesus' claim, counter-claimed by the Jews),
or the devil (a claim made by Jesus of the Jews). This section comes
to an end in verse 48 when the Jews accuse Jesus of being mad. At
this point Jesus picks up on a second aspect of the parable, the per-
manence which the son has in the father's house, which is interpreted in terms of eternal life. When the Jews dispute whether it is
possible that there should be eternal life, given that even Abraham
is dead, this opens the way for the final saying of self-revelation,
which itself authenticates the prophetic treatment of the *mashal* as a
whole. Lindars thus notes that John constructs the discourse so that
the reader does not lose sight of Abraham, whose status is at the
centre of the homily.

There are a number of points which we may marshal in support
of Lindar's explanation of the construction of this discourse. Firstly
that the dialogue implies, as it did in chapter 6, that the techniques
of diatribe were employed in the original delivery of this homily,
and that the narrative has preserved some reflection of these techniques in the process of questioning and dialogue. Secondly we may
note that the basis of the homily is a *mashal*, given in support of the
original saying. It is entirely conceivable that a homily in a setting
which is broadly Jewish-Christian should be based on a saying and
an accompanying *mashal* as we have observed when dealing with the
preaching of Hermas.[400] Finally we may note that the "homily" concludes with an oracle of self-disclosure entirely suited to a prophetic
exposition. Apart from laying out the argument of the discourse,
Lindars' claim to see the passage as homiletic is chiefly based on
subjective observations concerning the suitability of this technique to
preaching. We may claim to have given the argument here some
objective undergirding by seeing the Johannine method in the light
of other homiletic practices. We may also see that prophecy and
preaching intersect in the Johannine school even when the preach-

---

[400] 2.1.2.

ing is not based on Scripture but on a saying of the earthly Jesus, through the paraclete's bringing to remembrance of Jesus. We may finally note that prophecy and preaching intersect in that a homiletic process of expansion and application may be confirmed with a word of prophecy: that is to say that prophecy confirms prophecy.

2.2.3.2. Papias' ἐξεγήσεις of the Lord's λόγια as preaching

A further representative of the Asian school tradition who may illuminate our attempt to trace the development of the homily is Papias, who was prominent in Hierapolis in the early part of the second century.[401] We intend to argue that his comments on elements of the Gospels reflect the process of *diakrisis* of prophecy, and thus demonstrate that the same procedure as known before is still in play, but that the locus of *diakrisis* is moving away from the living voice of prophecy, even though prophecy is still practised, toward recorded written prophecies.

Absolute certainty about the social organisation of Papias' church is impossible, but it may be noted that Papias himself was rhetorically educated, since he treats the Gospels according the canons of ancient literary criticism.[402] He was moreover a collector of traditions received from the ancients, from whom he sought to learn.[403] This historical and rhetorical interest is the basis on which his church has been classed here among those of a scholastic orientation. However one may also note that Papias is at pains to stress the sources of his learning, which may indicate a concern to establish a succession of teachers to guarantee his own teaching, a typically scholastic concern. According to Körtner these teachers were *Wanderprediger*,[404] but there is no evidence of this being the case. Philip stands in the succession of Papias' teachers, and all the evidence indicates that Philip was settled in Hierapolis.

Also in this quoted succession lies John the Elder. However, although there are some indications that Papias is heir to some authentically Johannine tradition, such as is betrayed in the order in which he lists the disciples of the Lord in his prologue, which is

---

[401] On the date of Papias see Schoedel, "Papias", 236–237, 262–263 and references.
[402] On Papias as a rhetorician see Stewart-Sykes, "τάξει in Papias", and references.
[403] Papias at Eusebius *Historia ecclesiastica* 3.39.3.
[404] Körtner, *Papias*, 129–132.

the same of that of the fourth Gospel,[405] one cannot put too much
trust in the statement of Irenaeus that Papias was a hearer of John
the Apostle since this would appear to be a deduction made by
Irenaeus himself.[406] Although Papias is recorded as having reference
to *I John*[407] there is nothing particularly Johannine at a theological
level about the surviving fragments of Papias, and so although it
may be possible to speak of a school of John, on the grounds of the
absence of any peculiarly Johannine theological concerns we must
conclude that Papias was not a member;[408] John was undoubtedly
an honoured prophet in the Christian community of Hierapolis, but
he did not stand in the position of founder. We may therefore expect
that the preaching of Papias might differ formally from that of the
fourth evangelist despite their common Asian origin and scholastic
orientation. Papias thus represents a separate strand in the development of the Asian church, though a strand that would coalesce in
time with Johannine influence.

According to Eusebius, Papias composed five books of λογίων
κυριακῶν ἐξεγήσεως,[409] a title which has led to extensive discussion,
over the meaning both of *logia* and of *exegēsis*. We intend to argue
that this work was a homiletic collection, and in support of this interpretation we intend to argue that *logion* here has as its meaning "oracle" and that *exegēsis* is "interpretation" in the manner in which the
word was employed to refer to the interpretation of oracles in the
ancient world. This has a prima facie probability in that Hierapolis
was no stranger to prophetic religion; the daughters of Philip, well
known as prophets, were active there, and Papias has reference to
traditions handed down by them.[410] The seer of *Revelation* likewise
wrote a letter to Hierapolis. The rhetorical sophistication which has
been observed in the work of Papias may seem to fit ill with this

---

[405] So Hengel, *Johannine question*, 17.

[406] *Adversus haereses* 5.33.4. Multiple confusions may well have entered here. For
instance it is possible that Irenaeus has confused John the Apostle with John the
elder. It is also possible that Papias' chiliasm is connected with that of the seer of
the Apocalypse, but, as Körtner, *Papias*, 100–101, notes, this is a possibility only,
as the chiliasm represented by Papias' tradition is rather more developed.

[407] Eusebius *Historia ecclesiastica* 3.39.7.

[408] Cf. Schoedel, *Apostolic fathers*, 90, who denies that a Johannine school existed
at all.

[409] *Historia ecclesiastica* 3.39.1.

[410] *Historia ecclesiastica* 3.39.4, 3.39.9.

kind of prophetic religion, but as Schoedel observes, there is a "curious union of primitive Jewish Christian concerns and advanced Hellenistic literary pretensions".[411]

Apart from the regard in which prophecy was held in Asia, the suggestion that Papias' work was a work of the interpretation of oracles may be given lexical support. Although the lexical evidence does not necessitate the interpretation suggested here it is entirely possible. The fundamental reason for understanding the λογίων κυριακῶν ἐξεγήσεως as "Interpretation of the oracles of the Lord" derives from a recognition that the shape of Christian discourse in preaching might be the judgement and elucidation of a cited oracle. This shape is manifest in one of the surviving fragments of Papias' work, and thus gives the clue to the meaning of the title and the form of the contents.

The first term which we may examine in Papias' title is λόγια. According to Lightfoot the word was a technical term for a Gospel, and Papias' work was therefore a commentary on one of the Gospels.[412] But Baum points out that according to Papias Matthew was a σύνταξις τῶν κυριακῶν λογίων, and that therefore the singular λόγιον would not apply to a Gospel but to an isolated saying.[413] A second suggested meaning is to make the word equivalent to τὰ ὑπὸ τοῦ Κυρίου ἢ λεχθέντα ἢ πραχθέντα,[414] which is the manner in which Papias describes the contents of the Gospel of Mark.[415] However a report concerning τὰ λεχθέντα καὶ πραχθέντα is essentially the definition of a *chreia*,[416] and the point that Papias is making is that Mark is a *chreia* collection.[417] It is not used as an equivalent to λόγια in this passage of Papias, since only things which were said might be considered λόγια. A third suggestion is that of Kürzinger, followed here by Körtner, that the Κυρίου is used as an objective and not a subjective genitive, and that the λόγια are therefore reports about the Lord, rather than sayings to be attributed to the Lord.[418] Once again this is an attempt to conform the meaning of the term to make it

---

[411] Schoedel, "Papias", 268.
[412] Lightfoot, *Essays*, 176–77.
[413] Baum, "Papias als Kommentator", 259.
[414] So Munck, "Presbyters and disciples", 228.
[415] At *Historia ecclesiastica* 3.39.15.
[416] Hermogenes *Progymnasmata* 3: ἀπομνημόνευμα λόγου τινὸς ἢ πράξεως.
[417] So Stewart-Sykes, "τάξει in Papias", 492.
[418] Kürzinger, "Papias von Hierapolis: zu Titel und Art seines Werkes"; followed in part by Körtner, *Papias*, 151–167.

equivalent to a written Gospel, for all that Papias himself preferred the living voice. However Baum points out that in the mind of the second century the sayings of Scripture were to be attributed to the Lord, whereas (in conformity with rhetorical terminology) reports about the Lord are described as διηγήσεις.[419] The remaining option is that Papias' choice of the word reflects the usual usage of Greek literature, and that is that the term is intended to mean "oracles",[420] and that the oracles referred to are statements of the Lord, which are interpreted as sayings from God. Baum concludes that it is the sayings of the Lord which are intended and he finds some support in that the surviving material concentrates on what is said.[421] But in agreeing with Baum here we should emphasize that the oracular quality of the sayings are given particular prominence by the use of this term, that the sayings are understood as prophetic sayings, whether said by the Lord as a prophet or uttered by him through his prophets.

The second term to be examined is ἐξέγησις. There is no doubt that the term can refer to a narrative, and that is the sense in which Kürzinger chooses to take it here;[422] according to him Papias' work is a narrative of the deeds of the Lord. In part his interpretation depends on his suggestion of an objective genitive for Κυρίου, and our recognition that this is not the case weakens his argument. Baum further observes that, although ἐξέγησις may mean a narrative, that is not the usual sense of the word in this period, but rather that explanation or interpretation is the more common meaning.[423] Körtner argues along similar lines to Kürzinger at this point, suggesting that the word is used in parallel with διήγησις;[424] however, in recognising that when Papias states that one of the purposes of his writing is interpretation (ἑρμηνεῖαι), he decides in the end that the book was not a narrative pure and simple but a narrative commentary.[425] Schoedel responds to this that it is hard to understand what kind

---

[419] Baum, "Papias als Kommentator", 262–263.
[420] Herodotus *Historiae* 1.64; Plutarch *Fabius Maximus* 4.5 (of the Sibylline, which is indicative that the usage was still current at the time of Papias).
[421] Baum, "Papias als Kommentator", 273.
[422] Kürzinger, "Papias von Hierapolis: zu Titel und Art seines Werkes".
[423] Baum, "Papias", 268.
[424] Körtner, *Papias*, 159–162.
[425] Körtner, *Papias*, 163.

of work this may mean.[426] ἑρμηνεία is translated by Kürzinger as "Darstellung", with particular reference to a number of uses in Lucian. A similar use is found in Dionysius of Halicarnassus *De Compositione* 1; this usage has developed from the technical use of the term in rhetoric to refer to narratives. For Kürzinger this is further evidence that what we have is a new narration of the words of the elders. However Schoedel examines the use of the word in Lucian, and comes to the correct conclusion that the usage refers to "rhetorically effective literary compositions" rather than "narratives".[427] He then goes on to dismiss any possibility that Papias is employing the word in this sense. Given Papias' rhetorical training there is no reason why he might not see part of his role in confirming the truth of the oracles and making them real as putting them into a rhetorically actuating shape; given his rhetorical training it is moreover probable that his usage would reflect that of contemporary rhetoricians. But this still does not mean that Papias is referring to a narrative. Rather he means a rhetorically effective treatment demonstrating the truth of the oracles about the Lord and clarifying their content in the same manner.

But whilst rejecting the interpretation of ἐξέγησις as narrative and recognising that its purpose is explanation, it is not necessary to return with Baum to the idea that Papias' work was some kind of commentary on the Gospels, even if it accords with the testimony of Jerome that the work of Papias was *explanatio*.[428] Used in connection with λόγια it is quite probable that the ἐξέγησις to which Papias refers is the process of interpretation (*explanatio*) of oracles; this was a common enough classical usage, as the role of *exegētēs* was understood as that of oracle interpreter.[429] The discussion cannot be settled by lexicology alone, since the explanation offered here, whilst lexically possible, is not the only possible interpretation; even so it is an interpretation which accounts for both words employed by Papias and for their combination here, which accords with the points he makes in his preface about his purpose, namely that it is to confirm the truth of the oracles he treats, and which accords with

---

[426] Schoedel, "Papias", 269.
[427] Schoedel, "Papias" 269, n76.
[428] *De Viris illustribus* 18.
[429] As at Herodotus *Historiae* 1.78.

the prophetic orientation of Christianity at Hierapolis which we have already noted.

Further support for this interpretation may be lent by the observation that the form of Papias' work might well have been that of the confirmation of oracular statements from the tradition. According to Schoedel, who here follows Lightfoot, Papias' work consisted of a citation from a Gospel (a *logion*) followed by an interpretation and an illustration from the oral tradition.[430] If Schoedel and Lightfoot are correct we may perceive that this pattern is similar to the discussion of prophetic oracles known in the Pauline churches, with an oracle being discussed and its truth finally determined by reference to Scripture. But if this is the case then the final element is not illustrative, as Schoedel and Lightfoot assume, but a citation meant to demonstrate the truth of the oracle and its interpretation, in the manner that citation might be employed in the schools. This is in entire conformity with the interpretation of Papias' title which we have proposed, just as the procedure of the testing of prophetic speech is in conformity with the stated purpose of his work, namely a gathering of the traditions of the elders into a treatise together with their *hermeneia* for the purpose of confirming their truth. It may seem a little strange that the same Papias who voiced suspicion of the written word and a preference for the living voice should himself be an author; however if we see Papias in the context of a prophetic tradition we may so solve the contradiction. Papias prefers the living voice because, like any other prophet, the speaker might be interrogated in order to confirm the veracity of the oracle which has been spoken. However, when the oracle has passed into the written tradition the original speaker can no longer be questioned and so a procedure of proof must suffice in order to perform the same function of διάκρισις and interpretation.

We may seek to observe this procedure of determining the prophetic authenticity of λόγια in the remaining exegetical fragments of Papias. Before doing so, we may observe an exegesis attributed to "the elders" in Irenaeus at *Adversus haereses* 3.21.4 which might indicate a similar procedure of scholastic *diakrisis* of written oracles. This shows that the procedure attributed to Papias was far from foreign to the

---

[430] Schoedel, *Apostolic fathers*, 94, "Papias", 145, following Lightfoot, *Essays*, 158–159.

Asian tradition. Irenaeus is defending the virgin birth, and the understanding of the term παρθένος in *Isaiah* 7 to mean a virgin.

> But the elders have interpreted what Isaiah said thus . . .

Here follows a complete citation of *Isaiah* 7:10–17, and after the citation comes an atomizing interpretation.

> The Holy Spirit has, therefore, indicated carefully, through what is being said, his birth, which is from a virgin and his essence, that he is God, for this is what the name Emmanuel signifies. And he shows that he is a man, when he says 'butter and honey shall he eat', and in that he terms him a child also 'before he knows good and evil', for all these are the manifestations of a human infant. But that "he will not consent to evil, that he may choose that which is good", this is proper to God . . .

The manner in which the interpretation follows on from a citation, taking points in turn is perhaps illustrative of a homiletic *exegēsis* of Isaiah's prophetic *logion* given through the Holy Spirit.

We may thus turn to Papias' own ἐξεγήσεις. Whereas most of the fragments preserved from his book are brief comments, and tell us little about the form of the longer work from which they have been excerpted, fragment 1 is revealing of a larger context read in its context within the work of Irenaeus.

Irenaeus is arguing for the reality of the millennial Kingdom, and quotes a series of Scriptures concluding with the text "I shall not drink henceforth of the fruit of this vine until that day when I drink it new with you in my Fathers' Kingdom."[431] The text is interpreted by concentrating on two points, the drinking of wine and the reality of the resurrection of the flesh, which is a reality towards which the drinking points. This is related in turn to the blessing of Jacob which, Irenaeus argues, is a blessing for the millennial Sabbath.[432] It is in this context that he goes on to cite the tradition of "the elders who saw John", who bear witness to sayings of the Lord which concern the days which will come when:

> vineyards shall grow each with ten thousand vines, and on one vine ten thousand branches, and on one branch ten thousand shoots, and on every shoot ten thousand clusters, and in every cluster ten thousand

---

[431] *Adversus haereses* 5.33.1.

grapes, and every grape when pressed will give twenty-five measures of wine . . ."

Irenaeus goes on to say that

Papias, a man of the primitive period, who was a hearer of John and a companion of Polycarp, also bears witness to these things in the fourth of his books.

A further pair of citations are then added:

These things are credible to those who believe

and

When Judas the traitor did not believe and asked "How will such extraordinary growths be brought about by the Lord?" the Lord said "Those who are alive when they take place will see them."

This fragment is the basis of Lightfoot's suggestion that the shape of Papias' work is that of citation followed by interpretation and confirmation. However it needs to be shown that Irenaeus is actually referring to Papias when he talks of "the elders who saw John". This tradition of the elders may be traced back to Papias' writing since Irenaeus goes on to say that "Papias also bears witness to these things in writing . . ." For whereas Körtner suggests that the tradition is not to be limited to Papias but is the product of a wider Johannine school, and that in this case Papias is cited as a secondary witness,[433] Schoedel suggests that the literary context is such that the foregoing must be a citation of Papias, and that Papias' work is the source which Irenaeus employs at this point. When Irenaeus says that Papias also bears witness to these things in writing he is stating not that Papias bears secondary witness to the tradition but that Papias has committed the oral tradition to writing.[434]

But although Papias is Irenaeus' written source for the entire citation, the entire citation is not to be attributed to Papias, as is commonly the case. Rather the whole eschatological description is itself a citation made by Papias of an oracle of the Lord. The description of the millennial Kingdom is the λόγιον Κυρίου which he is intending to prove and interpret. This prophetic oracle concerning

---

[432] *Adversus haereses* 5.33.2.
[433] Körtner, *Papias*, 41–42.
[434] Schoedel, *Apostolic fathers*, 94.

the millennial Kingdom is itself possibly the product of prophetic preaching; thus the order in which the grape and the corn are found, together with the call of the grape to be taken and blessed, is indicative of a liturgical context.[435] Its possibly "midrashic" content[436] might also be the result of charismatic and prophetic exegesis since it shows remarkable parallels with contemporary apocalyptic literature, and because some elements can be derived from a treatment of the Hebrew text of Genesis.[437] This however need not have taken place within the assembly. In Papias' treatment however we have clear indication of the manner in which prophecy in a school might function homiletically.

What follows the oracle is Papias' further proof. He proceeds by supporting the oracle with two further citations, the saying of the Lord that this is not difficult to those who believe and the reply given to Judas that those who live shall see these things. These are further citations of oracles, which presumably are themselves already considered tested and true, against which to measure the oracle just given in order to be assured of its veracity. It is more than possible that Papias continued with his interpretation beyond the brief citation which we have. The grotesque report of Judas' swelling up and bursting, resulting in his death,[438] is also said to come from the fourth book of Papias' work and it is even possible that this story is an extension of the proof of the reply given to Judas, namely that whereas those who live shall see, those who do not believe would surely die.

Irenaeus is here proving a *thesis* by citation and the citation from Papias is one of his citations by way of proof; what follows is a further citation, of the prophecy of Isaiah of the millennial Kingdom.[439] Whether this rhetorical method was employed in Irenaeus' own preaching is impossible to say. Papias, by demonstrating the truth contained in the oracles, might likewise claim to be proving a *thesis*,

---

[435] So McGowan, "First concerning the cup".

[436] The word is that of Schoedel, *Apostolic fathers*, 94.

[437] On which note Gry, "Le Papias des belles promesses messianiques". In particular, at 116, Gry suggests that the number ten thousand is derived from *Genesis* 27:28 (where plenty (רֹב) of grain and wine becomes ten-thousand (רִבּוֹ) and at 114 where he suggests that the call to "take me" derives from הכלילי (*Genesis* 49:12) read as הכי לי לי.

[438] Fragment 5 (Kürzinger).

[439] It is even possible that the citation of *Isaiah* 11 is part of Papias' own ἐξέγησις.

namely the *logion*, through further citation. Schoedel and Lightfoot
are thus entirely justified in seeing the citation of Papias insepara-
bly from its context in Irenaeus since it is demonstrative of the same
millennial theology and the same rhetorical procedure. What is
different however is that Papias' procedure reflects preaching in his
community, since the interpretation offered here is in accordance
with the pattern of homiletic explanation of prophecy which we have
observed elsewhere in primitive Christianity. The process of discernment and proof of prophecy by further citation is one of the origins
of preaching, which procedure is here being applied to the oracles
of the Lord. As part of the demonstration of its veracity it is broken down into constituent parts, and the treatment is concluded by
the demonstration of its conformity with other oracular statements.
Thus Papias, within the school tradition, has adopted the procedure
of testing prophecy, and extends it not to the verbal prophecy of
the church but to the (probably written) prophecy of the Lord. By
virtue of his suspicion of the written word and in accordance with
the normal procedure for receiving prophecy the written oracle needs
to be tested. But Papias' very suspicion of the written oracle serves
to elevate its position in the liturgy of the church by becoming the
basis of a homiletic treatment. In time the procedure of confirming
the oracles of the Lord would inevitably lead to their being the subject of preaching and exposition.

2.2.3.3. *The prophetic communication of* Epistula apostolorum

The Johannine tradition was one which was to be mediated widely
in the Asian church, and in particular the practice of prophetic
preaching was to continue. One might well anticipate that the
Johannine school might exercise a fair degree of influence in Asian
Christianity beyond its own immediate setting in Ephesus. These
may be described as Johannine trajectories,[440] currents of theological
approach which extended through Asia, which nonetheless developed
in their own ways, and are not necessarily bound up to the recep-
tion of the text of the fourth Gospel. We intend to see the manner
in which Johannine prophetic preaching is manifested in other Asian
schools, and begin with a document the Johannine basis of which

---

[440] A term borrowed from Pervo, "Johannine trajectories".

is widely accepted, the anonymous, but Asian, *Epistula apostolorum*.[441]

Hills notes the great variety of forms exhibited in the early part of the *Epistula apostolorum*. In particular he notes the presence of hymnic and exhortatory elements within the epistolary framework, and concludes eventually that the reader is given "a series of brief expositions on historical, doctrinal and ethical topics held together by the glue of the dialogue form".[442] However dialogical elements may, as we have already seen, be more than simply a literary convention to link various expositions. We have noted that dialogue may reflect a liturgical setting as a teacher is questioned by his pupils (a dialogue reflected especially in the diatribe) and as a prophet in the Spirit is interrogated in order to confirm the truth of his inspiration and to examine the content of the prophecy. It is our suggestion here that this is the context reflected by *Epistula apostolorum*, and that, as in the case of the work of Hermas, the dialogical similarities between which and the *Epistula* so impressed Schmidt,[443] the dialogue reflects the delivery of prophetic messages in the assembly. Stewart-Sykes has already suggested that a dialogue is the proper way in which early Christianity presented revelation reports,[444] and this may now be explained with reference to the liturgical procedure for receiving and adjudicating revelation. In both *Epistula apostolorum* and Hermas' *Pastor* the prophecies have been redacted into a secondary literary form, but we suggest that in both cases the secondary form preserves the essence of the prophetic messages and reflects the manner in which the prophetic messages might be received. In support of this we intend to note the frequent prophetic speech forms to be found, the connection with the (prophetic) Johannine literature, and the exhortatory function of the dialogue. In this light we may also go on to understand the redactor's use of Scripture. The epistolary framework moreover is not inimical to this understanding, since the redactor of this dialogue is doing nothing unique in framing prophecies in an epistle; we may compare the καθολικὴ ἐπιστολή of Themiso,[445] which

---

[441] For the Asian Johannine provenance of this document see Stewart-Sykes, "Asian context" and Hill, "Epistula apostolorum".

[442] Hills, *Tradition*, 14.

[443] Schmidt, *Gespräche Jesu*, 206–7; note also Hills, *Tradition*, 22–23, 27–28, for similarities between the two.

[444] Stewart-Sykes, "Asian context", 427.

[445] Apollonius at Eusebius *Historia ecclesiastica* 5.18.5.

was itself most probably a prophetic collection. Just as Themiso's letter was prophetic, so *Epistula apostolorum* employs the form of an epistle to communicate its collection of speeches by the risen Christ.[446] Schmidt refers to these as a "Fiktion",[447] but the fictional setting lies in the address to the apostles, rather than in the epistolary form or in the content of the speeches. Within the epistolary setting we intend to argue that *Epistula apostolorum* should be viewed as a collection of prophecies, given in the name of the risen Christ, and reflecting the prophetic communication of the word of God experienced in the assembly of the redactor, a suggestion which also accounts for the inclusion of hymnic and credal material in the text. The revelation dialogue was beloved of the gnostics it is true,[448] but this is not the explanation for the use of the form here.[449] We may moreover suggest that this context is the reason for the very different tone of these dialogues and the dialogues in the Greek philosophical tradition.[450]

In understanding the *Epistula* as prophecy we may first note the frequent prophetic speech forms to be found. *Epistula apostolorum* may be seen as displaying the same "I" form of the word of prophecy which is exhibited by the extant Montanist oracles and by the fourth Gospel:

I am wholly in the Father and the Father is in me (17)

I am the word (17)

I am fully the right hand of the Father (19)

I am the hope of the hopeless . . . (21)

Secondly one may note the "amen" sayings:

Truly I say to you the flesh will arise (26)

Truly I say to you whoever will hear you and believe in me, he will receive from you the light of the seal through me . . . (41)

---

[446] So Schmidt recognizes this as a catholic epistle, but suggests that this is the superficial form only. Hills, *Tradition*, 11–14, shows that the epistolary form is more than superficial.

[447] Schmidt, *Gespräche Jesu*, 195.

[448] As originally noted by Schmidt, *Gespräche Jesu*, 206.

[449] Against Hornschuh, *Studien*, 92–97.

[450] Noted by Hills, *Tradition*, 15.

Hills suggests that the "amen" in this text functions to lend a saying a particular solemnity;[451] combined with predictive content, as it
is here, we may be justified in stating that it reflects a prophetic
delivery, given by a supernatural agency, the risen Christ. We may
moreover suggest that this prophetic practice derives from the tradition of the fourth Gospel. For although the redactor shows acquaintance with a wide range of what would become the canonical New
Testament the whole is viewed through a Johannine prism. Thus,
as Schmidt notes, not only is John at the head of the apostles but
the Jesus who speaks is the exalted Johannine Jesus.[452] It is the
Johannine nature of this Christ, rather than the frequent allusions
to the fourth Gospel,[453] which secures the Johannine character of
the document. This comes about because of the prophetic nature of
the speeches of Christ in the fourth Gospel, which character is likewise that of the speeches of Christ in the *Epistula*. This in turn
explains the common usage of the "I am" formula, and the manner in which the Christ of the fourth Gospel and the Christ of
Epistula apostolorum alike give extended speeches in a dialogical setting. Whereas both texts reflect the delivery of prophecy in the community the difference between the two lies in the nature of the
questioning, which in *Epistula apostolorum* is reverent, whilst that in
the fourth Gospel is often hostile, a situation which in turn reflects
the differing nature of the schools. The prophetic intent of *Epistula
apostolorum*, deriving from its Johannine roots, extends beyond its form
to its purpose and theological content. There are frequent references
to prophecy in the text, bound up to missionary proclamation and
teaching in the assembly. It is assumed that the apostles will preach
and prophesy,[454] and they are given peace and spirit and power so
to do.[455] The overall function of the piece may moreover be upheld
as prophetic, since Hills discovers in the redactional process of incor-
porating the prophetic discourses into their current shape an "earnest
exhortation".[456] Thus when a later redactor identified the book as

---

[451] Hills, *Tradition*, 25.
[452] Schmidt, *Gespräche Jesu*, 224; this assessment of the Johannine character of
Epistula apostolorum is upheld by Hills, *Tradition*, passim.
[453] Collected by Schmidt, *Gespräche Jesu*, 225–226.
[454] *Epistula apostolorum* 23.
[455] *Epistula apostolorum* 30.
[456] Hills, *Tradition*, 172.

an ἀποκάλυψις[457] we may conclude that this redactor was correct in his description; it is a prophetic revelation of the words of God.

It is in the light of the prophetic character of *Epistula apostolorum* that we may examine the use of Scripture. The chief source of authority in this community is the risen Christ, but nonetheless there are allusions to Old Testament Scripture. However it should come as no surprise to note that all the scriptural sources which are named are prophetic.[458] More striking is the use of New Testament traditions; here the units are free in their employment of the traditions. Insofar as written books are being employed, which would seem to be most likely, then this free employment and reshaping of the material may be described as "charismatic exegesis" comparable to that of the seer of *Revelation*, who freely alludes to the Hebrew prophets in his prophetic warnings and who readily adapts them to his own prophetic purpose.

An example of this may be provided by the section which deals with the parable of the ten virgins.[459] Jesus exhorts the disciples to be watchful like the five wise virgins of the parable; for the wise virgins were able to go into the bridegroom's chamber, whereas those foolish ones who slept were shut out. Thus far the exhortation is based on the Scripture. However, the disciples then demand to know who the five wise virgins are. The Lord answers by naming them as Faith, Love, Joy, Peace and Hope. These are the qualities of those who are to be leaders in the church. He goes on with an oracle of self-revelation:

> I am the Lord and I am the bridegroom, they have received me and have gone with me into the house of the bridegroom, and laid themselves down with the bridegroom and rejoiced.

The narrative thread of the parable is then picked up once again:

> But the five foolish slept, and when they awoke they came to the house of the bridegroom and knocked at the doors, for they had been shut; and they wept, because they were shut.

This leads to a discussion of the fate of those who were shut out, whose names are revealed to be Insight, Knowledge, Obedience, En-

---

[457] *Epistula apostolorum* 1.1; see Hills, *Tradition*, 11–12, for the retroversion from Ethiopic, and on the secondary nature of this title.
[458] Hills, *Tradition*, 31.
[459] *Epistula apostolorum* 43–45.

durance and Mercy.[460] The disciples are upset because of the fate of those who are shut out, but this, says the Lord, is a matter of divine justice and not in the hands of the disciples.

We may thus note that at times the text is followed and expanded, rather after the manner of the expansions of the text in the pseudo-Philonic homilies, but that eventually the expansion takes over. Although there are prophetic elements here, the prophecy of self-revelation is enmeshed with the reading of the scriptural text, and the whole is given shape through dialogue.[461] The fundamental interest moreover is paraenetic, for the naming of the virgins is not simply a matter of imagination but is indicative of an anti-gnostic struggle.[462] The use of Scripture is complex, indicative both of charismatic reading and homiletic expansion. But as such this is indicative of the fundamental communication strategy of *Epistula apostolorum* as simultaneously prophetic and scriptural, with overall paraenetic intent within the school setting. If *Epistula apostolorum* is indeed a product of the church of Smyrna, as Hill suggests,[463] then this is indicative of the way in which Polycarp can be simultaneously prophet and teacher.[464]

On the basis of the use which *Epistula apostolorum* makes of Scripture, and in particular on the basis of the numerous scriptural citations worked into the text, Schmidt suggests that the redactor was an officeholder in the church.[465] Certainly he is a preacher and a prophet, but the social organisation of this church would seem not be based on office since, as Schmidt himself notes, there is no trace of the Ignatian insistence upon the responsibility of officeholders.[466] We need not deduce from this silence that there were no officeholders in this community but rather that, if they existed, they were still fundamentally domestic and not relevant to the scholastic concerns of the redactor, just as the householders were of no concern to the prophet of Patmos. There is some indication that the teaching functions of

---

[460] According to the Coptic. The Ethiopic lists Knowledge, Wisdom, Obedience, Forbearance and Mercy.

[461] So Hornschuh, *Studien*, 21.

[462] So Hornschuh, *Studien*, 28–29.

[463] Hill, "Epistula apostolorum", 29–39.

[464] διδάσκαλος ἀποστολικὸς καὶ προφητικὸς γενόμενος ἐπίσκοπος (*Martyrium Polycarpi* 16.2).

[465] Schmidt, *Gespräche Jesu*, 214.

[466] Schmidt, *Gespräche Jesu*, 376–378.

members of the community were becoming bound up to some form
of institutional office at chapters 41–42 with the statement that they
will be "Fathers and *diakonoi* and workers"[467] but the emphasis of the
community's primary concern is not on office but on the mutual
relationship of the members of the community, who are told to love
one another and to obey one another[468] and on their mutual νουθεσία:

> If you see a sinner then admonish him between yourself and him. But
> if he does not listen to you then take with you another up to three
> and instruct your brother . . .[469]

This reflects the same scholastic ideal as the fourth Gospel of equal-
ity within the school and of mutual correction by the members of
the school. Just as the organisation of the apostles is that of a school,
the emphasis of the life of the community is likewise on teaching,
clearly considered to be a primary function of those who are leaders in the community; in conformity with this the disciples are to
be teachers delivering the word of Jesus and warning and rebuking.[470] Teaching is commanded also at 19 and 46, and in common
with the Johannine vision of the paraclete teaching through the disciples so the apostles of the *Epistula* recognize that, when they teach,
the risen Christ will be teaching through them.[471] As Hornschuh
notes, the message which they pass on is the same message which
was delivered at the beginning,[472] and so we may also see that this
community has the essential scholastic concern to maintain the traditional teaching. Teaching which consists of warning and rebuking
may be described as preaching when undertaken within a scholastic community, and so the teaching of Jesus within the *Epistula* may
be taken as typifying that which was prophetically delivered and discussed in ὁμιλία in the worshipping assembly of the redactor. *Epistula
apostolorum* thus provides us with a valuable example of an Asian
community which, whilst scholasticized, knows the practice of prophecy
as the fundamental means of the communication of the word of God
and engages in prophetic ὁμιλία.

---

[467] Cf. Hills, *Tradition*, 133, who seeks to deny an investment in office even here.
[468] *Epistula apostolorum* 18.
[469] *Epistula apostolorum* 48 (Coptic).
[470] *Epistula apostolorum* 42.
[471] *Epistula apostolorum* 42 (Coptic only); see Hills, *Tradition*, 133, for the reasoning behind preferring this reading to that of the Ethiopic.
[472] Hornschuh, *Studien*, 81.

2.2.3.4. *Melito's* Peri Pascha *as preaching?*

A further distinctively Johannine witness in Asia is provided by Melito of Sardis, whose work *Peri Pascha* is generally dated to the middle of the second century, and is widely considered a sermon.

The links between Melito and the Johannine school are summed up by Stewart-Sykes, who suggests that Melito is a Johannine Christian on grounds both historical and theological. His historical arguments are that in the letter of Polycrates recorded by Eusebius, where Melito is listed last among the apostolic worthies who await the resurrection in Asia, John the elder stands second in the list,[473] that the Quartodeciman passion chronology of which Melito was the heir is that represented in the fourth Gospel and that, in common with John, Melito might be considered a prophet, indeed that they stand in a common tradition of prophetic Asian Christianity. Theological traits found in common include the way in which the glorification of Jesus is not distinguished from the crucifixion, a common theory of typology, a common anti-gnostic and anti-docetic christology, and a common attitude towards Jews and Judaism, by which a repudiation of Judaism is a necessary concomitant of the acceptance of Christianity and by which the λόγος takes on the characteristics of, and thus supersedes, the νόμος.[474] Some of these aspects of Melito's Christianity will be taken up later in this section.

Whether Melito's church was organised on a scholastic basis is less easy to say since beyond *Peri Pascha* there is little evidence. However it can be said with certainty that Melito himself had undergone an extensive rhetorical education, as his work is marked by many of the stylistic devices of the second sophistic, such as extensive homoioteleuton (e.g. at *Peri Pascha* 73), homoiarcton (e.g. *Peri Pascha* 69), long series of two membered isocola with anaphora (e.g. at *Peri Pascha* 44), address to persons and objects not present (e.g. *Peri Pascha* 32, to the angel) exclamations with Ὦ followed by the genitive (e.g. *Peri Pascha* 97), as well as neologism and a sideways citation of Homer. That this is the case is not only demonstrable from *Peri Pascha*, since Grant has demonstrated that, in his *Apology* to Marcus Aurelius, Melito follows the advice laid down by Menander for an address of this kind, in dwelling on the history of the

---

[473] *Historia ecclesiastica* 5.24.
[474] So Stewart-Sykes, *Lamb's high feast*, 12–17.

imperial family and in pledging loyalty to the Emperor and to his succession.[475] In the same apology the profession of Christianity is described as a philosophy, but this may reflect the means by which Melito is seeking to commend Christianity to a philosophically minded emperor rather than the usual expression with Christianity might find in Melito's understanding.[476] We may also note the debt to stoic interpreters of Homer which is to be found in the fragment (probably by Melito) on baptism.[477] However it cannot be said that the church of Melito necessarily reflected the scholastic bias of its bishop; *Peri Pascha* is not particularly didactic in tone, but it must also be said that it is far from a typical sermon and as such it is little guide to the normal preaching of Melito's church.

When Bonner first published Melito's *Peri Pascha* he classified it as "a Good Friday Sermon".[478] This classification of *Peri Pascha* is one which has been consistently maintained since, most recently for instance by Siegert, Salzmann and Edwards.[479] A subtle variation on this theme is suggested by Hall, who proposes that *Peri Pascha* be divided at 46,[480] and that the first half, that is to say *Peri Pascha* before this point, is a homily for one of the Sabbaths preceding Passover.

Since Melito's tradition is Johannine, then we may reasonably expect that the shape that he might give to a homily would be the same as that which may be observed in the Johannine discourses. However a glance at *Peri Pascha* is sufficient for us to ascertain that it is not a synagogue homily of the Johannine type. At certain points scriptural texts emerge, and in particular at *Peri Pascha* 12 we may begin to see a citation from *Exodus* 12 where Melito explicitly refers to the text, saying several times φησίν, and sets forth the content of *Exodus* 12. But this is not a homily of the proemic type, as there is no atomization of the text under consideration. The text of *Exodus*

---

[475] Grant, "Five apologists", 6–7 with reference to fragment 1.

[476] Cf. Wilken, *Christians*, 83, who sees this as evidence of the scholastic basis of Melito's church.

[477] Fragment 8b in Hall, *Melito of Sardis on Pascha*. Grant, "Melito of Sardis on baptism", draws out the extent of the debt.

[478] Bonner, *Homily*, 19.

[479] Salzmann, *Lehren und Ermahnen*, 270; Edwards, "History of preaching", 188; Siegert, *Drei hellenistisch-jüdische Predigten* II, 18.

[480] Hall, "Melito in the light of the Passover haggadah", 36–37.

is soon left behind in a broader typological examination of the Hebrew basis of the Christian Pascha.

Apart from the homily, other suggestions along similar lines have been made; McDonald for instance suggests that the diatribe holds the key to the understanding of Melito's work.[481] McDonald makes his suggestion on the grounds that elements of the diatribe found their way into Christian preaching and because elements of rhetorical technique appear in Epictetus' *diatribai*. But whereas Melito's school tradition might make the admission of elements of the diatribe likely, there is no engagement with opponents who are present, nor indeed do the aims of *Peri Pascha* co-incide with those of the diatribe; the diatribe is a moral essay, essentially sumbouleutic in intent. *Peri Pascha* has no ethical content, and it is primarily an epideictic work. In the light of its epideictic intent Stewart-Sykes has suggested that its nearest equivalent in extant Graeco-Roman literature is a prose hymn of Aelius Aristides, which likewise takes off from a narrative base and concludes with a string of attributes anaphorically linked by οὗτος at the beginning of each asyndetic list. According to Stewart-Sykes "the etymological word-play, the story of creation leading to a hymning of the one who is first of all things, the repetition of οὗτος and the asyndeton are all reminiscent of *Peri Pascha*."[482]

Peri Pascha is comparable to a prose-hymn essentially because it is a liturgical document, functioning in the paschal celebrations of the Quartodecimans in the same way that the haggadah functioned in the Jewish seder, as the means by which those present might commemorate the events of salvation. He also notes that, within the Graeco-Roman world, sophists might deliver epideictic oratory as the accompaniment of liturgical rites, and suggests that this provides the means by which a sophist like Melito might function within a religious ritual passed down from Judaism.[483] Since *Peri Pascha* is principally a liturgical text it is not therefore principally a homily.

Having stated this much, it is also to be accepted that the delivery of *Peri Pascha* followed on from the reading of *Exodus* 12, as Melito makes clear in the opening lines of his work, and that it must therefore have functioned in some way as a homily on that text since

---

[481] McDonald, "Comments".
[482] Stewart-Sykes, *Lamb's high feast*, 73.
[483] Stewart-Sykes, *Lamb's high feast*, 129–130.

it stood in a position where a homily might be expected, and because in the earlier part at least it picks up elements from the reading. Although it is not a proem homily there were other homiletic models available in the Jewish ancestry of Melito's Christianity. Insofar as *Peri Pascha* at least in part may be seen as a liturgical homily it need not therefore be an exegetical proem homily, and the absence of any proemic treatment is not an objection to seeing that part of the work which relates directly to the text of *Exodus* as homiletic in some way. He concludes that the best comparison for this is the *Liber antiquitatum biblicarum* of ps-Philo.[484] We have observed already that the homily might have narrative shape and be an expansion and retelling of the biblical text, and that the *Liber antiquitatum biblicarum* might be just such a selection of haggadic material suitable for use in homilies. We have also observed a similar procedure in the pseudo-Philonic homilies on Jonah and Samson. Melito undertakes a comparable procedure in the first half of *Peri Pascha*. Beginning with a citation from the text he expands it and paraphrases it, introducing application alongside retelling and expansion. We have already suggested that the synagogue homily grew out of the targum, and that homilies in early Judaism might frequently have had a narrative shape.[485] It is quite possible that this kind of narrative homily was a relatively early development along the line which led from translation to exegesis, more suited to the assembly than the more scholastic proem homily. In Melito's community, under the influence of the Passover haggadah, it is possible to observe that a similar development has taken place. The narrative thrust is not restricted to that part of *Peri Pascha* which Melito explicitly describes as his *narratio*, for even in the part of the work which forms the liturgical haggadah proper, which Melito forms into his *probatio*, there is a strong narrative thrust which traces the history of salvation beginning with Adam.

On the basis that the delivery of *Peri Pascha* follows the reading, and on the basis of the comparative homiletic material Stewart-Sykes accepts the division of *Peri Pascha* into two halves which is proposed by Hall, without accepting Hall's classification of the first half as a synagogue homily for a Sabbath preceding Passover. Rather, he sug-

---

[484] Stewart-Sykes, *Lamb's high feast*, 108–109.
[485] 1.2.3.2 above.

gests, it is delivered in the first part of the Quartodeciman Pascha, at the vigil before midnight.[486] Thus although this part of the work provides only part of the rhetorical whole, namely the *narratio*, together with an explanation of the principles of typology, which Stewart-Sykes describes as a methodological digression, it may nonetheless be considered separately as a homily, albeit of a type peculiar to the liturgical celebration which it was accompanying, bound up to its accompanying reading from *Exodus* and the surrounding darkness of the paschal night to constitute a paschal liturgy of the word.

Three things are particularly noteworthy about this liturgical homily; the extensive influence of the second sophistic, the use to which Scripture is put, and the fact that for all the sophistication of Melito's rhetoric, and for all that he is well-acquainted with Scripture, prophecy continues to exercise an influence in his proclamation of the word of God.

We have already had cause to observe the influence of the second sophistic on preaching in the Hellenistic synagogue and have suggested that this is a parallel but distinct phenomenon from the influence exercised on preaching within the church. Melito is in any event a special case since, more than any other Christian writer of his generation, he displays evidence of an extensive sophistic education;[487] in part therefore the prominence of rhetoric in his work is as much a result of his own education and background as of any broader social movement leading to the imitation of contemporary sophists and the incorporation of rhetorical style in preaching more generally. It is also to be suggested that the peculiar occasion of Melito's rhetoric, the observation of the paschal feast, would also lead to the adoption of a more high-flown style than might otherwise be expected in a homily. Not only was the occasion suitable to a prose-hymnic style, but the liturgical tradition would likewise lead to the adoption of such a form on this occasion, and the hymnic activities of pagan sophists as hierophants on liturgical occasions would also lead Melito to the adoption of a particularly ornate style on this occasion. Sweeping conclusions about the influence of rhetoric on Christian preaching are not therefore to be drawn from this single

---

[486] Stewart-Sykes, *Lamb's high feast*, 176.

[487] See in particular the classic studies of Wifstrand, "Homily" and Halton, "Stylistic device".

work. Other primitive homilies such as Hippolytus' homily *In Psalmos* show a degree of rhetorical accomplishment, but somehow inhabit a different world than *Peri Pascha*; there the reasoning is ordered, exhibiting the world of the school much more closely. Although Edwards dates the influence of classical rhetoric on Christian preaching from Melito,[488] *Peri Pascha*, being a festal and liturgical homily, is something exceptional.

To turn to Melito's use of Scripture we may first note that the homily takes off from a reading of *Exodus* 12. Melito begins his homily with a fairly free citation of the text, which expands into a wider typological exegesis of the passage, by which the lamb of the Egyptian Passover is seen to be a type of Christ the lamb of God, whose sufferings and death extend protection to believers in the same way that the death of the lamb protected the Israelites from the angel. Melito's exegetical method here may be characterised as "historical typology" as the events of the new Testament are seen to be typified in the old Testament thus creating a correlation between the Old Testament events of liberation and the New Testament events of salvation. The events of *Exodus* are described as τύποι. These τύποι are temporary in effect; Melito compares them to sculptors' working models, and to metaphors (παραβολαί), which are of use only until the finished work has been made. The people of Israel are as the artist's model, a preliminary sketch for the Church. The Law is the comparison by which the Gospel is elucidated.[489] Typological exegesis is not however limited to the central text of *Exodus*. Christ is likewise seen to be present in other figures of the Old Testament, such as "Abel who is murdered, Isaac who is bound, Joseph who is sold, Moses who is exposed, David who is persecuted . . ."[490] Typology is thus the basis for thoroughgoing hermeneutic of realization, which is the basis in turn for Melito's homiletic use of Scripture, a making real of the events of the past to the ears and minds of his hearers.

Apart from this extended use of typology concentrating on *Exodus*, Scripture is also prominent in a collection of proof texts from *Deuteronomy, Psalms, Jeremiah* and *Isaiah*, where Melito states that the mystery of the Lord is proclaimed by the prophetic voice.[491] This

---

[488] Edwards, "History of preaching", 189.
[489] *PP* 40.
[490] *PP* 59.
[491] *PP* 61–64.

collection stands at the conclusion of what is effectively the *probatio* of Melito's declaration, immediately preceding the third of the doxologies which mark of the distinct sections of the work. Thus Scripture plays a part in Melito's *probatio*, functioning not only as the basis for his preaching but also as proof by means of citation, which is not only a typically scholastic procedure but is also prophetic, since the *probatio* is effectively a *diakrisis*. This collection of proof-texts however is to be found in the second half of the work, which according to Stewart-Sykes is delivered after midnight, as the paschal celebration nears its climax, and which functions liturgically as the direct festal and quasi-sacramental realization of the paschal mystery. There is however no contradiction here, rather this illustrates the complexity of Melito's work. The distinction which we might wish to make between the homiletic and the liturgical does not apply in the case of this second-century figure. As Mazza comments on another report of early Christian liturgy (*Acts* 20:7–12):

> Paul's words were not just what we could call a homily. It was the liturgical celebration itself, including at the same time liturgical text, proclamation, comment, homily, and physical action, all of which, lasting till dawn, had the characteristics of a vigil.[492]

Finally, and significantly, we may note that although Melito to an extent depends on the prophetic voice of old for the proof of his paschal oration the prophetic voice is not confined to the past, for his Christianity remains a Christianity of a prophetic type, and prophecy continues to exercise influence on preaching in his church. More than this, Melito was himself a prophet. Tertullian it is true disputes this claim, but the very fact that he needs to dispute it is an indication that the belief that Melito was a prophet was widespread.[493] Most telling as an example of this is the conclusion of *Peri Pascha*.

> Come all nations of men compounded with sins, and receive forgiveness of sins.
> For I am your forgiveness, I am the Passover of salvation . . .[494]

---

[492] Mazza, *Origins*, 105.

[493] The evidence is to be found in a citation of Tertullian by Jerome at *De viris illustribus* 24. Melito's interest in the subject is indicated by a work of his mentioned by Eusebius, a λόγος αὐτοῦ προφητείας (*Historia ecclesiastica* 4.26.4) which may be a collection of his own prophecies, or else a book concerning its practice.

[494] Melito *Peri Pascha* 103; Whereas this may be understood as *ethopoiia* this may

The similarity with the prophetic proclamation of the Johannine
Jesus, likewise given in the "I-form", is no co-incidence; here the
Christ-Spirit is speaking to the church through Melito, just as it had
spoken through the prophecy of John. In just the same way as in
the fourth Gospel there is a co-incidence of the Scriptural and the
prophetic in the communication of the word of God. Scripture is
moving to the centre of Christian communication but has not yet
ousted prophecy, even in the mind of the scholastic Melito. It is possible that the renewed interest in prophecy of the contemporary
Hellenistic world as witnessed by the writings of Plutarch and the
common practice of sophists operating as hierophants in the contemporary shrines made it possible for prophecy to continue to oper-
ate in Christianity, but these phenomena do not explain the existence
of the prophetic impulse in Melito's Christianity even if they account
for its continuance. For Melito communicates the word of God standing in the tradition of the fourth Gospel.

2.2.3.5. In Sanctum Pascha *as encomiastic homily*

In many ways comparable to Melito's *Peri Pascha* is a work preserved
among the spuria of Chrysostom, the author of which we shall refer
to as ps-Hippolytus in keeping with common usage. This work was
earlier believed to derive from the fourth century, but Cantalamessa
has argued that it is roughly contemporary with *Peri Pascha* and from
the same Asian milieu.[495] Cantalamessa's conclusions are broadly supported by Visonà, but Stewart-Sykes agrees with Rouwhorst that this
work is slightly later than that of Melito.[496] Further evidence for this

---

simultaneously be understood as prophecy, given in the "I form". Hawthorne,
"Christian Prophets and the Sayings of Jesus", 117, similarly regards this as an
example of prophecy.

[495] Cantalamessa, *Omelia*.

[496] Rouwhorst, "Quartodeciman Passover", 156–157; Stewart-Sykes, *Lamb's high
feast*, 25–26. Mazza, *Origins*, 105 n29, suggests that ps-Hippolytus precedes Melito,
on the grounds that the Scriptural reading is incorporated in the homily, and thus
that there is no distinction between reading, homily and sacrament. This is true of
Melito's period when, as we have seen, *Peri Pascha* functions both as liturgy and
homily; but the appearance of *Exodus* 12 in *In Sanctum Pascha* is, as we shall note
below, a repetition of the reading rather than the reading itself, the deliberate repetition being indicative of a greater concern that the text be interpreted with exactitude, as compared to the free rendition of *Exodus* 12 in Melito's work. Moreover
there is direct indication of further and subsequent liturgical action within *In Santum
Pascha*.

assertion will be noted here; in particular we shall observe the extent to which prophecy has ceased to be a live phenomenon in this community, alongside its increasing scholasticization betrayed principally through the dependence on Scripture.

Although later, *In Sanctum Pascha* has the same rough twofold outline as *Peri Pascha*, the first part likewise dealing in a typological manner with the Passover of Egypt as the Pascha of the Old Covenant, the second dealing with the new Passover and tracing the history of salvation from creation through incarnation to resurrection and glorification.[497] Although we argue here for a twofold outline Cantalamessa divides the work into three main parts, which he calls praeconium, exegesis and homily.[498] According to Cantalamessa the first sums up the themes of the work, the second is a close exegesis of *Exodus* 12, quoting the text in full and then dividing it up into verses for consideration, and the third is a more general treatment of the theme. What Cantalamessa calls the praeconium is a festal proemium to the homily as a whole rather than a separate undertaking and therefore we should continue to uphold the twofold nature of the work, a seriatim exegesis followed by an encomium of Pascha.

However, although the overall outline of *In Sanctum Pascha* is similar to *Peri Pascha* there are some distinct differences. A major difference lies in the fact that, whereas both begin by retelling the story of *Exodus* 12, which we may assume to have been a scriptural reading employed in these communities for the celebration of the paschal vigil, Melito's treatment is, as we have seen, a free retelling of the story. Ps-Hippolytus by contrast repeats the entire reading and then gives a preliminary typological exegesis of the whole. The repetition of the text is an indication of the extent to which Scripture is moving towards canonization in this school since as sacred text (θεία γραφή *IP* 6.1) it is not paraphrased until it has been repeated for the purpose of παραβολή and παράθεσις.[499] This is perhaps related to school practice, since according to Dionysius Thrax the process of explanation follows that of reading;[500] ps-Hippolytus ensures the proximity of explanation and reading by repeating the entire text.

---

[497] Hall, "Melito in the light of the Passover haggadah", 42–45; Visonà, *Pseudo Ippolito*, 49, also notes the same basic twofold shape.
[498] Cantalamessa, *Omelia*, 430.
[499] *In Sanctum Pascha* 5.2.
[500] Dionysius Thrax, *Ars grammatica*, 1.

Thus the initial repetition of the story is similar to that appearing in Melito's work, Melito describing it as a διήγημα, ps-Hippolytus as a χρεία,[501] but the attention which ps-Hippolytus shows to the details of the text is considerably greater. For having repeated the reading he announces καθ' ἕκαστον ἀκριβώσομεν τῶν ἀνεγνωσμένων (In Sanctum Pascha 6:2–3) and proceeds to do just that, atomizing the text for analysis and discussion. So for instance he deals with the significance of the tenth day of the month, the day on which the paschal lamb is selected, which he sees in the light of the decalogue as a sign that the lamb is selected under the old covenant. Melito does not even mention the selection of the lamb, even less go into detail concerning the significance of the day on which the choice is made.

For all this we should be clear that we are dealing with a homily delivered on a liturgical occasion and not a treatise. Visonà notes the elements in the work which allow us to classify this work as an actual homily, such as the reference to the preceding reading, the addresses to the audience as ἀγαπητοί, the calls to prayer in the course of the work, and the final reference to a concluding hymn, the Song of Moses.[502] Moreover he notes that the plan of exegesis set out at In Sanctum Pascha 7 does not altogether accord with the manner in which the homily concludes. There is still some fluidity and vitality left in the form.

The reference to the singing of the song of Moses with which the homily concludes is particularly significant in pointing us towards the manner in which the part which Scripture plays in the paschal vigil has grown since the time of Melito. On the assumption that this homily is part of the paschal vigil of this community, which given the continuity of shape with the work of Melito and the repeated references within In Sanctum Pascha to its liturgical setting would seem to be undeniable, it would seem that the song of Moses has now found its part alongside the reading of Exodus 12 within the vigil. What is interesting is that In Sanctum Pascha, whilst now a homily following on directly from the reading, is still enmeshed in the litur-

---

[501] IP 5.2: εἴπωμεν τί νόμος καὶ τί νόμου χρεία . . . Cf. Visonà's translation of the relevant passage: "diciamo innanzitutto che cos'è la legge, qual è la sua necessaria funzione . . ." The use of the term χρεία is not the only technical language in the work for the law is described, in the language of the rhetorical schools, as an οἰκονομία (IP 43).

[502] Visonà, Pseudo Ippolyto, 48.

gical action of the vigil by being sandwiched between the reading
and the song of Moses.

In addition we may note that *In Sanctum Pascha* shows considerably more acquaintance with the written New Testament than does
Peri Pascha, though the New Testament is given a rather freer treatment than the Old.[503] Stewart-Sykes suggests that it is under the
influence of the written New Testament, and in particular the New
Testament writings of paschal character such as *I Peter, John* 6 and
I Corinthians 11, all of which are cited, that the tradition has developed by which an original liturgy, the haggadah of Passover, has
developed into something which may be recognized as a festal
homily.[504] For the whole of *In Sanctum Pascha* is homiletic, by contrast to the highly liturgically charged second part of Melito's *Peri
Pascha*. He suggests that at first the boundaries between homily and
liturgy at Pascha were somewhat fluid and that an epideictic work,
being an act of remembrance, might also be perceived as liturgical;
however by the time of ps-Hippolytus the boundaries are beginning
to be erected and the homiletic celebration of the Pascha might be
seen as a separate event from its sacramental realization. So the
overall classification as homily applies to both parts of the work, the
treatment of *Exodus* 12 and the story of salvation; the festal opening
and conclusion, which are themselves intrinsic parts of the homily,
are all that remains of the liturgical haggadah in this community.
Cantalamessa had allowed the classification of "homily" only to this
second part of the work, but the preliminary typological exegesis
(classified by Cantalamessa simply as "exegesis") can hardly be separated from the broader homiletic treatment of salvation to be found
in the second part. This, together with the same heavy influence of
the rhetoric of the second sophistic on ps-Hippolytus as had been
observed in the case of Melito, enables us to see that the process of
scholasticization in the Asian church has continued to impact on the
manner in which the word of God is communicated. Prophecy as
a current phenomenon has disappeared, its exercise being restricted

---

[503] As noted by Visonà, 98–101. Cantalamessa, *Omelia*, 401–405, had suggested
that only the Old Testament was described as γραφή and that as such it alone was
canonical. However Visonà, *Pseudo-Ippolyto*, 99–101, observes that often New Testament
texts are quoted or alluded to alongside Old Testament scriptural citations, and
that as such may be seen to be on the way to canonization.

[504] Stewart-Sykes, *Lamb's high feast*, 137–138.

to the prophets of old whose words are contained in the Scriptures
(*In Sanctum Pascha* 9.28, 58.2); the people are to listen instead to the
reading of the law of Moses, which is described significantly with a
string of scholastic epithets as νηπίων παιδαγωγός (9.21, with none
of the negative inferences of *Galatians*) σοφὸν παιδευτήριον, ἀναγκαίον
γυμνάσιον, κοσμικὸν διδασκαλεῖον. (9.29–31)

In its rhetoric as in its use of Scripture, *In Sanctum Pascha* provides
an example of preaching from a scholasticized Asian community. It
had grown out of the paschal haggadah and its prophetic proof, and
thus derived from a slightly different root than other Asian homilies, but has nonetheless been subjected to the same process, and
thus becomes something recognizable both to ourselves and the original audience as a homily.

2.2.3.6. *The prophecy of the Montanists as Christian communication outside
the mainstream*

The emphasis on the Scriptures and the absence of any indication
of current prophecy in *In Sanctum Pascha* is to an extent the logical
conclusion to a process that began when the church became separated from the synagogue, and had therefore to adopt some synagogal procedures. But, as we have several times observed, this was
not a universal movement happening in a uniform manner or at a
uniform pace throughout the church. In particular it appears to have
had relatively little impact on the rural communities of Asia Minor
from which Montanism derived. Although it is difficult to see these
communities as scholastic, they are considered here precisely because
their interaction with scholastic Christian communities led to their
condemnation. As such we may observe the mode of communication
in Montanism as a further example of a practice akin to preaching.

Montanism was a prophetic movement originating in Phrygia in
the middle of the second century. Although marked in part by glossolalia, it cannot be held, as early studies sought to maintain, that
the Montanists were pure glossolalists, for there is reference in the
sources to the content of the Montanist prophecies,[505] though little
has survived, and in particular various oracles given by the Montanists
have been preserved, which are self-evidently not the products of
glossolalia, but are essentially paraenetic. As paraenetic prophets we

---

[505] Anonymous at Eusebius *Historia ecclesiastica* 5.16.10.

may suggest that the Montanists of Asia exercised their prophetic gifts in the context of worship, and that in these Asian communities their prophecies functioned as preaching. Recent studies have moreover shown that Montanism is rooted in the Christianity of Asia, rather than being a semi-pagan importation.[506] In particular we may suggest that the roots of this prophecy were Johannine, but that the Johannine witness had, by the time of this movement, been conflated with the circle of the seer of *Revelation*; evidence of this conflation may be found in the fact that Melito wrote on *Revelation*,[507] and yet he is clearly an heir of the Johannine school of Ephesus. The Montanists were avid readers of the apocalypse, and yet the pattern of their prophecy, their use of the "I am" form to authenticate their prophecy, and in particular their appeal to the paraclete as the basis of their prophetic activity are all Johannine. Thus Fiorenza is partly right in suggesting that there was a historical continuum of apocalyptic/prophetic Christianity originating with pre-Pauline traditions and running through *Revelation* and Papias to Montanism,[508] but she gives account of only part of the Montanist tradition. The roots of Asian Christian prophecy lie in the tradition of the fourth Gospel, and Montanism was a branch from the same tree as Melito of Sardis and *Epistula apostolorum*.

However, although a branch from this tree it has partly been grafted with the tradition underlying *Revelation* and with the prophecy of the daughters of Philip at Hierapolis, to which succession the Montanists laid explicit claim.[509] However, although heirs to these Asian prophetic traditions the Montanists also differed from the wider Asian church, particular in the social context of their prophesying. In contrast to the main leadership of the Asian church they were rural prophets,[510] and the accusation laid at their door by their anonymous opponent that they were unlearned[511] suggests that the Asian church's scholasticization had advanced in urban areas but that the Montanists had been left behind. This is borne out in what survives

---

[506] Trevett, "Apocalypse, Ignatius, Montanism"; Stewart-Sykes, "Asian context".
[507] Eusebius *Historia ecclesiastica* 4.26.
[508] Fiorenza, "Apokalypsis and propheteia", 152.
[509] For this appeal see Eusebius *Historia ecclesiastica* 5.17, quoting the anonymous' reply to the Montanist appeal to a prophetic succession.
[510] So Stewart-Sykes, "Original condemnation", 11–12.
[511] At *Historia ecclesiastica* 5.17.2 he refers to their ἀμαθία.

of their prophecy. Stewart-Sykes notes that the Montanist oracles are short and pithy, that eight probably authentic oracles survive which are not oracles of self-legitimation prefacing the speech, and that none of these is longer than a few lines.[512] Typical of these is Maximilla's prophecy: "After me there will no longer be a prophet, but the end."[513] Whereas it is possible that these oracles have been excerpted from longer discourses, the fact that they may be satisfactorily interpreted as they stand is indication that the complete oracles have been preserved. Should these oracles be contrasted to the length and complexity of the prophetic deliveries of the fourth Gospel and of Melito then the difference in prophecy caused by the social context of their delivery will be clear.

If the description given by Celsus of a Christian prophet at work is at all typical of Montanist prophecy one might expect the central oracle, containing the paraenetic content of the prophecy, to be prefaced by a self-introduction and concluded by a glossolalist display intended to authenticate the contents of the oracle which has been delivered.[514]

> Each one commonly and customarily says: "I am God" or "a son of God" or "a divine spirit and I have come. For the world is already perishing, and you, gentlemen, are ruined because of your offences. But I want to save you; and you will see me coming again with heavenly power. Blessed is he who has worshipped me now . . ." Then Celsus says "After they have brandished these words they subsequently add words that are unintelligible, and frenzied and totally obscure . . ."[515]

Celsus' report does not make it clear that this prophet is operating in a context of worship. The evidence for Montanist worship is scarce. One Montanist woman prophet at least sought the old prophetic privilege of offering the eucharist,[516] there is evidence that the Montanists as Quartodecimans kept the same Pascha as the great church, and Epiphanius briefly reports on Montanist worship, mentioning virgins clad in white and the burning of torches.[517] This, Stewart-

---

[512] Stewart-Sykes, "Original condemnation", 16.
[513] Fragment 6 according to the numbering of Heine, *Montanist oracles*. The others are 4, 9, 10, 12, 13, 14, and 15.
[514] On the mantic display as authenticating see Aune, *Prophecy*, 72, 359.
[515] Fragment 18 in Heine, *Montanist Oracles*; Origen *Contra Celsum* 7.9.
[516] So Firmilian in Cyprian *Epistulae* 75.10.
[517] Epiphanius *Panarion* 49.2.

Sykes suggests, is a report of the paschal vigil of the Montanists,[518] which explains the heightened eschatological expectation which is current at the celebration. However, although the evidence is scarce, there is sufficient here to enable us to see that Montanist worship mirrored that of the *Großkirche*, although differing perhaps in the extent to which eschatological expectation was expressed in worship and in the role of prophets (rather than householder-bishops) as celebrants. If this is the case then one might expect that the word of God would be delivered in worship in the same way that it was delivered in the worship of the *Großkirche*, but that the delivery would sound a distinctly prophetic note, as it had in the households of the Pauline communities and, more pertinently, as it did in the communities addressed by the seer of *Revelation*. There is also similarity between these prophecies and the prophecy of "John" in the nature of the exegesis employed.

In particular two oracles of the original Montanists have been shown to be exegetical reflections of Scripture. First of all Groh suggests that Maximilla's statement that God was ῥῆμα . . . καὶ πνεῦμα καὶ δύναμις[519] is a reflection of *I Corinthians* 2:4.[520] Although Stewart-Sykes suggests that it is more likely that an Old Testament text lies behind the statement, suggesting *Psalm* 32:6 (LXX) τῷ λόγῳ τοῦ Κυρίου οἱ οὐρανοὶ ἐστερεώθησαν καὶ τῷ πνεύματι τοῦ στόματος αὐτοῦ πᾶσα ἡ δύναμις αὐτῶν, or, more probably in view of the context, *Psalm* 67:12 (LXX) Κύριος δώσει ῥῆμα τοῖς εὐαγγελιζομένοις δυνάμει πολλῇ,[521] we have here, whichever text underlies the oracle, an allusion to Scripture uttered by a prophet in ecstasy, applying the past of the Scripture to the present experience of the congregation. As was the case with John's apocalypse the emphasis is not, however, on the Scripture but on the prophecy, not on the promise but on the fulfilment. This is exhibited by the other scriptural allusion which Groh observes in Montanist prophecy, the statement of Montanus that "Neither an angel (ἄγγελος), nor an ambassador (πρέσβυς) but I, the Lord God Father have come" which Groh suggests is an allusion to *Isaiah* 63:9: "Not an ambassador (πρέσβυς), nor a messenger

---

[518] "Asian context", 423–424.
[519] Oracle 5.
[520] Groh, "Utterance and exegesis", 79.
[521] Stewart-Sykes, "Asian context", 428 n73.

(ἄγγελος), but the Lord himself saved them . . ."[522] Isaiah is discussing
the past salvation of Israel, whereas Montanus concentrates on the
present experience of his hearers, the experience of the presence of
God through prophecy. This charismatic approach to Scripture
extends beyond the actual oracles. Montanus had named two vil-
lages "Jerusalem"[523] and the anonymous reports that Montanus first
received his revelations at a place called Ardabav.[524] Powell and
Tabbernee argue that the name Jerusalem is organisational in intent,
and that Jerusalem is intended to be the place from where the
prophets go out.[525] Ardabav is a name taken from *IV Ezra*, and is
intended to mean a place of revelation.[526] Biblical names are thus
provided for Asian places which perform a function parallel to those
performed by biblical places. This is reminiscent of the coded references of the apocalypse to Jezebel and Balaam as persons who
perform the functions within their communities of the Biblical figures
to whom allusion is made. A final similarity between the Montanists
and the seer may be noted in the manner in which Themiso, a later
leader of the Montanists, like John gathered a collection of prophecies into a letter sent around the Montanist communities.[527]

However, for all this similarity there is a vital difference between
the communities of the seer and those of the Montanists in the means
by which the prophecy is authenticated. Whereas John's prophecy
is unquestioned essentially because of the charismatic authority which
he wields, we may gather that the mantic displays which accompanied
Montanist prophecy provided the basis on which it was held not
possible to subject the prophecy to further interpretation. For all that
Montanus and his followers may have wielded charismatic author-

---

[522] Groh, "Utterance and exegesis", 90–91; for discussion of this passage as charismatic exegesis see also Trevett, *Montanism*, 81–83.

[523] So Apollonius at Eusebius *Historia ecclesiastica* 5.18.

[524] At Eusebius *Historia ecclesiastica* 5.16.

[525] Powell, "Tertullianists", 44; Tabbernee, "Revelation 21".

[526] So Preuschen, "Ardaf" supported by Trevett, *Montanism*, 25–26 and Stewart-
Sykes, "Asian Context", 434–435.

[527] Apollonius at Eusebius *Historia ecclesiastica* 5.18.5; there are further references
to collections of Montanist prophetic literature at Hippolytus *Refutatio* 8.19.1, 5;
Eusebius *Historia Ecclesiastica* 6.20.3; Theodoret *Haer. Fab. Comp.* 3.2. Although it is
not certain that the epistle was a prophetic collection, Stewart-Sykes, "Asian context", reckons this is the most probable characterization, and that in this sense
Themiso might be said to be imitating the apostle (μιμούμενος τὸν ἀπόστολον)
namely John, whose letters in *Revelation* are prophetic.

ity of a similar nature to that of John, glossolalia was necessary to authenticate the content of the prophecy. We may gather then that there was no critical examination of the prophecy in either set of communities, but the reasons for this lack of *diakrisis* are very different.

Even though there are similarities which are not fortuitous with mainstream Asian prophecy, Montanist prophecy must therefore be seen as a form of Christian communication lying outside the mainstream because of the manner in which the Montanists' prophecy was authenticated and because of the relative brevity of their utterances. Stewart-Sykes argues that the brevity of the oracles derives from the lack of education of the original prophets, which in turn derives from their rural setting, and that the Montanists had recourse to mantic behaviour to authenticate their prophecy because as marginalized individuals they would not otherwise expect their prophecy to secure a hearing.[528] In many ways the movement could thus be said to be harking back to an earlier period in the church's communication of the word of God, a period before the process of scholasticization had begun, but standing in the middle of the second century it is anomalous and anachronistic. The extent of this anomaly may once again be appreciated by comparing the oracles of the Montanists to the output of their fellow-Asian Melito, a prophet of a similar period, but crucially a prophet with an urban base. The Montanists thus provide us with a few examples and some insight into the communication of the word of God in second century Asia, but although their prophecy is related to other examples of similar prophetic communication, such as the fourth Gospel, the apocalypse and *Epistula apostolorum*, it does not help us to chart the development of the process by which the homily of the *Großkirche* came about.

But although Montanist prophecy lies outside the chief line of development the movement did give some indirect impetus to the development of the scriptural homily. For despite the denials of Ash that Montanism had anything to do with canonization,[529] there is some evidence, particularly in the introductory words of the anonymous anti-Montanist who fears lest he might be thought to be adding to the words of the new covenant, that there was some movement towards the idea that the age of revelation was closed. Certainly this

---

[528] Stewart-Sykes, "Original condemnation", 17.
[529] Ash, "Decline", 227–228.

was not absolutely established, otherwise the anonymous opponent
would not even imagine that anything he wrote might be taken as
having quasi-canonical authority, but the idea would appear to be
taking root that the apostolic writings were normative and complete.
For this reason Themiso is described as imitating the apostle when
he himself commits prophecy to writing in a circular letter,[530] since
he is seen as taking on an apostolic privilege. The move towards
informal canonization would come about as a result of the scholasticization of the church and its concentration therefore on the interpretation of written, as opposed to oral, prophecy. But the need to
oppose Montanism, as Paulsen persuasively argues, would tend to
give impetus to the idea of a closed canon of revelation.[531] In time
this would lead to formal canonization, but the process of canonization did not take place originally at an abstract theological level
but began in Christian communities who sought to convey the word
of God, and who found in written Scriptures both prophecy and
fulfilment, and who found, as a result of using the Scriptures to test
prophecy, that new prophecy was unnecessary. As the bishops became
intellectual leaders expounding set texts, the conflict with rural
Christianity claiming new revelation would be inevitable, and the
result of restricting preaching to the interpretation of existing prophecy
would lead in turn to functional canonization of old and new testaments alike.

2.2.3.7. *Schools, Scripture and the disappearance of prophecy in Asia*
It is not possible to be certain about the length of time which sep-
arates the paschal proclamations of Melito and ps-Hippolytus, but
the advance in scholasticization is clear in the manner in which the
paschal proclamation becomes more directly homiletic and the reference to Scripture more precise, as well as in the stark absence of
any prophetic speech form in ps-Hippolytus. It is also most probable that between the two stand the new prophecy and the reaction
which it provoked. The significance of Montanism for the develop-

---

[530] Apollonius at Eusebius *Historia ecclesiastica* 5.18.5; although Themiso might here
be seen to be encouraging a process of scholasticization similar to that which was
occurring in the *Großkirche* through the provision of written materials, because of
the rural setting of the majority of Montanists there was not the social basis of
basic education which scholasticization, and therefore canonization, required.
[531] Paulsen, "Bedeutung".

ment of the homily thus lies not in its revival of the prophetic spirit
(which had in any case never died out) but in the manner in which,
quite contrary to its aims and origins, it advanced the scholasticization of the church and the centring of Christian communication on
the canon of written Scripture. Thus originating in a variety of settings, both domestic and scholastic, the scholastic social setting of
Asian Christianity comes in the end to be dominant, with the result
that prophecy comes to an end as a way of communicating the word
of God in the assembly and is replaced by a concentration on what
has now become Holy Scripture.

2.2.4. *Scholastic preachers in Rome*

Having observed the developments of the Asian schools we go on
to examine preaching in the schools at Rome, where a similar process
of scholasticization and scripturalization combined with rhetorical
flourish, alongside certain more conservative elements, will be found.

The existence of teachers within the Roman churches was noted
in our study of Hermas. At the coming of Christianity to Rome there
were already a significant number of independent Jewish teachers in
the city, and as Christianity formed itself in part in relationship to
this Judaism so this gives rise to similarly independent Christian
teachers.[532] But although these teachers are independent, Hermas has
a vision of teachers as part of the overall harmony of churches[533]
presumably exercising functions of catechesis, as an example of whom
we may note Grapte, who is to teach the content of the visions to
the women and children.[534] However we have also noted something
of a protest from Hermas against scholastic orientation within the
church. Hence the teachers who, with the apostles, provide the foundation of the tower in the ninth *Similitude* are dead already; they are
manifestations of the past.[535] The teachers who remain within the
Roman church are those whose responses to questioning and whose
teaching is undertaken according to the desire of sinners and for
monetary gain.[536] In this way they correspond to the false prophet

---

[532] 2.1.2.
[533] *Vis.* 3.5.1.
[534] *Vis.* 2.4.3.
[535] *Sim.* 9.15.4; 9.16.5.
[536] *Sim.* 9.19.2–3.

whose mind likewise is on gain, and who answers the questions which are put to him rather than teaching through the medium of the Spirit.[537] We have already argued that the false prophet is a manifestation of scholastic orientation within the Roman churches, against which Hermas is protesting, and it is possible that the teaching according to the desire of the wicked at *Similitude* 9.19.3 is a process of oracular questioning like that put to the false prophet. It is interesting that Hermas himself, through his use of the revelation dialogue, reflects a situation where the prophet is questioned, since the dialogues reflect in turn the discussion which would accompany a vision report. However, Hermas clearly feels that there is something qualitatively different about this process of enquiry.

The diffuse nature of Roman Christianity in the second century with its corresponding lack of central authority meant that the existence of independent Christian teachers continued throughout the century, among whom we may note Cerdo, claimed by Irenaeus as the teacher of Marcion.[538] We may also note Epiphanius' report of scholastic activity within the Roman church, where there is a debate between Marcion and other Roman teachers on the meaning of the parable of the patch on the wineskin.[539] It would be erroneous to contrast these independent teachers with the official church, as Bardy does,[540] for among the decentralized churches of Rome the schools were simply households among others. The prominence of the schools in Rome, whereas partly the result of the attraction elicited by the imperial capital, came about also as a result of the diffuse nature of Roman Christianity which resulted in turn from its diffuse beginnings and the difficulty of enforcing any control on a large number of Christian households scattered across a large and changing city and population. If, with the benefit of hindsight, the heretics predominate among the Roman schools, this is the result of the nature of the philosophical activity which took place within them. The demise of the schools only begins with the establishment of a monarchical episcopate in Rome, at which point the households have taken on many scholastic functions in any event, to form something recognizable to us as the church. Bardy is correct in pointing to Victor

---

[537] *Mandate* 11.
[538] Irenaeus *Adversus haereses* 1.27.2; also Hippolytus *Refutatio* 10.19.
[539] Epiphanius *Panarion* 42.2.1–5.
[540] Bardy, "Écoles Romains", 511–512.

as the originator of this demise,[541] though the process did not end
with Victor; Callistus, who succeeded Victor, is seen by Hippolytus
in scholastic terms, and the Hippolytean school flourished into the
third century, and through its reconciliation with the wider church
maintained its peculiar scholastic orientation.

We may reasonably expect that preaching activity took place within
the Christian schools. Of these schools some remains of preaching
activity are extant from those of Justin, Valentinus and Hippolytus.

2.2.4.1. *Preaching in the school of Justin*

We have already had occasion to observe Justin's report on preaching. Since this is often cited as the first concrete information which
we have about preaching his report stands at the head of this section. Justin, when informing his hearers about the worship of the
Christians, states that there are readings of the memoirs of the apostles and of the prophets, which are followed by a word of νουθεσία
καὶ πρόκλησις given by the president, intending imitation of the good
contained therein.[542] The word προέστως, which Justin employs to
refer to the president, is significant, as it is used by Diogenes to refer
to the head of a philosophical school.[543] Thus we may see that leadership in the philosophical school on which this church is modelled
leads to leadership in the preaching activity undertaken. It is however also noteworthy that Justin would appear to have been head
of his own school rather than subject to a patron, since he appears
in the *Acta* of his martyrdom at the head of the martyrs, and knows
no Christian meeting place beside his own.[544]

Turning to the shape prescribed by Justin for the sermon we may
observe that at first sight this would indicate something like the word
of exhortation proposed by Wills as the normative shape of an early
Christian sermon, where a scriptural *exemplum* is held up as the basis
of ethical instruction;[545] Justin's account thus indicates that an *exemplum* is held up which the audience is then encouraged (through
νουθεσία καὶ πρόκλησις) to imitate (μιμεῖσθαι). However we may
compare to this account the actual exegesis of Scripture to be found

---

[541] Bardy, "Écoles Romains", 521–530.
[542] *I Apologia* 1.67.
[543] So Brent, *Hippolytus*, 404.
[544] *Acta Justini* 3.
[545] This pattern is proposed by Wills, "Form of the sermon".

in Justin' work. As an example of this we may take *Dialogus* 98, where Justin cites *Psalm* 22 at length and goes on to break it down into its constituent parts, showing that it has christological application, and demonstrating this application with reference to texts from the Gospels. On this Koester comments "Justin discloses valuable information about the activities of early Christian schools. Their work apparently included not only the detailed interpretation of passages from the Old Testament, but also critical work on its Greek text."[546] Even though the proem form is not exhibited here, for the blocks selected for exegesis are large ones rather than individual words or groups of words, such a scholastic treatment of a scriptural text may betray something of preaching activity in Justin's church where the Scriptures provide a platform for religious teaching. But if this is the case then there is some tension with the report of preaching at *I Apologia* 1.67 where, although the sermon follows on from the reading of the Scriptures, Justin implies that the significance which is drawn from the readings is ethical.

It is hard to be certain of the value of these witnesses because of the contexts in which they are to be found. As was suggested above, it is possible that given the apologetic motivation for Justin's writing he has picked upon the moral aspect of preaching in his description found in the *Apologia* because it might readily commend itself to a Graeco-Roman audience. As such it is possible to overemphasize the ethical content of Justin's preaching.[547] On the other hand the theological, and specifically christological, interpretation of *Psalm* 22 is found in the context of an anti-Jewish dialogue, and might therefore be dictated by that form and context. Moreover, the exegesis of *Psalm* 22 as it stands in the dialogue ends suddenly; this sudden conclusion is a possible indication that it has been excerpted from an independent source. In view of this sudden conclusion, it is quite possible that an ethical conclusion might have followed were this exegesis to provide the basis for a homily within the worshipping assembly. The ethical predominates in the preaching of Hermas, and it is therefore possible that some ethical content is expected of a preacher, in particular given the ethical emphasis of stoic and cynic

---

[546] Koester, *History and Literature*, 342.
[547] As do Salzmann, *Lehren und Ermahnen*, 249–253 and Ekenberg, "Urkristen predikan", 7.

teachers and the ethical content of the prophecy which was the first means of communication in the Christian assembly.

What is notable about the citation and treatment of the psalm is that there is an intersection of the psalm and the Gospel, as each part of the psalm is illustrated with Gospel material. This intersection is reminiscent of what Justin states concerning the readings at the synaxis, namely that they come from the prophets or from the memoirs of the apostles. The manner in which the words of the psalm and the gospel are intertwined is perhaps indicative of the manner in which Justin's preacher might employ the readings from the prophets and the Gospels to demonstrate his point, and confirms Senn's instinct in commenting on *Dialogus* 66 that "the juxtaposition of the prophets and apostles [in the readings at the liturgy] suggest a hermeneutic for Christian preaching";[548] the words of the prophet David and those of the Gospel provide mutual proof for one another. As such we may observe with Salzmann that the prophets who were read were the prophets of the Old Testament, rather than contemporary or recent Christian prophets.[549] Even though Christian prophets are still flourishing in Rome at the time of Justin,[550] their activities and proclamation are not found in this scholastic setting.

Even though the treatment of the psalm appears to share a hermeneutic with the preaching described by Justin we cannot be certain that this scriptural treatment is directly indicative of Justin's manner of preaching, given the absence of a proem form or any other independently demonstrated homiletic form. Nonetheless we may reasonably anticipate that such a scriptural treatment might provide the groundwork for preaching, given the scholastic orientation of Justin's community, and given the abrupt conclusion of the exegesis, which indicates that it has been included from another source, which source may be homiletic.

If we are correct in seeing Justin's treatment of the psalm at this point, with the possible addition of an ethical conclusion, as indicative of preaching in this school, we may also see that although there is some correspondence with the word of exhortation the form is rather more complex than that mapped out by Wills. This lends

---

[548] Senn, *Christian liturgy*, 75.
[549] Salzmann, *Lehren und Ermahnen*, 247.
[550] *Dialogus* 82.

support to our earlier conclusion that the form might be considered
homiletic but that its purer literary manifestations are idealisations,
and that in an actual homily a more complex use of the pattern,
like that found in *Hebrews*, might be expected. Quite apart from its
moral aims we may observe that preaching in this school, like that
which we have already noted from Asia, was closely bound up to
close exegesis of scriptural texts. It is the text which provides the
basis of the homily and the prophecy which is examined is written
prophecy from the past, its proof demonstrated not by inspired and
prophetic *diakrisis* but by the demonstration of its fulfilment, a fulfilment
itself demonstrated from a literary text.

2.2.4.2. *Preaching in the school of Valentinus*

A rather different representation of preaching at Rome in a school
setting is provided by Valentinus.[551] Two fragments are preserved by
Clement which are, he states, derived from ὁμιλίαι. Although it is
possible that the term ὁμιλία here refers to philosophical dialogue,
the content and style do not seem to suit this setting. Here, therefore, is perhaps the first use of the term to refer to preaching, whether
the usage be that of Clement or of Valentinus. It is hardly co-incidental that both Clement and Valentinus derive from a school setting which might know the kind of *homilia* which is found in stylized
form in the diatribe, but the usage here does not lead to the conclusion to which Norden came that the term derived from the schools.
The practice of ὁμιλία has been observed in Christian households,
and these households are as likely to be the origin for the application of the term once Christianity became scholasticized.

Although the fragments of Valentinus are too brief to allow us to
draw any significant conclusions about the nature of preaching in
this school they are valuable nonetheless as rare examples of material where there is external evidence of homiletic origin. There are
some additional gnostic texts which, according to Salzmann, are
"predigtartig" but which cannot be proven to be homiletic.[552]

The first is found at *Stromata* 4.89.1–3

> From the beginning you are immortal
> and (καί) children of everlasting life;

---

[551] On Valentinus as a Roman teacher see Markschies, *Valentinus gnosticus?*, 388–389.
[552] Salzmann, *Lehren und Ermahnen*, 326.

And (καί) you would have death apportioned (μερίσασθαι) to you
so that you could spend (δαπανήσετε) it and lavish it
so that death may die in you (καὶ ἀποθάνῃ ὁ θάνατος ἐν ὑμῖν)
and through you (καὶ δι᾽ ὑμῶν);
for when you dissolve (λυήτε) the world
you will not be dissolved (καταλύησθε);
have lordship over the creation and over everything perishable (κυριεύετε
τῆς κτίσεως καὶ φθορᾶς ἁπάσης.)

Immediately noticeable is the exalted style of the address and the
marks of Asianist rhetoric, with short cola or which some are homoi-
oteleutic, the paratactic καὶ and paronomasia. Markschies, who takes
Peri Pascha to be a homily, thus compares the style of this fragment
to that of Melito.[553] It is not necessary to hold that *Peri Pascha* is a
homily to observe the stylistic points which they share in common,
which is indicative of the widespread influence of the second sophistic in the period and the appropriation of the style of the rhetorical schools by Christian teachers, and an indication that an address
to the congregation is an appropriate manifestation of this style in
a scholastic ecclesial setting.

The second immediately noticeable aspect of this homiletic fragment
is the manner in which, in making a theological point, the preacher
engages with the audience, addressing them directly and applying
the theological point directly to them. This is at some remove from
the rather unqualified ethical prescripts which were given by the
prophetic Paul, but shares something in common with the exhortation pattern which Wills suggested might be the mark of a homily.
But it is not a simple use of the pattern, for the exhortation is not
a direct imperative, nor is there a conclusion directly drawn, rather
there is an inference which the audience might pick up which is of
a theological rather than an ethical nature. Although Markschies is
right in stating that the material is too fragmentary to deduce with
certainty the complete absence of paraenesis from this homily,[554] the
heightened style does indicate that this fragment may come from the
conclusion, where we would anticipate some element of paraenesis
were it to be present. The absence of ethical material stands in contrast to Justin's insistence on the ethical content of preaching, even

---

[553] Markschies, *Valentinus gnosticus?*, 127, 137 n121.
[554] Markschies, *Valentinus gnosticus?*, 126 n64, in response to Orbe, "Los hombres
y el creador", 6.

though we might suspect that Justin overstates this in the *Apologia*, and significantly coheres with the tendency to shift meaning from the ethical to the intellectual plain found in the scriptural exegesis of *Evangelium veritatis*, a document of Valentinian provenance.[555]

The possibility that this homiletic fragment is a conclusion drawn from a scriptural basis raises the question of what the scriptural basis might have been. Two suggestions have been made. Orbe suggests that the parable of the prodigal son may lie behind this statement,[556] whereas Jeremias suggests that the curse of Adam may lie behind this homiletic fragment.[557] This latter hypothesis is found attractive by Markschies, who recognizes the possibility that the words as they stand might have been addressed to Adam and Eve. Although the congregation, rather than the primal couple, is being addressed in the fragment as it stands, he feels it possible that this is an application of the words originally addressed to Adam and Eve, growing out of a homiletic treatment of the original story.

Markschies is less convinced by Orbe's suggestion, which is based on two verbal parallels between the fragment and the parable, namely the request for a share of his lot (μέρος) made by the son, which Orbe believes corresponds to the sharing (μερίσασθαι) in death found in the homily, and the spending (δαπανᾶν) of the birthright which, according to Orbe, corresponds to the expenditure of death which the immortal soul undertakes.[558] On the basis of these verbal parallels he suggests that the fragment is effectively an allegorical treatment of the parable, with the Son as the one who consumes death, that is to say earthly life. In rejecting this thesis Markschies observes that there is no other use of the parable elsewhere in Valentinus' work, nor any other allegorical treatment.[559] This lack of comparable material is as likely to be the result of the fragmentary state of our knowledge as it is of any failure in Orbe's argument. More prob-

---

[555] On which see Williams, *Biblical interpretation*, 197–198; as an example of this de-ethicizing exegesis we may note with Williams, *Biblical interpretation*, 100–102, the manner in which *Matthew* 5:48, a statement that the father's perfection should be followed by the disciple, is turned into a metaphysical statement about the perfection of the father in being. An ethical exhortation has become a theological statement without impact upon the lives of the hearers.

[556] Orbe, "Los hombres y el creador", 7–12.

[557] G. Jeremias, in conversation, cited by Markschies, *Valentinus gnosticus?*, 146.

[558] Orbe, "Los hombres y el creador", 7–8.

[559] Markschies, *Valentinus gnosticus?*, 140 n143.

lematic is the fact that this is not the only scriptural reference observed by Orbe; he also notes the possible use of *John* 8:44 as a text imputing the creation of death to the demiurge,[560] and, lying behind the suggestion that the gnostic might govern the earth, *Genesis* 1:26–28.[561] This leads one to wonder which of these texts the homily intends to treat; the possible reference to *Genesis* leads back to Jeremias' suggestion but even then it cannot be said with certainty that the homily is based on this Scripture. The reference to the parable of the prodigal son may be a passing reference only, or it is possible that Valentinus has tied the parable to the creation narrative in his homily, but we can speak only of possibilities, not of certainties.

There is moreover another possibility, in that Clement explains this fragment of Valentinus as indicating that death is the creation of the demiurge, whereas a class saved by nature has come to abolish death. Clement then says that Valentinus therefore employs the Scripture "nobody shall see the face of God and live." Markschies suggests that this is a misrepresentation of Valentinus' statements here, and therefore is disinclined to see the citation of *Exodus* as deriving from Valentinus at all, even less to associate it with this homily.[562] But it would be strange were Clement to seek out and point out the citation of this text at this point if it were entirely unconnected to the foregoing homily, since it is hardly necessary for his argument. Even if the distinction between the creator of death and the Saviour is falsely imputed to Valentinus by Clement, as Markschies suggests, the citation would seem to belong in a homily on immortality, whether it is the basis of the homily or a text adduced to support a point being made. In view of the implied contradiction between the text and the overall thrust of the earlier contents of the homily the latter is more probable; conceivably the text is introduced, in diatribal style, as a difficulty to be placed in the way of the argument, a difficulty answered with recourse to a distinction between creation and salvation. There can be no assurance here, but the use of Scripture in building the homily appears to be assured, even if Valentinian interpretation tended towards the free and unliteral, and even if the precise manner in which Scripture is employed is inaccessible to us.

---

[560] Orbe, "Los hombres y el creador", 7.
[561] Orbe, "Los hombres y el creador", 12–14.
[562] Markschies, *Valentinus gnosticus?*, 149–152.

The second fragment is found at *Stromata* 6.52.3–53.1 and is said
by Clement to have come from a homily περὶ φίλων.

> Many of those things written in popular books (δημοσίαις βίβλοις)
> are found written in the church of God.
> For those things which are held in common (κοινά)
> are the words which come from the heart,
> and the law which is written on the heart.
> This is the people of the beloved,
> who are beloved and who love him.

Since friendship was a common philosophical theme which was taken
into the Christian tradition, certainly through the Johannine corpus
though conceivably more widely through the appropriation by
Christians of the model of the school, it is hardly surprising to find
that it is treated by Valentinus. Markschies however suggests that
the content of the homily indicates that the friendship indicated is
the friendship of God.[563] Certainly that is the content of the tiny
fragment preserved for us, though it is far from impossible that this
is simply one part of a wider treatment of friendship within the
school and the relationship with God involved in being in the school.
One indication of this is the word κοινά, regularly found in the context of the discussion of philosophical friendship to mean those things
held in common by members of a school, which is here employed
with a quite different meaning, namely the unity between the words
coming from the heart of God's people and the law which is written on their hearts. This perhaps indicates that the vocabulary of
philosophical friendship is being employed as part of an extended
image for the relationship between God and the gnostic.

This fragment may be compared with the earlier fragment in that
still there is anaphoric construction and some homoiarcton, though
the literary artifice is less obvious here. There is not the same direct
address to the audience either, which is perhaps an indication that
the more hymnic and exalted style is reserved for the address to the
audience which might conclude a homily whereas this fragment is
derived from the argument of the middle.

The equation of the law written upon human hearts with that
which is written down is an indication of the hermeneutical principles which allowed the Valentinians to sit, in the manner observed

---

[563] Markschies, *Valentinus Gnosticus?*, 191–192.

by Williams, relatively lightly upon those texts which would come to form the New Testament; and yet because the statement is itself an echo of Scripture then we may conclude that the school was not cut adrift from Scripture altogether, indeed that the text had centrality in the school even to the extent that further texts were produced. There was as yet no established hermeneutic upon which a preacher might draw, and so the interpretative liberty of Valentinus was perhaps not unusual in the first part of the second century. It would seem that, as the century progressed and Christianity was forced to define itself more closely in relationship to the text, this interpretative liberty became restricted. As such Valentinus' school would stand out all the more in that its tendencies would differ from the general direction which Christian preaching was taking, but nonetheless we may uphold the general fidelity of Valentinus to Scripture. In Irenaeus' eyes the Valentinians recognized the Scriptures (by contrast to the Marcionites) but perverted the interpretation;[564] that is to say their beliefs were scripturally justified, but only according to a hermeneutic which was no longer available to the church.

In time it is possible that preaching would itself contribute towards the functional canonization of Scripture in the Christian church, indeed it is even possible that the different hermeneutical strand represented by Valentinus was itself an impetus towards canonization, though the internal dynamic of formative Christianity, which needed to anchor the proclamation of the will of God in a text, would be of itself sufficient.

Whatever the differences between Valentinus and the emerging catholic church, we may nonetheless see him as a typical preacher within a scholastically understood ecclesial setting on the basis of these two fragments. He is concerned with the exegesis of Scripture, emphasizes philosophical friendship and employs rhetorical flourish in communicating to his audience within the assembly.

2.2.4.3. *Preaching in the school of Hippolytus*
The anchorage of preaching to the scriptural text had been made fast in Rome by the beginning of the third century, to judge from the manner in which the preaching of Hippolytus is closely wedded to Scripture. At this point we are entering onto the history, as opposed

---

[564] *Adversus haereses* 3.12.12.

to the prehistory, of preaching. Hippolytus is reported to have numbered Origen among his audience when preaching,[565] and with Origen
the triumph of preaching over prophecy is complete.

In writing of Hippolytus we must make it clear that we are dealing with an author from roughly the end of the second century who
is a leader within a school setting in Rome, and that this author is
the earlier of the two who are represented within the Hippolytean
corpus, whom Brent recognises as the author of the *Elenchus*. There
has been extensive discussion in the past whether the corpus of works
attributed to Hippolytus is to be assigned to one author or to two.
The solution adopted here is that of Brent, according to whom there
are two authors, the latter of whom succeeded the former as head
of a Roman school.[566] That Hippolytus represents a church in a
school setting is evident from many of his comments. For instance
he refers to the school of Callistus somewhat slightingly,[567] whereas
he refers to his own church as a school of grace and the members
as μαθηταί.[568] Apart from these internal indications we may note the
interest which he has in the concept of *diadochē*, which Brent suggests is derived from the philosophical literature,[569] and indeed may
refer to Brent's explanation of the statue, previously supposed to
have been of Hippolytus, as a statue of wisdom which was a cen-
trepiece of the school of Hippolytus.[570]

Hippolytus in his time had renown as a preacher, yet little remains
of his work. Extant in Greek there is a homily on the Psalms reconstructed from among the catenae by Nautin,[571] and one on David
and Goliath extant in Georgian. Of the homiletic origin of these
pieces there is no doubt. A homily on the theophany has been passed
down among the works of Hippolytus, as has one on Lazarus' four
days in the tomb, neither of which are generally ascribed to Hippolytus,
but which have both found recent champions ready to defend their
authenticity.[572] The very difficulty in distinguishing Hippolytus' work

---

[565] Eusebius *Historia ecclesiastica* 6.14.10; Jerome *De viris illustribus* 61.
[566] For the argument see Brent, *Hippolytus*, passim. For a sympathetic critique of
Brent, with some modifications to his hypothesis, see Stewart-Sykes, "Integrity".
[567] *Ref.* 9.7, 9.12.
[568] *In Ps* 12; 17.
[569] Brent, *Hippolytus*, 263–265.
[570] Brent, *Hippolytus*, 51–114.
[571] In Nautin, *Dossier*, 166–183.
[572] So Siegert, *Drei hellenistisch-jüdische Predigten* II, 19–20, suggests that, since a pri-

from that of later generations is further indication that, with this figure, preaching as it was later known was established, with the triumph both of Scripture and of the second sophistic though the scholasticization of Christian communication.

The homily *In Psalmos* is not entirely complete but may be understood as indicating a controversy at the time of Hippolytus about the place of prophecy in the church, perhaps caused by the reaction to Montanism in Rome, which caused some to disdain the role of prophecy altogether.[573] Hippolytus is essentially supportive of the practice of prophecy, as long as it is carried out within the ordered worship of the church. The fact that there is a controversy may perhaps be an indication that the succession of Roman prophets had not died out with Hermas. But for all that Hippolytus is a supporter of the prophets there is no indication that Hippolytus' school setting knows anything of the activity of prophets; Stewart-Sykes notes that the language formerly applied to prophecy is in the *Traditio apostolica* applied to the preaching activity of the church.[574] What is of fundamental importance for Hippolytus is that there should be order in the church, that pupils should be obedient to their teacher! As such the informality which was associated with prophetic delivery in the household has disappeared to be replaced by a picture more akin to that presented by Hermas in the eleventh *Mandate*.

Although the controversy over the role of prophecy may in part be due to the arguments at Rome concerning the recognition of Montanism it is also possible that the reaction to gnosticism may have played a role. Valentinus' preaching, we noted, was fundamentally scriptural, though the lack of an established hermeneutic meant that a rather free interpretation of the Scriptures was possible, in particular with regard to the New Testament, which was not as yet in any way canonized. Irenaeus however informs us of the prophetic practice of a different gnostic group, the Marcosians.[575] He regales the reader with a description of the lascivious tendencies of

---

mary reason for suspecting the authenticity of the homily on the theophany is the sophistication of the rhetoric, the discovery of Melito's *Peri Pascha* means that the question should be revisited, whereas Frickel, "Hippolyt von Rom: als Prediger verkannt", seeks to defend the authenticity of that on Lazarus. We do not employ either homily in this study because of the uncertainty of attribution.

[573] For discussion and references see Stewart-Sykes, "Hermas the prophet", 47–55.
[574] Stewart-Sykes, "Hermas the prophet", 61 n78.
[575] Irenaeus *Adversus haereses* 1.13.1–7.

Marcus, who preyed particularly on wealthy women, pursuing both
their money and their virtue, and concludes that he was demoni-
cally possessed, and that this is the means by which he prophesied.
Although the tale may be embellished there are no grounds to doubt
that Marcus prophesied and encouraged prophecy within his group.
If this was the case then some kind of external control on prophecy
would be needed all the more, and Scripture would provide precisely such a control, alongside an insistence on the rule of faith and
on the true succession of teachers. The theme of succession and the
move towards scriptural canonization both appear in *In Psalmos*,
superficially as means by which prophecy might be undergirded,
though actually as elements to which it must be subordinated.

In Psalmos is a rhetorically correct work, with clearly delineated
propositio, narratio and *probatio*, with the intention of demonstrating that
the Psalms should be read in the church given that their true meaning is apprehended. This true meaning is to be understood by reference to the rhetorical force of the psalms (δύναμις);[576] having shown
this, then, according to Hippolytus, their true meaning is clear. He
makes it clear that his homily has reference to a reading within the
church by referring to the reading of the psalms that had preceded
his homily; as such we may see that they are approaching something akin to canonical status in this setting. This in turn indicates
the primacy of Scripture in the school setting of Hippolytus. The
extent to which he dwells on the titles of the psalms is a further
indication of the scholastic orientation of this community. The text
has primacy in teaching, and the detail of the text is of significance,
as well as the broad sweep of the narrative. We may see that in this
community at least the exegetical homily following the reading of
Scripture is established as the primary locus of edification.

Scripture comes to the fore in the *narratio* of the homily, which is
based on the removal of the ark under David to Jerusalem. Hippolytus
points out that the manner in which the praises of God were sung
pointed both to order and to inspiration in the worship of the
Israelites. This is then employed as a means by which a lesson for
the church may be derived, namely that in the church likewise there
must be ordered worship, and the writings of Paul are brought in
to support the argument. This narrative and probative use of Scripture

---

[576] *In Psalmos* 1.

may indicate that the proemic treatment of Scripture need not by this stage be the only means by which Scripture might provide the basis of a homily in the church, since there is no indication that either reading took place prior to the homily. Light is thus cast back on the method of Justin, for whom a detailed treatment of *Psalm* 22 might, we indicated, provide the basis for a scriptural homily. In a latter part of the homily Hippolytus turns to two psalms which had been read earlier, and uses them to show the fundamental divine inspiration behind the psalms, in that the first two psalms are indicative of the birth and the passion of Christ. Not only is Scripture the base material for Hippolytus' preaching, but the scriptural status of some material needs to be defended.

The subject matter of this homily, and the context (the homily is occasioned by the dispute over the role of prophecy in the church) are indications that the prophetic homily did not disappear without a fight. However, much as we may be assured that prophets continued to function in some Roman churches, we have no remains of their activity. In time the language of prophecy, along with its paraenetic function, was absorbed into a church which was by now firmly based on a scholastic model of organisation. The content of this homily is an indication of the extent of scholasticization and of the extent to which Scripture has become central to the concerns of the preacher.

There is however some indication within the school of Hippolytus that some of the earlier informality had survived. In the section devoted to meals *Traditio apostolica* discusses the manner in which conversation should be carried out at table,[577] or rather forbids conversation altogether, as the suggestion is made that the meal should take place in silence with the exception of an exhortation given by the bishop, and questions which should then be addressed to him. His answers are heard in silence, and silence is then maintained until a further question is asked of the bishop.[578] Herein is an indication that an attempt is being made to control the philosophical ὁμιλία which had previously marked the table of the Hippolytean school,

---

[577] *Traditio apostolica* 28.

[578] The interpretation of *Traditio apostolica* here is that of Dix, *Treatise*, 47, here preferred to that of Botte, *Tradition apostolique*, 70–71. The versions are unclear and each seems to introduce its own confusion. The extent to which this interpretation conforms to *Mandate* 11 of Hermas is the reason for preferring it.

through the insistence on the prerogative of the bishop to speak. The contribution of the people, any of whom might previously have participated, is restricted to asking questions of the bishop and to listening obediently to his answers in a manner chillingly reminiscent of the operation of the false prophet in the eleventh *Mandate* of Hermas. It is difficult to be sure of the stage of development within the school which this section represents, but that such provision should be necessary indicates that there is still some expectation on the part of the participants that they should be free to speak, and the reliance on the bishop alone to be the arbiter of truth may indicate that this section derives from a relatively early stage in development. It is also significant that the bishop's exhortations come at the direct request of the audience, which indicates that there is still some direct engagement between the two parties, as opposed to the stylized rhetorical questions of the diatribe.

The scholastic setting and scriptural basis of Hippolytus' preaching is of some encouragement in exploring Salzmann's suggestion that *In Danielem* may contain homiletic material.[579] Although this commentary is the work of the second figure of the Hippolytean corpus, it is instructive nonetheless to see what it might teach us concerning the further development of preaching in this school.

In the light of the findings of the first chapter of this work it is clear that we must proceed with caution in mining homilies from a non-homiletic work, but it may be that the differences between this commentary and preaching are not as marked as those between other commentaries and potential homilies. Junod studies the distinctions between the commentaries and the homilies of Origen,[580] but the distinctions which he makes in the case of Origen do not actually help us when attempting to do the same with the work of Hippolytus. According to Junod, the commentaries of Origen are marked by the aim of exploring every detail of the text, whereas the aim of the homilies is to build up the church. Junod suggests that the distinction is partly due to the mixed nature of the audience of the homilies, as opposed to the purely scholastic audience of the commentaries.[581] Since, on the basis of *In Psalmos*, the audience of

---

[579] Salzmann, *Lehren und Ermahnen*, 381–386.
[580] Junod, "Wodurch unterscheiden".
[581] Junod, "Wodurch unterscheiden", 53–57.

Hippolytus would appear to have been a fairly sophisticated audience, reflecting the social homogeneity of the Roman congregations of the period and the scholastic organisation of the church of Hippolytus, the difference between the commentary and the homily may be less marked than in the case of Origen. *In Psalmos* goes into great detail on the titles of the psalms, which may be seen as a detail belonging more to the commentary form; and yet this is a homily. *In Danielem*, unlike the commentaries of Origen, does not go into the detail of every part of the text; rather, in a manner which Bardy suggests would accord with a homiletic approach, selected parts only of the text are treated.[582] Moreover, according to Bardy, the commentary has a pastoral aim. In studying this prophetic text Hippolytus is concerned to combat problems in the Roman church resulting from an over-eager expectation of the parousia. His interest is therefore not "purely" scientific.[583] Dunbar agrees that one of the aims of Hippolytus' interest in the prophecies of the end-time was a concern lest people be led astray by apocalyptic prophecy, but suggests that further to this there is a concern to build up the church under persecution, and in particular to assist the Roman church in coping with the Severan persecution by seeing this persecution in the light of the trials which must be endured before the coming of the end-time.[584] Dunbar makes it clear that these trials are not equated with the eschatological trials, but nonetheless eschatological trials may provide a context in which Hippolytus' hearers might understand their own trials. Such a direct association with the Severan persecution is unnecessary;[585] the passage at *In Danielem* 1.25.2 where the Jewish elders' search for Susanna is interpreted as a type of the trials of the church fits as well with individual and sporadic persecution as with a generalized persecution, but the point that *In Danielem* might be seen as a pastoral work to support persecuted Christians may still be made.

But although the line between commentary and homily may be less marked in the work of Hippolytus than in that of Origen, nonetheless we may suggest that the form in which the material of the commentary may be found does not reflect the method of a

---

[582] Bardy, *Hippolyte*, 10.
[583] Bardy, *Hippolyte*, 10–18.
[584] Dunbar, "Hippolytus of Rome".
[585] So Brent, *Hippolytus*, 277–279.

preacher even if it is adaptable to a preacher's need. Brief citations
of the text are followed by brief exegetical comments. Although these
comments may provide the raw material out of which a homily may
be constructed this is not a homiletic form.

However in the moral conclusions to each part of the homily we
may see the hand of a preacher at work:

> Therefore, with hearts ever alert and living wisely, imitate (μιμήσασθε)
> Susanna, and take your pleasure in the garden. Wash yourselves in
> never-failing water, wipe away every stain from yourselves, and sanc-
> tify yourselves in the celestial oil so that you can present a pure body
> to God. Light your lamps and watch for the bridegroom, so that you
> can receive him when he knocks; you can receive him, and sing hymns
> to God through Christ, to whom be glory for ever Amen. (1.23)

The concluding doxology is also indicative of homiletic inspiration,
if not of homiletic delivery.

One also catches hints of the diatribe in the manner in which the
author addresses the hearer/reader:

> But someone might say: Impossible! Now sir, what is impossible to
> God? Did he not, in the beginning, bring the whole creation out of
> nothing? (1.8)

We may thus note the union of exposition and exhortation with diatribal style, dressed with liturgical elements. The prominence of *exempla* is some indication that, if *In Danielem* were certainly homiletic,
Wills' "common pattern" might actually be found. Even so this is
simply one example of preaching in a church which was now almost
universally scholasticized:

> Now look (ἰδὲ σύ)! Babylon today is the world. The satraps are its
> powers (ἐξουσίαι), Darius is their king, the pit is hell and the lions are
> its torturing angels. Imitate (μίμησαι) Daniel! Do not fear the Satraps,
> and do not submit yourself to any human decree. Then, if you are
> thrown into the lions' den, you will be protected by the angel, you
> will tame the beasts; they shall bow low before you as before a serv-
> ant of God. No mark shall be found upon you but you will be pulled,
> living, from the pit and participate in the resurrection. You will be
> master over your enemies, and you shall live always giving thanks to
> God, to whom be glory and power for ever and for ever. Amen. (3.31)

This Hippolytus is a presbyter, an office which has now been transformed from an office of patronage within an unqualified household
into a teaching office. The presbyter's homily is uninterrupted and

the interruptions replaced with purely stylized diatribal interjections, as it has absorbed prophetic paraenesis alongside exegesis of the oracles. And just as was the case in Papias' Hierapolis, the oracles are scriptural and the *diakrisis* is interpretation.

2.2.4.4. *Peter's sermon in* Acta Petri *as typical preaching in scholasticized households*

We may conclude our treatment of preaching in the Christian schools of Rome with a sermon from *Acta Petri*. This is probably a more typical homily in the scholastic setting than any other examined in this chapter because, whilst showing some rhetorical colour in keeping with a scholastic setting, it is nonetheless not preserved because of its particular brilliance or significance. But although reflective to an extent of scholastic concerns it nonetheless reflects a school which is still in transition from the household.

Acta Petri make a number of references to Peter preaching, describing this as encouraging and exhorting the congregation.[586] However most important is the scene at *Acta Petri* 20 where Peter enters a Christian assembly in the household of Marcellus to find the Gospel is being read. He rolls up the scroll and proceeds to deliver a sermon on the Gospel, stating that he will explain what has just been read. In this popular account we may see some reflection of the manner in which a homily might be preached in this particular setting, beginning with the Scriptures, which by now are coming to include the New Testament; Peter states his intention to enable his hearers to understand the Scriptures, and his purpose in preaching to explain them. The homily falls broadly into four parts, which may be roughly characterized as *propositio, narratio, probatio* and *exhortatio*.

Peter begins by setting out his reasons for preaching:

> You must know how the holy scriptures of our Lord should be proclaimed (pronuntiari) . . . we should first learn to know the will of God, that is his goodness . . .

He then explains this statement by reference to the polymorphy of Jesus, before turning to the *narratio* of the transfiguration, which would appear to have been the scriptural incident which was being read. That a homily standing broadly in the Jewish tradition might have

---

[586] So e.g. *Acta Petri* 30.

a narrative basis has already been suggested, and we have observed in this respect the retelling of the scriptural story in ps-Philo as well as Eleazer haModai's use of narrative to enthrone a scriptural text.[587] As such Peter is being obedient simultaneously to the canons of classical rhetoric and the expectations of a Jewish preacher.

> And now I will explain (exponam) to you what has just been read to you. Our Lord wished me to see his majesty on the holy mountain, but when I, with the sons of Zebedee, saw the brilliance of his light, I fell as one dead, and closed my eyes, and heard his voice, such as I cannot describe; I thought that I had been blinded by his radiance . . . and he gave me his hand and lifted me up. And when I stood up I saw him in such a form as I was able to comprehend.

From this experience he deduces that God's mercy means that Jesus was human in appearance for the sake of our salvation and understanding, whilst being divine. Here further scriptural citation is introduced by way of support for the statements which are made.

> So, my dearest brethren, as God is merciful, he has borne our weaknesses and carried our sins, as the prophet says "He himself bears our sins and is afflicted for us; yet we thought him to be afflicted and stricken with wounds." For "he is in the Father and the Father in him". He is himself the fullness of all majesty, who has shown us all his goodness.

This is cause for comfort to the congregation. The *probatio* then gives way to praise as a long list of the qualities of God follows:

> This God who is both great and small, beautiful and ugly, young and old, appearing in time and yet in eternity . . .

Not only should we note the high rhetoric of this almost hymnic passage, but may note the manner in which Peter, after an asyndetic catalogue, concludes with a benediction similar in form and function to the "homiletic benedictions" uncovered by Jewett in the Pauline correspondence,[588] and demonstrating the manner in which, in this period, the homily was still closely wedded to the liturgy.

> This is the Jesus whom you have, the door, the light, the way the bread, the water, the life . . . He is all things and there is no other greater than he. To him be praise for ever and ever. Amen.

---

[587] 1.2.1.2 above.
[588] Jewett, "Form and function".

As we observed, the situation described is transitional from the household to the school, for although the physical location described is a private house, albeit a large one since it has colonnades, the situation described may be understood as scholastic since the Scriptures are being read (apparently from rolls), because of the rhetorical care of Peter's preaching (demonstrated not only in the structure of his preaching but in such elements of style as the asyndetic catalogue with which his homily concludes) and since Marcellus has set apart his house with a sprinkling of water for religious functions. Scriptures are being read in a dedicated place, yet the dedicated place is still the dining room (*triclinium*), indicative of a similar setting to that presumed in the Emmaeus pericopē, and is still part of Marcellus' house. Peter thus stands in the position of sophist within a household, under Marcellus' patronage. In its scholastic elements it reflects the situation of the time of redaction rather than the fictional first century setting, at which point it is only to be expected that the original households had undergone some social development, but the surprise is the extent to which the original household is still intact. If *Acta Petri* derive from the third century this is further evidence that the transition was far from chronologically uniform. But although the transition from unqualified οἶκος to οἶκος θεοῦ, encouraged in the first century by *I Peter*, is still not complete, the transition from prophecy to preaching is accomplished.

2.2.4.5. *Scholasticization in Rome*

In Asia it was observed that the school had come to be prominent in the self-understanding of the church by the middle of the second century and that, although progression towards universal scholasticization was uneven, in particular because Montanism is a rather uncomfortably conservative prophetic movement, by the end of the second century the process was near to being universal, and that the actual result of Montanism was to throw the church back even more thoroughly upon the scriptural text. Hippolytus' homily *In Psalmos* is an indication that the same happened at Rome and that, although there are survivals in Rome of the old prophetic spirit, even those communities which are still recognizable as households have nonetheless adopted scholastic procedures by the beginning of the third century, with the corresponding impact on preaching in these households.

2.2.5. *Preaching and prophecy in Tertullian's Africa*

We have already observed that in the brief accounts of worship contained in Tertullian's works there is reference to preaching, though
no content has survived.[589] *Apologeticum* 39.3 speaks of *exhortatio* in the
assembly, based on the Scriptures, and *De Anima* 9 states that Scripture
is read and that there are addresses after the scriptural reading. We
might reasonably conclude from these references that the African
church, at the earliest time at which we know it, was already entirely
scholasticized, and that Scripture, and preaching based upon Scripture,
had become the uniquely privileged manner in which the word of
God was communicated in the assembly. The possibility that the
African version of the Old Testament was based on a Jewish text
might be seen as further evidence of a synagogalizing tendency in
African Christianity if not of a synagogal origin.[590]

There is however some evidence of the continued survival, or perhaps the revival, of prophetic procedures. The account of worship at
De Anima 9 is occasioned by Tertullian's report of a sister who has
visions in the liturgy. After the dismissal of the people (*dismissa plebe*)
she would report her visions and these visions would be examined
and tested so that their veracity might be established.

This process of testing, albeit taking place outside the assembly,
is one which we might anticipate since, in keeping with the pattern
of examination discerned elsewhere, we might expect that prophecy
would be examined and tested. Tertullian does not state exactly who
undertook the testing, simply stating that the reports were made
"nobis." This may be a reference to a Montanist group within the
Carthaginian church,[591] or may be a more formal group, perhaps
made up of *seniores* within the church, among whom Tertullian may
be numbered, charged with the task of testing prophecies on behalf
of the church.[592] A third possibility is that the earlier pattern had
been for an official group to test prophecies but that this practice
had died out, yet was maintained or revived by the Montanist group
within the church and, because it was being undertaken by a group
without official sanction in the church, it took place away from the

---

[589] 1.1.4.
[590] So Quispel, "African Christianity before Minucius Felix and Tertullian"; the
discussion of Tertullian's scriptural text is at 257–265.
[591] Rankin, *Tertullian and the church*, 35–36; Trevett, *Montanism*, 173.

main assembly. That the testing of the prophecy, and presumably its further communication, takes place outside of the main assembly, rather than being the task of a prophet or teacher or bishop within the assembly, is an indication that the process described is that of a sub-group within the Carthaginian church and is thus a pre-occupation of that group and not of the whole church. That the process should take place at all however is an indication that at one point prophecy had been delivered and tested as part of the regular pattern of worship in the African church. The absence of the *plebs* may indicate that the testing of prophecy had traditionally been a function of the patrons of the church, the *seniores*, and that Tertullian as *senior* and sympathizer with the new prophecy is maintaining that tradition, but it is equally possible that the testing takes place after worship because it is a concern of those sympathetic to the new prophecy alone. As *senior*, Tertullian would be a leader in that process as in that group.

The manner according to which the prophecies were tested may perhaps be gathered from the "multiple warrants" for Christian faith gathered from Tertullian's writings by Guerra.[593] These are Scripture, reason, the superior moral behaviour of Christians, spiritual testimony and tradition. As Guerra points out, none of these has total priority over the others, but are employed by Tertullian as he requires them. In testing the validity of spiritual testimony we may suggest that conformity with the other possible warrants of faith was sought, and that prophetic revelation tested by Scripture might generate charismatic exegesis. Further to this, a prophecy once determined as true could become the subject of further discussion. To illustrate this argument we may take four oracles (two of which are cited contiguously and are therefore treated together) quoted and discussed by Tertullian, on the assumption that these are oracles delivered not by Phrygian Montanists but by Carthaginian prophets at the time of Tertullian.[594]

---

[592] So Tabbernee, "To pardon or not to pardon".

[593] Guerra, "Polemical Christianity", 109.

[594] Following therefore Tabbernee, "To pardon or not to pardon", whose case may be strengthened by observing *De anima* 58.8, which speaks of the frequent admonitions of the paraclete (presumably within the Carthaginian community), and *De ieiunio* 13.5, which states that the paraclete might issue instructions for a fast. Cf. Robeck, *Prophecy in Carthage*, 117, 115, 125 who seeks a Phrygian origin for each of the prophecies treated here.

> The church can pardon sin, but I will not do it, lest they commit fur-
> ther sin. (*De pudicitia* 21.7)

The context of this oracle is Tertullian's argument that the church
should not forgive. A diatribal objector states that the church has
power to forgive sin, at which point Tertullian agrees, but quotes
this oracle to argue that even though the church may have the
power, it is not a power which the Spirit exercises, and that the
church should not therefore exercise it. Both Tabbernee and Robeck
see this as charismatic exegesis, whilst differing over the text at
issue.[595] But much as it is possible to see scriptural background in
any statement concerning the forgiveness of sins, this is not the realization of a text but a paraenetic statement of the paraclete. Nonetheless
the diatribal discussion continues with a treatment of Scripture. This
scriptural discussion once again is not charismatic exegesis, but is a
demonstration of the validity of the prophecy through answering the
possible scriptural objection that the power of forgiveness was given
to Peter. Immediately after quoting the oracle Tertullian says (perhaps in the persona of the objector):

> But what if a false prophetic spirit said this?

Immediately he responds that this cannot be the case, "as the destroyer
would rather have commended himself by his clemency and he would
have set others in the way of sin". A further argument for the truth
of this prophecy is then added, in that if a false spirit were claiming the ability to forgive fornication, then he would not in turn be
withholding the forgiveness for fear of leading others astray. Tertullian
then forestalls a possible objection that the power of forgiveness was
given to Peter by suggesting that this power was given to Peter alone,
that such power was not given to the church, because it is on Peter
that the church is subsequently built. Thus he sees that Peter subsequently looses the gentiles from the law, as he set free the lame
man in the temple from disease, whilst binding Christians to keep
those elements of the moral law which remained, as he had bound
Ananias to death. Scripture is proven from scriptural narrative, and
the purpose of the discussion is to demonstrate the validity of the
oracle, which is shown not to contradict Scripture.

---

[595] Tabbernee, "To pardon or not to pardon"; Robeck, *Prophecy in Carthage*, 117.

In this discussion we can see the way in which an oracle might be discussed in the context of a hostile objection, a claim that it was not the paraclete which had spoken through a prophet, but a false spirit. Two arguments are presented which demonstrate the internal consistency of the oracle and its conformity to Scripture. In the first event it is argued that were the spirit a false one then what is said would not be consistent with the machinations of a deceptive spirit, and secondly it is suggested that the oracle's apparent contradiction of Scripture can be resolved.

At *Adversus Praxean* 8, Tertullian is dealing with the Valentinian doctrine of emanation, and wishes to put distance between his idea of the projection of the Son from the Father and that of Valentinus, whose emanations are separate from their source. It is in this context that he cites this oracle.

> God put forth his word as a root puts forth a shoot and as a spring puts forth a river and as the sun puts forth a ray. (*Adversus Praxean* 8.5)

More clearly than the other examples cited here, this oracle is an example of charismatic exegesis, for all three images are derived from *Sirach* 24, which compares wisdom to a tree spreading out its branches and to a river running over, and the teaching of wisdom to the brightness of the dawn.[596] This prophecy is based on Scripture, and is brought into the present by comparing the Son of God to the wisdom of God. Tertullian then goes on to argue that it is proper to see the ray as the offspring of the sun and the river as the offspring of the spring, and points out that just as there are two things in each of his examples, that is to say that the spring and the river are different things, nonetheless they are conjoined. The point of this is to establish both the separate existences of the Father and the Son, and to anchor their unity of *substantia*. In this further discussion of the oracle we may see that the prophecy is being shown to be coherent with the principles of reason and of the tradition of the faith, and that it is being proved in the process of expansion. We may thus deduce something of the manner in which it might have been discussed in the community. However Tertullian then goes on to suggest that the Spirit might be a third derived principle from the original Godhead, like an irrigation canal cut from a river. In this

---

[596] An observation of Skarsaune, "Scriptural interpretation", 433 n119.

further expansion Tertullian is not only arguing for a Trinity of persons in the Godhead, but is carrying out further charismatic exegesis. For at *Sirach* 24:30–31 Ben Sira himself speaks, and states that "like a rivulet from her (Wisdom's) stream" he chose to water his garden. It is this scriptural writing which Tertullian is picking up, and just as Ben Sira compares wisdom to prophecy so Tertullian prophetically interprets and expands this verse in order to show the existence of the Spirit, derived from the Godhead and speaking prophetically in the church.

The discussions of oracles here presumably illustrate the manner in which they might be discussed within the *ecclesiola in ecclesia* which Tertullian describes at *De anima* 9. They are expanded through Scripture and through the generation of further charismatic exegesis and are defended on the grounds of conformity with Scripture and of internal consistency. We might hypothesize that such discussions of oracles took place in the main assembly of the African church at a time earlier than that of Tertullian when prophecy was delivered and tested in the church, and that the discussion then followed the lines indicated in the discussions of these oracles, namely that scriptural exegesis, whether charismatic or not, was the basis on which they were expanded and applied. We might further speculate that here as elsewhere the testing of prophecy through Scripture caused Scripture to predominate in the Carthaginian community and eventually to supplant prophecy as the privileged locus of inspiration; it is even possible that Tertullian's realization that Scripture did not exhaust the communication made by God to God's people was a cause of his attraction to the new prophecy in Carthage. Our final pair of oracles may perhaps illustrate this possibility.

> It is good for you to be publicly exposed. For he who is not exposed among men is exposed in the Lord. Do not be disturbed; righteousness brings you before the public. Why are you disturbed when you are receiving praise? There is opportunity when you are observed by people.

And also elsewhere:

> Do not seek to die on soft beds, or in miscarriages, and in mild fevers but in martyrdoms, that he who has suffered for you may be glorified. (*De fuga* 9.4)

The treatment of these contiguous oracles is somewhat different from those above. Rather then being subjected to proof, they are assumed to be true, since they appear already to have been accepted into the canon of accepted prophetic utterance, and are therefore employed together not to launch an argument but to cap an argument. Tertullian is arguing against fleeing persecution and uses Peter and John as *exempla*. He has quoted and interpreted a number of scriptural passages in support of his argument, and the oracles, cited in close proximity, are the final crown of the argument. The manner in which they are cited together is reminiscent of the manner in which we observed that the Thessalonian correspondence cited paraenetic oracles in close proximity to one another. There it was suggested that the manner in which they were cited together was reflective of the practice of the church at worship;[597] here too we may suggest that the manner in which scriptural *exempla*, scriptural texts and prophetic oracles are found together is reflective of preaching. The context is paraenetic rather than homiletic and the overall function of *De fuga*, which is an individual paraenesis, dictates the form and the content of this passage, but the methods of a preacher may nonetheless be seen in the use of material. The oracle does not need to be proved, but rather it is used because it is established truth which fits in with the interpretation of Scripture which Tertullian is proposing. As such we may have some reflection of the methods of a preacher in the African church, combining proven prophecy with Scripture, including the use of scriptural *exempla*, in building up the faith of his hearers.

In noting Tertullian's description of the process of testing prophecy and in observing his discussions of oracles in this light it was noted that this was in keeping with a regular procedure known elsewhere. We may thus have a degree of assurance that the probative discussion of oracles reflects the *sermo* of the prophetic circle at Carthage of which he was a member. But the pattern of development which has led to the procedure described taking place outside the main assembly, and thus the nature and genesis of preaching in the African church before Tertullian, can only be hypothesized.

2.2.6. *The Alexandrian school tradition*

We have observed the process of scholasticization with its corresponding impact on preaching in the cities of Asia and in Rome.

---

[597] 2.1.1.

When the Alexandrian church emerges into the light of history early
in the third century it does so as a scholastically formed Christian
community, the church functionally equivalent to a school.[598] Although
it is only possible to guess at the basis for this scholastic formation,
it is not impossible that a similar process of scholasticization had
taken place in Alexandria as in Rome and in the Asian cities. The
strong Jewish influence to be found in Alexandria, and in particular the large number of synagogues, together with the possibility that
Christianity in Alexandria formed itself in a Jewish matrix,[599] might
be indication that this Christianity was synagogal from the start, but
the necessity of patronage in order to support the schools might also
indicate that there was a strong domestic element within Alexandrian
Christianity. The role of the householder as patron might account
for the power accorded to the Alexandrian presbyters up to the time
of Nicaea.[600] But whatever the obscurity of early Alexandrian Christianity, when Origen emerges from this Christian milieu as the first
patristic preacher of whose output anything of substance remains, he
emerges as representative of a Christianity thoroughly scholastic in
its orientation.

We know little however of Origen's antecedents as preachers. For
in keeping with our ignorance concerning Alexandrian Christian origins there are no remains of preaching from an earlier period.
Whereas *Barnabas* is often attributed to an Alexandrian milieu and
has even been claimed as a homily,[601] both assertions are so uncertain that nothing can be built upon these suppositions. *Epistula ad
Diognetum* similarly has been widely claimed as Alexandrian,[602] and
the final chapters as a fragment of a homily.[603] Barnard thinks these
latter chapters a homily on the grounds of their apparent address
to Christians and on the grounds of the high-flown rhetorical style

---

[598] See for some discussion Bardy, "Origines" and van den Hoek, "'Catechetical'
school".

[599] So Pearson, "Earliest Christianity in Egypt", 145–151.

[600] On which see Telfer, "Episcopal succession".

[601] By Barnard, "Is the Epistle of Barnabas a paschal homily?" Barnard picks up
on various baptismal and paschal aspects of the work, rather confusingly since there
is no evidence for an association of baptism and Pascha at this time. He does not
argue at all for the classification as a homily.

[602] Marrou, *A Diognète*, 265–267, goes so far as tentatively to suggest the name
of Pantaenus as author.

[603] Barnard, "Enigma".

of these chapters. His arguments however do not convince, for not only are these neither necessary nor sufficient grounds to classify the chapters as a homily, but both the style and the mode of address may be seen as appropriate ways in which triumphantly to conclude a protreptic discourse. Seeing the closing chapters in this light is preferable to seeing them as fragments of a homily as it enables us to make sense of the document overall.[604]

One other document deriving from Alexandrian Christianity before Origen which might be a homily is Clement's *Quis dives salvetur*. This is described by Quasten as "a homily ... which however seems not to be a sermon delivered in a public service"![605] Butterworth is slightly clearer in suggesting that the work has the form of a homily, but that it is a desk-homily or a homily revised for publication.[606] His grounds for suggesting that it is a desk-homily are essentially that it is too long to be a homily. However, we do not know what length would be expected in a sermon in the Alexandrian setting of Clement and may recall that in the synagogues of Philo's Alexandria discourse on the law might fill an entire day. There are certainly grounds for seeing the work as a homily, in particular the manner in which it is grounded on a seriatim exegesis of *Mark* 10:17–31. Clement does not state that this reading had immediately preceded his treatment of the text, indeed there are some indications that this has not been read, for instance he states that he repeats the words of Scripture, which until now (ἄχρι νῦν) had troubled the audience.[607] This is an indication that the passage is known from outside the context of an assembly. However his address is to the committed, for he states that he is not concerned with those who are not initiated.[608] The prayer for grace before beginning his treatment of Scripture[609] might indicate a liturgical context, but need not do so.

The context of delivery might well be a particular occasion in the life of the Alexandrian Christian community, conceivably a controversy over the Gospel in question which might prompt a particular

---

[604] Thus in agreement on the unity and purpose of *Ad Diognetum* with Rizzi, *Questione dell'unità*.

[605] Quasten, *Patrology*, II 15.

[606] Butterworth, *Clement of Alexandria*, 263.

[607] *Quis dives salvetur* 4.

[608] *Quis dives salvetur* 2.

[609] *Quis dives salvetur* 4.

address within Clement's school. If a particular occasion is at issue this may explain the preservation of the homily. Clearly Clement is concerned that the wealthy should continue to offer patronage to the school and to individual Christian teachers, which is the basis for his suggestion that the wealthy should adopt, as it were, a teacher and trainer.[610] Just as Hermas' teaching of a second repentance might be interpreted as a ploy for retaining the social support of the wealthy, so the final emphasis in *Quis dives salvetur* might be read as an attempt to keep the wealthy in the church in order that they might continue to support the school.

This would mean that this is an atypical homily since addressed to a particular occasion, but formally may nonetheless be indicative to some extent of the manner in which an Alexandrian preacher in a scholastic setting might address his audience. In particular we may observe the manner in which, as in *In Sanctum Pascha*, the Scripture is repeated before its atomizing interpretation. The difference between this and ps-Hippolytus' work however lies in the fact that exhortation is much more closely bound up to exegesis. The text is followed through and treated in small sections, but the corresponding application follows at every point, rather than being gathered into any kind of appendix. The second half of the work, roughly from the 28th chapter on, leaves the text behind altogether and deals generally with salvation and repentance. This broader thematic treatment may be homiletic, but there is no basis on which we might know this to be the case. However, the scholastic treatment of Scripture in the earlier part of the work is what one would expect, demonstrating the same emphasis and exegetical form as that found in Origen's preaching, and so at this point perhaps the work is more typical of a homily. Alongside the emphasis on understanding Scripture, there are some indications of scholasticization in the use of the common diatribal metaphors of the athlete[611] and the pilot,[612] and in the *ēthopoïia* of the courtroom[613] followed immediately by a sudden address to an fictitious member of the audience,[614] concluding with a catalogue and a citation. Here we are transported to Clement's schoolroom.

---

[610] *Quis dives salvetur* 41.
[611] *Quis dives salvetur* 3.
[612] *Quis dives salvetur* 26.
[613] *Quis dives salvetur* 23.
[614] *Quis dives salvetur* 24.

Can you too rise above your riches? Say so then; Christ does not drag
you away from your riches, the Lord is not jealous! But can you see
yourself overcome by them and dragged down? Leave them behind,
throw them away, despise them, bid them farewell and run away! "If
your right eye causes you to stumble, cut it out quickly."

2.2.7. *The triumph of the school*

Origen thus emerges from a scholasticized Christianity. His preaching not only reflects that background but underscores it in the subsequent history of preaching.

This is the point at which a history of preaching might begin,
and is thus the point at which this prehistory concludes. In the
absolute primacy given to Scripture in Origen's preaching we may
observe the final triumph of scholasticization. However, although
Scripture has primacy, certain elements of the earlier preaching tradition emerge in his work, as they do in later preachers. In particular the relationship between exegesis and exhortation is to be
observed. The ethical functions of the earliest prophecy, now transferred to preaching, have not been lost. So following on from the
exegetical part of Origen's sermons an ethical conclusion is present.
The same phenomenon may be found centuries later in the sermons
of Chrysostom. But Scripture is now used as the basis of exhortation, rather than being used, as *II Clement* had used it, to support
the content of exhortation or, as it had been used in the Pauline
communities, to test the validity of prophetic exhortation. It is the
voice of God in the written word which is now to be obeyed rather
than the unmediated voice of the Spirit as heard from Paul and
from John of Patmos.

CHAPTER THREE

SOME CONCLUSIONS

3.1. *An underpinning hypothesis, from prophecy to preaching*

From the beginning the word of God was communicated to believers within the Christian assembly; this meets the broad, functional definition of preaching proposed at the beginning of this work, even though it was not preaching as we would now recognize it. Rather than scriptural preaching, prophecy would appear to have been the most primitive form of Christian communication, and prophecy was supplemented by the examination of prophecy to establish whether it was true prophecy, and expansion and application of the prophetic messages, which might itself be seen as an inspired speech-activity. This took place around the table of the earliest Christian households and therefore, although prophecy might have taken place at some length, in particular since oracles may have been given in series, and although the examination of the prophecies might also have been lengthy, the prevailing mode of communication would have been conversational. The need for the testing of prophetic messages meant that from an early period both prophecy and the testing of prophecy were bound up to the use of Scripture since Scripture could provide some external basis for the critical examination of prophecy. In addition the process of examination undergone by prophecy might also be practised on Scripture itself. Herein lies one of the origins of Christian preaching: for when prophecy was delivered it was necessary that the prophecy be judged, interpreted and expounded. Thus it is in this process, it is suggested, that the origins of the homily lie, rather than in synagogal preaching or in the practice of the Hellenistic schools, though the conversation which might take place in the meals of the Hellenistic schools is socially comparable to that which took place at Christian tables in the celebration of the Lord's Supper. The practice of the synagogue and the schools however did impact at a later stage upon the development of preaching out of these origins, as Scripture came to replace the living voice, and the process of expansion and application was applied to the written word.

We have observed that prophecy is most prominent in a household setting. Although this medium of communication is suitable for
delivery in this context, since the household was also the most primitive form of ecclesial organisation it is in part inevitable that the
most primitive form of communication would take place within it.
However when the household develops into a synagogue or school
prophecy continues to be practised. And yet this social development
combines with the theological development of a growing respect paid
to the written canon, as is appropriate in a scholastic social organisation, with the eventual result that Scripture comes to dominate
prophecy to such an extent that the prophetic voice disappears altogether. It is in this way that Graeco-Roman schools, and the synagogue in particular, come in time to influence the communication
of the word of God in Christianity. This phenomenon has been
termed "scholasticization", a term intended to describe the process
by which the loose organisation of the communication of the word
of God in the earliest households through prophecy, and through
reactions to prophecy which are themselves prophetic, is replaced
by systematic communication through the reading and interpretation
of Scripture in part under the influence of preaching in the synagogue and in part as the result of the models available for delivery
and discussion within the schools, as the churches formed themselves
along these essentially scholastic lines. Just as the synagogue homily
had grown from the targum, and was controlled by Scripture, so
the same scriptural control comes about within Christianity, even
though Christians tended not to adopt the same forms as those of
early Judaism, just as Jewish preaching developed along its own lines.

So we may observe that in the Pauline households, as in that of
Hermas, Scripture plays a relatively minor role in the communication of the word of God. In the school of John it provides the basis
for prophetic communication, and in that of Hippolytus it has complete dominance; and yet in neither the Johannine nor the Hippolytean
communities is Scripture simply retold, but it is reapplied. The movement from unqualified οἶκος to οἶκος θεοῦ is thus marked by a movement towards scripturally based communication.

This is shown in the change in the nature of ethical exhortation.
We have seen that the ethical content of second century preaching
has been overestimated through the assumption that *II Clement* was
a homily and through an over-literal reading of Justin's report, and
that Ekenberg's belief that the growth in the prominence of ethical

paraenesis led to the decline of prophecy[1] is actually the very opposite of the truth, in that the later homilies which we have uncovered show little or no ethical interest, whereas in the first century
prophecy was capable of being a vehicle for paraenesis. Insofar as
ethical exhortation is found in the preaching of the second century
there is development away from the unmediated and undisputed
command of God given through prophecy. Although Wills' "common homiletic pattern"[2] has not been shown to be homiletic in the
first two centuries it undoubtedly existed in the realm of early Christian
moral discourse, and may be characterized as the demand of God
made in Scripture from which the exhorter must draw conclusions.
As such it is ready to make an entree into the sermon when the
sermon becomes the predominant mode of Christian discourse.

This drowning out of the prophetic voice however only comes
about in the third century, even though the process which led to it
began in the first. The process was gradual and uneven, and the
speech forms of prophecy continued in many places to influence the
manner in which Scripture was treated. In Rome and Asia the decline
of prophecy may well be linked to the rise and condemnation of
gnosticism, and more particularly of Montanism. However, even had
Montanism never come along, it is perhaps inevitable, given the
social development that the church underwent, and given the need
for the authentication of prophetic messages, that Scripture would
come to achieve primacy among the theological resources of the
church, and that as a result the scriptural homily, ultimately derived
from Jewish models and anchored in the church as a result of synagogalization, would achieve primacy at the last. It is this process
which we have sought to trace here.

The corollary of this narrative is that the rise of preaching meant
the decline of prophecy. At several points in this work there has
been occasion to observe the structures of authority in various seg-
ments of early Christianity because of the way in which changes in
the means and manner of communication impact on these structures. But in observing the widespread and ultimately universal phenomenon which has been termed scholasticization there has been no
consistent attempt to trace the rise of the teacher or the decline of

---

[1] Ekenberg, "Urkristan predikan", 9, 23, 31.
[2] Proposed in "Form of the sermon" and discussed at 1.2.1.4 above.

the prophet, nor to correlate the two with the phenomenon of episcopacy. The reason for this is that although scholasticization ultimately led to the decline of prophecy the relationships between
prophet and teacher and that obtaining between the functions of
prophecy and teaching and the household-based officers of the church
(and the functions which these officers might exercise) is not uniform. In particular we should beware of seeing charisma and office
as mutually exclusive forces. In the treatment of the Revelation to
John above there was occasion to criticize the assumptions of Satake
and Fiorenza, who infer from the prophetic nature of John's authority either that he is challenging the structures of episcopacy (so
Fiorenza) or that such structures do not exist (so Satake).[3] It was
suggested then that rather than not existing and rather than being
challenged by the prophetic order they functioned entirely differently
and did not come into John's purview. There is no conflict because
the levels of authority differ; in particular John's exhortations do not
impinge directly upon the function of governance. Elsewhere however Hermas who is a prophet is also a householder; here there is
no conflict because there is cohesion between traditional and charismatic legitimation.[4] Hermas however does have occasion to criticize
the scholasticization of other Roman churches,[5] whereas in the community of *Epistula apostolorum*, where Schmidt finds no trace of hierarchy "in the catholic sense", there is the beginning of a hierarchy
based on the teaching office alongside the practice of prophecy.[6]
Here it seems the functions of teaching and prophecy merged into
one another. In the Roman community of *Traditio apostolica* we should
note that the fundamental conflict was between teacher and household-based patron-presbyter[7] whereas Justin is both teacher and
patron.[8] The co-incidence of roles in some communities, and the triumph of the teacher over patrons (elsewhere) is what leads to
Countryman's observation of the intellectual role of so many early
catholic bishops.[9] Order may derive from the resolution of conflict

---

[3] See 2.1.3 above with reference to Satake *Gemeindeordnung* and Fiorenza, "Apokalypsis
and propheteia".
[4] Contra Jeffers, *Conflict at Rome* with Stewart-Sykes, "Hermas the prophet".
[5] Note the discussion of *Mandate* 11 at 2.1.2 above.
[6] Note Schmidt, *Gespräche Jesu*, 376–378 and the discussion at 2.2.3.3 above.
[7] So Stewart-Sykes, "Integrity".
[8] See the discussion at 2.2.4.1 above.
[9] See Countryman, "Intellectual role".

but need not do so. There may be conflicts between prophecy and *episkopē*, though there is no evidence that this ever actually took place,[10] and much evidence that the two co-existed. Thus Polycarp and Melito were prophetic bishops and the Montanists, prophetic Christians par excellence, had offices. Nonetheless there was certainly conflict between teaching and prophecy, to which Hermas bears witness, and conflict between teaching and *episkopē* based on patronage is revealed in *Traditio apostolica*, but these are not necessary conflicts. Thus, if the conclusion of this work is that preaching originated in prophecy and in time replaced it, and the corollary of this conclusion is that the decline of prophecy was caused by the rise of preaching through the establishment of a working scriptural canon and the corresponding necessity that the preacher be qualified to interpret this text, we may go on from there to note that the corollary has a corollary, namely that prophecy did not decline because of the rise of the episcopate. It is true that the establishment of the practice of preaching meant that the communication of the word of God in the assembly would be restricted to one person rather than to one person at a time; thus the presbyter who delivers *II Clement* gives both the prophecy and its *diakrisis*.[11] It is also true that this one person would normally have been the bishop (though may be a presbyter insofar as the two are distinguished) but this does not mean that the bishop overcame the prophet, rather that the function of exhortation, which had formerly been that of the prophet, became that of the bishop because of the change in the nature of that exhortation and the need for exhortation to receive external validation, and so the functions and qualifications of the bishop changed in turn in order to accommodate the new responsibilities of this office.

But although scriptural preaching derives from scholasticization, the process of scholasticization did not at first necessitate complete abandonment of the household model and its characteristic modes of discourse, in part because of the natural conservatism of any liturgical movement and in part because of the close relationship between the household and the school, including the common practice in both of domestic *homilia*. Thus we may observe the case of *Acta Petri*, where a fully-fledged sermon is found in a transitional social setting,

---

[10] Cf. Trevett, "Prophecy and anti-episcopal activity" who attempts to see this occurring at Philadelphia.

[11] See the discussion of *II Clement* at 2.2.2.4 above.

and the Pastoral Epistles, where a synagogalized community nonetheless still knows the practice of prophecy. The use of Scripture brought about de facto scholasticization, which in turn brought about preaching. Only when the process is complete is it possible, though still not necessary, to move out of the house into the basilica.

Thus to summarize the proposal of this work, we may state that prophecy, and accompanying discussion which intended to prove the content of the prophecy, was the earliest form of Christian communication and that this took place within households. This stage of communication is exemplified in the Pauline writings, in *Pastor Hermae* and in the churches addressed by the seer of the apocalypse. Its content may vary, but is often ethical. Scripture could be employed in the process of *diakrisis*, and the interpretation of Scripture might also be a prophetic task. Although the content of prophecy was often paraenetic, prophecy within the assembly was not the only possible medium of paraenesis, and so without indicators that delivery took place within the assembly we cannot assume that there is an equation of paraenesis and preaching or paraenesis and prophecy, and for this reason we demurred from classifying *James* or *II Clement* as homiletic, and were uncertain about the relationship of *Hebrews*, despite its self-identification in homiletic language, to communication in the assembly. In the case of *II Clement* however, which was, we argued, a pre-baptismal *Mahnrede*, it was possible to observe that the same process of proof and expansion which was applied to prophetic messages was applied to the *credo* of a community. This is significant because it shows that the procedure applied to prophecy might be applied to other speech-forms within the assembly. It is also noteworthy in that the procedure of *diakrisis* here is not undertaken through conversation but is the work of one *presbuteros*. A similar picture of *diakrisis* taking place with regard to non-prophetic material (though the speakers in this case are also prophets) is James' determination of the report of Paul and Barnabas in *Acts*. The final stage of development comes when the process of *diakrisis* applied to prophecy becomes applied to Scripture itself. It is at this stage of development that it becomes necessary to borrow forms from the synagogue and the school in order to meet this new rhetorical occasion. The completed process may be found in the work of Hippolytus and that of the anonymous author of *In sanctum Pascha*. The process took place in differing ways and in differing time-scales, but typical mediating positions might be those of John, who in the sixth chapter

of his Gospel prophesies on the basis of Scripture, and Papias, who
applies the process of *diakrisis* (which he calls *exegēsis*) to oral reports
of prophecy, which are in the process of becoming Scripture. The
process of organizing the church as a scholastic institution, necessary as a result of the tensions deriving from competition between
householders in the household church, received impetus from the
scripturalization of prophecy, and the increasing emphasis on written Scripture led in turn to further scholasticization. For a time
prophecy and Scriptural preaching can co-exist as they do in reality
in the work of Melito and as they do in theory only in Justin's vision
of the church. But the whole direction of the church makes prophecy
increasingly redundant, leaving the Montanists in Asia outside the
church and the new prophets of Africa outside the assembly.

3.2. *Smyrna as* exemplum

The process as a whole may be well exemplified with reference to
the church in Smyrna. We suggested above that from the remains
that we hold we may trace some movement from the household
church over which Polycarp presided to a fully-fledged scholastic
community in the third century.[12] The seer of *Revelation* directed an
oracle to the church at Smyrna which brooked no opposition, but
by the time of Polycarp the household converses concerning the
prophetic messages it receives. Thus it is in the household context
that Polycarp is instructed by Ignatius ὁμιλίαν ποιεῖν about κακοτεχνίαι.[13] Here, we suggested above, ὁμιλία means conversation.[14] At
the end of this investigation we can flesh out the picture of what
this meant in the practice of Polycarp's community.

Given that the origin of preaching grew in part out of the practice of discerning the meaning and validity of prophetic addresses,
a technique which in time became transferred to other communications, such as the *credo* of the church of *II Clement*, and in time
Scripture, one might anticipate that this διάκρισις would involve a
measure of conversation. We have met a number of ὁμιλίαι taking
place in the context of house-churches, which we may envisage as

---

[12] 2.
[13] Ignatius *Ad Polycarpum* 5.1.
[14] 1.1.4; note also the discussion of this passage at 1.2.4.4.

a kind of prophetic table-talk. In particular we may note that the ὁμιλία of *Acta Pauli* was conducted entirely in prophetic speeches. Some development was discerned in the community out of which Luke-Acts grew, but in the Emmaeus narrative it was to be observed that, even though the Scriptures are the basis of the conversation, conversation is still a primary means of discovering the word of God. This is the ὁμιλία in which Polycarp is to participate. But if this is the case, how does the instruction given to Polycarp to make ὁμιλία specifically against κακοτεχνίαι connect with prophecy, if the κακο-τεχνίαι are not themselves the subject of prophecy?

Broadly there are two interpretations of the word as used here. The first is that recently supported by Schoedel (though according to Lightfoot going back to Cureton[15]) as a reference to trades which are improper for a Christian. Schoedel argues that the phrase is to be taken in the context of the prior instruction that slaves should not have their freedom purchased from the common fund, in order that they might not become slaves of ἐπιθυμία, and that it is thus a reference to trades and professions whose object is to bring pleasure.[16] This reading of the instruction in context does not however take account of the social context of the instruction not to buy freedom for slaves, which is to ensure that the net of patronage is not spread too widely.[17] The freed slaves would not be engaging in trade but become part of a *clientela*, and the ἐπιθυμία is therefore not that of any prospective customer, but that of the patron. Lightfoot is correct in seeing that "in a list of practical exhortations we need not look for any close connexion with the preceding or following topics."[18]

The alternative suggestion is that of Lightfoot, who reads the state-ment here in the light of the other Ignatian usage of κακοτεχνία at *Ad Philadelphios* 6, where he suggests that Ignatius has reference to the "schismatical designs of the false teachers."[19] More specifically, in view of the connection of these κακοτεχνίαι with the Devil at this point, he suggests that sorcery in particular was intended, seeing the term as equivalent to the Latin *maleficia*.

---

[15] Lightfoot, *Apostolic fathers* II.2, 347.
[16] Schoedel, *Ignatius*, 271; similarly Bartelink, *Lexicologisch-semantische studie*, 121; Camelot, *Ignace d'Antioche*, 174.
[17] On which see Harrill, "Ignatius *ad Polycarpum* 4.3".
[18] Lightfoot, *Apostolic fathers* II.2, 347.
[19] Lightfoot, *Apostolic fathers* II.2, 346.

Lightfoot's interpretation enables us to make sense of the following instruction to converse against these evil arts, for the particular magic which might be intended would be divination or any other form of false prophecy. This false prophecy, says Ignatius, should be unmasked by Polycarp in the conversation which follows. The ὁμιλία would always follow the prophecy and Polycarp is being exhorted to ensure that prophecy achieved through κακοτεχνίαι is recognized as such through his ὁμιλία, which would of necessity take place after the prophetic message is delivered. Further support for this interpretation may be gathered from the use in *Ad Philadelphios* 6, for in this letter Ignatius is dealing with those seeking a charismatic legitimation to break away from the control of the bishop.[20] There he tells us of his own prophecy, which was to do nothing without the bishop, and we can reasonably assume that this came out in the context of prophetic ὁμιλία like that described in *Acta Pauli*. The ὁμιλία is charismatic, but is an opportunity to expose social strategies (like that of freeing slaves in order to add to one's *clientela*) masquerading as charismata.

We may also gather, in the light of the following instructions given Polycarp to προσλαλεῖν to the sisters and παραγγέλειν to the brethren, that a number of teaching and communication functions which would later be separated out take place simultaneously in the assembly as it gathers around the table.

ὁμιλία in the church of Smyrna of the early second century is conversation. However, by the late third century, at which point the church, as we have seen, is fully scholasticized in keeping with the culture of Smyrna as a centre of rhetorical education, the term has changed its meaning utterly; thus when *Vita Polycarpi* refers to the ὁμιλίαι of Polycarp[21] and to ὁμιλίαι from presbyters in the context of worship[22] we can only understand the term here to refer to sermons. Prophecy in this community is solely visionary in inspiration,[23] and *paraklēsis* is preaching.[24] Even so it is noteworthy that in the liturgy there are a number of ὁμιλίαι from the presbyters at Polycarp's ordination, following on from the teaching of the bishops. This cus-

---

[20] So Trevett, "Prophecy and anti-episcopal activity".
[21] *Vita Polycarpi* 12.
[22] *Vita Polycarpi* 22.
[23] *Vita Polycarpi* 10, 17, 20, 21.
[24] *Vita Polycarpi* 24.

tom might well have come about from a situation like that represented by *Acta Pauli*, where the original prophecy is then followed by two further treatments. The custom of delivering ὁμιλίαι in turn has thus led to the situation where the individual speeches making up the ὁμιλία have lengthened but are still delivered in turn.

3.3. *From* homilia *as converse to* homilia *as discourse*

In the light of this conclusion we may finally turn to the question of the origin of the term ὁμιλία to refer to preaching, thus offering one final proof of the proposed narrative. We have observed that the normal meaning of *homilia* is "conversation", and enquired into how it came to refer to addresses. We have seen that Norden's thesis is founded on insufficient evidence, and has held court for far too long.[25] An alternative may be suggested, namely that although the term is scholastic in origin, having reference to the debate and converse that would take place in that particular domestic setting, the practice derives not from the schools but from domestic Christianity and the *diakrisis* of prophecy. This *diakrisis* would originally be collective and conversational, but with the growing authority of Scripture would become truncated, and easily in time be transferred to an individual as arbiter of the scriptural tradition in an increasingly scholasticized church. Because of the practice of the schools of discussing addresses which were given there was a continuing place for ὁμιλία as the church became scholasticized, as through scholasticization the term ὁμιλία could be adopted to refer to what had always taken place. It thus relates to scholasticization, but has nothing to do with the tone of "familiar speech" as Norden would have it. But as the church becomes further scholasticized, when oral prophecy is finally replaced by written prophecy, then the dialogue becomes a monologue, ὁμιλία and διάλεξις become indistinguishable, and only the term, together with certain diatribal elements such as imaginary objections and rhetorical questions, remain as reminders of the manner in which the earliest churches spoke to themselves. Originally employed to describe the diacritical process of discussing prophecies and Scriptures at table, and borrowed in imitation of the

---

[25] 1.1.4.

other schools, it stands at the last with a new meaning when the
practice of *diakrisis* and *homilia* have disappeared. By the time of
Origen the relationship between exegesis and exhortation has changed.
No longer is Scripture used to check the content of exhortation;
rather exhortation derives from Scripture. Prophecy has become
preaching, and ὁμιλία has become homily.

BIBLIOGRAPHY

Primary texts

As in the text, Latin titles of works are employed, except where such a title would be unusual and clumsy.

The following are the principal editions employed; the use of other editions is clearly noted in the text or notes.

Scriptural sources

Novum Testamentum, *The Greek New Testament*, K. Aland et al. edd. (Stuttgart: UBS, 1983)

Vetus Testamentum (Graece), *Septuaginta*, A. Rahlfs ed. (Stuttgart: Wüttembergische Bibelanstalt, 1935)

Jewish sources

Aristeas, *Epistula*, H.StJ. Thackeray ed. in H.B. Swete *An introduction to the Old Testament in Greek* (Cambridge: Cambridge UP, 1900) 519–574

Esther Rabbah, S. Dunsky ed., *Midrash rabbah: Esther* (Montreal: Canadian Jewish Congress, 1962)

Dead Sea Scrolls, F.G. Martínez and E.J.C. Tigchelaar edd., *The Dead Sea scrolls: study edition* (Leiden: Brill, 2000)

Genesis Rabbah, J. Theodor ed., Ch. Albeck rev., *Bereschit Rabba* (Jerusalem: Wahrmann, 1965)

Josephus, *Antiquitates Judaicae* 4, H.StJ. Thackeray ed. (London: Heinemann, 1930)

———, *Contra Apionem*, H.StJ. Thackeray ed. (London: Heinemann, 1926)

Mishnah *Megillah*, *Die Mischna: Megilla*, L. Tetzner ed. (Berlin: Töpelmann, 1968)

Mishnah *Ta'anith*, *Die Mischna: Taanijot*, D. Correns ed. (Berlin: de Gruyter, 1989)

Pesiqta deRab Kahana, W.B. Braude, I.J. Kapstein edd. (Philadelphia: JPS, 1975)

Philo, *Apologia*, F.H. Colson and G.H. Whitaker edd. (London: Heinemann, 1929)

———, *De mutatione nominum*, F.H. Colson and G.H. Whitaker edd. (London: Heinemann, 1934)

———, *De sacrificiis Abeli et Caini*, F.H. Colson and G.H. Whitaker edd. (London: Heinemann, 1927)

———, *De somniis*, F.H. Colson and G.H. Whitaker edd. (London: Heinemann, 1934)

———, *De specialibus legibus*, F.H. Colson ed. (London: Heinemann, 1937)

———, *De vita Mosis*, F.H. Colson ed. (London: Heinemann, 1935)

———, *Legum allegoriae*, F.H. Colson ed. (London: Heinemann, 1925)

ps-Philo, *Liber antiquitatum biblicarum*, D.J. Harrington, Charles Perrot, Pierre-Maurice Bogaert edd., *Ps-Philon: Les antiquités bibliques* I (Paris: Cerf, 1976)

———, *De Jona*, Folker Siegert ed., *Drei hellenistisch-jüdische Predigten* I (WUNT 20; Tübingen: Mohr, 1980)

Sifre Deuteronomy, L. Finkelstein ed., *Siphre ad Deuteronomium* (Berlin: Jüdischer Kulturbund in Deutschland, 1939)

Talmud Babli: Betzah (Yom tob), L. Goldschmidt ed., *Der Babylonische Talmud* 3 (Berlin: Calvary, 1899)

Talmud Babli: Sanhedrin, L. Goldschmidt ed., *Der Babylonische Talmud* 7 (Berlin: Calvary, 1903)

Talmud Babli: Sotah, L. Goldschmidt ed., *Der Babylonische Talmud* 5 (Leipzig: Otto Harrassowitz, 1912)

Talmud Yerushalmi: Sotah, J. Neusner ed., *The Talmud of the land of Israel: Sotah* (Chicago: University of Chicago, 1984)

Talmud Yerushalmi: Hagiga, J. Neusner ed., *The Talmud of the land of Israel: Hagiga and Moed Katan* (Chicago: University of Chicago, 1985)

Testamenta xii patriarchum, M. de Jonge ed., *The testaments of the twelve patriarchs* (Leiden: Brill, 1978)

Tosefta, M.S. Zuckermandel ed. (Pasewalk: np, 1880)

Christian sources

Acta Johannis, E. Junod and J-D Kaestli edd. (Turnhout: Brepols, 1983)

Acta Justini, H. Musurillo ed., *The acts of the Christian martyrs* (Oxford: Clarendon, 1972)

Acta Pauli, Léon Vouaux ed., *Les Actes de Paul et ses lettres apocryphes* (Paris: Letouzey et Ané, 1913)

Acta Petri, Léon Vouaux ed., *Les actes de Pierre* (Paris: Letouzey et Ané, 1922)

Acta Thomae, M. Bonnet ed. in R.A. Lipsius and M. Bonnet edd., *Acta apostolorum apocrypha* (Leipzig: Mendelssohn, 1891)

Ad Diognetum, Henri Marrou ed., *A Diognète* (Paris: Cerf, 1997)

Canones apostolorum (versio Latina), Erik Tidner ed., *Didascaliae apostolorum, canonum ecclesiasticorum, traditionis apostolicae versiones Latinae* (TU 75; Berlin: Akademie, 1963)

Constitutiones Apostolorum, M. Metzger ed., *Les constitutions apostoliques* (Paris: Cerf, 1985–1987)

Epistula apostolorum (Coptic), Carl Schmidt ed., *Gespräche Jesu mit seinen Jüngern nach der Auferstehung* (TU 43; Leipzig: Hinrichs, 1919)

Martyrium Polycarpi, P.Th. Camelot ed., *Ignace d'Antioche, Polycarpe de Smyrne: lettres, martyre de Polycarpe* (Paris: Cerf, 1951)

Passio Pionii, H. Musurillo ed., *The acts of the Christian martyrs* (Oxford: Clarendon, 1972)

Vita Polycarpi, J.B. Lightfoot ed., *The apostolic fathers* II.3 (repr; Peabody MA: Hendrickson, 1989) 432–465

Barnabas, *Epistula*, Klaus Wengst ed., *Schriften des Urchristentums* (Zweiter Teil) (Darmstadt: Wissenschaftliche Buchgesellschaft, 1984)

I Clement, Clément de Rome: Épître aux Corinthiens, A. Jaubert ed. (Paris: Cerf, 1971)

II Clement, Klaus Wengst ed., *Schriften des Urchristentums* (Zweiter Teil) (Darmstadt: Wissenschaftliche Buchgesellschaft, 1984)

Clement of Alexandria, *Stromata*, O. Stählin ed., L. Früchtel rev. (Berlin: Akademie, 1985)

———, *Quis dives salvetur*, G.W. Butterworth ed., *Clement of Alexandria: The exhortation to the Greeks, the rich man's salvation* (London: Heinemann, 1919)

Epiphanius, *Panarion*, Karl Holl ed., *Epiphanius II* (Leipzig: Hinrichs, 1922)

Eusebius, *Historia ecclesiastica*, E. Schwartz ed., *Eusebius Werke II: die Kirchengeschichte* (Leipzig: Hinrichs, 1903, 1908)

Hermas, *Pastor*, R. Joly ed., *Hermas: le pasteur* (Paris: Cerf, 1958)

Hippolytus, *Refutatio omnium haeresium*, M. Marcovich ed. (Berlin: de Gruyter, 1986)

———, *Homilia in Psalmos*, Pierre Nautin ed. in *Le Dossier d'Hippolyte et de Meliton dans les Florileges Dogmatiques et chez les Historiens Modernes* (Paris: Cerf, 1953)

———, *Traditio apostolica*, B. Botte ed., *La Tradition Apostolique de Saint Hippolyte* (Münster: Aschendorff, 1963)

———, *Commentarius in Danieliem*, Gustav Bardy ed., *Hippolyte: commentaire sur Daniel* (Paris: Cerf, 1947)

ps-Hippolytus, *In sanctum Pascha*, Guiseppe Visonà ed., *Pseudo Ippolyto: In Sanctum Pascha: studio edizione commento* (Studia Patristica Mediolanensia 15; Milan: Vita e Pensiero, 1988)

Ignatius, *Epistulae*, P.Th. Camelot ed., *Ignace d'Antioche, Polycarpe de Smyrne: lettres, martyre de Polycarpe* (Paris: Cerf, 1951)

Irenaeus, *Adversus haereses* 1, A. Rousseau and L. Doutreleau edd., *Irénée de Lyon: contre les hérésies* 1.2 (Paris: Cerf, 1979)

———, *Adversus haereses* 3, A. Rousseau and L. Doutreleau edd., *Irénée de Lyon: contre les hérésies* 3.2 (Paris: Cerf, 1979)

———, *Adversus haereses* 5, A. Rousseau ed., *Irénée de Lyon: contre les hérésies* 5.2 (Paris: Cerf, 1969)

Jerome, *De viris illustribus*, A. Ceresa-Gastaldo ed. (Florence: Nardini, 1988)

Justin, *I Apologia*, M. Marcovich ed. (Berlin: de Gruyter, 1994)

———, *Dialogus*, E.J. Goodspeed ed., *Die ältesten Apologeten* (Göttingen: Vandenhoek und Ruprecht, 1914)

Melito, *Peri Pascha*, S.G. Hall ed., *Melito of Sardis on Pascha* (Oxford: Clarendon, 1979)

Papias, *Fragmenta*, R.M. Hübner ed. in J. Kürzinger *Papias von Hierapolis und die Evangelien des Neuen Testaments* (Regensburg: Pustet, 1983)

Fragmenta Montanista, Ronald E. Heine ed., *The Montanist Oracles and Testimonia* (NAPSPMS 14; Macon GA: Mercer UP, 1989)

Tertullian, *Opera*, various edd. (2 vols) (Turnhout: Brepols, 1954)

Theodoret, *Haereticorum Fabularum Compendium*, PG83

Theophilus, *Ad Autocylum*, M. Marcovich ed. (Berlin: de Gruyter, 1995)

Classical sources

Aristotle, *Rhetorica* J.H. Freese ed. (London: Heinemann, 1926)

———, *Rhetorica ad Alexandrum*, H. Rackham ed. (London: Heinemann, 1937)

Cicero, *De officiis*, W. Miller ed. (London: Heinemann, 1913)

Dio Chrysostom, *Oratio 71*, H.L. Crosby ed. (London: Heinemann, 1951)

Dionysius of Halicarnassus, *De compositione*, S. Usher ed. (London: Heinemann, 1985)

———, *Thucydides*, S. Usher ed. (London: Heinemann, 1974)

Dionysius Thrax, *Ars grammatica*, Jean Lallot ed. (Paris: CNRS, 1989)

Emporius, *De ethopoiia*, Karl Halm ed., *Rhetores Latini minores* (Leipzig: Teubner, 1863)

Epictetus, *Dissertationes*, W. Oldfather ed. (London: Heinemann, 1925–1928)

Hermogenes, *Progymnasmata*, H. Rabe ed. (Leipzig: Teubner, 1913)

———, *De methodo*, H. Rabe ed. (Leipzig: Teubner, 1913)

Herodotus, *Historiae*, C. Hude ed. (Oxford: Clarendon, 1927)

Iamblichus, *De vita Pythagorica*, J. Dillon and J. Hershbell ed., *Iamblichus: on the Pythagorean way of life* (Atlanta GA: Scholars, 1991)

ps-Isocrates, *Ad Demonicum*, G. Norlin ed. (London: Heinemann, 1928)

Philodemus, *De libertate dicendi*, David Konstan et al. edd., *Philodemus: on frank criticism* (Atlanta: Scholars, 1998)

Philostratus, *Vitae sophistarum*, W.C. Wright ed. (London: Heinemann, 1921)

Plutarch, *Fabius Maximus*, B. Perrin ed. (London: Heinemann, 1916)

———, *Quaestiones conviviales*, P.A. Clement, H.B. Hoffleit edd. (London: Heinemann, 1969)

Polybius, *Historiae*, W.R. Paton ed. (London: Heinemann, 1922)

Quintilian, *Institutio oratoria*, H.E. Butler ed. (London: Heinemann, 1920–1922)

Suetonius, *Augustus*, J.C. Rolfe ed. (London: Heinemann, 1914)

Xenophon, *Memorabilia*, E.C. Marchant ed. (London: Heinemann, 1923)

Secondary studies

Agourides, Savas C., "The origin of the Epistle of St. James" *GOTR* 9 (1963) 67–78
Albl, M.C., *And Scripture cannot be broken* (NovT Supp 96; Leiden: Brill, 1999)
Anderson, Graham, *The second sophistic: a cultural phenomenon in the Roman Empire* (London: Routledge, 1993)
Anderson, G.W., "Canonical and non-canonical" *The Cambridge history of the Bible* I P.R. Ackroyd and C.F. Evans edd. (Cambridge: Cambridge UP, 1970) 113–158
Anderson, Paul, *The christology of the fourth gospel* (Valley Forge PA: Trinity, 1997)
Ash, James L., "The decline of ecstatic prophecy in the early church" *Theological Studies* 37 (1976) 227–252
Ashton, John, *Understanding the fourth gospel* (Oxford: Clarendon, 1991)
Atkinson, K., "On further defining the first-century CE synagogue: fact or fiction" *NTS* 43 (1997) 491–502
Attridge, H.W., "New covenant christology in an early Christian homily" *Quarterly Review (Methodist)* 8 (1988) 89–108
————, *The epistle to the Hebrews* (Philadelphia: Fortress, 1989)
————, "Paraenesis in a homily (λόγος παρακλήσεως): the possible location of, and socialization in, the "Epistle to the Hebrews" Leo G. Perdue and John G. Gammie edd., *Paraenesis: act and form* (Semeia 50; Atlanta: SBL, 1990) 211–226
Aune, D.E., "The social matrix of the Apocalypse of John" *BibRes* 24 (1981) 16–32
————, *Prophecy in early Christianity and the ancient Mediterranean world* (Grand Rapids: Eerdmans, 1983)
————, "The prophetic circle of John of Patmos" *JSNT* 37 (1989) 103–116
Baasland, E., "Der 2 Klemensbrief und frühchristliche Rhetorik: 'die erste christliche Predigt' im Licht der neureren Forschung" *ANRW* II 27.1, W. Haase ed. (Berlin: de Gruyter, 1993) 78–154
Bacher, W., *Die Proömien in der alten Jüdischen Homilie* (Leipzig: Hinrichs, 1913)
Baeck, Leo, "Greek and Jewish preaching" *The pharisees and other essays* (NY: Schocken 1947) 109–122
Bailey, J.L., and Vander Broek, L.D., *Literary forms in the New Testament* (London: SPCK, 1992)
Balzer, Klaus, *The covenant formulary* (ETr) (Philadelphia: Fortress, 1971)
Bamberger, Bernard, "Philo and haggadah" *HUCA* 48 (1977) 153–185
Bardy, Gustav, "Les Écoles Romaines au second siècle" *RHE* 28 (1932) 501–532
————, "Aux origines de l'école d'Alexandrie" *RechScR* 27 (1937) 65–90
————, *Hippolyte: commentaire sur Daniel* (Paris: Cerf, 1947)
Barnard, L.W., "Is the Epistle of Barnabas a paschal homily?" in *Studies in the apostolic fathers and their background* (Oxford: Blackwell, 1966) 73–86
————, "The enigma of the Epistle to Diognetus" in *Studies in the apostolic fathers and their background* (Oxford: Blackwell, 1966) 165–174
Barnes, T.D., *Tertullian: a historical and literary study* (Oxford: Clarendon, 1971)
Barrett, C.K., "The flesh of the Son of Man: John 6:53" *Essays on John* (Philadelphia: Westminster, 1982) 37–49
Bartelink, G.J.M., *Lexicologisch-semantische studie over de taal van de Apostolische Vaders* (Utrecht: J. Beyer, 1952)
Bauckham, Richard, *The climax of prophecy* (Edinburgh: Clark, 1993)
————, *The theology of the book of Revelation* (Cambridge: Cambridge UP, 1993)
Bauer, Walter, *Der Wortgottesdienst der ältesten Christen* (Tübingen: Mohr, 1930)
Baum, Armin Daniel, "Papias als Kommentator evangelischer Aussprüche Jesu" *NovT* 38 (1996) 257–276
Beare, F.W., *The first epistle of Peter*³ (Oxford: Blackwell, 1970)
Berger, Klaus, "Hellenistische Gattungen im Neuen Testament" *ANRW* II 25.2, Wolfgang Haase ed. (Berlin: De Gruyter, 1984) 1031–1432

Best, Ernest, *I Peter* (Grand Rapids: Eerdmans, 1971)
————, *Commentary on the first and second epistles to the Thessalonians* (London: Black, 1972)
Betz, H.D., "Ursprung und Wesen christlichen Glaubens nach der Emmauslegende" *ZTK* 66 (1969) 7–21
Beyschlag, K., *Clemens Romanus und der Frühkatholizismus* (Tübingen: Mohr, 1966)
Bjerkelund, Carl J., *Parakalô: Form, Funktion und Sinn der Parakalô-Sätze in der Paulinischen Briefe* (Bibliotheca Theologica Norvegica 1; Oslo: Universitetsforlaget, 1967)
Black, C. Clifton, "The rhetorical form of the Hellenistic Jewish and early Christian sermon: a response to Lawrence Wills" *HThR* 81 (1988) 1–19
Bloch, P., "Studien zur Aggadah" *Monatschrift für die Geschichte und Wissenschaft des Judenthums* 34 (1885) 166–184, 210–224, 257–269, 383–404
Bonner, Campbell, *The homily on the passion by Melito Bishop of Sardis and some fragments of the apocryphal Ezekiel* (Studies and Documents 12; London: Christophers, 1940)
Borgen, Peder, "The unity of the discourse in John 6" *ZNW* 50 (1959) 277–278
————, *Bread from Heaven: an exegetical study of the concept of manna in the Gospel of John and the writings of Philo* (NovT Supp 10; Leiden: Brill, 1965)
Boring, M. Eugene, *The continuing voice of Jesus* (Louisville KY: WKJP, 1991)
Bornemann, W., "Der erste Petrusbrief: eine Taufrede des Silvanus?" *ZNW* 19 (1919) 143–165
Bornkamm, G., "Die eucharistische Rede in Johannesevangelium" *ZNW* 47 (1956) 161–169
————, "Der Paraklet im Johannesevangelium" *Geschichte und Glaube* (erster Teil) (gesammelte Aufsätze 3) (München: Chr Kaiser, 1968) 68–89
Botte, Bernard, *La Tradition Apostolique de Saint Hippolyte* (Münster: Aschendorff, 1963)
Bowersock, G.W., *Greek sophists in the Roman Empire* (Oxford: Clarendon, 1969)
Bowker, J.W., "Speeches in Acts: a Study in proem and yelammedēnu form" *NTS* 14 (1967–68) 96–111
Bradshaw, Paul, *The search for the origins of Christian worship* (London: SPCK, 1992)
Branick, Vincent P., "Source and redaction analysis of I Corinthians 1–3" *JBL* 101 (1982) 251–269
————, *The house church in the writings of Paul* (Wilmington: Michael Glazier, 1989)
Brent, Allen, *Hippolytus and the Roman church in the third century* (VigChr Supp 31; Leiden: Brill, 1995)
Brilioth, Yngve, *A brief history of preaching* (ETr) (Philadelphia: Fortress, 1965)
Brown, R.E., "The Paraclete in the Fourth Gospel" *NTS* 13 (1967) 113–131
Brox, N., "Προφητεία im ersten Timotheusbrief" *Biblische Zeitschrift* 20 (1976) 229–232
————, *Der erste Petrusbrief* (EKK 21; Zürich: Benzig, 1979)
————, *Der Hirt des Hermas* (Göttingen: Vandenhoek u Ruprecht, 1991)
Bruce, F.F., *The Acts of the apostles³* (Leicester: Apollos, 1990)
Buchanan, G.W., *Hebrews* (NY: Doubleday, 1972)
Bultmann, Rudolf, *Der Stil der paulinischen Predigt und die kynisch-stoische Diatribe* (FRLANT 13; Göttingen: Vandenhoek und Ruprecht, 1910)
Burgess, Theodore Chalon, *Epideictic Literature* (Chicago: Chicago UP, 1902)
Burtchaell, James Tunstead, *From synagogue to church* (Cambridge: Cambridge UP 1992)
Butterworth, G.W., *Clement of Alexandria: The exhortation to the Greeks, the rich man's salvation* (London: Heinemann, 1919)
Camelot, P.Th., *Ignace d'Antioche, Polycarpe de Smyrne: lettres, martyre de Polycarpe* (Paris: Cerf, 1951)
Camp, Claudia V., "Paraenesis: a Feminist Response" Leo G. Perdue and John G. Gammie edd. *Paraenesis: act and form* (Semeia 50; Atlanta: SBL, 1990) 243–260

Campbell, R. Alastair, *The elders: seniority within earliest Christianity* (Edinburgh: Clark, 1994)

Cantalamessa, R., *L'Omelia 'In S. Pascha' dello ps-Ippolyto di Roma* (Milan: Vita e Pensiero, 1967)

Cargal, Timothy B., *Restoring the diaspora: discursive structure and purpose in the Epistle of James* (SBLDS 144; Atlanta: Scholars, 1993)

Carroll, Thomas K., *Preaching the word* (Wilmington: Michael Glazier, 1984)

Chow, John K., *Patronage and power: a study of social networks at Corinth* (JSNT Supp 75; Sheffield: JSOT, 1992)

Church, Christopher L., *A Forschungsgeschichte on the Literary Character of the Epistle of James* (Diss Southern Baptist Theological Seminary, 1990)

Collins, John J., *Between Athens and Jerusalem: Jewish identity in the Hellenistic diaspora* (NY: Crossroad, 1983)

Collins, Raymond F., "The unity of Paul's paraenesis in I Thess. 4:3–4: I Cor. 7:1–7, a significant parallel" *NTS* 29 (1983) 420–429

Conley, Thomas M., *Philo's rhetoric: studies in style, composition and exegesis* (Center for Hermeneutical Studies Monograph 1; Berkeley: GTU, 1987)

Cosby, M.R., *The rhetorical composition and function of Hebrews 11 in the light of example lists in antiquity* (Mercer UP: Macon, 1988)

Cothenet, E., "Prophetisme et ministere" *La Maison Dieu* 107 (1971) 29–50

———, "Les prophètes Chrétiens comme exégètes charismatiques" in J. Panagopoulos ed. *Prophetic vocation in the New Testament and today* (NovT Supp 45; Leiden: Brill, 1977) 75–107

Countryman, L. William, "The intellectual role of the early catholic episcopate" *Church History* 48 (1979) 261–268

Culpepper, R. Alan, *The Johannine school: an evaluation of the Johannine-school hypothesis based on an investigation of the nature of ancient schools* (SBLDS 26; Missoula Mont: Scholars, 1975)

Dahl, Nils, "Form-critical observations on early Christian preaching" *Jesus in the memory of the early church* (Augsburg: Fortress, 1976) 30–36

Daube, David, "Example and precept: from Sirach to R. Ishmael" in *Tradition and interpretation in the New Testament: essays in honor of E. Earle Ellis* G.F. Hawthorne and Otto Betz edd. (Grand Rapids: Eerdmans, 1987) 16–21

Davids, P.H., *The epistle of James* (Exeter: Paternoster, 1982)

———, "The epistle of James in modern discussion" *ANRW* II 25.5 W. Haase ed. (Berlin: de Gruyter, 1988) 3621–3645

De Witt, Norman W., "Organisation and procedure in Epicurean groups" *Classical Philology* 31 (1936) 205–211

den Boeft, J., "Are you their teacher?" *StPatr* 21 E.A. Livingstone ed. (Leuven: Peeters, 1989) 60–65

Dekkers, E., "ΠΡΟΦΗΤΕΙΑ-Praefatio" *Mélanges offerts à Mademoiselle Christine Mohrmann* (Utrecht: Spectrum, 1963) 190–195

Delling, Gerhard, *Worship in the New Testament* (ETr) (London: DLT, 1962)

Dibelius, Martin, *James* (ETr) (Philadelphia: Fortress, 1976)

Dillon, J. and Hershbell, J., *Iamblichus: on the Pythagorean way of life* (Atlanta GA: Scholars, 1991)

Dix, Gregory, *The treatise on the Apostolic Tradition of St Hippolytus* (London: SPCK, 1937)

Doeve, J.W., *Jewish hermeneutics in the synoptic gospels and Acts* (Assen: van Gorcum, 1954)

Donfried, K.P., "False presuppositions in the study of Romans" in K.P. Donfried ed. *The Romans debate* (Peabody MA: Hendrickson, 1991) 102–125

———, "The theology of Second Clement" *HThR* 66 (1973) 487–501

———, *The setting of Second Clement in early Christianity* (NovT Supp 38; Leiden: Brill, 1974)

Dunbar, David G., "Hippolytus of Rome and the eschatological exegesis of the early church" *WTJ* 45 (1983) 322–339

Dunn, J.D.G., "John 6: A eucharistic discourse?" *NTS* 17 (1971) 328–338

——, "Prophetic 'I'-sayings and the Jesus tradition: the Importance of testing prophetic utterances within early Christianity" *NTS* 24 (1978) 175–198

Edwards, O.C., "History of preaching" W.H. Willimon and Richard Lischer edd. *Concise encyclopaedia of preaching* (Louisville: WJKP, 1995)

Ekenberg, Anders, "Urkristen predikan" in Alf Härdelin ed. *Predikohistoriska perspektiv* (Uppsaala: Skeab Verbum, 1982) 7–39

Ellingworth, Paul, *The Epistle to the Hebrews* (Grand Rapids: Eerdmans, 1993)

Elliott, John H., *A home for the homeless: A social-scientific criticism of I Peter, its Situation and Strategy* (Minneapolis: Fortress, 1991)

Ellis, E.E., "Exegetical patterns in I Corinthians and Romans" *Prophecy and hermeneutic in early Christianity* (Grand Rapids: Eerdmans, 1978) 213–220

——, "How the New Testament uses the Old" *Prophecy and hermeneutic in early Christianity* (Grand Rapids: Eerdmans, 1978) 147–172

——, "The role of the Christian prophet in Acts" *Prophecy and hermeneutic in early Christianity* (Grand Rapids: Eerdmans, 1978) 129–144

——, "Biblical interpretation in the New Testament church" *Mikra* M.J. Mulder ed. (Assen: van Gorcum, 1974) 653–724

Ellul, Danielle, "Antioche de Pisidie: Une Predication, trois credos" *Filologia Neotestamentaria* 5 (1992) 3–11

Finkel, Asher, *The Pharisees and the Teacher of Nazareth* (Leiden: Brill, 1964)

Fiorenza, E. Schüssler, "Apokalypsis and propheteia: Revelation in the context of early Christian prophecy" in *The Book of Revelation: Justice and Judgment* (Philadelphia: Fortress, 1985) 133–156

Fischel, H., "The use of sortites in the Tannaitic period" *HUCA* 44 (1973) 119–151

Forbes, Christopher, *Prophecy and inspired speech in early Christianity and its Hellenistic environment* (Peabody MA: Hendrickson, 1997)

Forbes, P.B.R., "The structure of the Epistle of James" *Evangelical Quarterly* 44 (1972) 147–153

Freedman, H. and Simon, M., *Midrash Rabbah* (9 vols) (London: Soncino, 1939)

Freudenthal, J., *Die Flavius Josephus beigelegte Schrift über die Herrschaft der Vernunft* (Breslau: Schletter, 1869)

Frickel, J., "Hippolyt von Rom: als Prediger verkannt" in *Stimuli* G. Schöllgen and C. Schoffen ed. (JAC Ergänzungsband 23; Münster: Aschendorff, 1996) 129–40

Furnish, V.P., "Prophets, apostles and preachers: a study of the biblical concept of preaching" *Interpretation* 17 (1963) 48–60

Gammie, J.G., "Paraenetic literature: towards the morphology of a secondary genre" Leo G. Perdue and John G. Gammie edd. *Paraenesis: act and form* (Semeia 50; Atlanta: SBL, 1990) 41–77

Gärtner, B., *John 6 and the Jewish Passover* (Coniectanea Neotestamentica 17; Lund: Gleerup, 1959)

Gertner, M., "Midrashim in the New Testament" *JJS* 7 (1962) 267–292

Gillespie, Thomas W., *The first theologians: A Study in early Christian prophecy* (Grand Rapids: Eerdmans, 1994)

Ginzberg, Louis, *Legends of the Jews* (Etr) I (Philadelphia: JPS, 1909); III (Philadelphia: JPS, 1911)

Goldberg, Arnold, "Petiha und Hariza: zur Korrektur eines Missverständnis" *JSJ* 10 (1979) 211–218

Grant, R.M., "Melito of Sardis on baptism" *VigChr* 4 (1950) 33–36

——, "Five Apologists and Marcus Aurelius" *Vigiliae Christianae* 42 (1988) 1–17

——, and Graham, H.H., *The Apostolic fathers II: first and second Clement* (New York: Nelson, 1965)

Grässer, E., "Der Hebräerbrief 1938–1963" *ThR* 30 (1964) 138–226

————, *Der Glaube im Hebräerbrief* (Marburg: Elwert, 1965)

————, *An die Hebräer* (Zürich: Benzig, 1990)

Groh, Dennis E., "Utterance and exegesis: biblical interpretation in the Montanist crisis" in *The Living Text: Essays in Honor of Ernest W. Saunders* D.E. Groh and Robert Jewett edd. (Lanham: UP America, 1985) 73–95

Gry, L., "Le Papias des belles promesses messianiques" *Vivre et Penser* 3 (1944) 112–124

Guerra, Anthony J., "Polemical Christianity: Tertullian's search for certitude" *SCent* 8 (1991) 109–123

Guthrie, George H., *The structure of Hebrews: a text-linguistic analysis* (NovT Supp 73; Leiden: Brill, 1994)

Hahnemann, G.M., *The Muratorian fragment and the development of the canon* (Oxford: Clarendon, 1992)

Hall, S.G., "Melito in the light of the Passover haggadah" *JTS* (ns) 22 (1971) 29–46

————, "Paschal baptism" *StEv* 6 (TU 112; Berlin: Akademie, 1973) 239–251

Halton, Thomas, "Stylistic device in Melito *Peri Pascha*" in *Kyriakon: Festschrift Johannes Quasten* Patrick Granfield and Josef A. Jungmann edd. (Münster: Aschendorff, 1970) 249–255

Harrill, J. Albert, "Ignatius *ad Polycarpum* 4.3 and the corporate manumission of Christian slaves" *JECS* 1 (1993) 107–142

Harrington, D.J., Perrot, Charles, Bogaert, Pierre-Maurice, *Ps-Philon: Les Antiquités Bibliques* 2 (Paris: Cerf, 1976)

Harris, William V., *Ancient literacy* (Cambridge MA: Harvard UP, 1989)

Hawthorne, G.F., "Christian prophets and the sayings of Jesus: evidence of and criteria for" *SBL seminar papers* 1975 (Vol. 2) (Missoula: Scholars, 1975) 105–129

Heine, Ronald E., *The Montanist oracles and testimonia* (NAPSPMS 14; Macon GA: Mercer UP, 1989)

Heinemann, Joseph, "The triennial lectionary cycle" *JJS* 19 (1968) 41–48

————, "Preaching in the Talmudic age" *EncJud* 13 (NY: Macmillan, 1971) 994–998

————, "The proem in the aggadic midrashim" *Studies in aggadah and folk literature* Joseph Heinemann and Dov Noy edd. (Scripta Hierosolymitana 22; Jerusalem: Magnes, 1971) 100–122

————, and Petuchowski, Jakob J., *Literature of the synagogue* (NY: Behrman, 1975)

Hemer, C.J., "The address of I Peter" *ET* 89 (1977–78) 239–243

Hengel, Martin, *The Johannine question* (ETr) (London: SCM, 1989)

Henne, P., *L'unité du Pasteur d'Hermas* (Paris: Gabalda, 1992)

Hill, C.E., "The Epistula Apostolorum: an Asian tract from the time of Polycarp" *JECS* 7 (1999) 1–53

Hill, David, "Christian prophets as teachers or instructors in the church" in J. Panagopoulos ed. *Prophetic vocation in the New Testament and today* (NovT Supp 45; Leiden: Brill, 1977) 108–130

————, "Prophecy and prophets in the Revelation of Saint John" *NTS* 18 (1971–1972) 401–418

————, *New Testament prophecy* (London: Marshall Morgan and Scott, 1979)

Hills, Julian, *Tradition and composition in the* Epistula Apostolorum (Minneapolis: Fortress, 1990)

Hirschmann, Marc, "The preacher and his public in third century Palestine" *JJS* 42 (1991) 108–114

Hornschuh, Manfred, *Studien zur Epistula Apostolorum* (Patristische Texte und Studien 5; Berlin: de Gruyter, 1966)

Hughes, G., *Hebrews and hermeneutics* (Cambridge: Cambridge UP, 1979)

Jacobson, Howard, *A commentary on pseudo-Philo's liber antiquitatum biblicarum* I (Leiden: Brill, 1996)

Jay, Eric G., "From presbyter bishops to bishops and presbyters" *SCent* 1 (1981) 125–162

Jeffers, James L., "Pluralism in early Roman Christianity" *Fides et Historia* 22 (1990) 4–17

———, *Conflict at Rome: social order and hierarchy in early Christianity* (Minneapolis: Fortress, 1991)

Jeremias, J., "Joh 6, 51c–58—redaktionell?" *ZNW* 44 (1952–1953) 256–257

Jewett, R., "The form and function of the homiletic benediction" *AngThR* 51 (1969) 18–34

Johnston, G., *The Spirit Paraclete in the Gospel of John* (Cambridge: Cambridge UP, 1970)

Jones, A.H.M., *The Greek city from Alexander to Justinian* (Oxford: Clarendon, 1940)

Judge, E.A., "The Early Christians as a scholastic community" *Journal of Religious History* 1 (1960) 4–15, 125–137

Junod, Éric, "Wodurch unterscheiden sich die Homilien des Origenes von seinen Kommentaren?" in *Predigt in der alten Kirche* E. Mühlenberg and J. van Oort ed. (Kampen: Kok Pharos, 1994) 50–81

Käsemann, E., "Das Formular einer neutestamentlichen Ordinationsparänese" *Exegetische Versuche und Besinnungen I* (Göttingen: Vandenhoek und Ruprecht, 1965) 101–108

Kennedy, G., *The art of persuasion in ancient Greece* (Princeton: Princeton UP, 1963)

Klauck, H-J., "Hellenistische Rhetorik im Diasporajudentum" *NTS* 35 (1989) 451–465

Koester, Helmut, *History and literature of early Christianity* II (Philadelphia: Fortress, 1982)

Knopf, R., *Die Lehre der zwölf Apostel, die zwei Clemensbriefe* (Tübingen: Mohr, 1920)

Körtner, U.H.J., *Papias von Hierapolis: ein Beitrag zur Geschichte des frühen Christentums* (FRLANT 133; Göttingen: Vandenhoek und Ruprecht, 1983)

Krüger, G., "Bemerkungen zum zweiten Klemensbrief" *Studies in early Christianity* S.J. Case ed. (New York: Century, 1928) 419–431

Kürzinger, J., "Papias von Hierapolis: zu Titel und Art seines Werkes" *BZ* 23 (NF) (1979) 172–186

———, *Papias von Hierapolis und die Evangelien des Neuen Testaments* (Eichstätter Materialien 4; Regensburg: Pustet, 1983)

Lampe, Peter, *Die Stadtrömischen Christen in den ersten beiden Jahrhunderten* (WUNT 2.18; Tübingen: Mohr, 1987)

Lane, William L., "Hebrews: a Sermon in Search of a setting" *SWJTh* 28 (1985) 13–18

———, *Hebrews 1–8* (WBC 47a) (Dallas: Word, 1991)

Lauterbach, Jacob Z., *Mekilta de-Rabbi Ishmael* II (Philadelphia: JPS, 1933)

le Déaut, Roger, *La nuit pascale* (Analecta Biblica 22; Rome: Pontifical Biblical Institute, 1963)

Leaney, A.R.C., "I Peter and the Passover: an Interpretation" *NTS* 10 (1963–64) 238–251

Lebram, J.H.C., "Die literarische Form des vierten Makkabaerbuches" *VigChr* 28 (1974) 81–96

Lieu, Judith, *The second and third epistles of John* (Edinburgh: Clark, 1986)

Lightfoot, J.B., *Essays on the work entitled 'Supernatural Religion'* (London: Macmillan, 1889)

———, *The apostolic fathers* I.2 (London: Macmillan, 1889)

———, *The apostolic fathers* II.2 (London: Macmillan, 1889)

Lindars, Barnabas, *Behind the fourth gospel* (London: SPCK, 1971)

———, *The Gospel of John* (London: Marshall Morgan and Scott, 1972)

———, "The rhetorical structure of Hebrews" *NTS* 35 (1989) 382–407

Lindemann, Andreas, *Die Clemensbriefe* (Tübingen: Mohr, 1992)

Litfin, Duane, *Saint Paul's theology of proclamation: I Corinthians 1–4 and Greco-Roman rhetoric* (Cambridge: Cambridge UP, 1994)

Lohse, E., "Paraenesis and kerygma in I Peter" in *Perspectives on I Peter* C.H. Talbert ed. (Macon GA: Mercer UP, 1986) 37–55

MacDonald, Margaret Y., *The Pauline churches: a socio-historical study of institutionaliza-tion in the Pauline and deutero-Pauline writings* (Cambridge: Cambridge UP, 1988)

Mack, Burton L., *Rhetoric in the New Testament* (Minneapolis: Fortress, 1990)

Mack, Hananel, *The aggadic midrash literature* (ETr) (Tel Aviv: MOD, 1989)

Maier, Harry O., *The social setting of the ministry as reflected in the writings of Hermas, Clement and Ignatius* (Dissertations SR 1; Waterloo, Ontario: Wilfred Laurier UP, 1991)

Malherbe, Abraham, "Exhortation in First Thessalonians" *NovT* 25 (1983) 238–256

———, *Moral exhortation: a Greco-Roman sourcebook* (Philadelphia: Westminster, 1986)

———, *Social aspects of early Christianity*[2] (Philadelphia: Fortress, 1983)

Mann, Jacob, *The Bible as read and preached in the old synagogue* I (Cincinnati: Private Publication, 1940)

Markschies, C., *Valentinus gnosticus?* (Tübingen: Mohr, 1992)

Marmorstein, A., "The background of the aggadah" *HUCA* 6 (1929) 141–204

Marrou, Henri, *A Diognète* (Paris: Cerf, 1997)

———, *The history of education in antiquity* (ETr) (London: Sheed and Ward, 1956)

Martin, R.P., *James* (Word Biblical Commentary 48) (Waco TX: Word, 1988)

März, Claus-Peter, *Der Hebräerbrief* (Würzburg: Echt, 1989)

Maybaum, S., *Die ältesten Phasen in der Entwicklung der jüdischen Predigt* (Berlin: Itzkowski, 1901)

Maynard-Reid, Pedrito U., *Poverty and wealth in James* (Maryknoll: Orbis, 1987)

Mazza, Enrico, *The origins of the eucharistic prayer* (Collegeville: Liturgical, 1995)

McDonald, J.I.H., *Kerygma and didache: the articulation and structure of the earliest Christian message* (Cambridge: Cambridge UP, 1980)

———, "Some comments on the form of Melito's Paschal Homily" *StPatr* 12 (TU 115; Berlin: Akademie, 1975) 104–112

McGowan, A., "'First regarding the cup': Papias and the diversity of early eucharis-tic practice," *JTS* (ns) 46 (1995) 551–7

Meeks, Wayne, *The first urban Christians: the social world of the Apostle Paul* (New Haven: Yale UP, 1983)

Merklein, Helmut, "Der Theologe als Prophet: zur Funktion prophetischen Redens im theologischen Diskurs des Paulus" *NTS* 38 (1992) 402–429

Meyer, A., *Das Rätsel des Jakobusbriefes* (Giessen: Töpelmann, 1930)

Michaels, J. Ramsey, *Interpreting the Book of Revelation* (Grand Rapids: Baker, 1992)

Moore, George Foote, *Judaism in the first centuries of the Christian era* (Cambridge MA: Harvard UP, 1927)

Morris, Leon, "The saints and the synagogue" *Worship, theology and ministry in the early church* Michael J. Wilkins and Terence Paige edd. (JSNT Supp 87; Sheffield: Sheffield Academic, 1992) 39–52

Müller, Ulrich B., *Prophetie und Predigt im Neuen Testament: Formgeschichtliche Untersuchungen zur urchristlichen Prophetie* (SNT 10; Gütersloh: Mohn, 1975)

Munck, Johannes, "Presbyters and disciples of the Lord in Papias: exegetic coments on Eusebius Ecclesiastical History III.39" *HThR* 52 (1959) 223–243

Nautin, Pierre, *Le Dossier d'Hippolyte et de Méliton dans les florilèges dogmatiques et chez les historiens modernes* (Paris: Cerf, 1953)

Norden, E., *Antike Kunstprosa*[3] (Leipzig: Teubner, 1918)

Old, Hughes Oliphant, *The reading and preaching of the scriptures in the worship of the Christian church* I (Grand Rapids: Eerdmans, 1998)

Olivar, Alexandre, "Preparacion e improvisacion en la predicacion patristica" *Kyriakon: Festschrift Johannes Quasten* II Patrick Granfield and Josef A. Jungmann edd. (Münster: Aschendorff, 1970) 736–767

———, *La predicacion Cristiana antigua* (Barcelona: Herder, 1992)

Orbe, A., "Los hombres y el creador según una homilia de Valentin" *Gregorianum* 55 (1974) 5–48, 339–368

Osiek, Carolyn, *Rich and poor in the Shepherd of Hermas: a social-exegetical investigation* (CBQMS 15; Washington: Catholic Biblical Association, 1983)

Panagopoulos, J., "Die urchristliche Prophetie" in J. Panagopoulos ed. *Prophetic vocation in the New Testament and today* (NovT Supp 45; Leiden: Brill, 1977) 1–32

Paulsen, H., "Die Bedeutung des Montanismus für die Herausbildung des Kanons" *VigChr* 32 (1978) 19–52

Pearson, Birger A., "Earliest Christianity in Egypt: some observations" in B.A. Pearson and J.E. Goehring ed. *The roots of Egyptian Christianity* (Philadelphia: Fortress, 1986) 132–157

Perdue, Leo G., "Paraenesis and the Epistle of James" *ZNW* 72 (1981) 241–256

———, "The death of the sage and moral exhortation: from ancient near eastern instructions to Graeco-Roman paraenesis" Leo G. Perdue and John G. Gammie edd. *Paraenesis: act and form* (Semeia 50; Atlanta: SBL, 1990) 81–109

Pervo, R.I., "Johannine trajectories in the Acts of John" *Apocrypha* 3 (1992) 47–68

Petuchowski, J.J., "A Sermon attributed to R Ele'azar HaModa'i" *HUCA* 48 (1977) 243–264

des Places, E., "Style parlé et style oral chez les écrivains grecs" *Mélanges Bidez* (AIPHO 2; Brussels: Institut pour Philologie et Histoire Orientales, 1934) 267–286

Popkes, W., *Adressaten, Situation und Form des Jakobusbriefes* (Stuttgart: Katholisches Bibelwerk, 1986)

Powell, Douglas, "Tertullianists and Cataphrygians" *VigChr* 29 (1975) 33–54

Praetorius, W., "Die Bedeutung der beiden Klemensbriefe für die älteste Geschichte der kirchlichen Praxis" *ZKG* 33 (1912) 347–63; 501–28

Preuschen, E., "Ardaf: IV Esra 9,26 und der Montanismus" *ZNW* 1 (1900) 265–266

Quacquarelli, Antonio, *Retorica e liturgia antenicena* (Ricerche Patristiche 1; Rome: Desclée, 1960)

Quasten, J., *Patrology* II (Utrecht: Spectrum, 1953)

Quinn, Jerome D., "Paraenesis and the Pastoral Epistles: lexical observations bearing on the nature of the sub-genre and soundings on its role in socialization and liturgies" Leo G. Perdue and John G. Gammie edd. *Paraenesis: act and form* (Semeia 50; Atlanta: SBL, 1990) 189–210

———, *The Letter to Titus* (New York: Doubleday, 1990)

Quispel, G., "African Christianity before Minucius Felix and Tertullian" *Actus: studies in honour of H.L.W. Nelson* J. den Boeft and A.H.M. Kessels edd. (Utrecht: Instituut voor klassieke Talen, 1982) 257–335

Rankin, David, *Tertullian and the church* (Cambridge: Cambridge UP, 1995)

Reese, James M., "A semiotic critique: with emphasis on the place of the Wisdom of Solomon in the literature of persuasion" Leo G. Perdue and John G. Gammie edd. *Paraenesis: act and form* (Semeia 50; Atlanta: SBL, 1990) 229–242

———, *Hellenistic influence on the Book of Wisdom and its Consequences* (Analecta Biblica 41; Rome: Pontifical Biblical Institute, 1970)

Reicke, Bo, "A synopsis of early Christian preaching" *The root of the vine* A. Fridrichsen ed. (London: Dacre, 1953) 128–160

Reiling, J., *Hermas and Christian prophecy: a study of the eleventh Mandate* (Leiden: Brill, 1973)

Richter, G., "Zur Formgeschichte und literarischen Einheit von Joh 6 31–58" *ZNW* 60 (1969) 21–55

Rizzi, Marco, *La questione dell'unità dell' "Ad Diognetum"* (Studia Patristica Mediolanensia 16; Milan: Vita e Pensiero, 1989)

Robeck, Cecil M. "Irenaeus and prophetic gifts" in *Essays on apostolic themes: Studies in honor of Howard M. Ervin* Paul Elbert ed. (Peabody MA: Hendrickson, 1985) 104–114

———, *Prophecy in Carthage: Perpetua, Tertullian and Cyprian* (Cleveland OH: Pilgrim, 1992)

Robinson, J.A.T., *Redating the New Testament* (London: SCM, 1976)

Ropes, J.H., *The epistle of James* (ICC; Edinburgh: Clark, 1916)

Rordorf, Willy, "Was wissen wir über Plan und Absicht der Paulusakten?" *Oecumenica et patristica* D. Papeandrou, W.A. Bienert, K. Schäferdiek edd. (Stuttgart: Kohlhammer, 1989) 71–82

Rouwhorst, G.A.M., "The Quartodeciman Passover and the Jewish Pesach" *Questions Liturgiques* 77 (1996) 152–173

Saldarini, A.J., "Last words and deathbed Scenes in rabbinic literature" *JQR* 68 (1977) 28–45

Salzmann, Jorg Christian, *Lehren und Ermahnen: zur Geschichte des christlichen Wortgottesdienstes in der ersten drei Jahrhunderten* (WUNT 2 Reihe 59; Tübingen: Mohr, 1994)

Sarason, R.S., "The petihtaot in Leviticus Rabbah: 'Oral homiles' or 'redactional constructions'" *JJS* 33 (1982) 557–567

Satake, A., *Die Gemeindeordnung in der Johannesapokalypse* (WMANT 21; Neukirchen: Neukirchener Erziehungsverein, 1966)

Schäfer, Peter, "Der synagogale Gottesdienst" *Literatur und Religion des Frühjudentums* (Gütersloh: Mohn, 1973) 391–413

Schenke, Ludger, "Die formale und gedenkliche Struktur von Joh 6,26–58" *BZ* 24 (1980) 21–41

———, "Die literarische Vorgeschichte von Joh 6, 26–58" *BZ* 29 (1985) 68–89

Schille, G., "Katechese und Taufliturgie: Erwägungen zu Hebr. 11" *ZNW* 51 (1960) 112–131

Schmeller, T., *Paulus und die Diatribe* (Münster: Aschendorff, 1987)

Schmidt, Carl, *Gespräche Jesu mit seinen Jüngern nach der Auferstehung* (TU 43; Leipzig: Hinrichs, 1919)

Schmidt, E.G., "Diatribe und Satire" *Wissenschaftliche Zeitschrift der Universität Rostock* 15 (1966) 507–515

Schnackenburg, Rudolf, *The Gospel according to Saint John* I (ETr) (Tunbridge Wells: Burnes and Oates, 1968)

Schneelmelcher, W., *New Testament apocrypha* II (ETr) (Louisville KY: WKJP, 1992)

Schneider, Carl, *Geistesgeschichte des antiken Christentums* II (Munich: Beck, 1954)

Schnelle, U., *Antidocetic christology in the Gospel of John* (ETr) (Minneapolis: Fortress, 1992)

Schoedel, W.R., *The apostolic fathers V: Polycarp, Martyrdom of Polycarp, Fragments of Papias* (Camden NJ: Nelson, 1967)

———, *Ignatius of Antioch: A commentary on the letters* (Philadelphia: Fortress, 1985)

———, "Papias" *ANRW* II.27.1 W. Haase ed. (Berlin: de Gruyter, 1993) 235–270

Schürmann, Heinz, "Joh 6, 51c—ein Schlüssel zur johanneischen Brotrede" *BZ* 2 (1958) 244–262

Schutter, William L., *Hermeneutic and composition in I Peter* (WUNT 30, 2 Reihe; Tübingen: Mohr, 1989)

Schütz, Werner, *Geschichte der christlichen Predigt* (Berlin: de Gruyter, 1972)

Sedgwick, W.B., "The origins of the sermon" *HJ* 45 (1946) 158–164

Senn, Frank C., *Christian liturgy: catholic and evangelical* (Minneapolis: Fortress, 1997)

Sieben, H.J., "Die Ignatianen als Briefe: einige formkritische Bemerkungen" *VigChr* 32 (1978) 11–18

Siegert, Folker, *Drei hellenistisch-jüdische Predigten* I (WUNT 20; Tübingen: Mohr, 1980)

———, *Drei hellenistisch-jüdische Predigten* II (WUNT 61; Tübingen: Mohr, 1992)

Simonetti, Manlio, *Biblical interpretation in the early church* (ETr) (Edinburgh: Clark, 1994)

Skarsaune, Oskar, "The development of scriptural interpretation in the second and third centuries—except Clement and Origen" *Hebrew Bible/Old Testament: the history of its interpretation* I M. Sæbø ed. (Gottingen: Vandenhoeck und Ruprecht, 1996) 373–442

Smith, D. Moody, "The presentation of Jesus in the Fourth Gospel" in *Johannine Christianity* (Edinburgh: Clark, 1987) 175–189

Smalley, Stephen, *John: evangelist and interpreter* (Exeter: Paternoster, 1978)

Stanley, C.D., "Pearls before swine: did Paul's audiences understand his biblical quotations?" *NovT* 41 (1999) 124–144

Stanton, G.R., "2 Clement VII and the origin of the document" *Classica et Mediaevalia* 28 (1969) 314–320

Stegemann, Christa, *Herkunft und Entstehung des sogenannten zweiten Klemensbriefes* (Diss: Bonn, 1974)

Stegner, William Richard, "The ancient Jewish synagogue homily" *Greco-Roman literature and the New Testament* (SBL Sources for Biblical Study 21: Atlanta: Scholars, 1988) 51–70

Stein, E., "Die homiletische Peroratio im Midrasch" *HUCA* 8–9 (1931–1932) 353–371

Stendahl, K., *Paul among Jews and gentiles* (Philadelphia: Fortress, 1976)

Sterling, G.E., "The school of sacred laws: the social setting of Philo's treatises" *VigChr* 53 (1999) 148–164

Stern, David, *Midrash and Theory: ancient Jewish exegesis and contemporary literary studies* (Evanston IL: Northwestern UP, 1996)

Stevenson, J.S., "St. James' sermon notes" *ET* 24 (1923) 44

Stewart-Sykes, A., "τάξει in Papias: again" *JECS* 3 (1995) 487–492

———, "Papyrus Oxyrhynchus 5: a prophetic protest from second century Rome" *Studia Patristica* 31 E.A. Livingstone ed. (Leuven: Peeters, 1997) 196–205

———, "The Asian origin of *Epistula Apostolorum* and of the new prophecy" *VigChr* 51 (1997) 416–438

———, "The christology of Hermas and the interpretation of the fifth Similitude" *Augustinianum* 37 (1997) 273–284

———, "Hermas the prophet and Hippolytus the preacher: the Roman homily and its social context" in M.B. Cunningham and P. Allen edd. *Preacher and audience: studies in early Christian and Byzantine homiletics* (Leiden: Brill, 1998) 33–63

———, *The Lamb's high feast* (VigChr Supp 42; Leiden: Brill, 1998)

———, "The original condemnation of Asian Montanism" *JEH* 50 (1999) 1–22

———, "The integrity of the Hippolytean ordination rites" *Augustinianum* 39 (1999) 97–127

Stowers, Stanley K., "Social status, public speaking, and private teaching: the circumstances of Paul's preaching activity" *NovT* 26 (1980) 59–92

———, *The diatribe and Paul's letter to the Romans* (SBLDS 57; Atlanta: Scholars, 1981)

———, *Letter writing in Greco-Roman antiquity* (Philadelphia: Westminster, 1986)

———, *A rereading of Romans* (New Haven: Yale UP, 1994)

Strack, H.L., and Stemberger, G., *Introduction to the Talmud and Midrash* (ETr) (Edinburgh: Clark, 1991)

Suggs, M.J., "Wisdom of Solomon 2:10–5: a homily on the fourth servant song" *JBL* 76 (1957) 26–33

Swetman, James, "On the literary genre of the "Epistle" to the Hebrews" *NovT* 11 (1969) 261–269

Tabbernee, William, "Revelation 21 and the Montanist new Jerusalem" *AustBR* 37 (1989) 52–60

———, "To pardon or not to pardon: North African Montanism and the forgiveness of sins" *Studia Patristica* forthcoming

Telfer, W., "Episcopal succession in Egypt" *JEH* 8 (1952) 1–13

Theissen, G., *The social setting of Pauline Christianity* (ETr) (Philalphia: Fortress, 1982)

Thomas, J.C., "The order of the composition of the Johannine Epistles" *NovT* 37 (1995) 68–75

Thuren, L., "Risky rhetoric in James" *NovT* 37 (1995) 262–284

Thyen, H., *Der Stil der jüdisch-hellenistischen Homilie* (FRLANT 65 (NF47); Göttingen: Vandenhoek und Ruprecht, 1955)

Trebilco, Paul, *Jewish communities in Asia Minor* (Cambridge: Cambridge UP, 1991)

Trevett, Christine, "Prophecy and anti-episcopal activity: a third error combatted by Ignatius?" *JEH* 34 (1983) 1–18

——, "Apocalypse, Ignatius, Montanism: seeking the seeds" *VigChr* 43 (1989) 313–338

——, *Montanism: gender, authority and the new prophecy* (Cambridge: Cambridge UP, 1996)

Turner, Max, "The Spirit of prophecy and the power of authoritative preaching in Luke-Acts: a question of origins" *NTS* 38 (1992) 66–88

Urman, Dan, "The house of assembly and the house of study: are they one and the same?" Dan Urman and P.V.M. Flesher edd. *Ancient synagogues: historical analysis and archaeological discovery* 1 (Studia Post-Biblica 47; Leiden: Brill, 1995) 232–255

Usener, H., *Epicurea* (Leipzig: Hinrichs, 1887)

van den Hoek, Annewies, "The 'catechetical' school of early Christian Alexandria" *HThR* 90 (1997) 59–87

van Henten, Jan Willem, "Datierung und Herkunft des vierten Makkabaerbuches" *Tradition and re-interpretation in Jewish and early Christian literature* J.W. van Henten, H.J. de Jonge, P.T. van Rooden, J.W. Wesselius edd. (Leiden: Brill, 1986) 136–149

van Unnik, W.C., "A formula describing prophecy?" *NTS* 9 (1963) 86–94

——, "A Greek characteristic of prophecy in the fourth gospel" in *Text and interpretation* E. Best and R. Wilson edd. (Cambridge: Cambridge UP, 1979) 211–229

Vanhoye, Albert, *The structure and message of the Epistle to the Hebrews* (Subsidia Biblica 12; Rome: Pontifical Biblical Institute, 1989)

Vermes, Geza, *The Dead Sea Scrolls in English*[4] (Harmondsworth: Penguin, 1995)

Verner, David C., *The household of God: the social world of the pastoral epistles* (SBLDS 71; Chico: Scholars, 1983)

Visonà, Guiseppe, *Pseudo Ippolyto: In Sanctum Pascha: studio edizione commento* (Studia Patristica Mediolanensia 15; Milan: Vita e Pensiero, 1988)

Vouaux, Léon, *Les Actes de Paul et ses lettres apocryphes* (Paris: Letouzey et Ané, 1913)

——, *Les actes de Pierre* (Paris: Letouzey et Ané, 1922)

Ward, R.B., "Partiality in the assembly: James 2:2–4" *HThR* 62 (1969) 87–97

Wendland, P., "Philo und die kynisch-stoische Diatribe" *Beiträge zur Geschichte der griechischen Philosophie und Religion* Paul Wendland and Otto Kern edd. (Berlin: Reimer, 1895) 3–75

——, *Die hellenistisch-römische Kultur* (Tübingen: Mohr, 1912)

Wengst, Klaus, *Schriften des Urchristentums* (Zweiter Teil) (Darmstadt: Wissenschaftliche Buchgesellschaft, 1984)

Wessel, W.W., *An enquiry into the origin, literary character, historical and religious significance of the Epistle of James* (diss. Edinburgh 1953)

Wifstrand, A., "Stylistic problems in the Epistles of James and Peter" *STh* 1 (1948) 170–182

——, "The homily of Melito on the passion" *VigChr* 2 (1948) 201–223

Wilamowitz-Moellendorff, U., *Antigonos von Karystos* (Berlin: Weidmanische Buchandlung, 1881)

Wilken, R.L., "Collegia, philosophical schools, and theology" in *Early church history: the Roman Empire as the setting of primitive Christianity* S. Benko and J.J. O'Rourke edd. (London: Oliphants, 1971) 268–291

——, *The Christians as the Romans saw them* (New Haven: Yale UP, 1984)

Williams, Jacqueline A., *Biblical Interpretation in the gnostic Gospel of Truth from Nag Hammadi* (SBLDS 79; Atlanta: Scholars, 1988)

Wills, Lawrence, "The form of the sermon in Hellenistic Judaism and early Christianity" *HThR* 77 (1984) 277–299

Windisch, Hans, *Taufe und Sünde im ältesten Christentum bis auf Origenes* (Tübingen: Mohr, 1908)
———, *Der Hebräerbrief* (Tübingen: Mohr, 1913)
———, "Das Christentum des zweiten Klemensbriefes" *Harnack-Ehrung* (Leipzig: Hinrichs, 1921) 119–134
Winston, David, *The Wisdom of Solomon* (NY: Doubleday 1979)
Wuellner, Wilhelm, "Haggadic homily genre in I Corinthians 1–3" *JBL* 89 (1970) 199–204
Young, Steve, "Being a man: the pursuit of manliness in the Shepherd of Hermas" *JECS* 2 (1994) 237–255
York, A.D., "The targum in the synagogue and in the school" *JSJ* 10 (1979) 75–86
Zunz, Leopold, *Die gottesdienstlichen Vorträge der Jüden historisch entwickelt* (Frankfurt: Kauffmann, 1892)

INDEX OF ANCIENT TEXTS

1. Scriptural sources

2. *Jewish sources*

3. Christian sources

4. Classical sources

INDEX OF MODERN AUTHORS

SUPPLEMENTS TO VIGILIAE CHRISTIANAE

36. Vinzent, M. *Pseudo-Athanasius, Contra Arianos IV*. Eine Schrift gegen Asterius von Kappadokien, Eusebius von Cäsarea, Markell von Ankyra und Photin von Sirmium. 1996. ISBN 90 04 10686 3

37. Knipp, P.D.E. *'Christus Medicus' in der frühchristlichen Sarkophagskulptur*. Ikonographische Studien zur Sepulkralkunst des späten vierten Jahrhunderts. 1998. ISBN 90 04 10862 9

38. Lössl, J. *Intellectus gratiae*. Die erkenntnistheoretische und hermeneutische Dimension der Gnadenlehre Augustins von Hippo. 1997. ISBN 90 04 10849 1

39. Markell von Ankyra. *Die Fragmente. Der Brief an Julius von Rom*. Herausgegeben, eingeleitet und übersetzt von Markus Vinzent. 1997. ISBN 90 04 10907 2

40. Merkt, A. *Maximus I. von Turin*. Die Verkündigung eines Bischofs der frühen Reichskirche im zeitgeschichtlichen, gesellschaftlichen und liturgischen Kontext. 1997. ISBN 90 04 10864 5

41. Winden, J.C.M. van. *Archè*. A Collection of Patristic Studies by J.C.M. van Winden. Edited by J. den Boeft and D.T. Runia. 1997. ISBN 90 04 10834 3

42. Stewart-Sykes, A. *The Lamb's High Feast*. Melito, *Peri Pascha* and the Quartodeciman Paschal Liturgy at Sardis. 1998. ISBN 90 04 11236 7

43. Karavites, P. *Evil, Freedom and the Road to Perfection in Clement of Alexandria*. 1999. ISBN 90 04 11238 3

44. Boeft, J. den and M.L. van Poll-van de Lisdonk (eds.). *The Impact of Scripture in Early Christianity*. 1999. ISBN 90 04 11143 3

45. Brent, A. *The Imperial Cult and the Development of Church Order*. Concepts and Images of Authority in Paganism and Early Christianity before the Age of Cyprian. 1999. ISBN 90 04 11420 3

46. Zachhuber, J. *Human Nature in Gregory of Nyssa*. Philosophical Background and Theological Significance. 1999. ISBN 90 04 11530 7

47. Lechner, Th. *Ignatius adversus Valentinianos?* Chronologische und theologiegeschichtliche Studien zu den Briefen des Ignatius von Antiochien. 1999. ISBN 90 04 11505 6

48. Greschat, K. *Apelles und Hermogenes*. Zwei theologische Lehrer des zweiten Jahrhunderts. 1999. ISBN 90 04 11549 8

49. Drobner, H.R. *Augustinus von Hippo:* Sermones ad populum. Überlieferung und Bestand - Bibliographie - Indices. 1999. ISBN 90 04 11451 3

50. Hübner, R.M. *Der paradox Eine*. Antignostischer Monarchianismus im zweiten Jahrhundert. Mit einen Beitrag von Markus Vinzent. 1999. ISBN 90 04 11576 5

51. Gerber, S. *Theodor von Mopsuestia und das Nicänum*. Studien zu den katechetischen Homilien. 2000. ISBN 90 04 11521 8

52. Drobner, H.R. and A. Viciano (eds.). *Gregory of Nyssa: Homilies on the Beatitudes*. An English Version with Commentary and Supporting Studies. Pro ceedings of the Eighth International Colloquium on Gregory of Nyssa (Paderborn, 14-18 September 1998) 2000 ISBN 90 04 11621 4

53. Marcovich, M. (ed.). *Athenagorae qui fertur*. De resurrectione mortuorum. 2000. ISBN 90 04 11896 9

54. Marcovich, M. *Origines: Contra Celsum Libri VII*. ISBN 90 04 11976 0 *In preparation.*

55. McKinion, S. *Words, Imagery, and the Mystery of Christ*. A Reconstruction of Cyril of Alexandria's Christology. 2001. ISBN 90 04 11987 6

56. Beatrice, P.F. *Theosophia, An Attempt at Reconstruction*. ISBN 90 04 11798 9 *In preparation.*

57. Runia, D.T. *Philo of Alexandria:* An Annotated Bibliography 1987-1996. 2001. ISBN 90 04 11682 6

58. Merkt, A. *Das Patristische Prinzip*. Eine Studie zur Theologischen Bedeutung der Kirchenväter. 2001. ISBN 90 04 12221 4

59. Stewart-Sykes, A. *From Prophecy to Preaching*. A Search for the Origins of the Christian Homily. 2001. ISBN 90 04 11689 3